DRAWING THE BODY

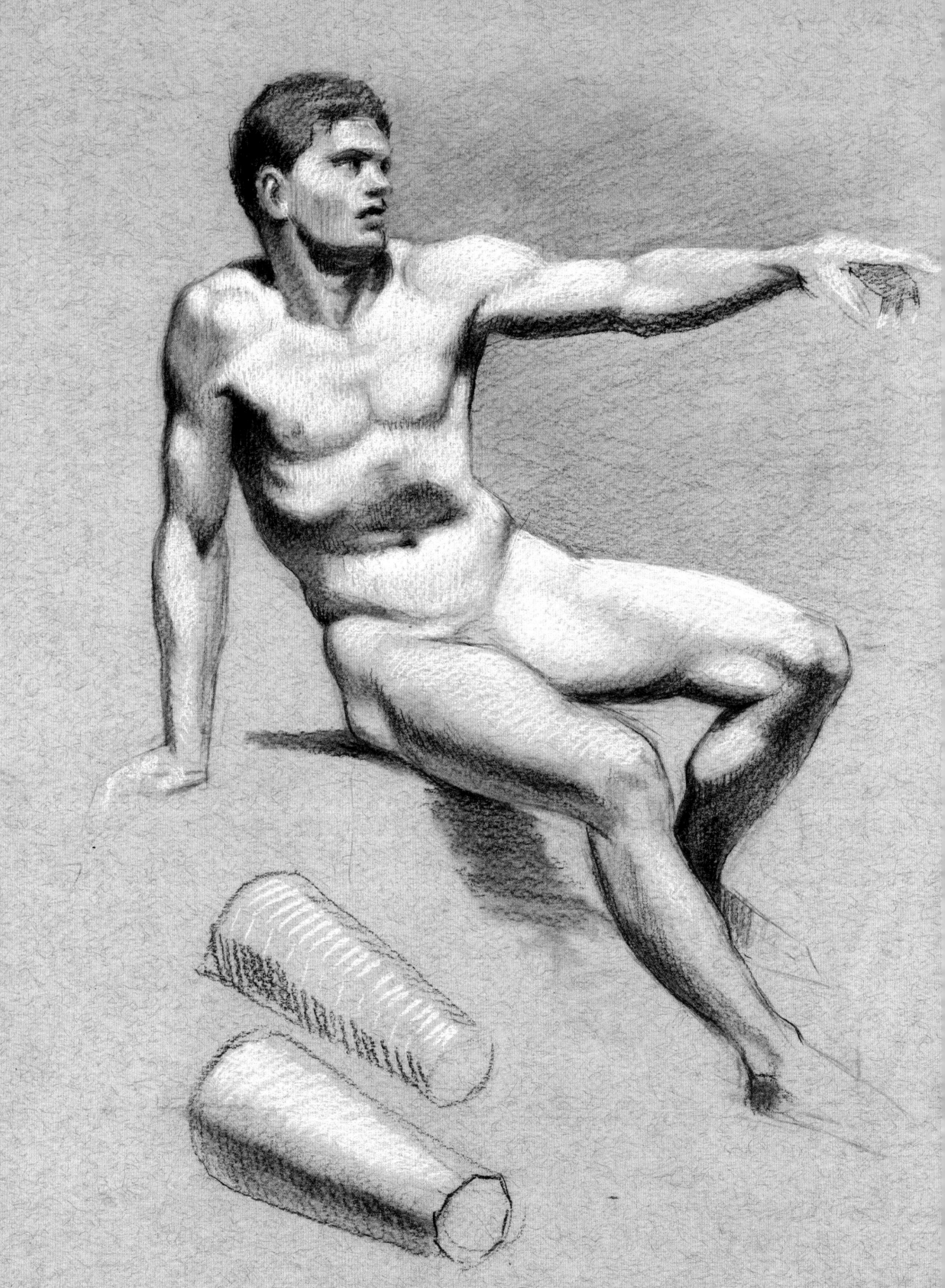

DRAWING
THE
BODY

READING THE HUMAN FORM IN ART

ROBERTO OSTI

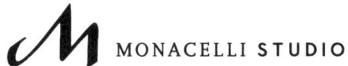
MONACELLI STUDIO

Editor: Carla Sakamoto
Consulting Editor: James Waller
Designer: Jennifer K. Beal Davis
Production Director: Michael Vagnetti
Cover design by Jennifer K. Beal Davis

Library of Congress Control Number: 2024940643

ISBN: 978-1-58093-645-3

Printed in China

Monacelli
A Phaidon Company
111 Broadway
New York, NY 10006

www.phaidon.com/monacelli

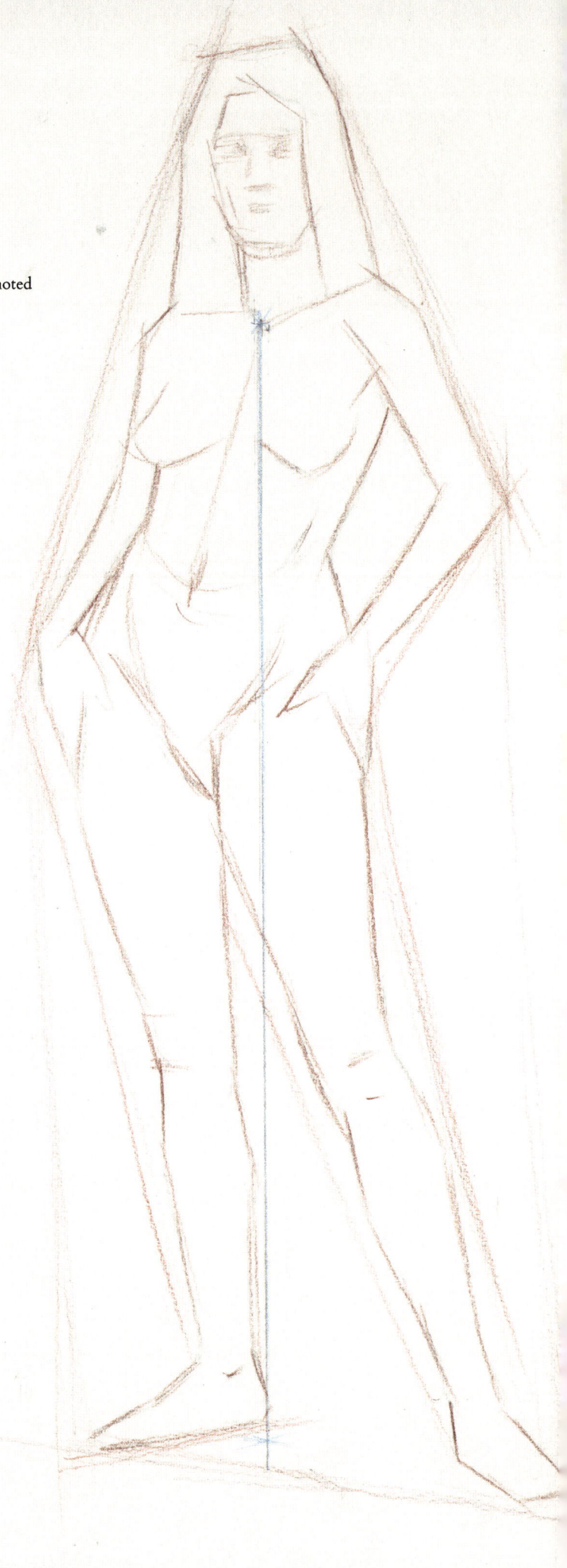

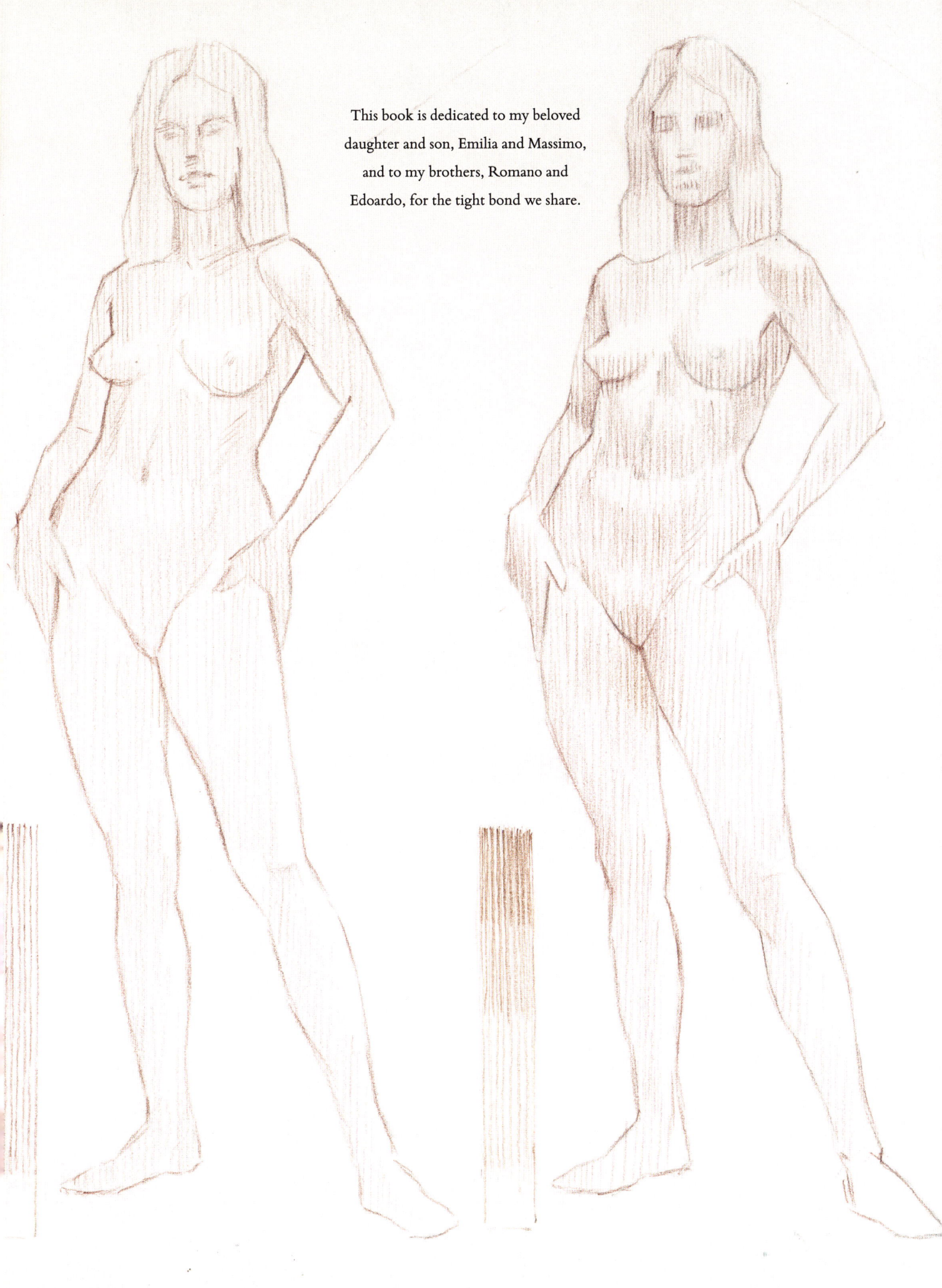

This book is dedicated to my beloved
daughter and son, Emilia and Massimo,
and to my brothers, Romano and
Edoardo, for the tight bond we share.

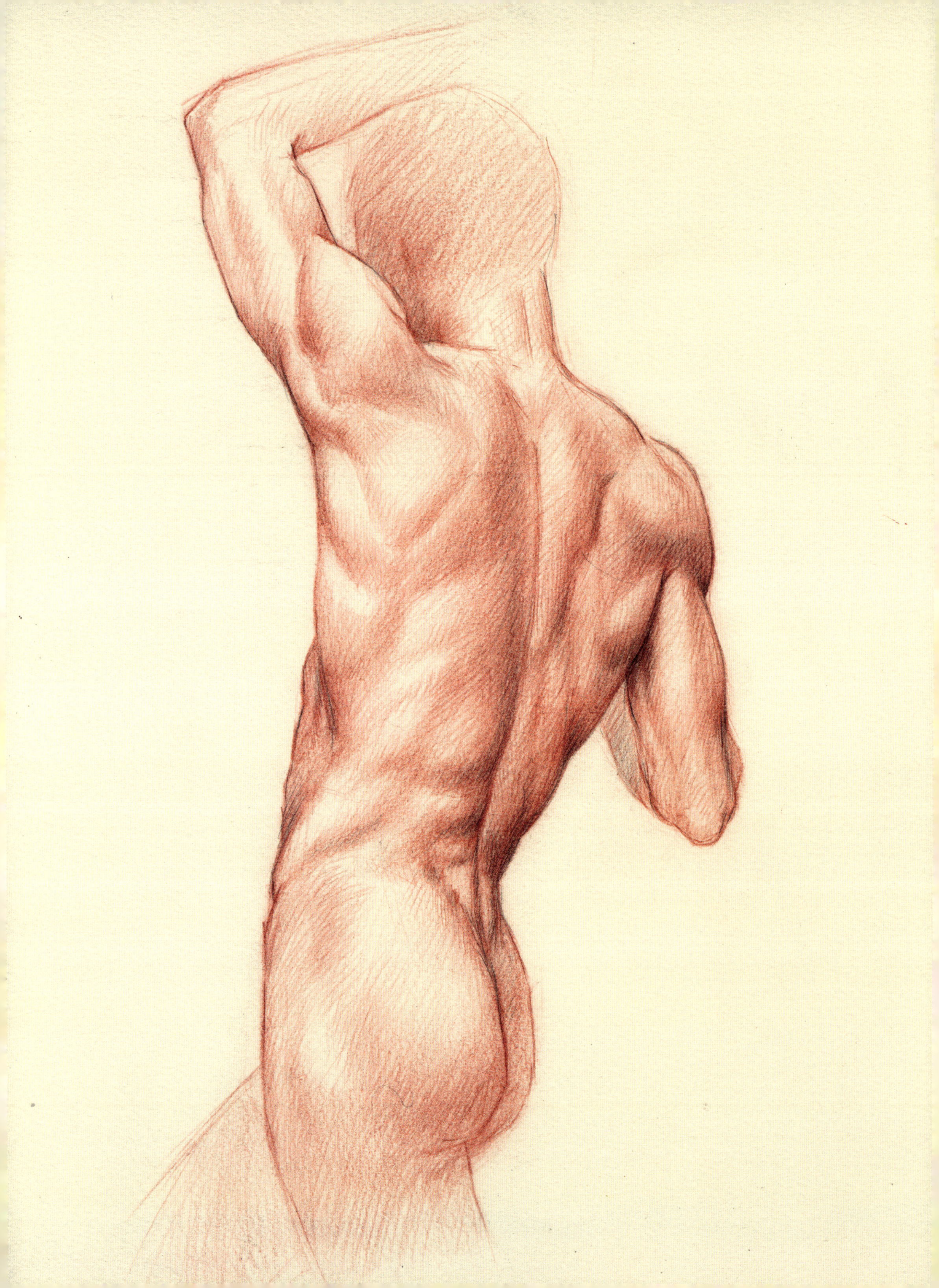

CONTENTS

ACKNOWLEDGMENTS

I first want to express my gratitude to the many readers of my previous two books, *Basic Human Anatomy* and *Dynamic Human Anatomy,* whose feedback was instrumental in the creation of *Drawing the Body*.

I want to thank Michael Vagnetti, production director at Monacelli, for suggesting I do a third book to complete the series. Many thanks also to Carla Sakamoto, senior editor at Monacelli, for encouraging me throughout the laborious period of the book's production.

A special acknowledgment is due to James Waller for lending his professional ethic and expertise and for masterfully editing this book, giving it stylistic continuity with the previous two books, which he also edited.

I want to thank the New York Academy of Art, where I teach Anatomical Drawing, Figure Drawing and Light on Form, for awarding me the Venture Fund Grant, an important acknowledgment and validation of my academic efforts from the foremost American graduate school dedicated to figurative art.

I also want to thank Massimo Demma, friend and fellow artist, for lending his expertise regarding the images that needed digital intervention.

Finally, I thank Andrea Morani and Vilidian Vilks, two professional and dedicated models who were great sources of inspiration and from whom I commissioned many photographic reference images for the book.

FOREWORD

by Michael Grimaldi

It is no small coincidence that the in-depth study of anatomy paralleled—and was influenced by—the understanding of linear perspective. When Filippo Brunelleschi (1377–1446) worked out the mechanisms of linear perspective, artists developed a visual language in which the musculoskeletal system could be understood spatially, studied thoroughly, quantified, and eventual broadly codified by Leon Battista Alberti (1404–1472). Pioneered by Leonardo, Michelangelo, and Vesalius, a revitalization of anatomical understanding blossomed, challenging traditional medical theories established a millennium prior—theories based not on the direct study of anatomical structures but rather on clinical examination, animal study, and assumption. This nexus between the arts and sciences fundamentally changed the how the body was perceived and understood, and it gave birth to the modern era.

Roberto Osti's latest book, *Drawing the Body: Reading the Human Form in Art*, is a unique and invaluable resource for figurative artists. For many, even those thoroughly invested in arts and medical education, the relationship of anatomy to drawing remains elusive and often disconnected. Osti skillfully links the study of anatomy and drawing through simultaneous, thorough, and holistic comparison. The functional, morphological, and kinesiological aspects of the human form are considered spatially while pragmatic strategies for their effective interpretation are explored through drawing. *Drawing the Body* will help students gain an advanced knowledge of anatomy and develop the tools and strategies to effectively interpret the form and function of the human body.

Michael Grimaldi is the director of the departments of Drawing and Anatomy at the New York Academy of Art.
michael-grimaldi.com

INTRODUCTION
by Roberto Osti

Unlike many figurative artists I know, I believe that Marcel Duchamp's revolutionary assertion of the supremacy of the conceptual over the retinal in art was an epochal event. Duchamp's radical questioning of the concept of art and of art's social role opened a door to new creative horizons.

But the dogmatism that ensued and persisted in the art world for decades afterward can be compared to the separation of spirit and matter that ousted the Classical principle of kalokagathia—loosely defined as a harmonious balance between the moral, physical, and spiritual—when art was Christianized following the demise of the Roman Empire and Classical culture.

Duchamp's excision of *techne* (skill) from the complex process of artmaking denied the "retinal" pleasure derived from observing the technical mastery that a well-executed artwork can elicit. Paradoxically, it also negated the importance that the conceptual component at the base of each technical approach has in the creative process. Only the final result of the technical process is visible in a finished artwork, not the steps leading to it, but these steps are the fundamental scaffolding on which we can superimpose aesthetics, provide a vehicle for narrative, and transcend the physical. The effect on a viewer of an artwork where technical mastery and conceptual content intertwine, can be compared to the overwhelming beauty of a couple engaged in a passionate tango dance.

This is essentially a book of exercises. It was inspired by the many requests for further technical information I have received from artists who purchased my previous books, *Basic Human Anatomy* (Monacelli Studio, 2016) and *Dynamic Human Anatomy* (Monacelli Studio, 2021). The step-by-step demos here will give you access to the foundational figure drawing techniques and reveal the complex interaction between the technical and creative processes. To complement the drawing sequences in the book, I have prepared a number of videos that demonstrate the various techniques in further detail. You can watch these videos, and draw along with me, by visiting this web pages:

robertoosti.com/drawing-the-body/
Password: dr4w1n9

MATERIALS LIST

The following art supplies will enable you to perform the exercises in this book. (With some of the more challenging exercises near the end of the book, I have included specific materials lists.)

PAPER

- Strathmore Drawing, white, in medium or vellum surface, series 400
- Strathmore charcoal, white and/or toned
- Ingres-type paper by Fabriano, Hahnemühle or Canson
- Strathmore Bristol series 300 or 400 in medium or vellum surface
- Other types of paper, toned or white, for charcoal and pastel, such as Canson Mi-teintes and Fabriano Tiziano

OTHER TOOLS

- Chamois cloth
- Kneaded eraser
- Mechanical eraser such as Factis Mechanical by General's
- Pencil sharpener(s): For sharpening, I prefer a thin, sharp small knife (about three inches long) and fine-grade sandpaper, which together permit you to completely shave off the wood casing to free about 1½ inches of graphite; to sharpen it into a long, conical point; and then to use a small piece of the sandpaper to finish the point. Of course, you can use a regular pencil sharpener for graphite or colored pencils instead.

DRAWING TOOLS

- Charcoal pencils: Wolff's carbon in B, 2B, 4B, and 6B grades, or General's in hard, medium, soft, and extra soft grades
- Non-compressed charcoal sticks from Nitram in H, HB, B, and B+ grades
- Pitt Pastel pencils or sticks in black, white, and sanguine red
- Oil-based Pitt Pastels in black (hard, medium, soft, and extra soft grades) and sanguine red. A word of caution: you cannot use these oil-base pastels in conjunction with regular pastels of any brand.
- Graphite pencils in HB, B, 2B, and 4B grades
- White chalk in pencils or sticks by Generals, Pitt Pastel, Conte, or Cretacolor
- Lead holders by Caran d'Ache (Fixpencils), Koh-I-Noor (Technigraph Lead Holders,) or Faber-Castell (TK 9400 lead holder). I find these lead-holders very useful; they carry leads of the same length and thickness as a wooden pencil, but the lead holder doesn't grow shorter as the lead is used, always ensuring a good grip. You buy the lead separately in any grade you need.
- Colored pencils: I particularly like to work with Faber-Castell Polychromos colored pencils, in Venetian red, India red, caput mortuum (a purplish brown color), Pompeian red, black, and white. These pencils' hardness permits you to obtain thin, sharp lines. Caran d'Ache is also an excellent brand, with high pigment concentration, though their pencils are a bit softer than Faber-Castell's Polychromos.

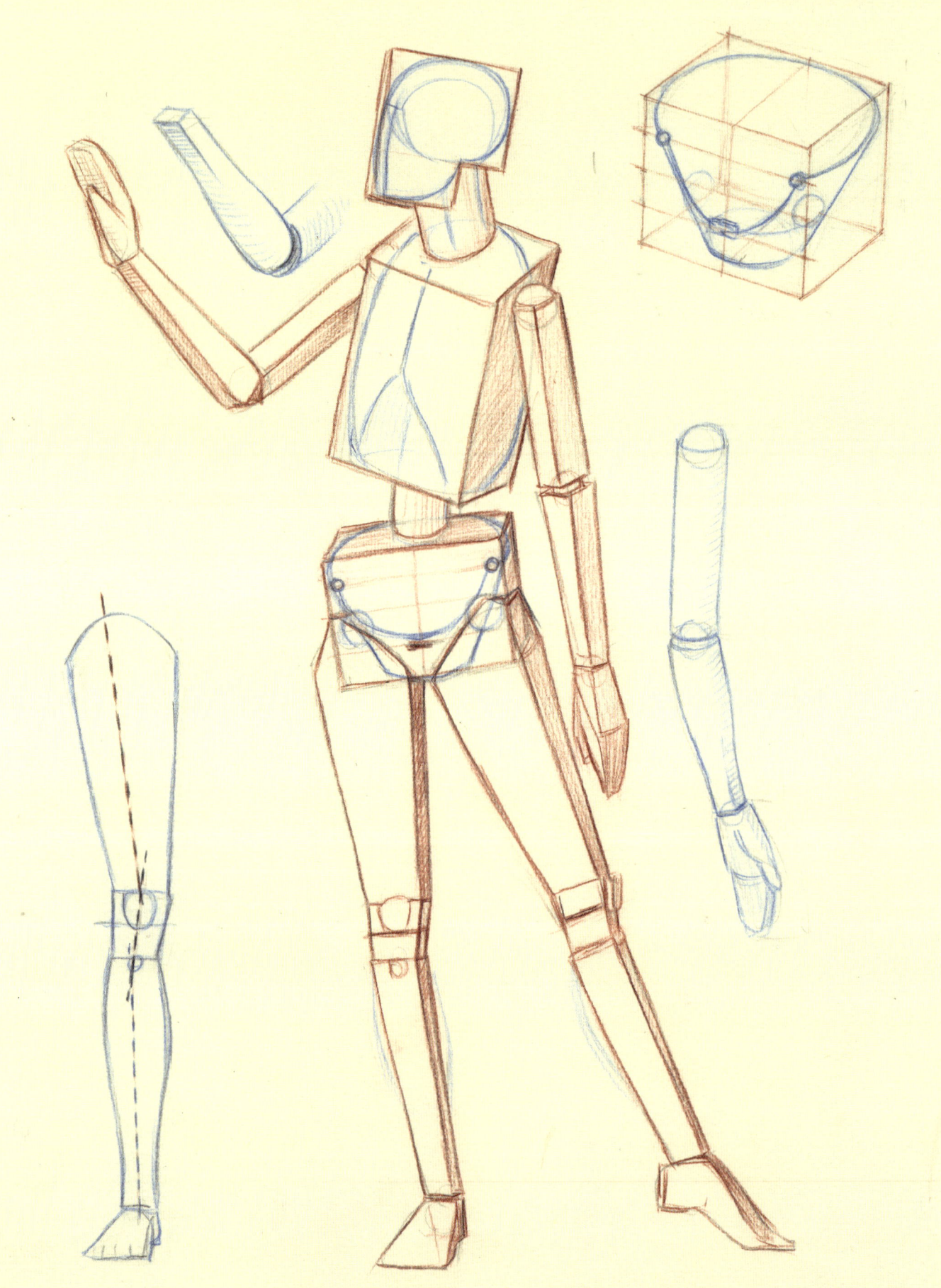

CHAPTER 1

STEREOMETRY

In this first chapter, you will learn to draw the human figure rendered as stereometric volumes, with exercises of increasing complexity.

Not everybody is familiar with the term *stereometry,* but virtually all artists have seen or drawn the human body rendered as "block figures." Many examples of stereometric rendering of the human figure can be found in books and online, but the great majority of these drawings are created intuitively, without explaining or following the core principle of this method, which in my opinion can be defined as *proportional relationships*. When drawing the human body with this approach, you need to consider how the various parts that compose it (head, ribcage, pelvis, limbs) are typically related to each other in terms of size and location. For example, the midpoint of the figure is at about the level of the pubic bone; the hands are never bigger than the head; the feet are about the same size of the head or a bit bigger; and the height of the pelvis is about the same height as that of the head.

Understanding proportional relationships helps you create more accurate figure drawings

Understanding these proportional relationships greatly helps you create figure drawings, both from life and from imagination, that are structurally and anatomically more accurate. By doing the exercises that follow, you will learn as you draw, assimilating the stereometric method more easily and in a way directly connected to its practical application. Typically, stereometric figures are rendered as three-dimensional angular solids (cubes and cuboid forms) that conform to the maximum height, width, and depth of each segment of the body. In addition to these angular visualizations, I have included more rounded stereometric renderings that more closely suggest the body's organic forms and that are easier to draw.

The exercises in this chapter are organized in four levels:

- **LEVEL 1** (exercises 1.1–1.11): Typical stereometric proportions of the female and male figures in a "control" position, in front, side, and back views
- **LEVEL 2** (exercises 1.12–1.15): Figures in various static poses
- **LEVEL 3** (exercises 1.16–1.17): Dynamic poses and dynamic flows
- **LEVEL 4** (exercises 1.18–1.24): Foreshortened poses

LEVEL 1
TYPICAL STEREOMETRIC PROPORTIONS

The eleven exercises that follow are designed to guide you through the proportional relationships of the male and female human figures. By doing the exercises, you will come to understand how the various segments of the body (head, ribcage, and pelvis for the axial skeleton and arms and legs for the appendicular skeleton) relate proportionally to each other.

To complete these exercises, copy each reference drawing on the gridded page to the right. You can also draw on a sheet of tracing paper positioned over the gridded page; this way, you can practice copying each reference drawing as many times as you like, each time using a new sheet of tracing paper.

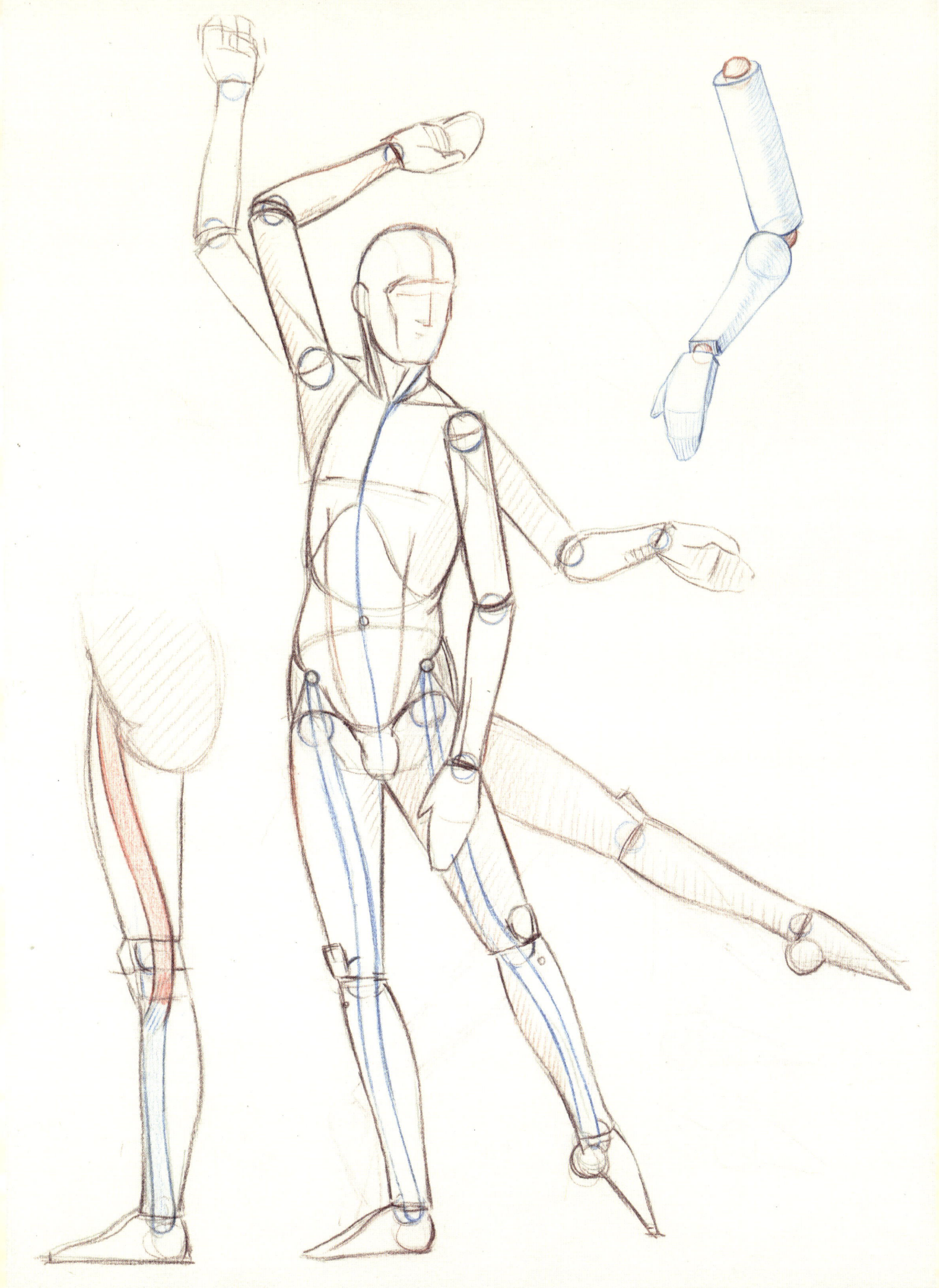

MALE FIGURE, FRONT VIEW

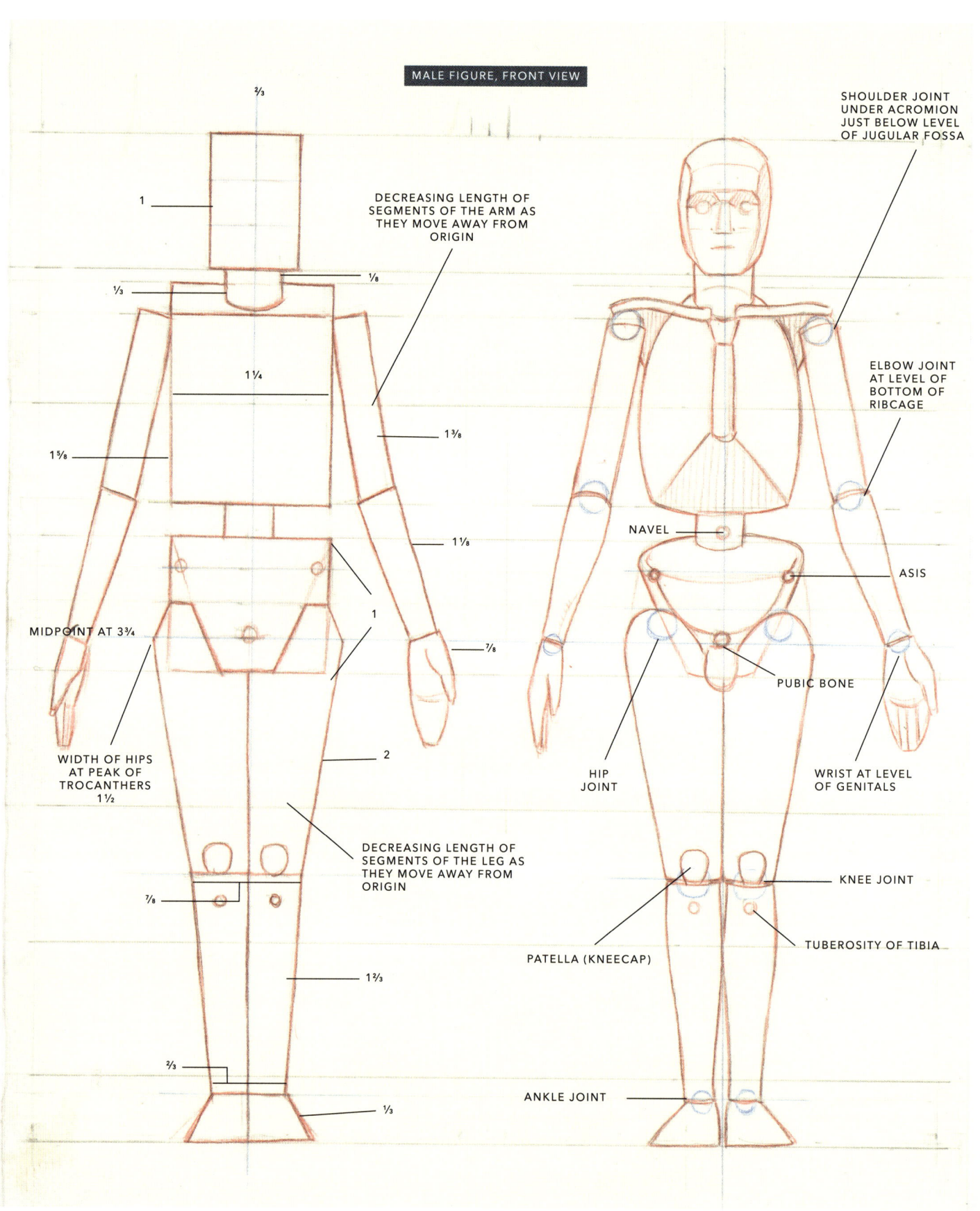

2/3

1

1/3

DECREASING LENGTH OF SEGMENTS OF THE ARM AS THEY MOVE AWAY FROM ORIGIN

1/8

1 1/4

1 3/8

1 5/8

1 1/8

MIDPOINT AT 3 3/4

1

7/8

WIDTH OF HIPS AT PEAK OF TROCANTHERS 1 1/2

2

DECREASING LENGTH OF SEGMENTS OF THE LEG AS THEY MOVE AWAY FROM ORIGIN

7/8

1 2/3

2/3

1/3

SHOULDER JOINT UNDER ACROMION JUST BELOW LEVEL OF JUGULAR FOSSA

ELBOW JOINT AT LEVEL OF BOTTOM OF RIBCAGE

NAVEL

ASIS

PUBIC BONE

HIP JOINT

WRIST AT LEVEL OF GENITALS

KNEE JOINT

PATELLA (KNEECAP)

TUBEROSITY OF TIBIA

ANKLE JOINT

CREATING A SCALE FOR THE STEREOMETRIC PROPORTIONS

To perform the exercises 1.1 through 1.5 and 2.1 through 2.10, you will need to prepare a scale to establish the size of the various segments of the stereometric figures. For this purpose, I have prepared a step-by-step video that will guide you through the process. You will find this video at this link: https://robertoosti.com/drawing-the-body/ pwd: dr4w1n9

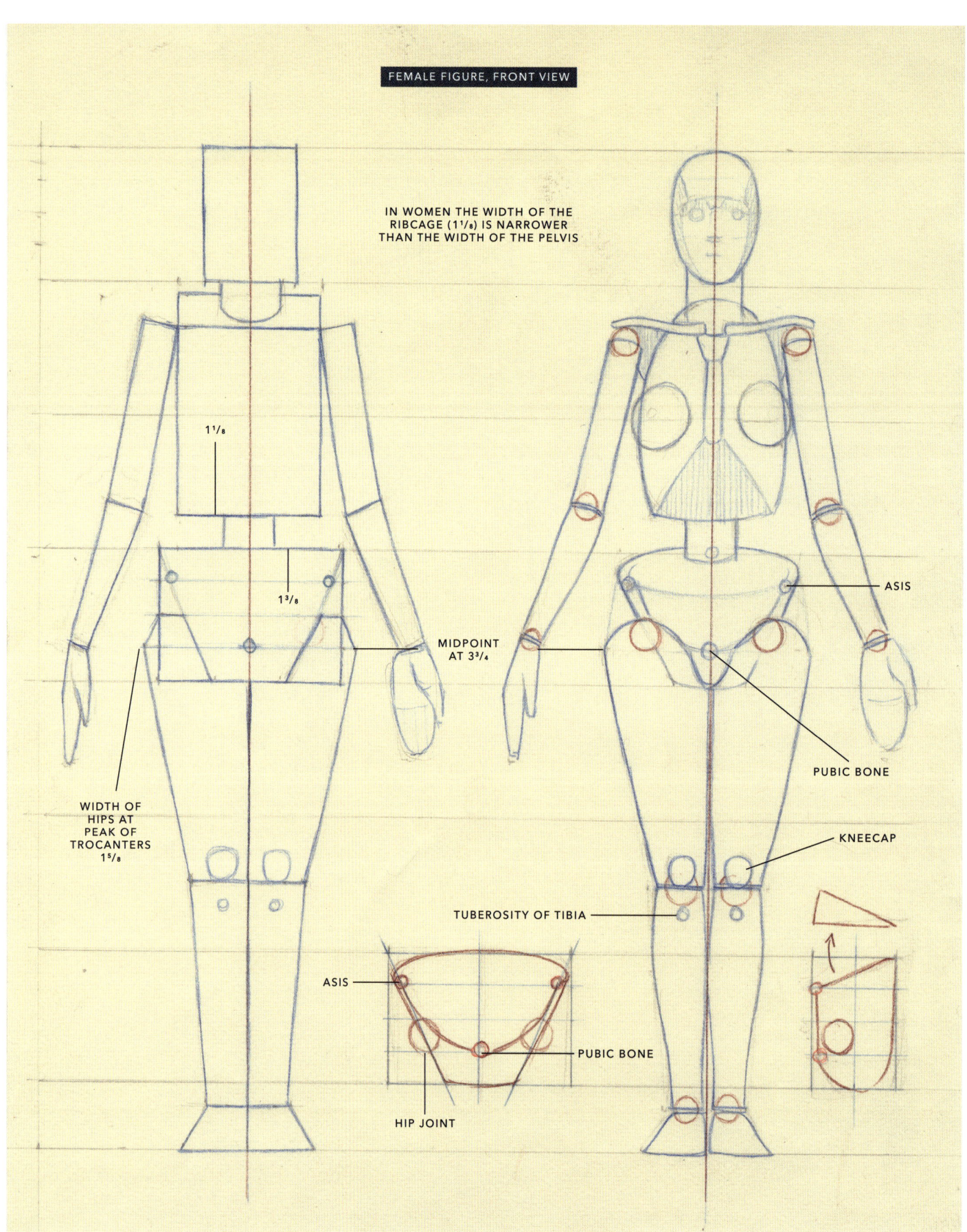

FEMALE FIGURE, FRONT VIEW

IN WOMEN THE WIDTH OF THE RIBCAGE (1¹⁄₈) IS NARROWER THAN THE WIDTH OF THE PELVIS

1¹⁄₈

1³⁄₈

MIDPOINT AT 3³⁄₄

WIDTH OF HIPS AT PEAK OF TROCANTERS 1⁵⁄₈

ASIS

PUBIC BONE

KNEECAP

TUBEROSITY OF TIBIA

ASIS

PUBIC BONE

HIP JOINT

EXERCISE 1.3

ANGULAR AND ROUNDED STEREOMETRY, MALE AND FEMALE FIGURES, SIDE VIEWS

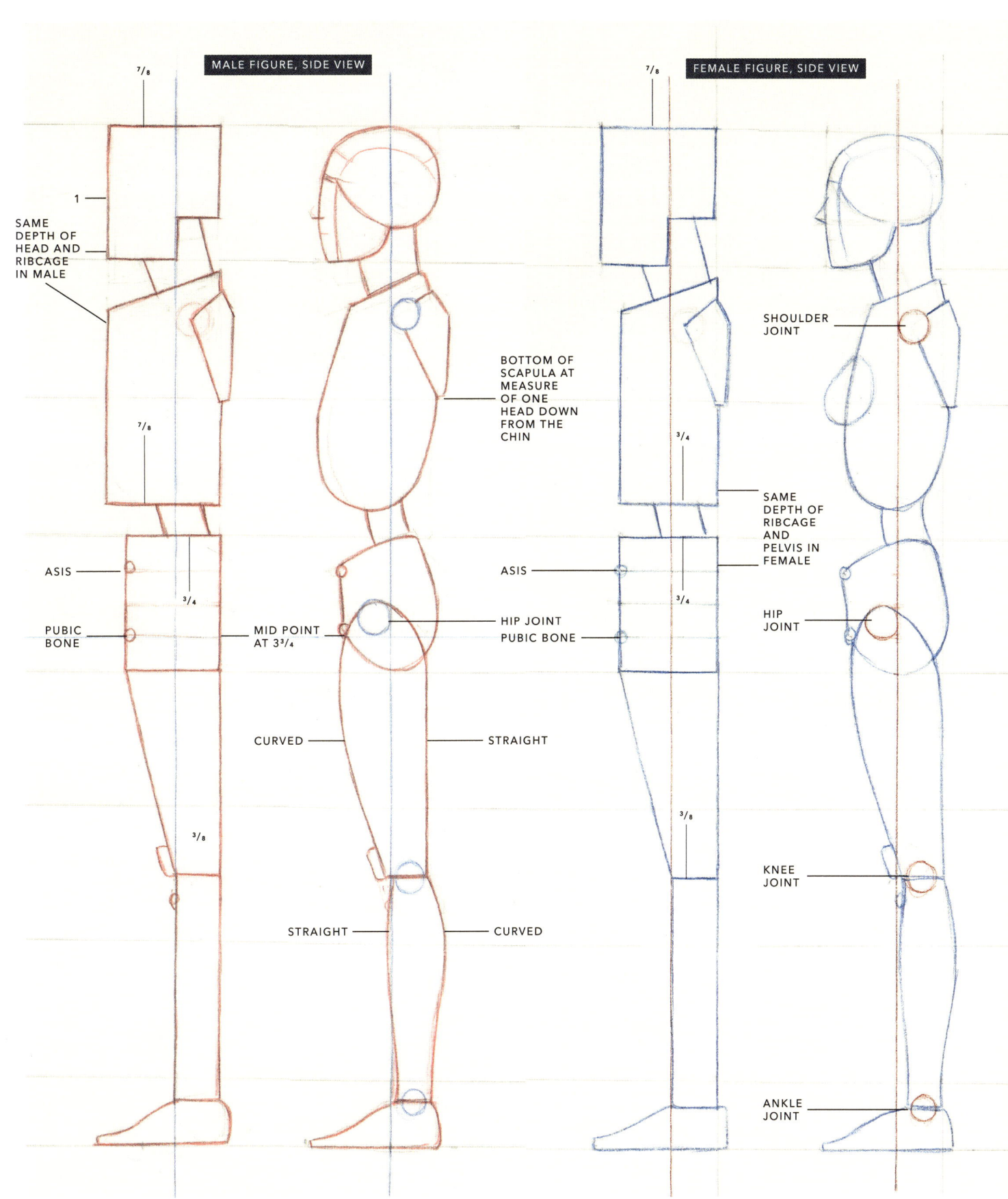

MALE FIGURE, SIDE VIEW

$^7/_8$

1

SAME DEPTH OF HEAD AND RIBCAGE IN MALE

$^7/_8$

$^3/_4$

ASIS

PUBIC BONE

MID POINT AT 3$^3/_4$

CURVED — STRAIGHT

$^3/_8$

STRAIGHT — CURVED

BOTTOM OF SCAPULA AT MEASURE OF ONE HEAD DOWN FROM THE CHIN

HIP JOINT PUBIC BONE

FEMALE FIGURE, SIDE VIEW

$^7/_8$

$^3/_4$

ASIS

$^3/_4$

$^3/_8$

SHOULDER JOINT

SAME DEPTH OF RIBCAGE AND PELVIS IN FEMALE

HIP JOINT

KNEE JOINT

ANKLE JOINT

ANGULAR AND ROUNDED STEREOMETRY, MALE FIGURE, BACK VIEW

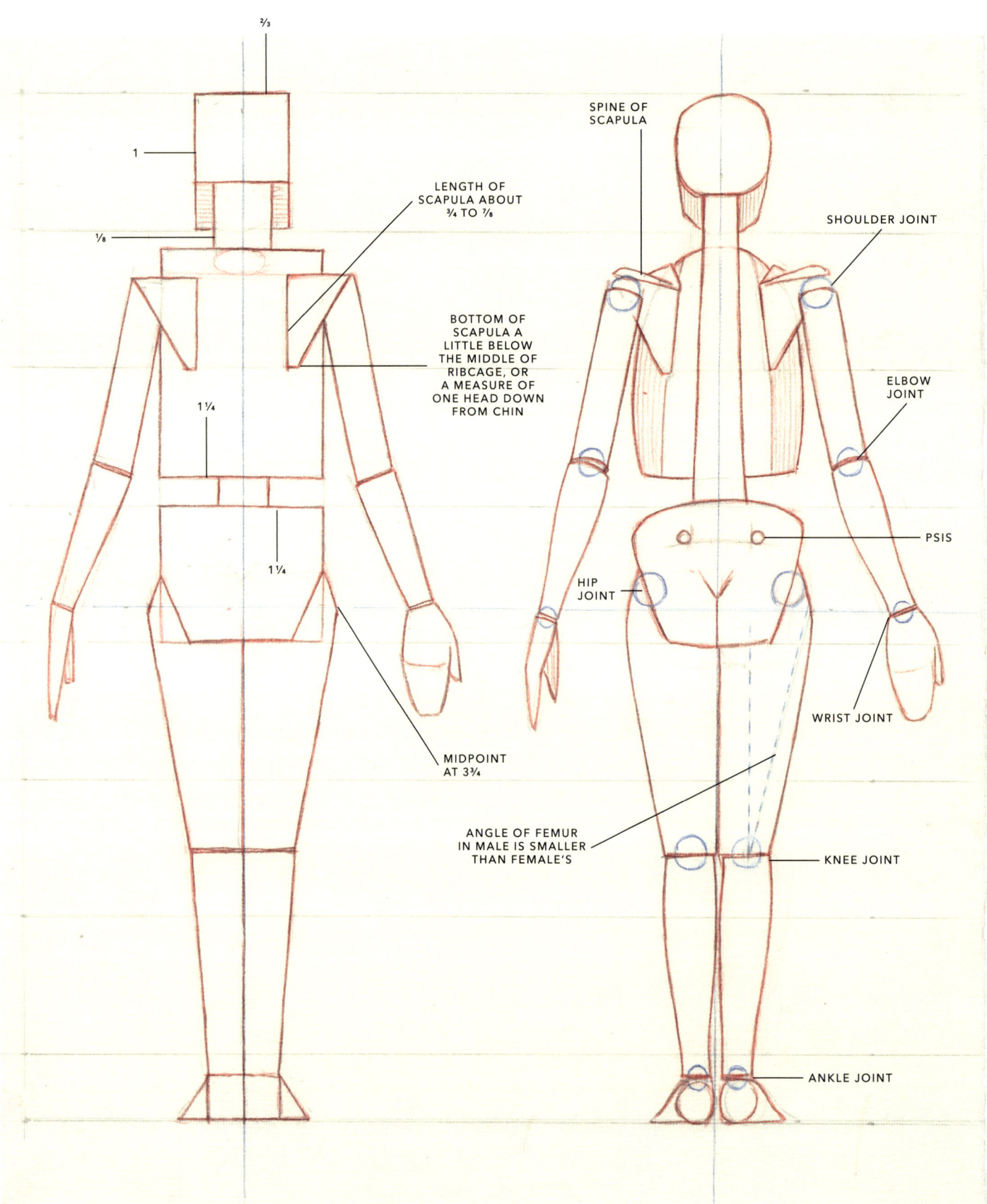

²/₃

1

¹/₈

LENGTH OF
SCAPULA ABOUT
¾ TO ⅞

BOTTOM OF
SCAPULA A
LITTLE BELOW
THE MIDDLE OF
RIBCAGE, OR
A MEASURE OF
ONE HEAD DOWN
FROM CHIN

1¼

1¼

MIDPOINT
AT 3¾

ANGLE OF FEMUR
IN MALE IS SMALLER
THAN FEMALE'S

SPINE OF
SCAPULA

SHOULDER JOINT

ELBOW
JOINT

PSIS

HIP
JOINT

WRIST JOINT

KNEE JOINT

ANKLE JOINT

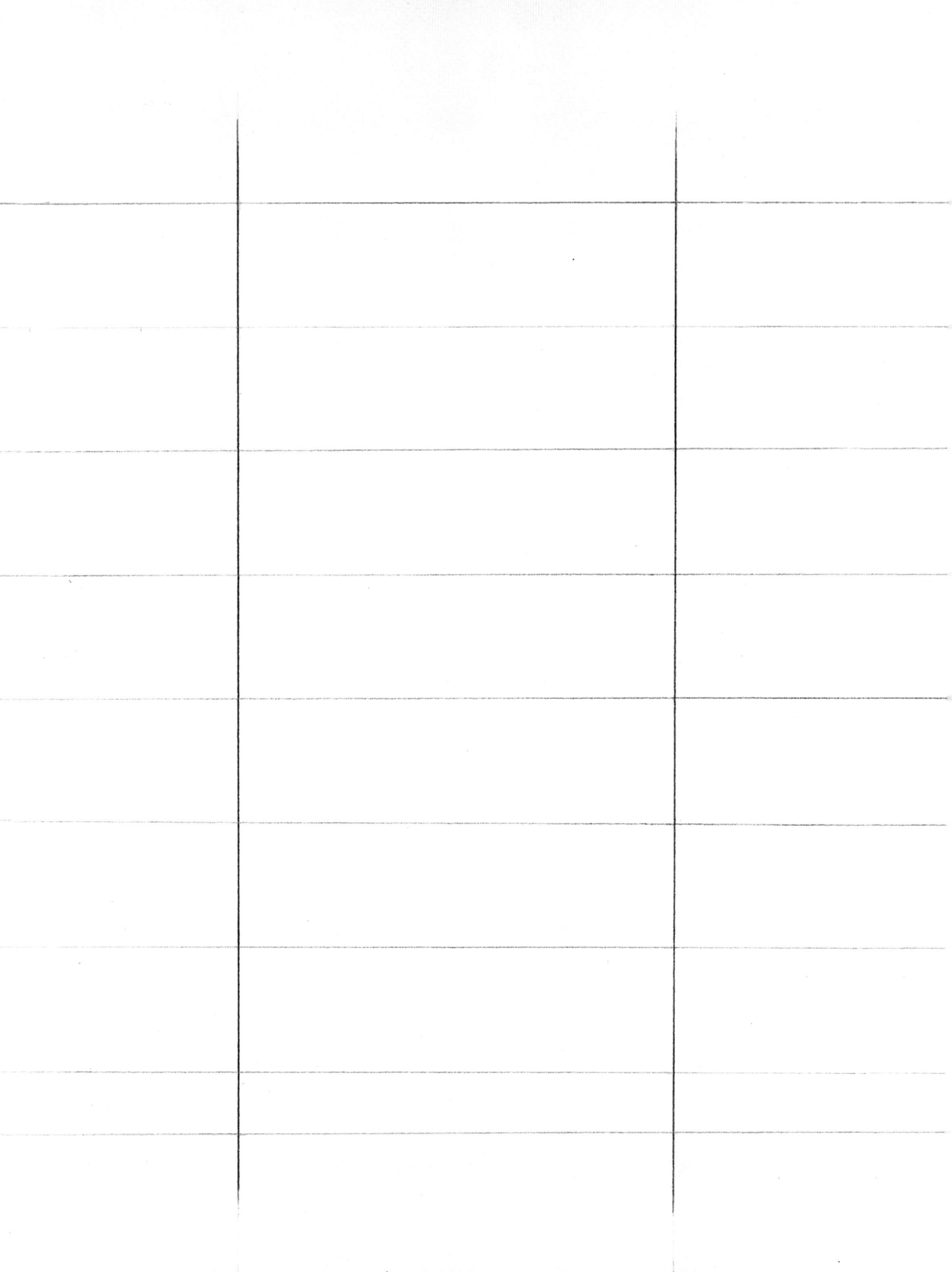

EXERCISE 1.5
ANGULAR AND ROUNDED STEREOMETRY, FEMALE FIGURE, BACK VIEW

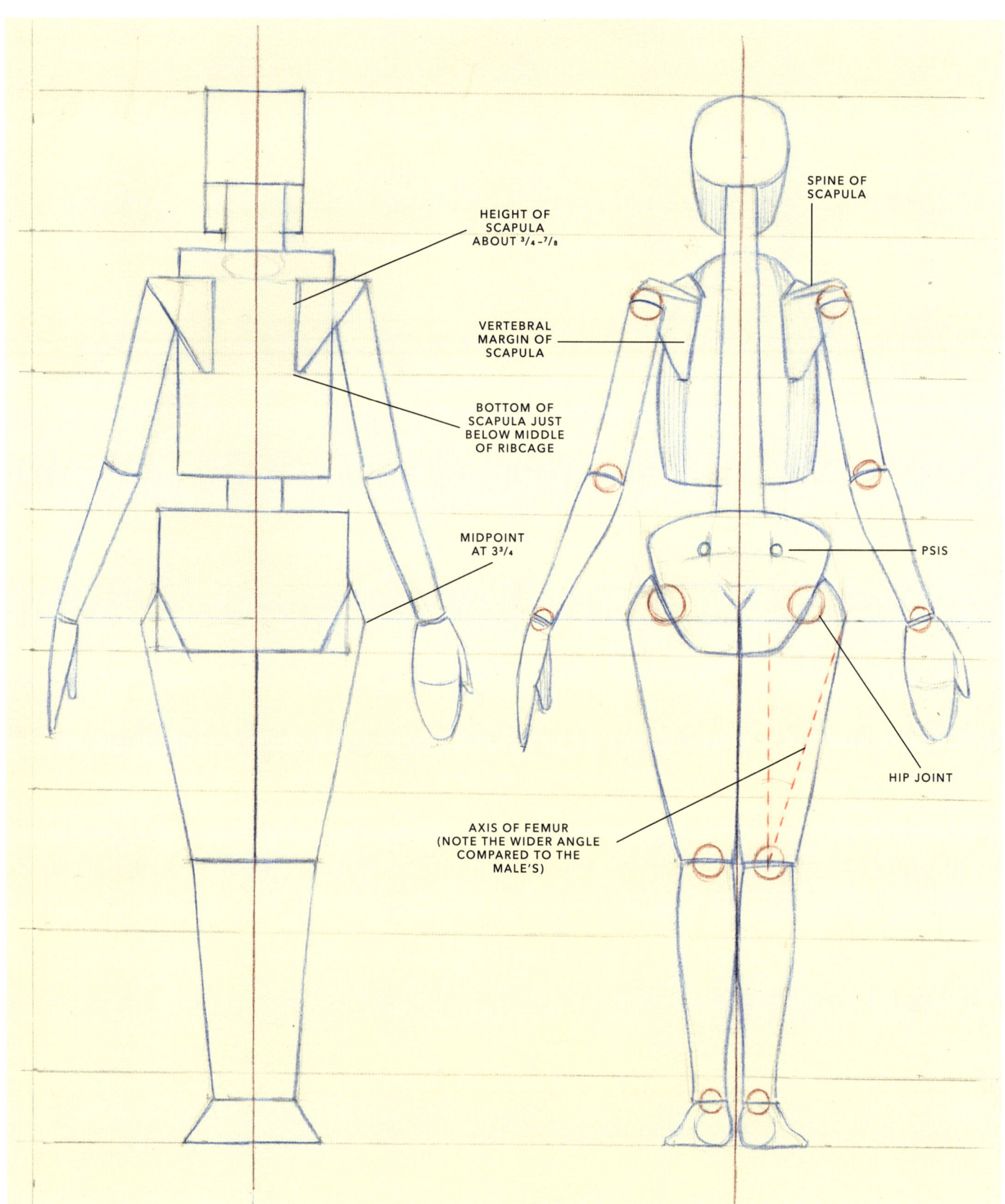

HEIGHT OF
SCAPULA
ABOUT $^{3}/_{4}$ - $^{7}/_{8}$

VERTEBRAL
MARGIN OF
SCAPULA

BOTTOM OF
SCAPULA JUST
BELOW MIDDLE
OF RIBCAGE

MIDPOINT
AT 3$^{3}/_{4}$

SPINE OF
SCAPULA

PSIS

HIP JOINT

AXIS OF FEMUR
(NOTE THE WIDER ANGLE
COMPARED TO THE
MALE'S)

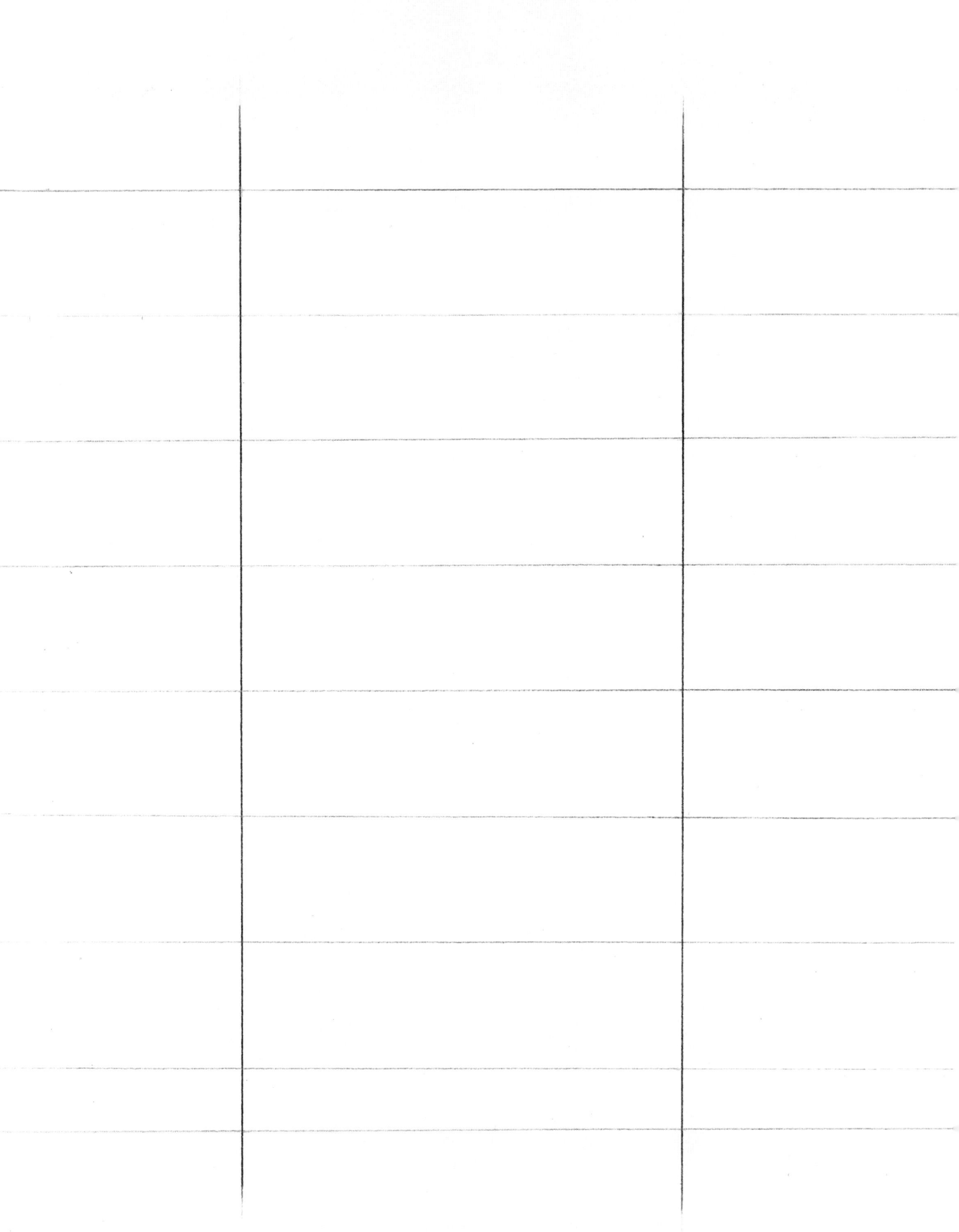

SEQUENCE: DRAWING THE ROUNDED STEREOMETRIC FIGURE

Do this exercise on the page opposite or, for a greater challenge, on regular unlined drawing paper or a page from a sketchbook dedicated to these exercises.

STEP 1

DRAW THE HEAD FIRST

By drawing the head first, you establish the unit of measurement used to determine the size of all the other segments of the body, each of which will be a fraction of, a multiple of, or the same size as the measure of the head.

Draw a circle of a size of your choice, add the measure of the radius at the base of the circle. Then draw the outline of the face by connecting the circle to the added measure with two curved lines.

You have now obtained an upside-down egg shape, divided in three equal segments. At the line at the base of the top third, mark the eyebrows, and at the line of the top of the second third mark the base of the nose.

STEP 2

DRAW THE AXIAL SKELETON

Following the illustration on page 28, draw a vertical axis along which you will mark the measures of four heads. The first measure is for the head, the second and third for the neck, the ribcage, and the space between the bottom of the ribcage and the top of pelvis, and the fourth measure is for the pelvis. (These segments, considered together, are known as the *axial skeleton*.) Further define the image by doing the following:

- Draw the head as an upside-down egg, and mark the lines for the eyebrows and the base of nose as shown in step 1.

- Draw the ribcage as an upright egg in the space between the second and third head measures, leaving a measure of about one-third of one head between chin and top of ribcage for the neck and about one-quarter of the measure

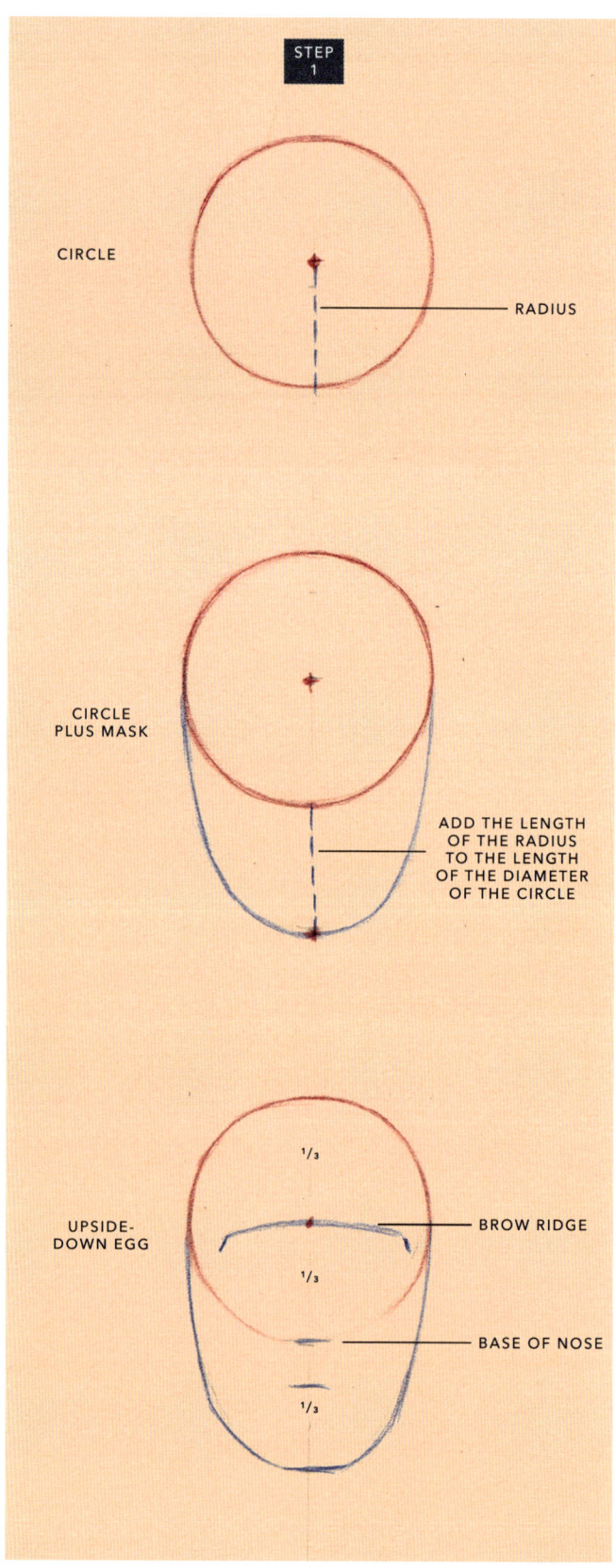

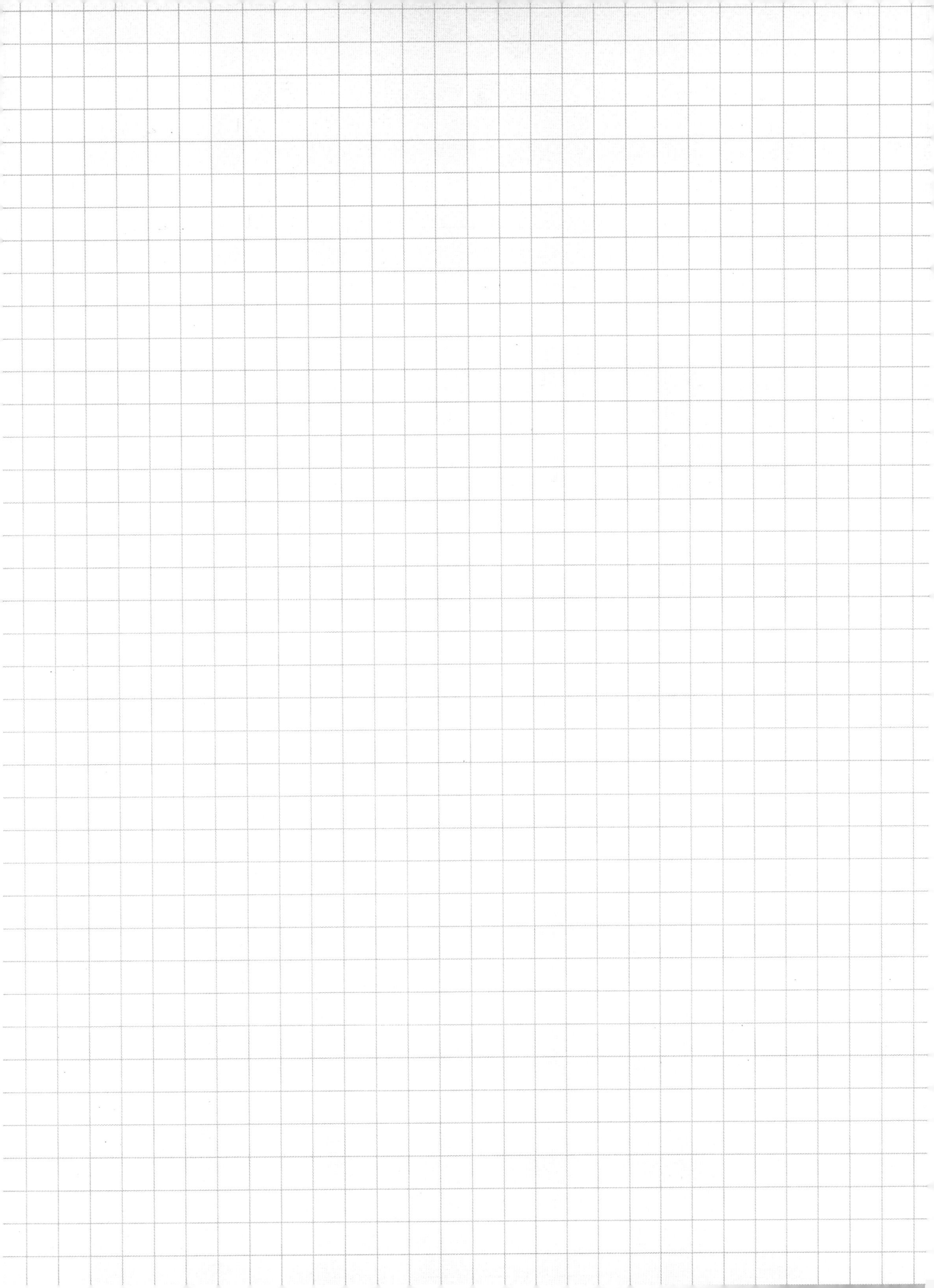

of one head for the space between the bottom of ribcage and the top of pelvis. The width of the ribcage is 1 ¼ head measures, or a bit more than the height of one head.

- Draw the pelvis as a bucket and divide it in four equal horizontal segments. Place dots indicating the anterior superior iliac spines (ASIS's) at the line of the base of the first quarter and a dot for the pubic bone at the line of the top of the lower quarter. The width of the pelvis is the same as the width of the ribcage in the male proportions (1 ¼ heads).

STEP 3

ESTABLISH THE HEIGHT OF THE FIGURE

The pubic bone marks, with good approximation, the midpoint of the figure. By doubling the measure that goes from the top of the head to the pubic bone along the figure's central axis, you can fairly accurately establish the height of the legs and thus the entire figure.

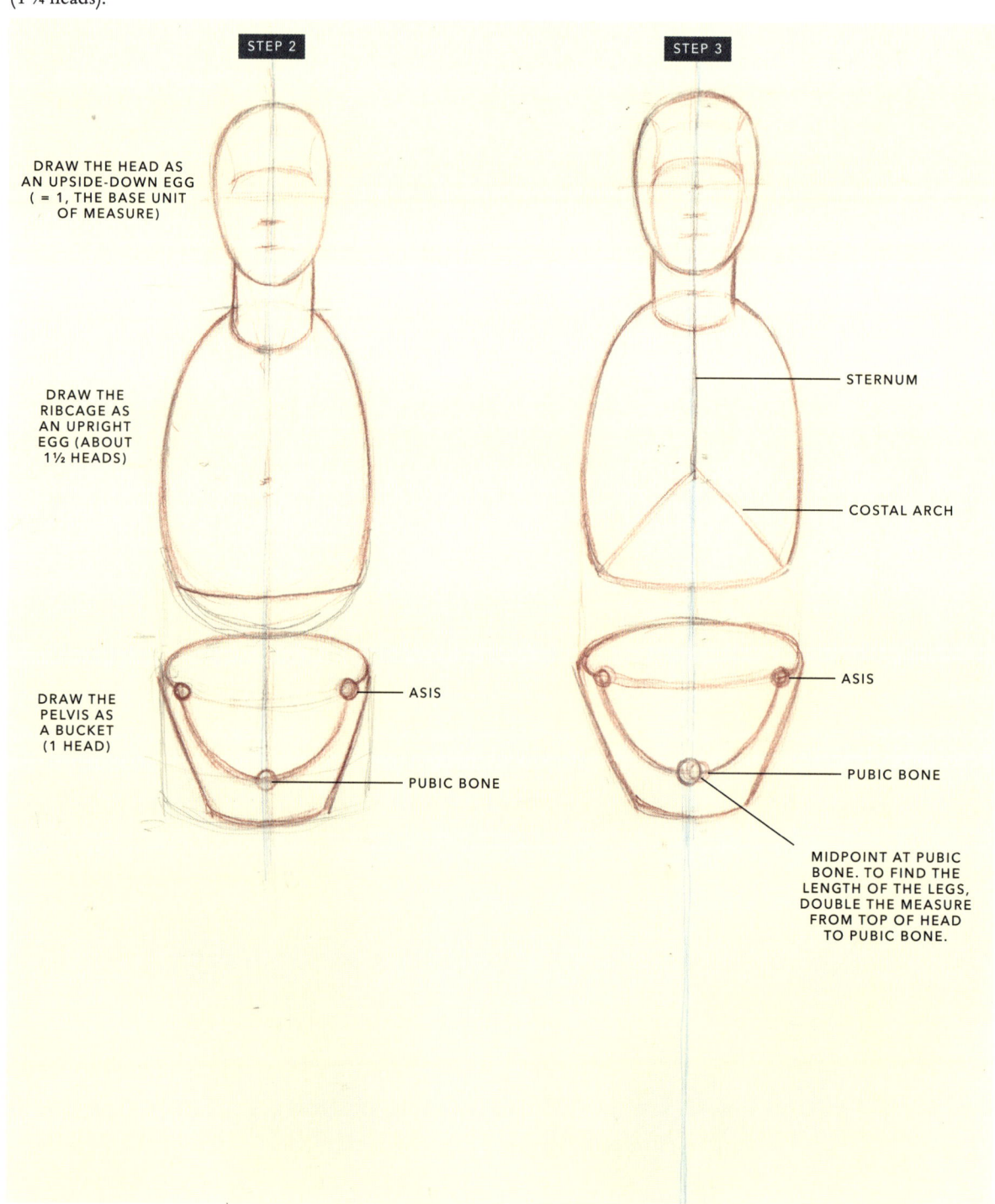

STEP 2

DRAW THE HEAD AS AN UPSIDE-DOWN EGG (= 1, THE BASE UNIT OF MEASURE)

DRAW THE RIBCAGE AS AN UPRIGHT EGG (ABOUT 1½ HEADS)

DRAW THE PELVIS AS A BUCKET (1 HEAD)

ASIS

PUBIC BONE

STEP 3

STERNUM

COSTAL ARCH

ASIS

PUBIC BONE

MIDPOINT AT PUBIC BONE. TO FIND THE LENGTH OF THE LEGS, DOUBLE THE MEASURE FROM TOP OF HEAD TO PUBIC BONE.

STEP 4

BEGIN DRAWING THE APPENDICULAR SKELETON—LEGS

The skeleton of the extremities—the legs including the feet and the arms including the hands—is known as the *appendicular skeleton*. Begin drawing it by adding the lower limbs and feet to the axial skeleton. The thighs start at the mid-level of the height of the pelvis, or halfway between iliac spines and pubic bone. The length of the thighs is the measure of two heads. The length of the lower legs, including the feet, is also two heads.

STEP 5

FINISH DRAWING THE APPENDICULAR SKELETON—ARMS

Then draw the arms. First, add the clavicles by drawing a horizontal line at the level of the pit of the neck. Then attach the arms below the clavicles at the shoulders. The upper arm is about the same length as the ribcage, with the elbow joint at the same level as the bottom of the ribcage. The wrist is at the level of the genitals, and the hand reaches down to about mid-thigh.

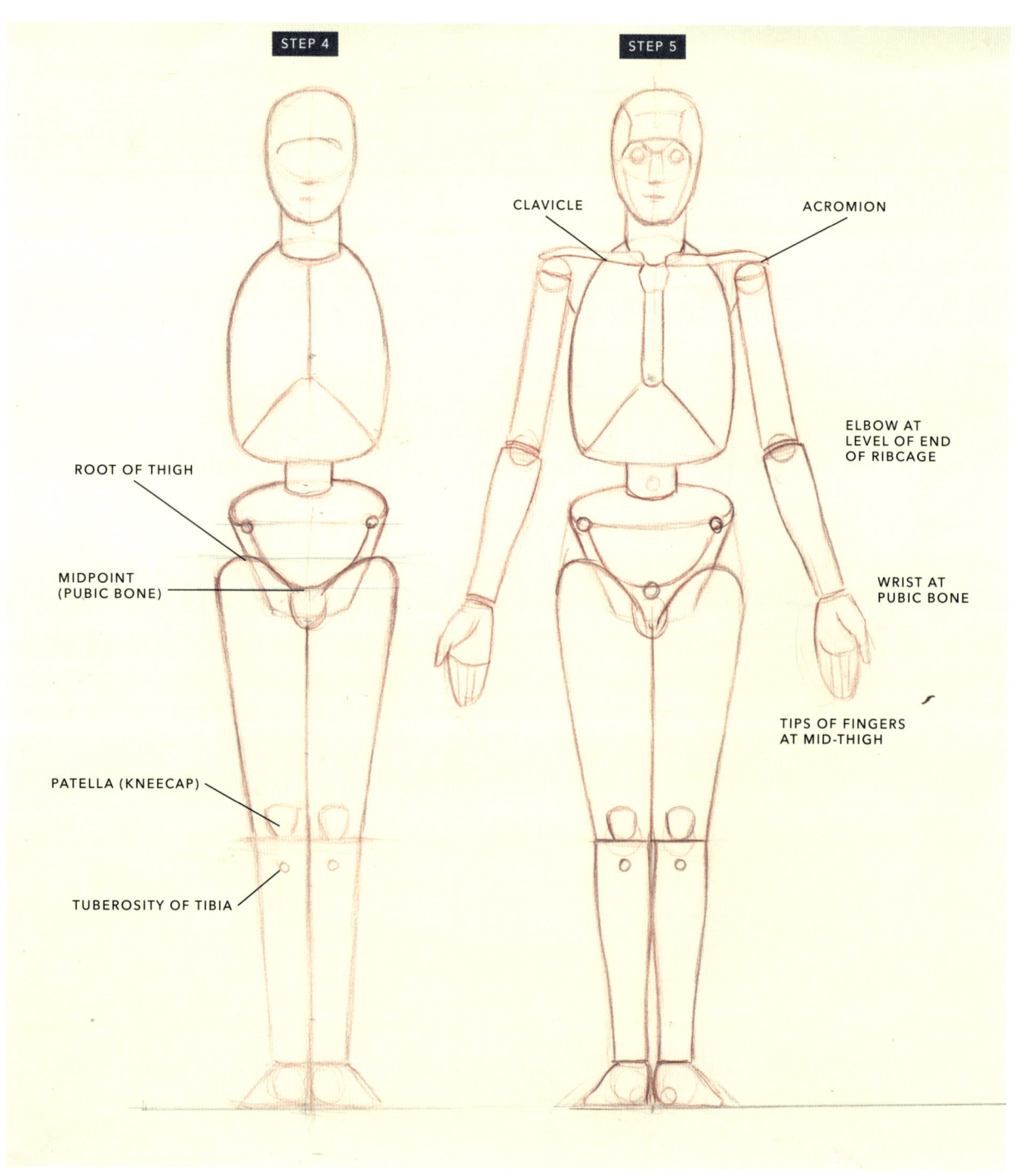

STEP 4

STEP 5

CLAVICLE

ACROMION

ROOT OF THIGH

MIDPOINT
(PUBIC BONE)

ELBOW AT
LEVEL OF END
OF RIBCAGE

WRIST AT
PUBIC BONE

PATELLA (KNEECAP)

TUBEROSITY OF TIBIA

TIPS OF FINGERS
AT MID-THIGH

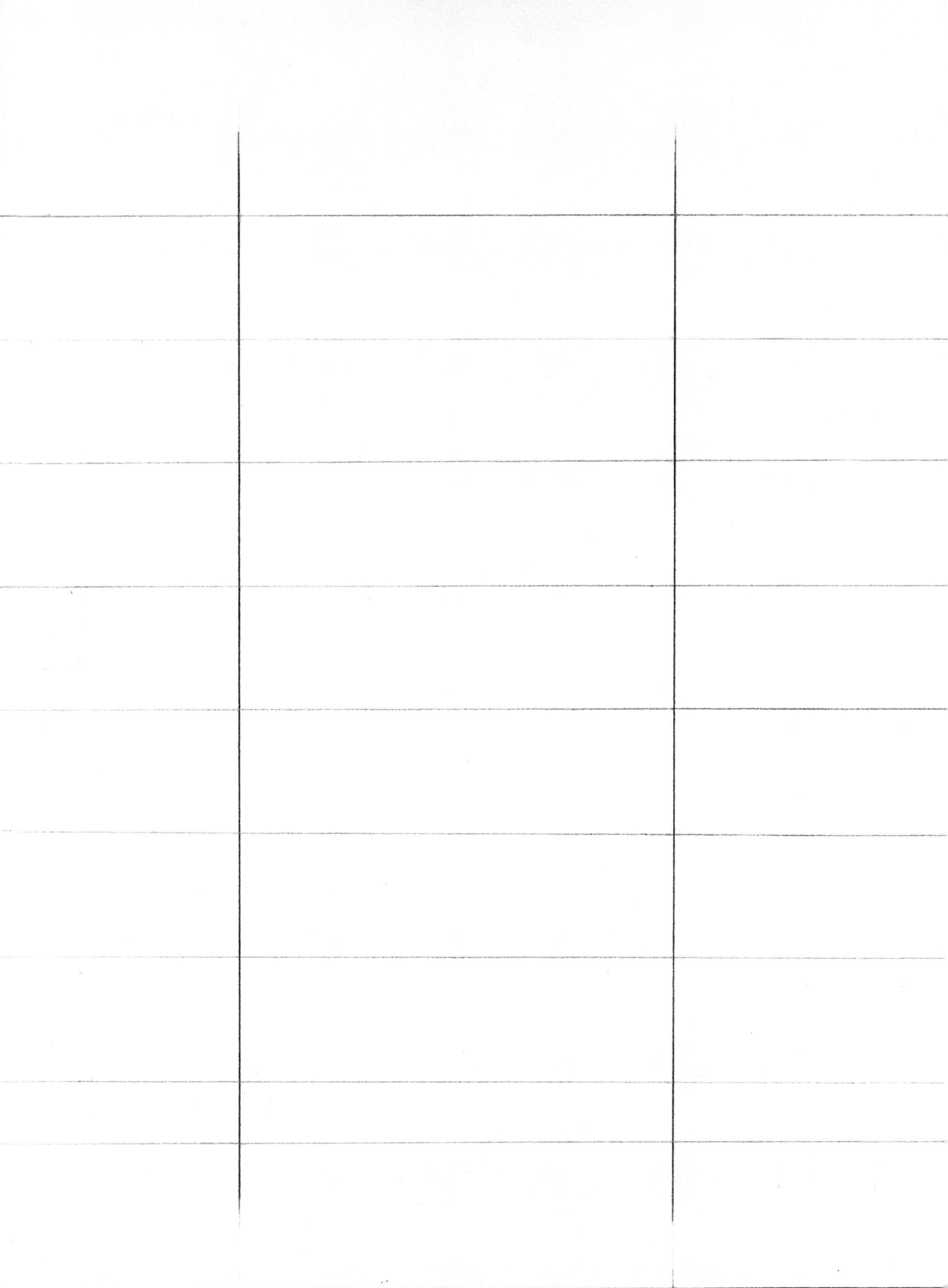

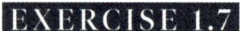

COMPARING MALE AND FEMALE PROPORTIONS

Copying the drawings below will help you understand the typical proportional relationships of the male and female bodies.

In the male, the width of the ribcage is about the same as the width of the pelvis, whereas in the female the ribcage is narrower than the pelvis. Because of their proportionally wider pelvis, the hip joints in women are farther apart than in men, and the shafts of the femurs and therefore of the thighs are positioned at a more pronounced angle, producing another typical difference between male and female figures.

The difference in the width of the female and male pelvis can also create a wider or narrower "U" shape at the inguinal ligament—which forms the line that connects the iliac spines via the pubic bone and that frames the bottom of the abdomen.

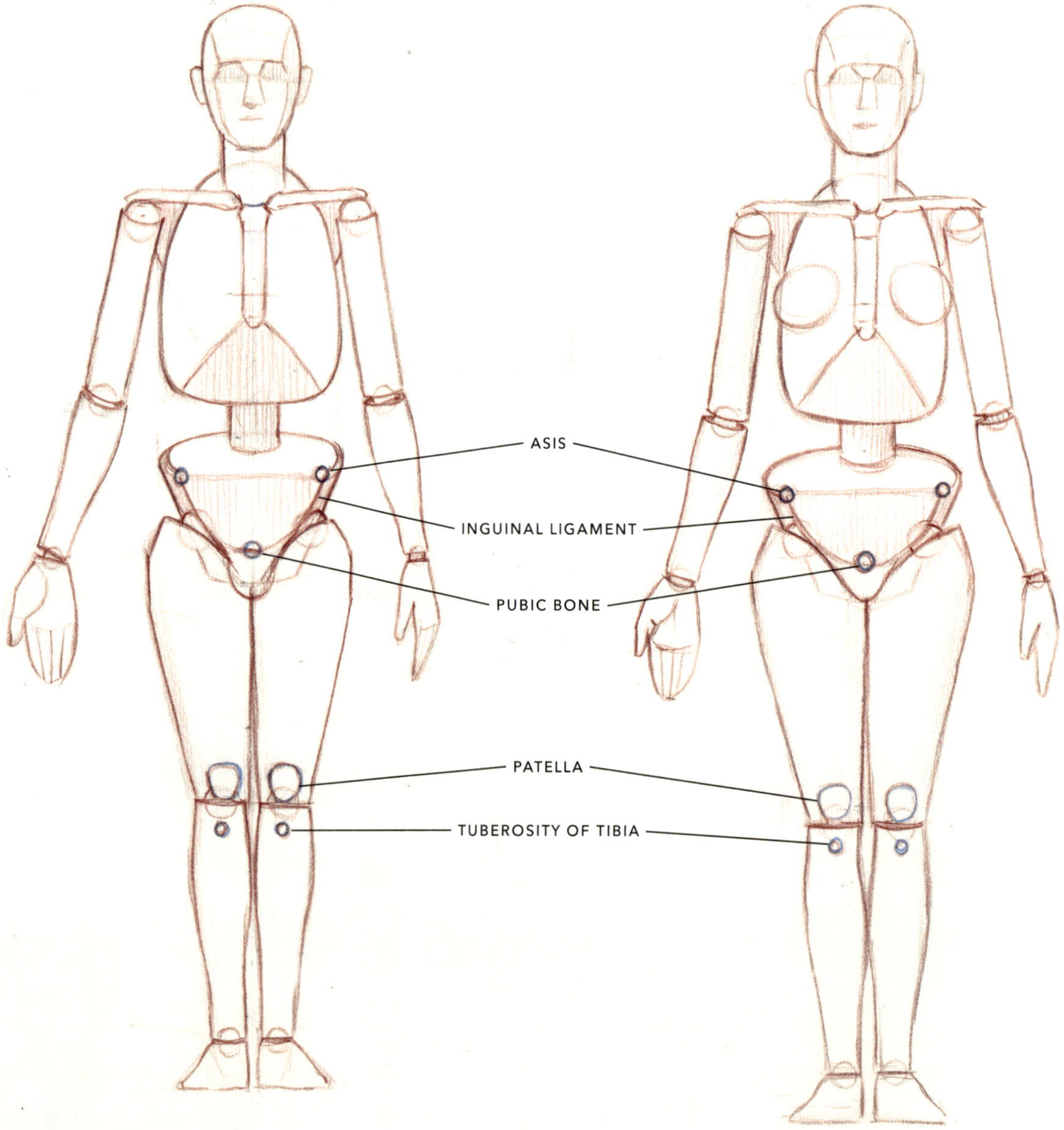

ASIS

INGUINAL LIGAMENT

PUBIC BONE

PATELLA

TUBEROSITY OF TIBIA

PROPORTIONS RELATING THE HEAD TO THE BODY AND THE BODY'S LANDMARKS

The drawing below helps you visualize the proportional relationships between the head and the rest of the body. As you can see, the head is the basic unit of measure, defined as "1," and the various parts of the body are therefore fractions or multiples of the measure of one head, or they are equal to it. We can also use the same method to compare the parts of the body other than the head to each other.

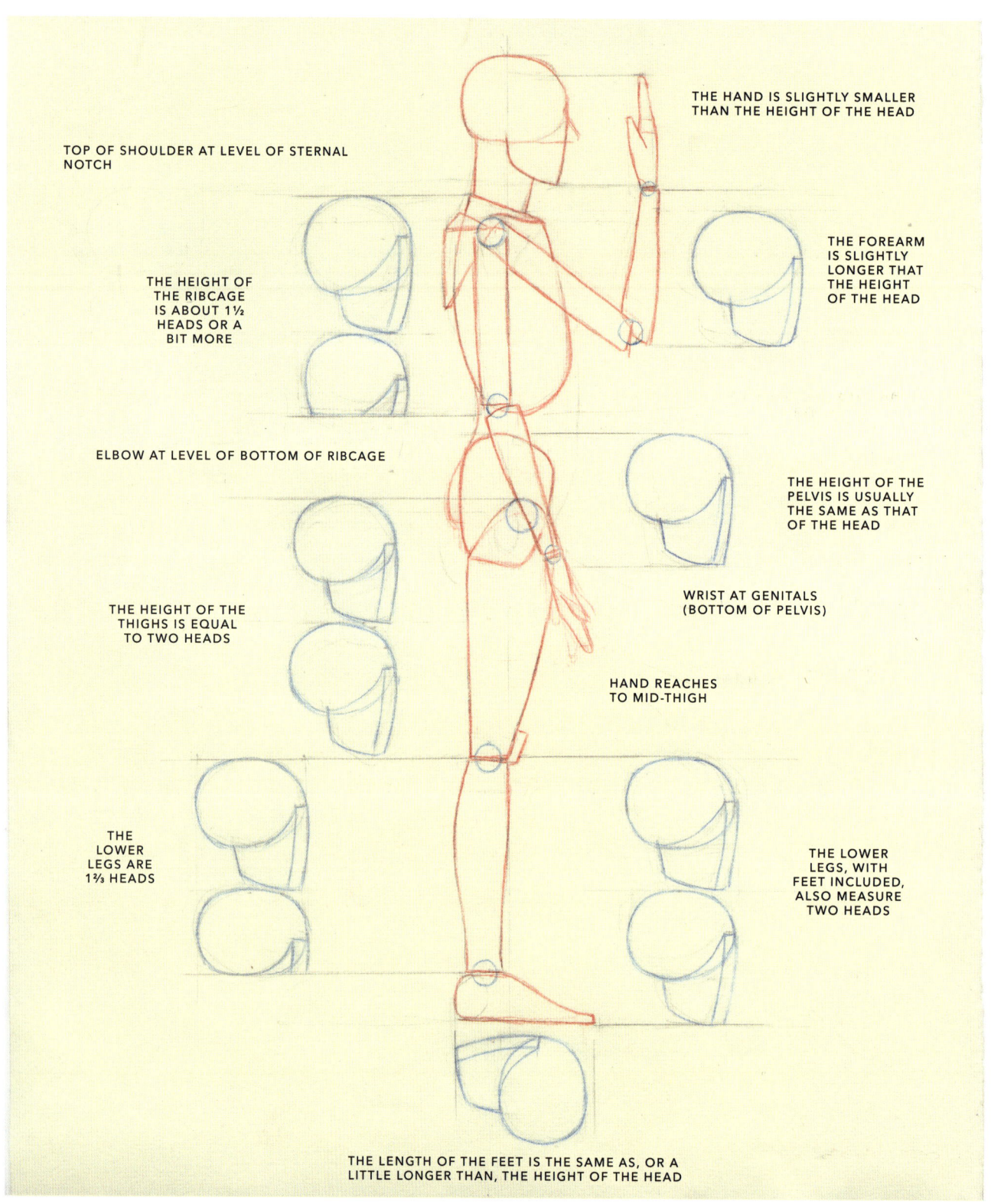

TOP OF SHOULDER AT LEVEL OF STERNAL NOTCH

THE HEIGHT OF THE RIBCAGE IS ABOUT 1½ HEADS OR A BIT MORE

ELBOW AT LEVEL OF BOTTOM OF RIBCAGE

THE HEIGHT OF THE THIGHS IS EQUAL TO TWO HEADS

THE LOWER LEGS ARE 1⅔ HEADS

THE HAND IS SLIGHTLY SMALLER THAN THE HEIGHT OF THE HEAD

THE FOREARM IS SLIGHTLY LONGER THAT THE HEIGHT OF THE HEAD

THE HEIGHT OF THE PELVIS IS USUALLY THE SAME AS THAT OF THE HEAD

WRIST AT GENITALS (BOTTOM OF PELVIS)

HAND REACHES TO MID-THIGH

THE LOWER LEGS, WITH FEET INCLUDED, ALSO MEASURE TWO HEADS

THE LENGTH OF THE FEET IS THE SAME AS, OR A LITTLE LONGER THAN, THE HEIGHT OF THE HEAD

EXERCISE 1.9

THE MAIN LANDMARKS OF THE BODY

Shown in the drawings below, the *skeletal landmarks* are points on the surface of the body where the skeleton is visible or palpable; they are usually recognizable, presenting themselves as small regular bumps (the iliac spines, malleoli, and tibial tuberosity) or as straight, uniform lines (the tibia, the sternum). The skeletal landmarks are useful for visualizing the skeletal structure, and recognizing them can help you create more accurately proportioned, solid, and properly articulated figure drawings. To become familiar with the basic landmarks, copy the drawings freehand a few times.

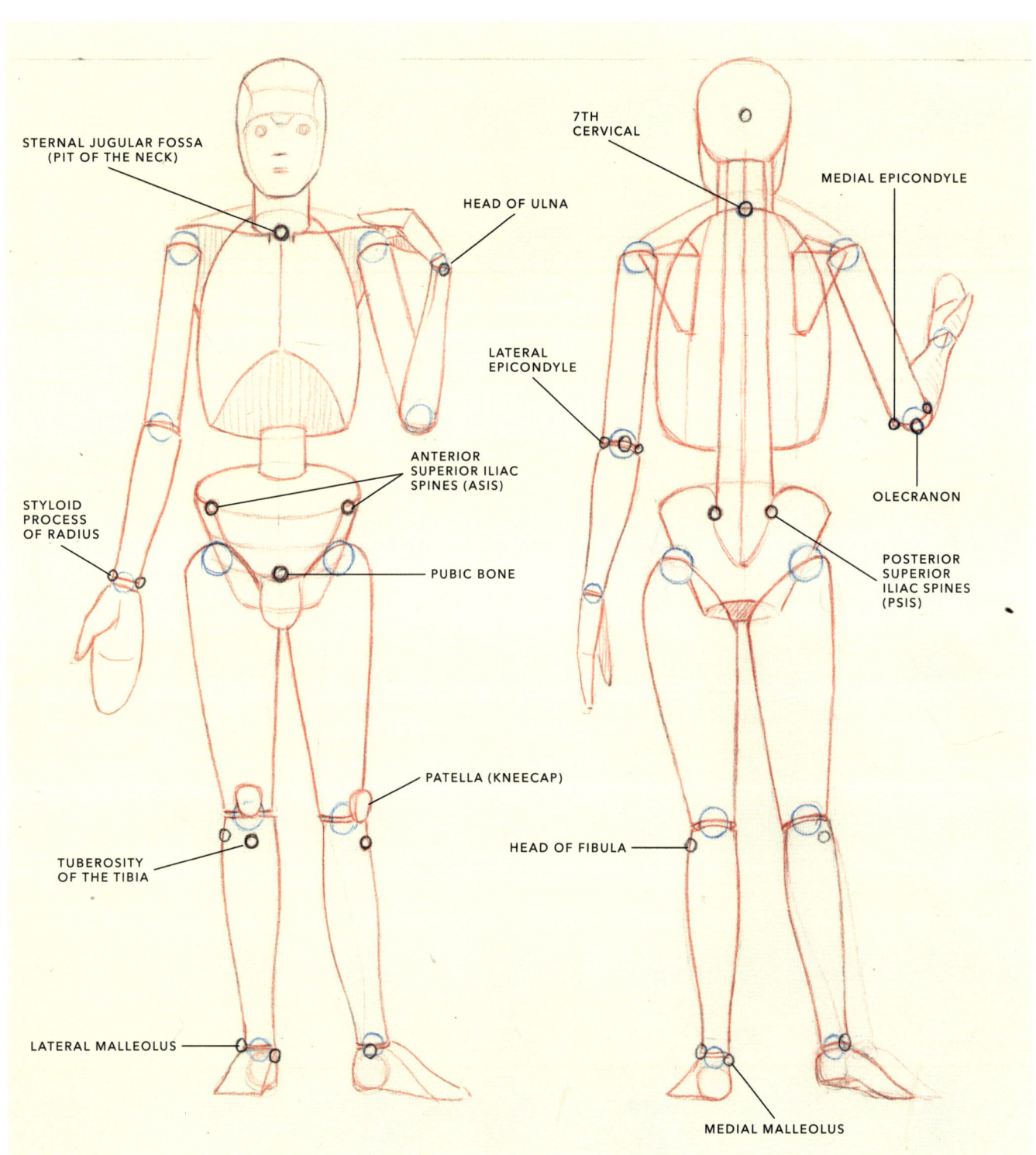

DRAWING THE PELVIS

The pelvis has a very complex form, but for our purposes, we need only its height, depth, and width as well as the positions of the essential landmarks, excluding all the rest. The pelvis can be conceptualized as a marshmallow or a bucket over which we mark the position of the ASIS's, pubic bone, iliac crest, and acetabulum. The drawings below and on page 40 show a few possible approaches to blocking in the essential form of the pelvis. Copy them for this exercise.

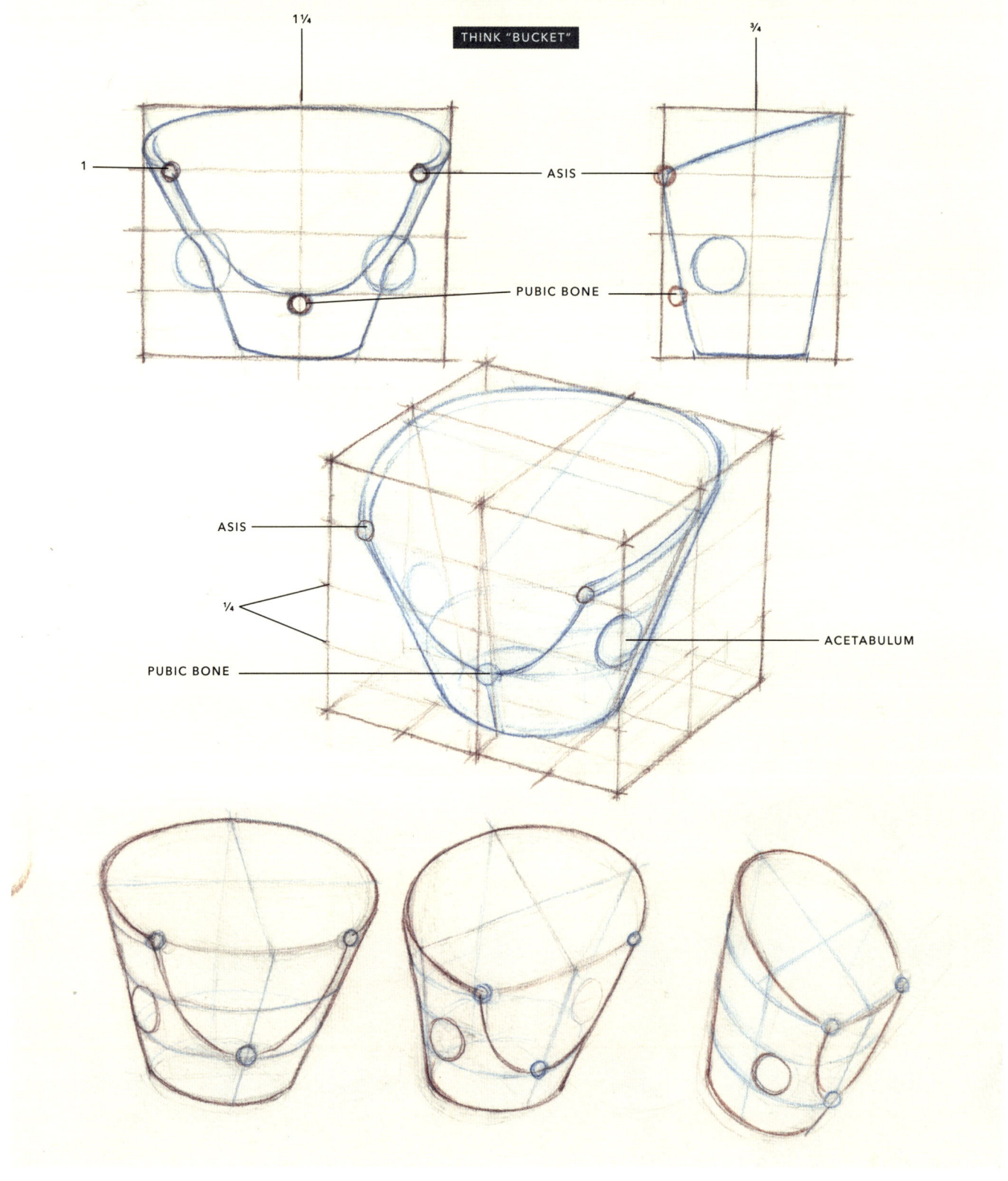

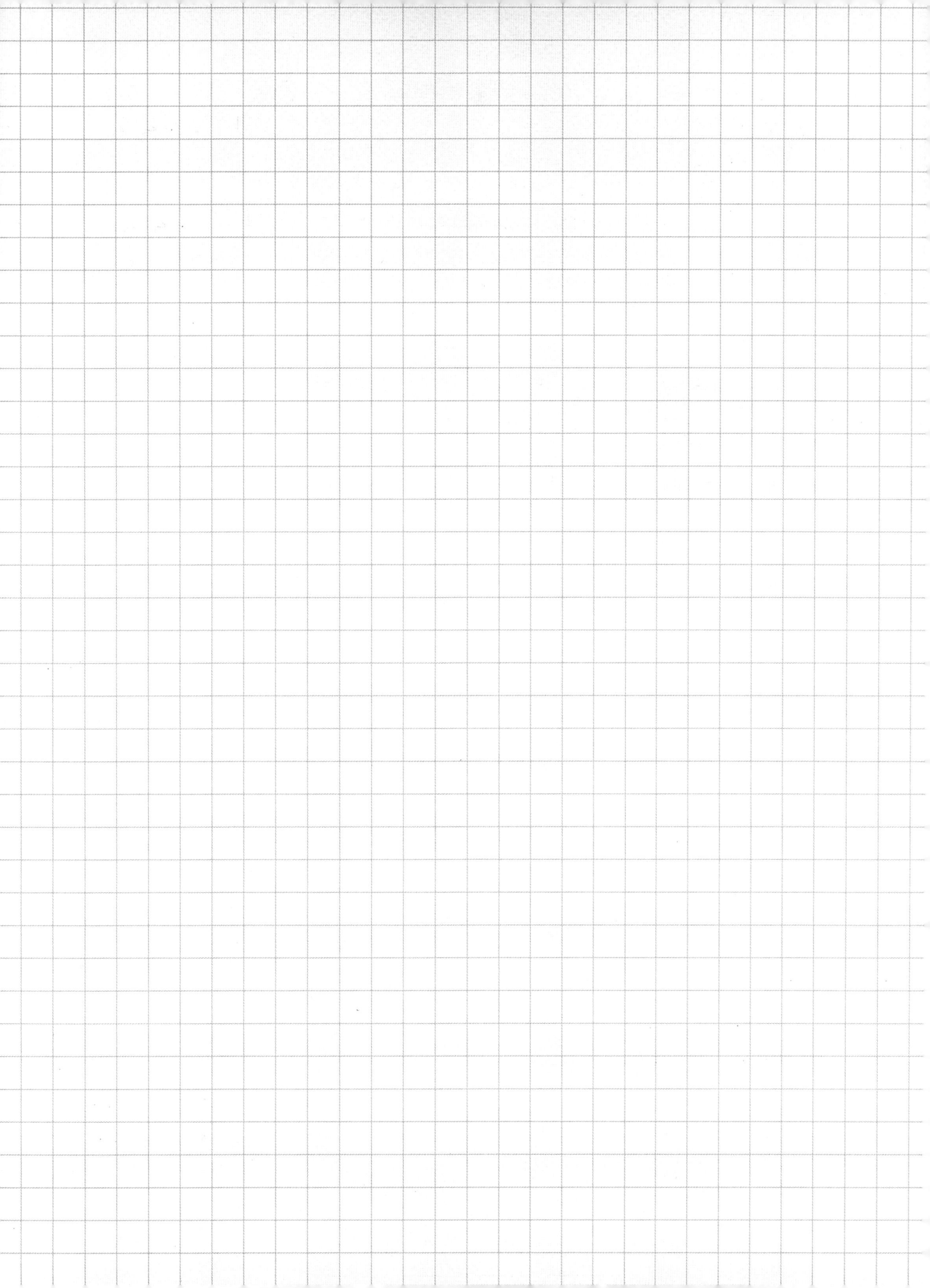

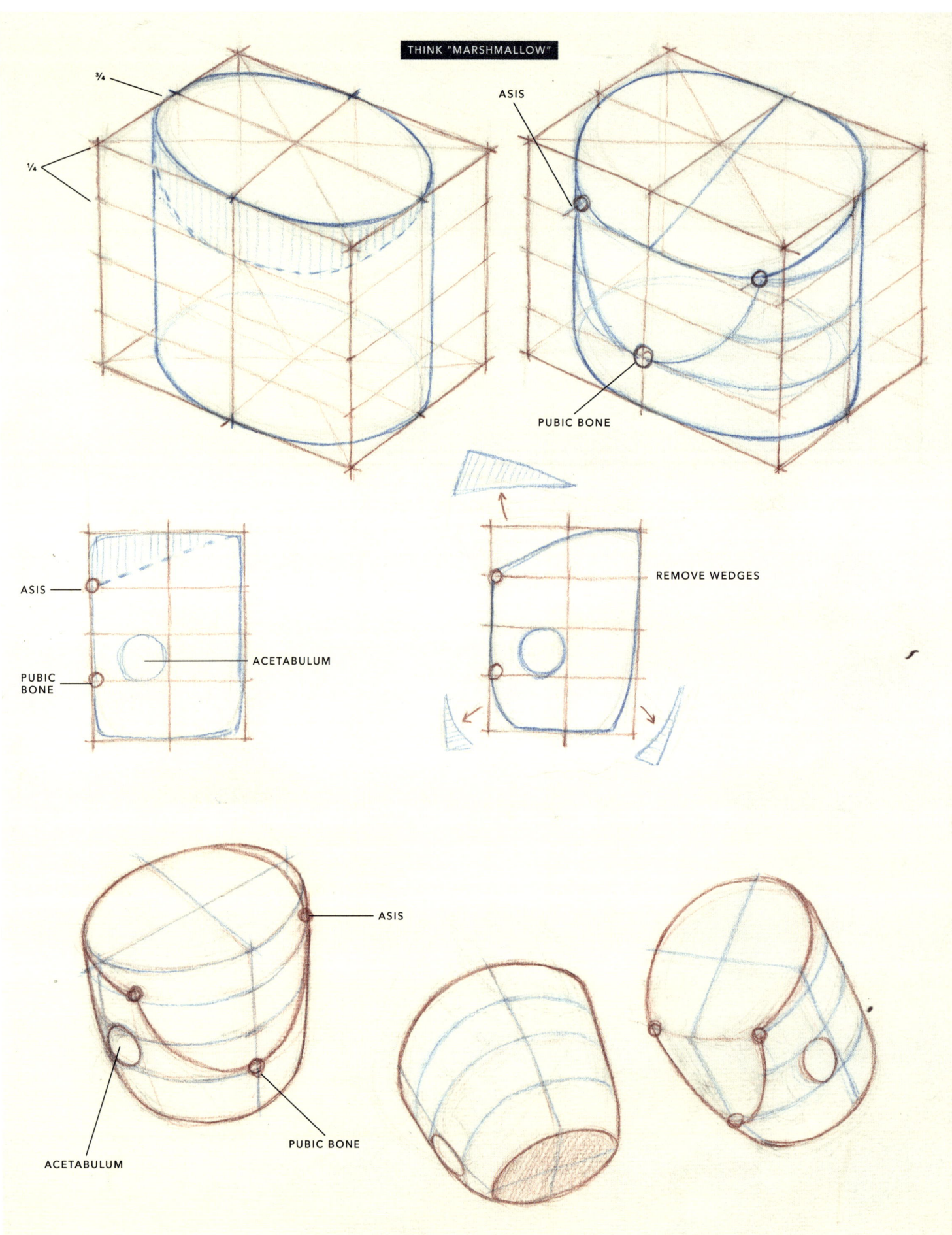

¾

¼

ASIS

PUBIC BONE

ASIS

PUBIC BONE

ACETABULUM

REMOVE WEDGES

ASIS

PUBIC BONE

ACETABULUM

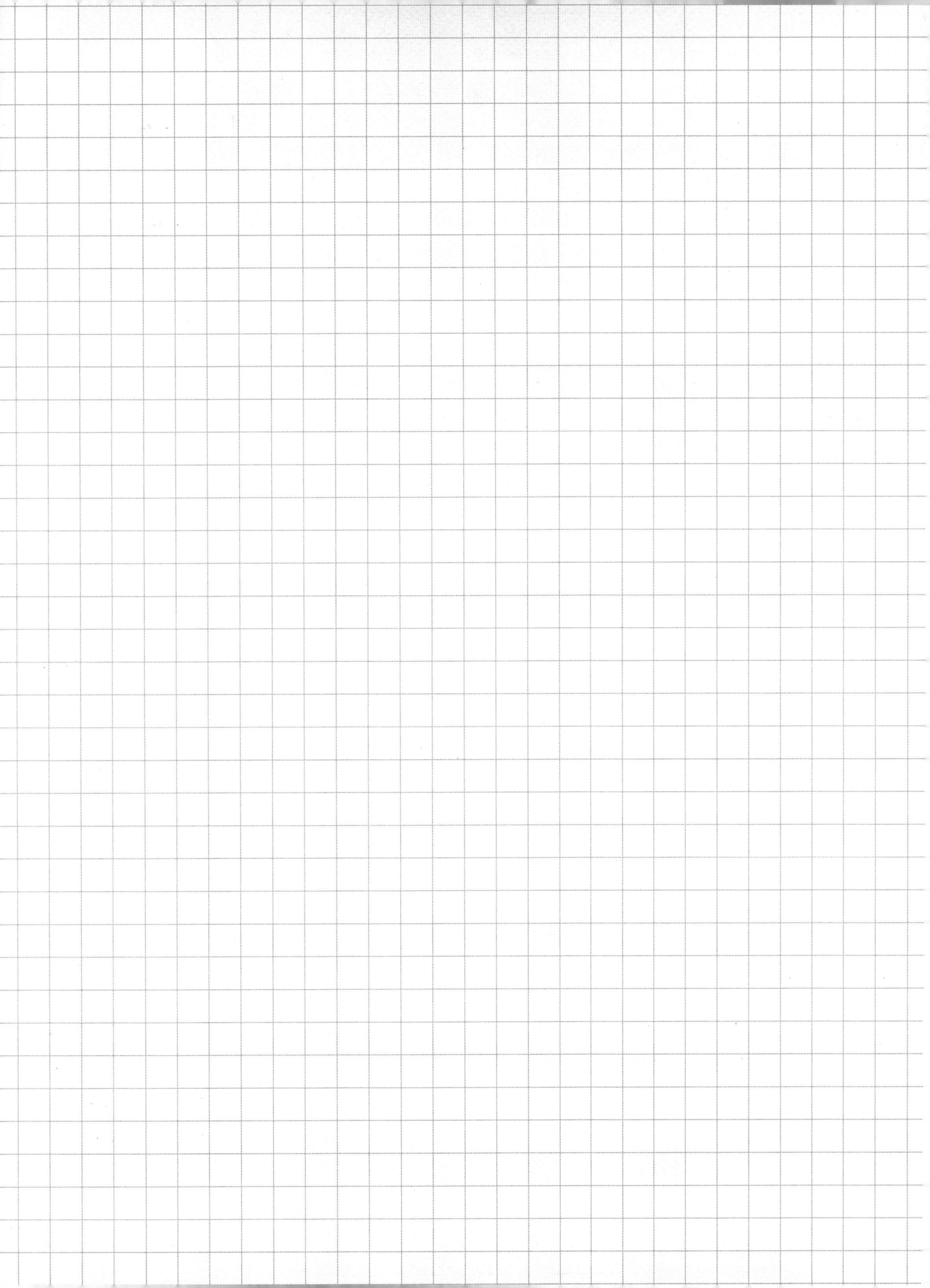

EXERCISE 1.11
REVIEW AND EXPERIMENT

Let's take some time now to review the material we have studied so far and to experiment with some slightly more complex poses. Draw a few male and female figures in both angular and rounded stereometry, giving them a sense of movement, as in the drawings below and on page 44. You can start by copying these four figures and then draw your own from imagination or using reference photos of models as inspiration. Try drawing figures in a three-quarters view, slightly flexing, extending, abducting the limbs, or turning the head, hips, and torso. Practice drawing with and without the help of a grid.

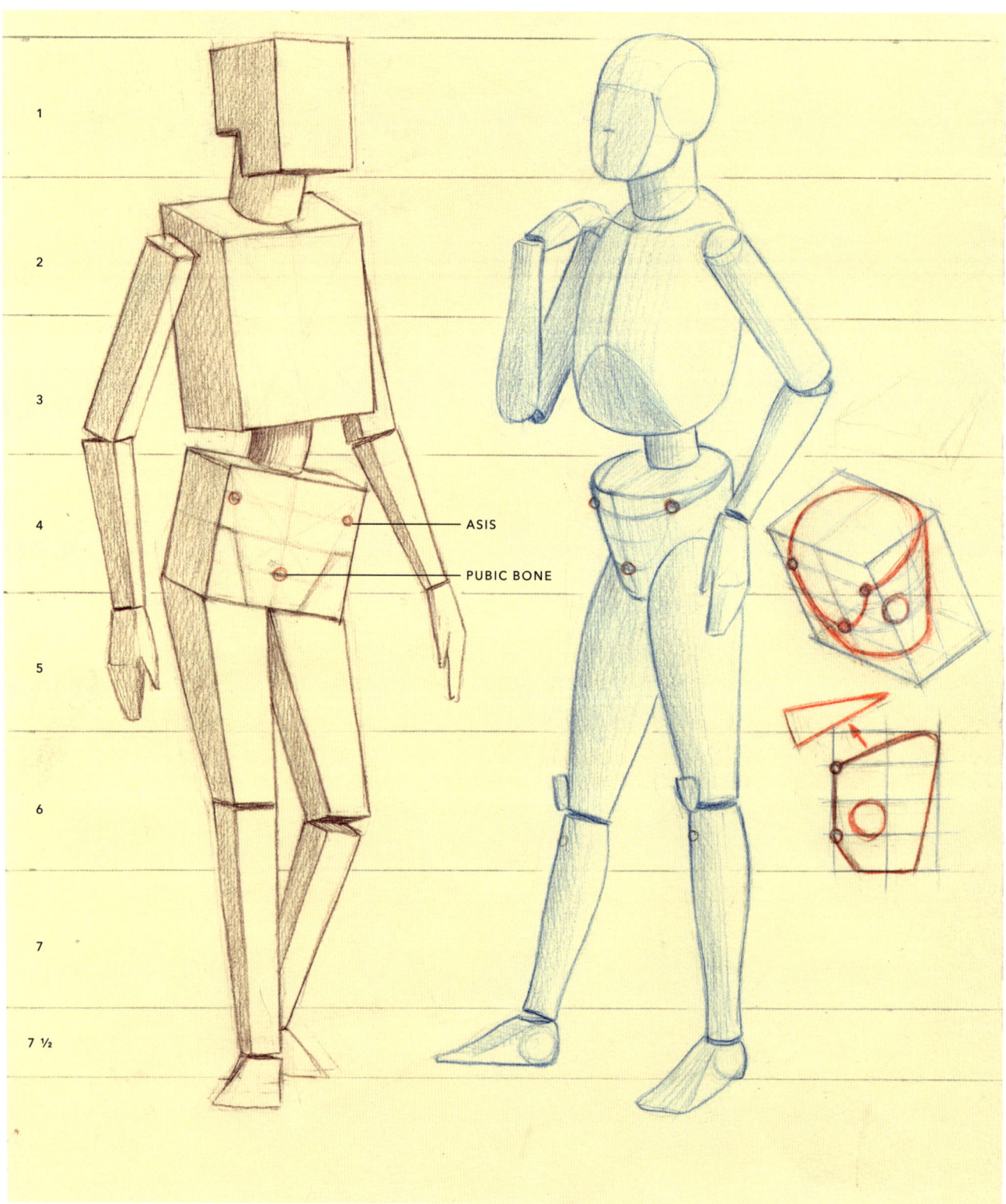

ASIS

PUBIC BONE

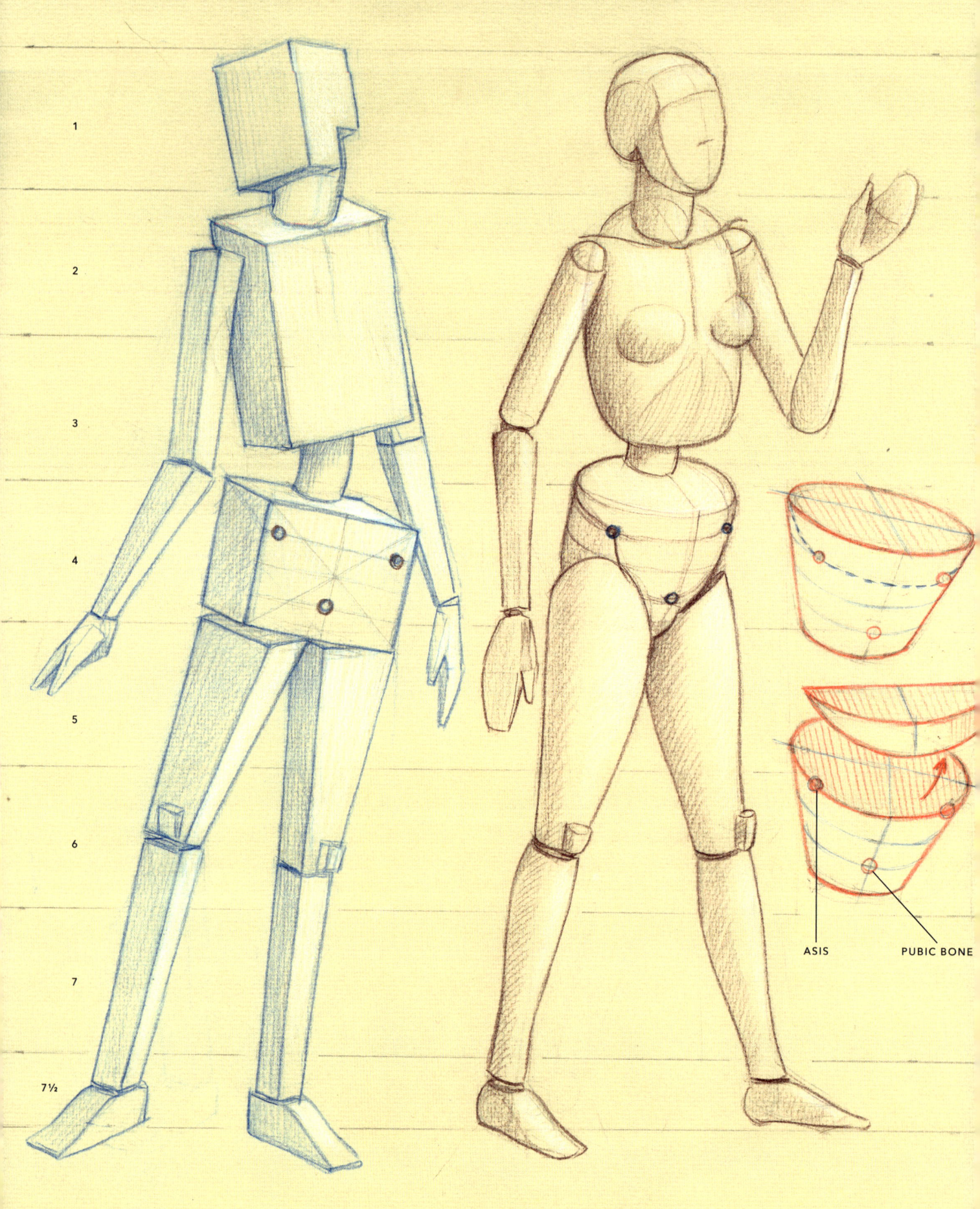

1

2

3

4

5

6

7

7½

ASIS PUBIC BONE

LEVEL 2

STATIC POSES AND THE USE OF LANDMARKS

In this level, we practice the use of the skeletal and soft landmarks we studied in the previous level, which is an essential skill to capture the model's pose, the body's structural integrity, proportional relationships, and finally, to help understand how the various segments of the body connect at the joints—a very important skill to obtain more convincing drawings of figures in static, dynamic, and foreshortened poses.

SEQUENCE: USING SKELETAL LANDMARKS

To practice using the skeletal landmarks to properly align segments of the body, copy the figures at right and on pages 48 and 50, following the steps explained below.

STEP 1

DRAW THE PELVIS

Start drawing the pelvis; the horizontal alignment of the iliac spines reveal its tilt. Now draw the ribcage; the sternum gives you the tilt of the ribcage in relation to the pelvis.

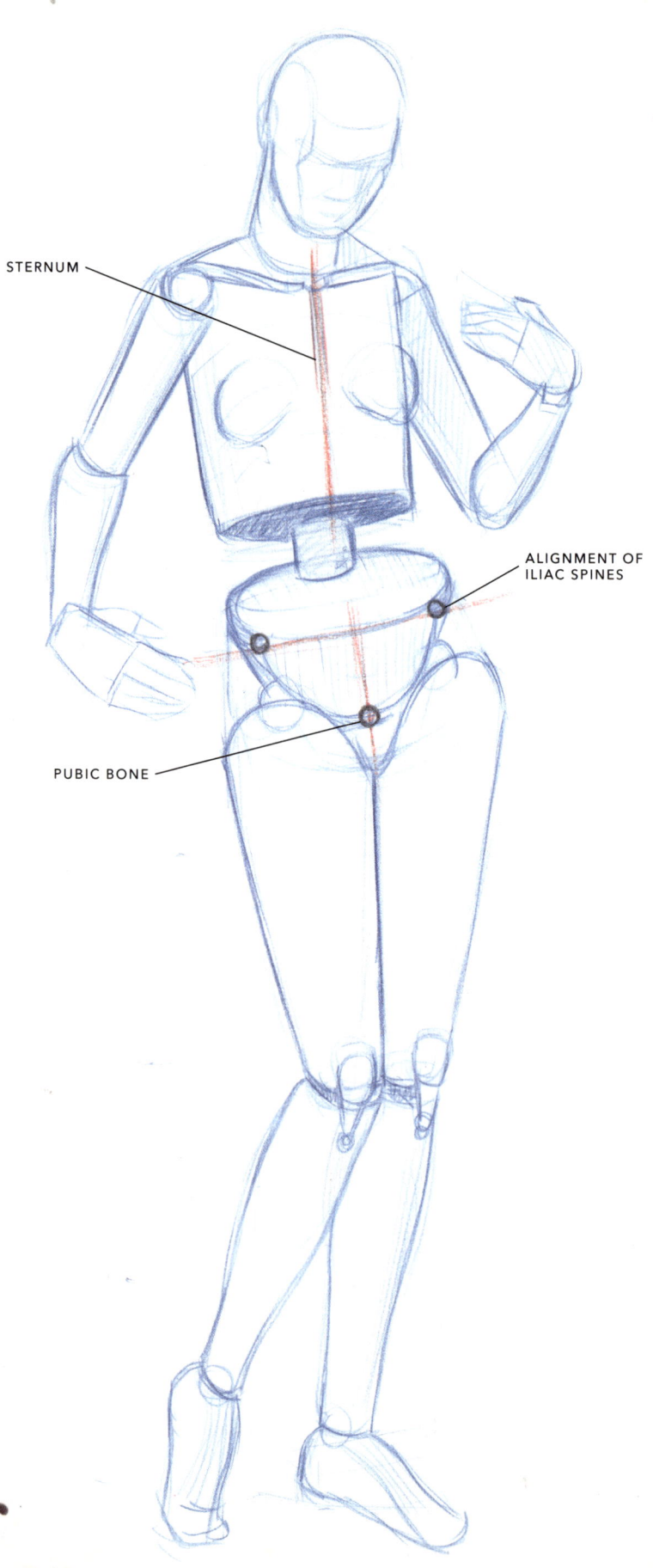

STERNUM

ALIGNMENT OF ILIAC SPINES

PUBIC BONE

STEP 2

POSITION THE JOINTS

The clavicles can help you determine the positions of the shoulder joints in relation to the ribcage. Pay attention to the tilt of the ribcage (revealed by the angle of the sternum) as well as the pelvic tilt (revealed by the angle of alignment of the iliac spines).

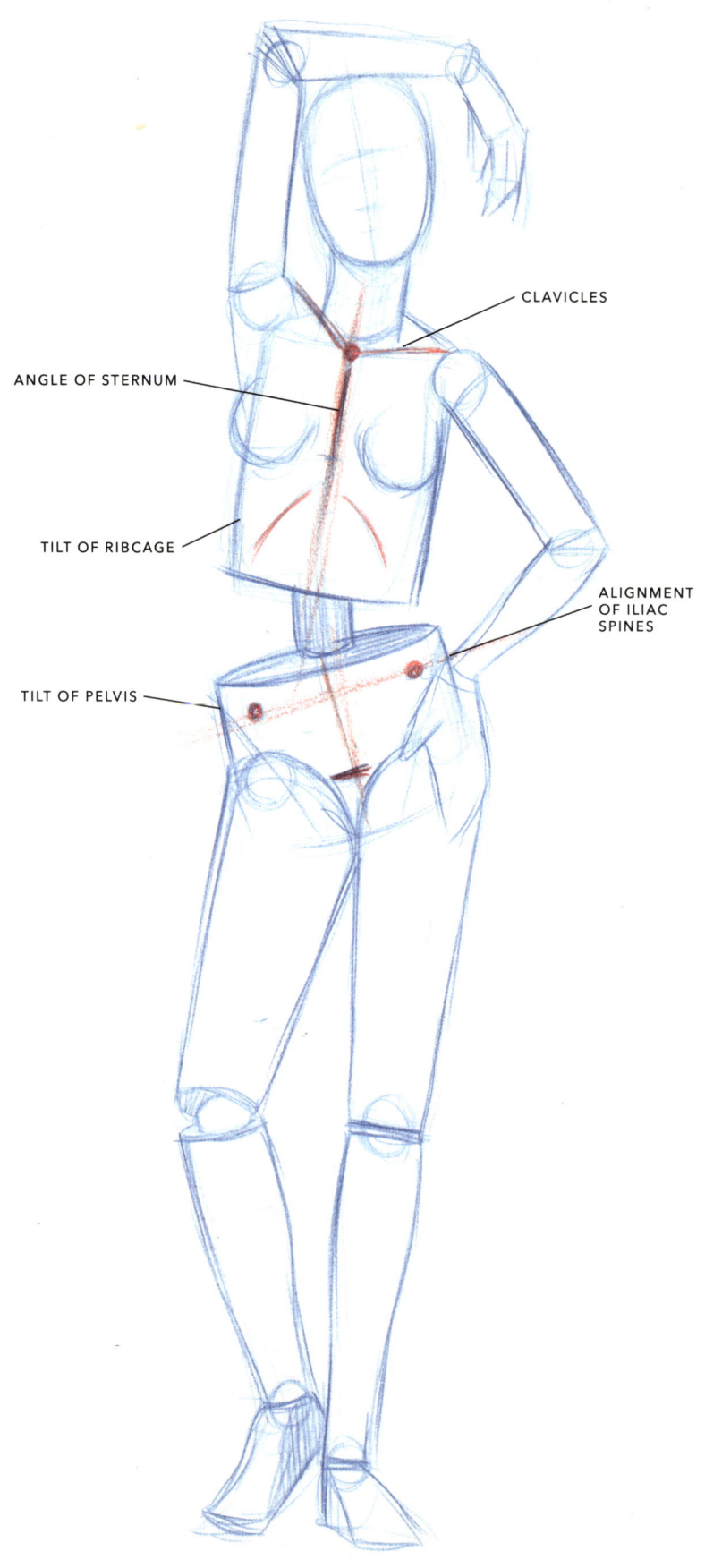

CLAVICLES

ANGLE OF STERNUM

TILT OF RIBCAGE

ALIGNMENT OF ILIAC SPINES

TILT OF PELVIS

STEP 3

ADD AXES TO ALIGN ALL THE BODY PARTS

Now add the axes of the head, arms, and legs to properly align all the segments of the body.

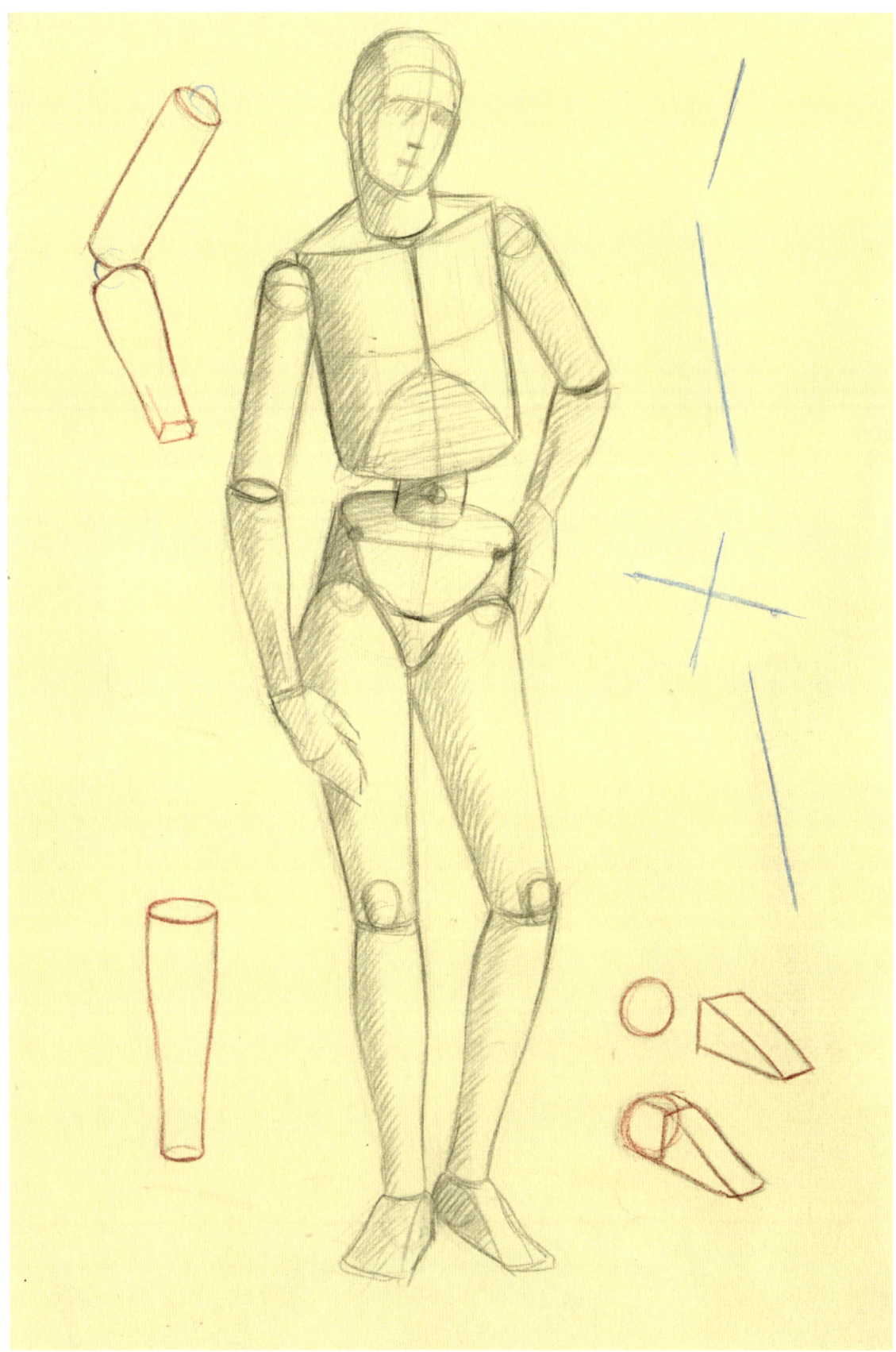

STEREOMETRIC STRUCTURE OF PELVIS AND LEGS

This exercise focuses on the stereometric structure of the pelvis and the positioning of the iliac spines (ASIS's), pubic bone, and hip joints.

STEP 1

BLOCK IN THE PELVIS

Start by blocking in the pelvis. Align the iliac spines to visualize the tilt of the pelvis, then proceed to attach the ribcage and legs to it and to gradually add the other segments of the body.

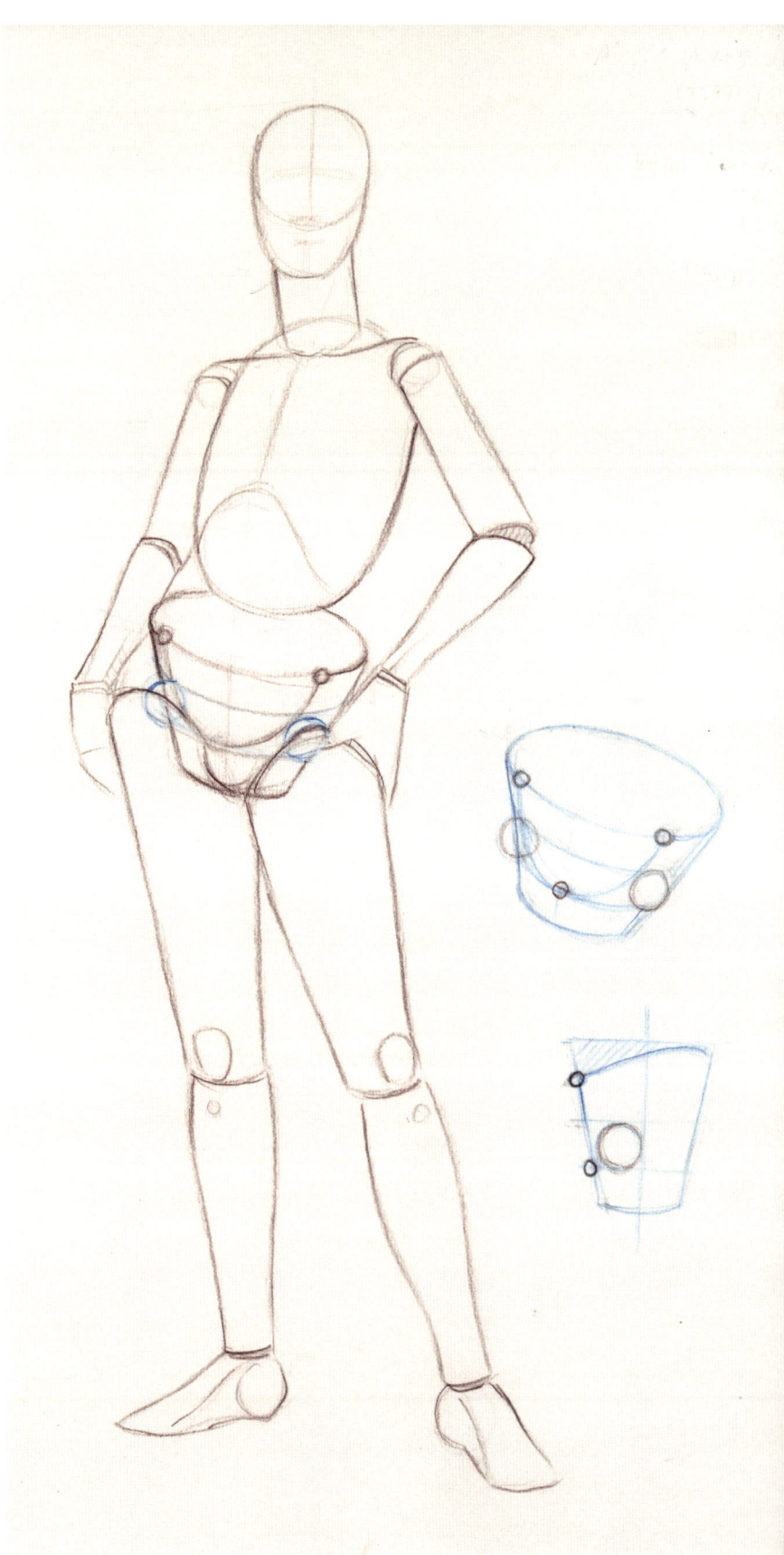

STEP 2

DIVIDE THE LEG INTO SPECIFIC SEGMENTS

The image below deconstructs the leg into its components, revealing more segments and axes: the volumes of thigh, the box of the knee, and the forms of the lower leg, ankles, and feet. Breaking down the lower limb into more specific segments helps you gradually move toward a more organic rendering of the leg. Note: The term *Cupid's bow* describes the pathway created by the sartorius muscle, the goosefoot (or pes anserinus, a small area on the medial side of the head of the tibia where the sartorius, gracilis, and semitendinosus muscles insert), and the medial face of the tibia, culminating in the medial malleolus.

As you copy the reference image, consider how the various segments of the stereometric figure align with each other and how they connect at the joints. For example, note that the top of the thigh is halfway between the iliac spine and the pubic bone. Note, too, the carrying angles of the various segments of the leg and the position of the hip joint in relation to the other landmarks of the pelvis.

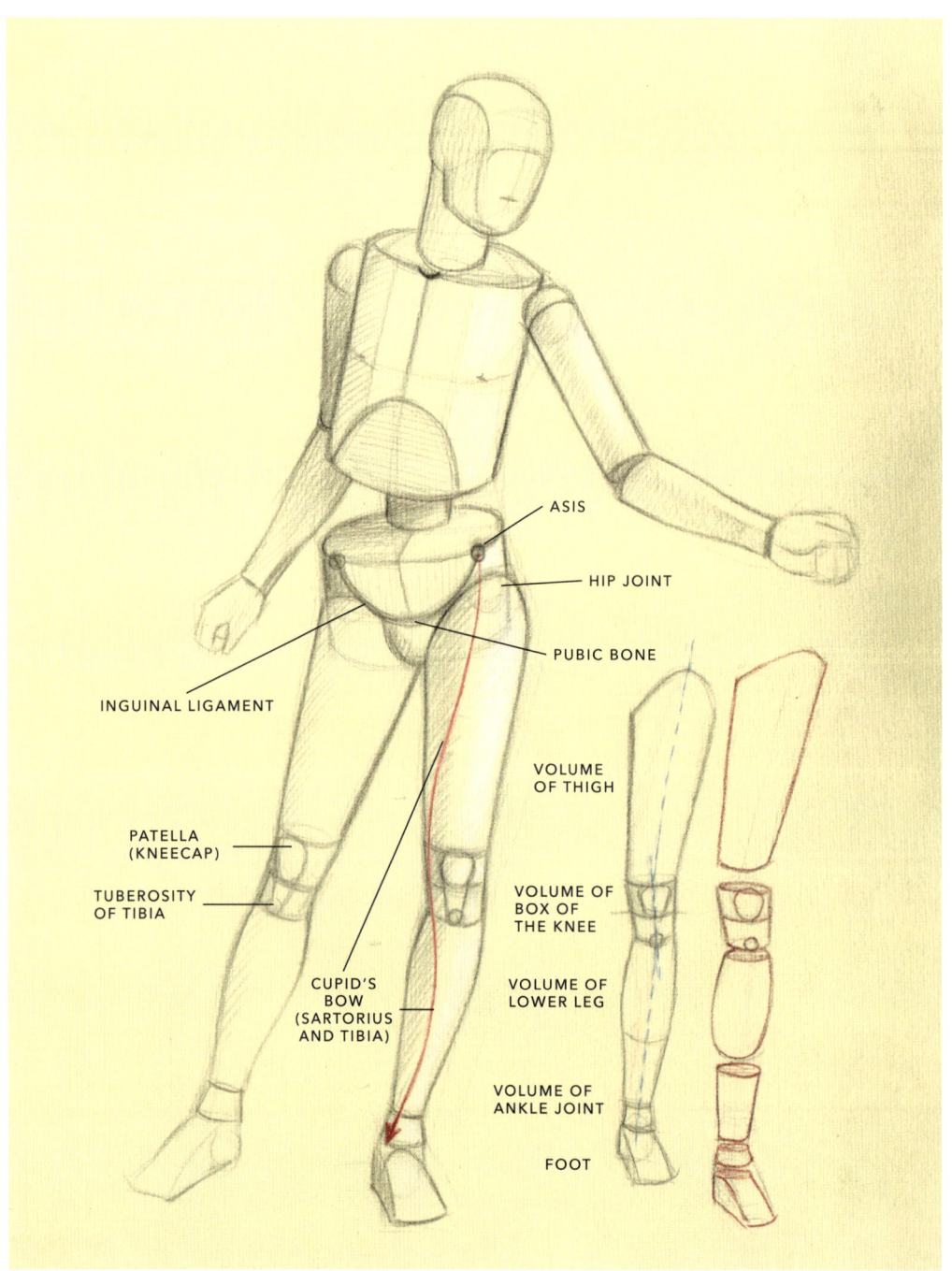

THE LINE OF THE CENTER OF GRAVITY

The line of center of gravity (LCG) is an imaginary vertical line that goes through the center of the body from the top of the head to the base of the pelvis, where it exits, falling between the feet. (See the figure in profile at right). You can use this imaginary line is to properly align the pose with the ground and the segments of the figure with each other.

To make this alignment easier, you can project the LCG outside the figure at the top of the torso (instead of the top of the head), more specifically at the jugular fossa on the front of the ribcage (figure on page 58) and at the bump of the 7th cervical vertebra on the back of the ribcage (figure on page 60). By dropping the LCG from either of these two landmarks down to the ground, you can perceive the body's orientation in relation to this line, which permits you to capture the alignment of the body's segments accurately.

The drawings on the following pages also show how to further subdivide the main stereometric volumes into smaller forms: the volumes of the quadriceps, adductors, calves, shin, ankles, deltoid, and hamstrings. This subdivision allows you to see how much space each of these smaller forms occupies in the segment of the body it belongs to and to draw it more accurately. See the landmarks chart (page 36) as well as chapter 2, on skeletal and muscular structure, for more details.

During life drawing sessions, you can use a plumb line to help you better visualize the LCG. Meanwhile, to become more familiar with the LCG, copy the drawings in this exercise.

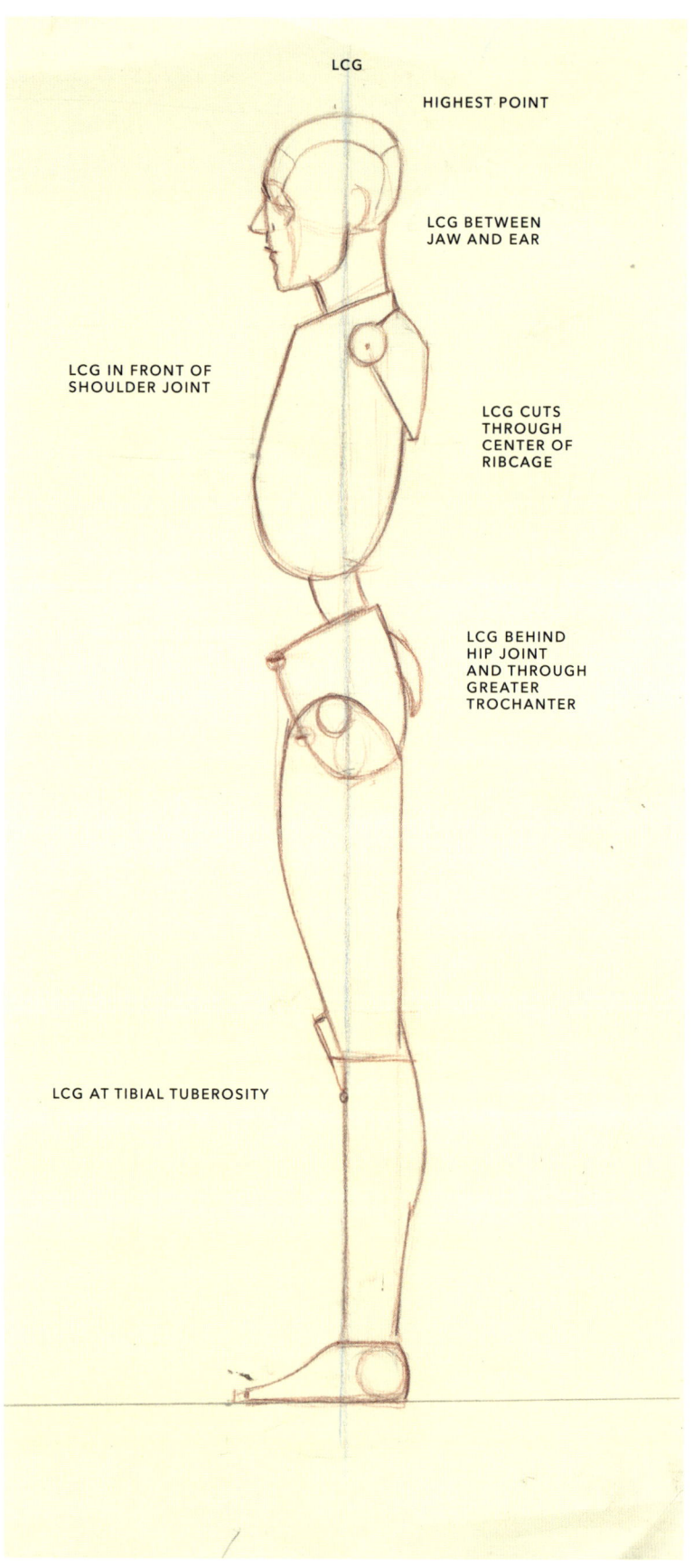

LCG

HIGHEST POINT

LCG BETWEEN JAW AND EAR

LCG IN FRONT OF SHOULDER JOINT

LCG CUTS THROUGH CENTER OF RIBCAGE

LCG BEHIND HIP JOINT AND THROUGH GREATER TROCHANTER

LCG AT TIBIAL TUBEROSITY

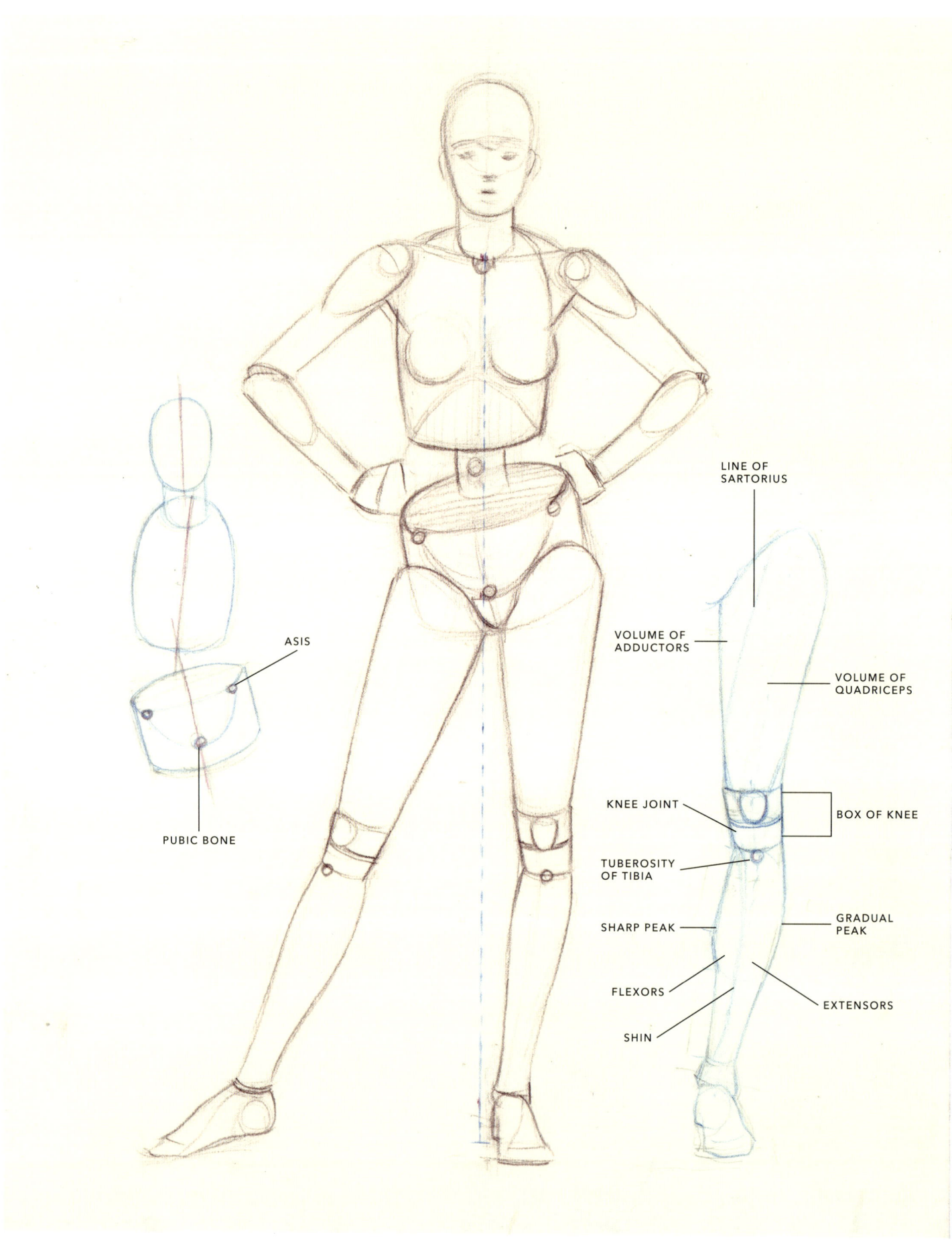

LINE OF
SARTORIUS

VOLUME OF
ADDUCTORS

VOLUME OF
QUADRICEPS

ASIS

PUBIC BONE

KNEE JOINT

BOX OF KNEE

TUBEROSITY
OF TIBIA

SHARP PEAK

GRADUAL
PEAK

FLEXORS

EXTENSORS

SHIN

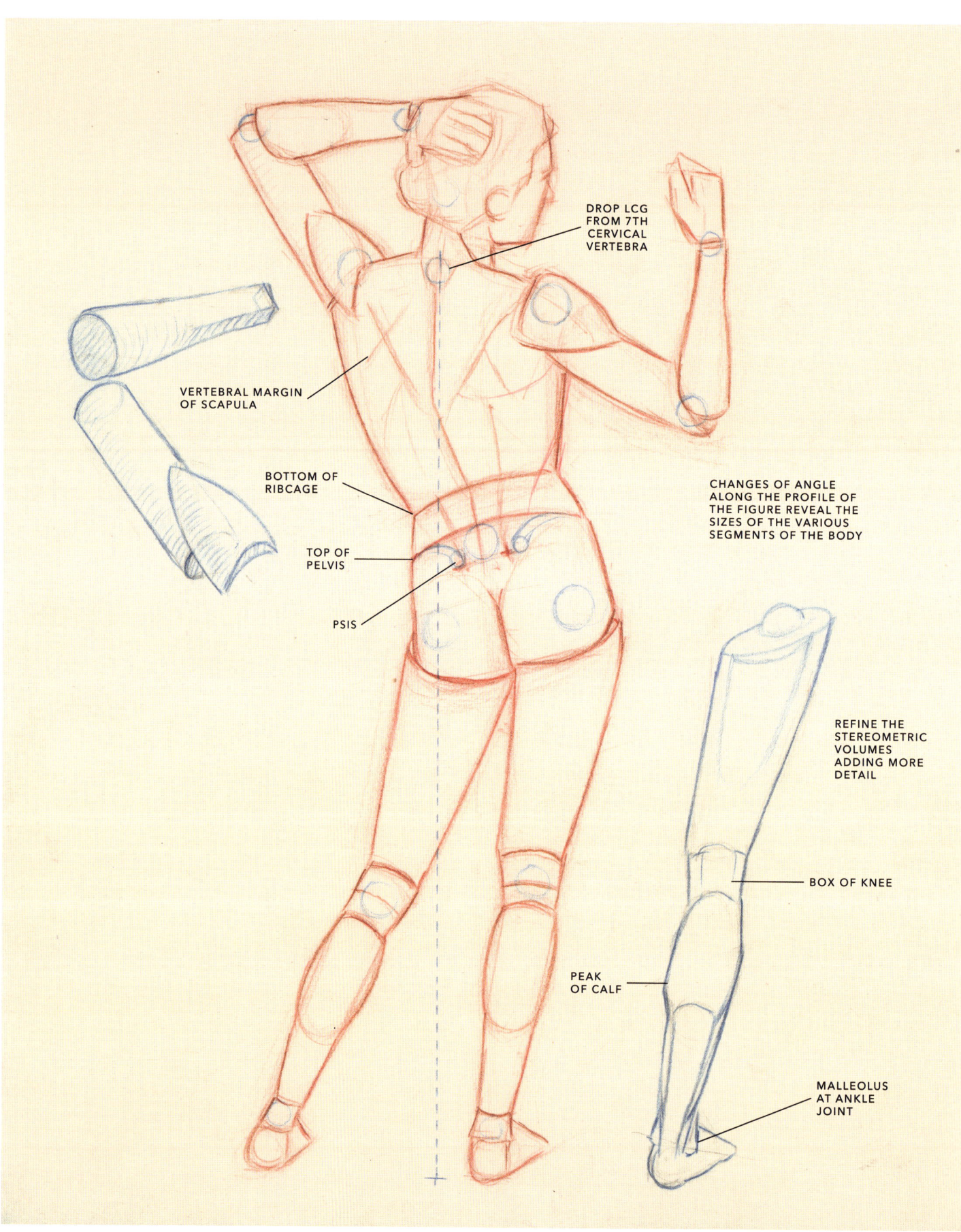

DROP LCG
FROM 7TH
CERVICAL
VERTEBRA

VERTEBRAL MARGIN
OF SCAPULA

CHANGES OF ANGLE
ALONG THE PROFILE OF
THE FIGURE REVEAL THE
SIZES OF THE VARIOUS
SEGMENTS OF THE BODY

BOTTOM OF
RIBCAGE

TOP OF
PELVIS

PSIS

REFINE THE
STEREOMETRIC
VOLUMES
ADDING MORE
DETAIL

BOX OF KNEE

PEAK
OF CALF

MALLEOLUS
AT ANKLE
JOINT

Create a few drawings of stereometric figures to review the various topics we have discussed for levels 1 and 2: proportional relationships, the body's axes and their alignments, landmarks, joints, and the line of center of gravity. (A summary of these features and their locations appears in the drawings on page 64.)

Start sketching your figures loosely, as you see in the drawing below, then refine your drawings by gradually adding smaller and more specific forms to the main stereometric volumes, as in the drawing at right.

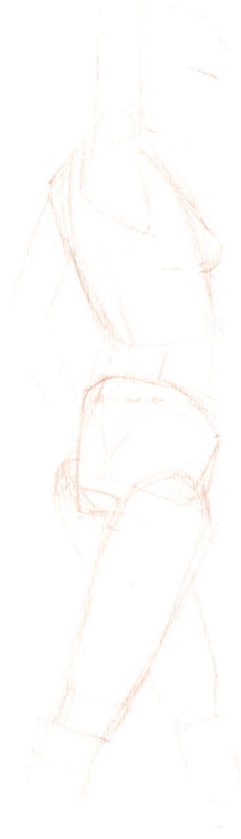

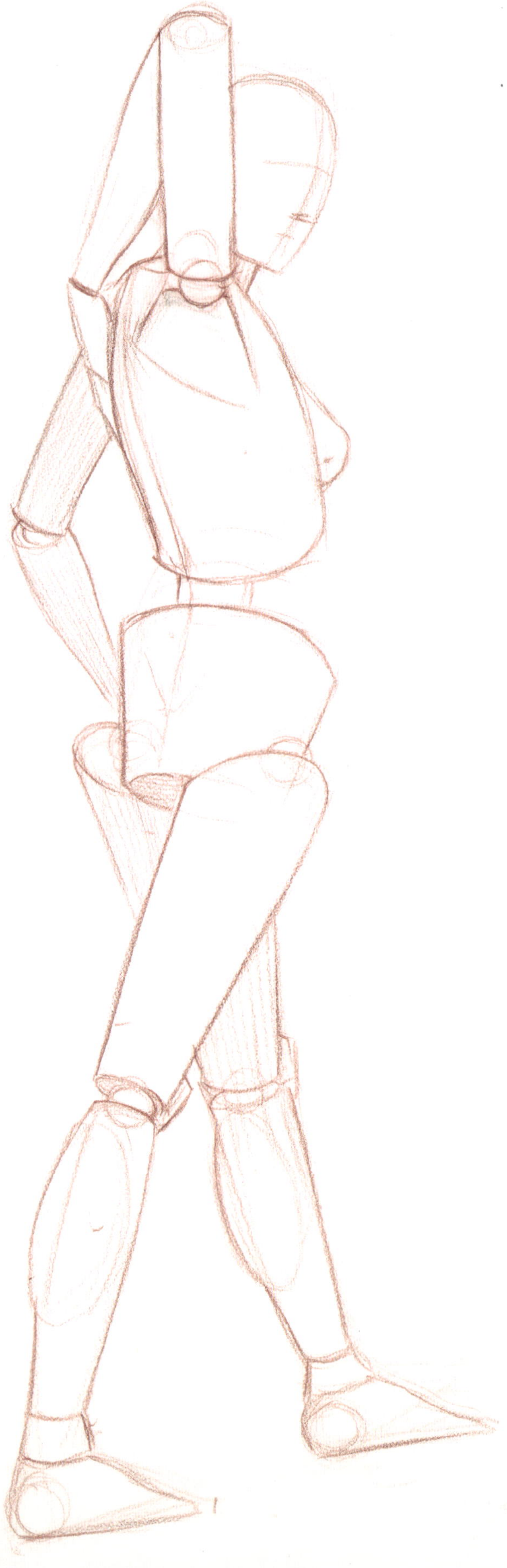

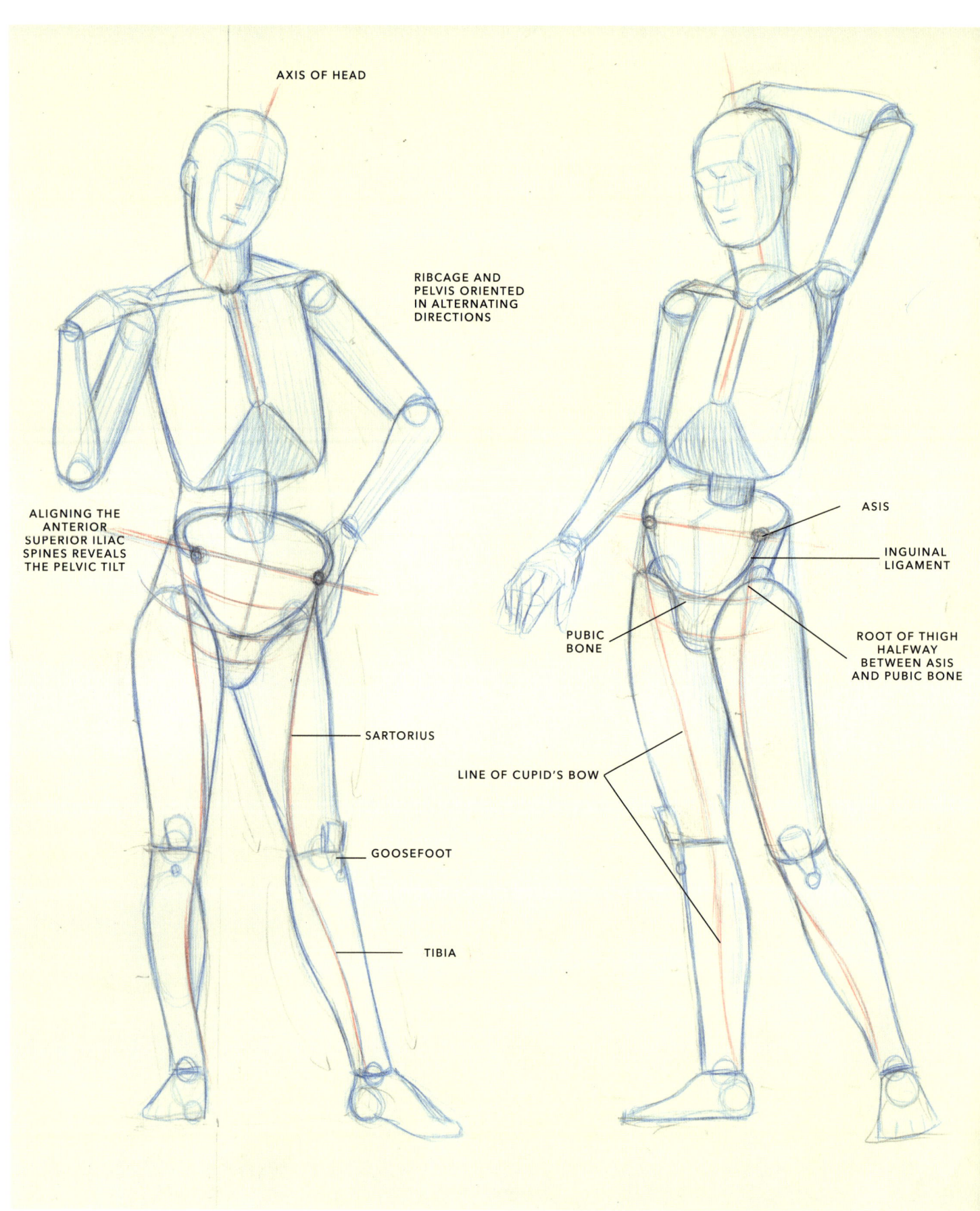

AXIS OF HEAD

RIBCAGE AND
PELVIS ORIENTED
IN ALTERNATING
DIRECTIONS

ALIGNING THE
ANTERIOR
SUPERIOR ILIAC
SPINES REVEALS
THE PELVIC TILT

ASIS

INGUINAL
LIGAMENT

PUBIC
BONE

ROOT OF THIGH
HALFWAY
BETWEEN ASIS
AND PUBIC BONE

SARTORIUS

LINE OF CUPID'S BOW

GOOSEFOOT

TIBIA

LEVEL 3

DYNAMIC POSES

You have now acquired the sufficient knowledge to start moving your figures consistent with the possibilities of the skeletal and muscular structures. With the following exercises, you start to impart a sense of dynamism, movement, and life to the stereometric figures.

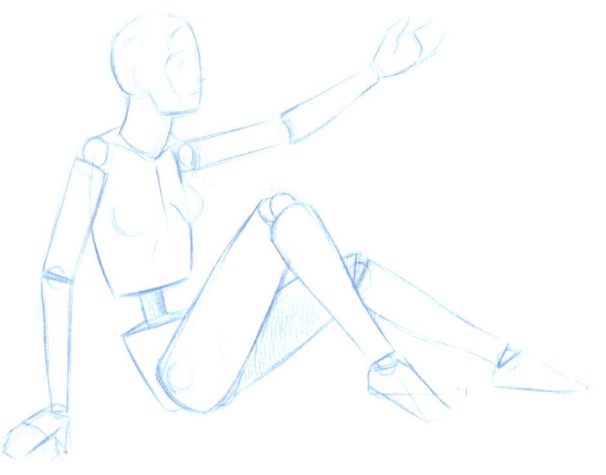

ERCISE 1.16
DYNAMIC POSES

Copy the reference images on these pages, paying attention to the overlapping of the various volumes and to how they connect with each other at the joints. Then create a few figures of your own from imagination.

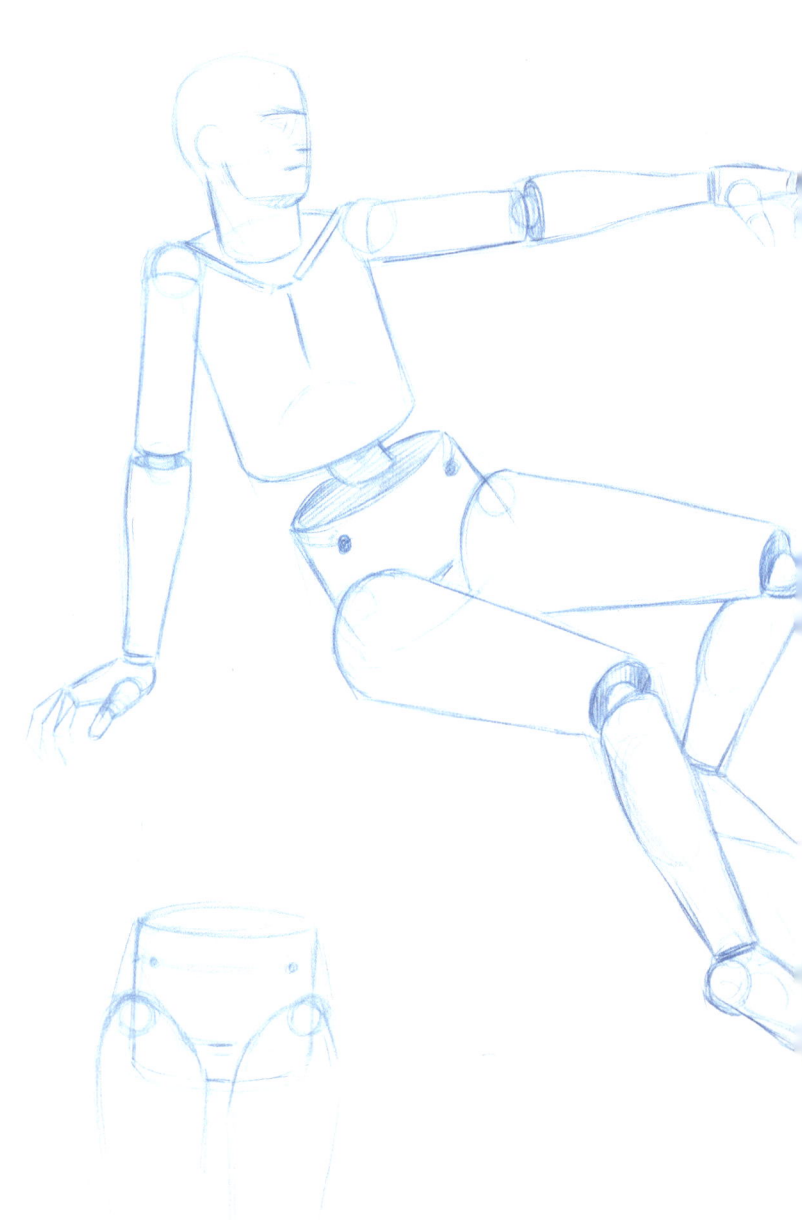

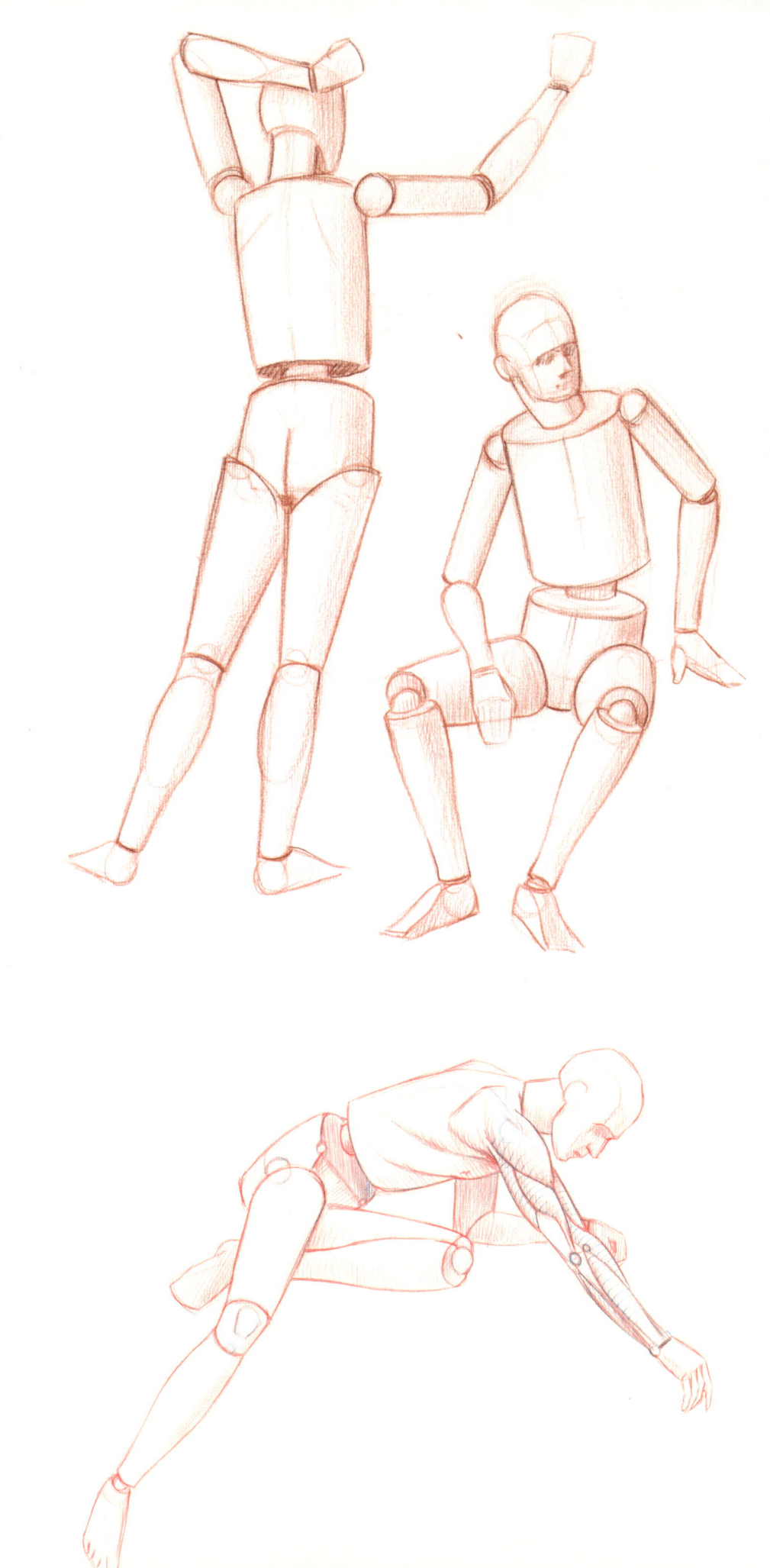

EXERCISE 1.17
DYNAMIC FLOWS

The exercises on these and the following pages introduce dynamic flows. These lines of flow are innumerable and impossible to classify, but the examples here give you an idea how you can learn to notice and capture various patterns of movement, pathways of flow between anatomical structures, and lines of action.

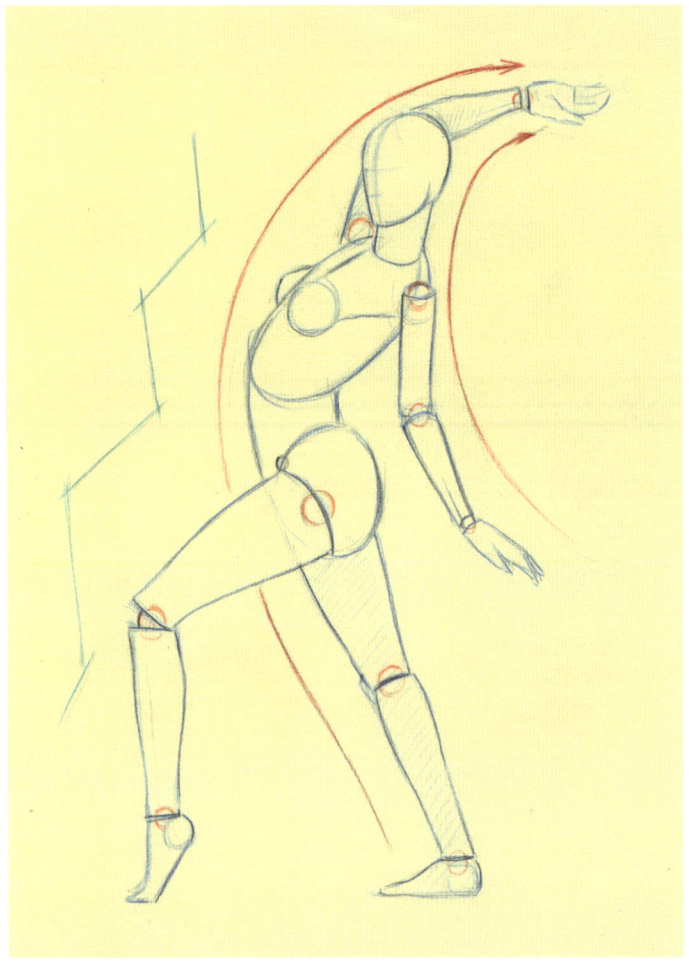

LINES OF ACTION IN FIGURE WITH ARCHING BACK

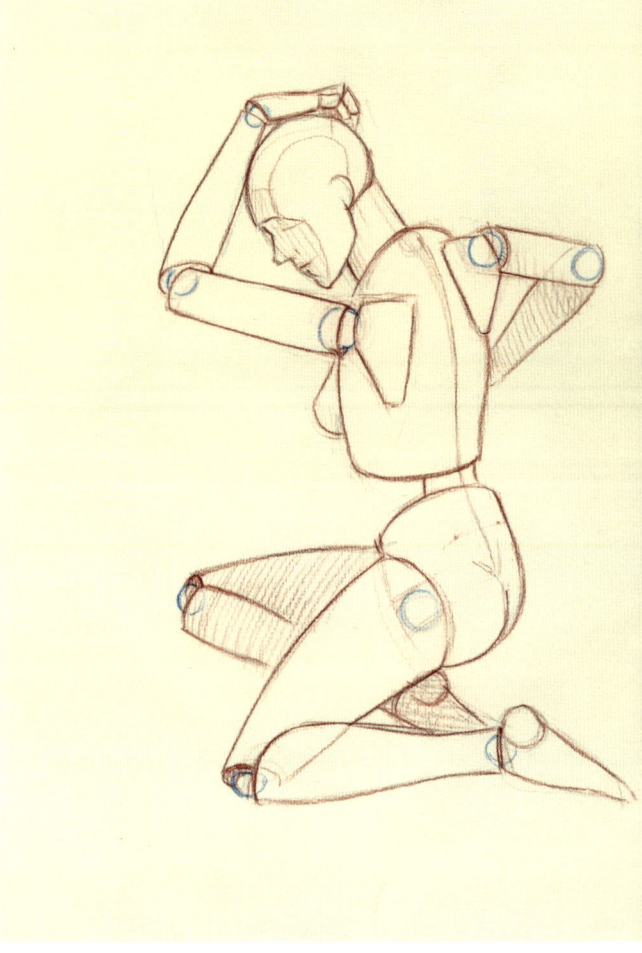

ZIGZAG PATTERN ON CROUCHING FIGURE

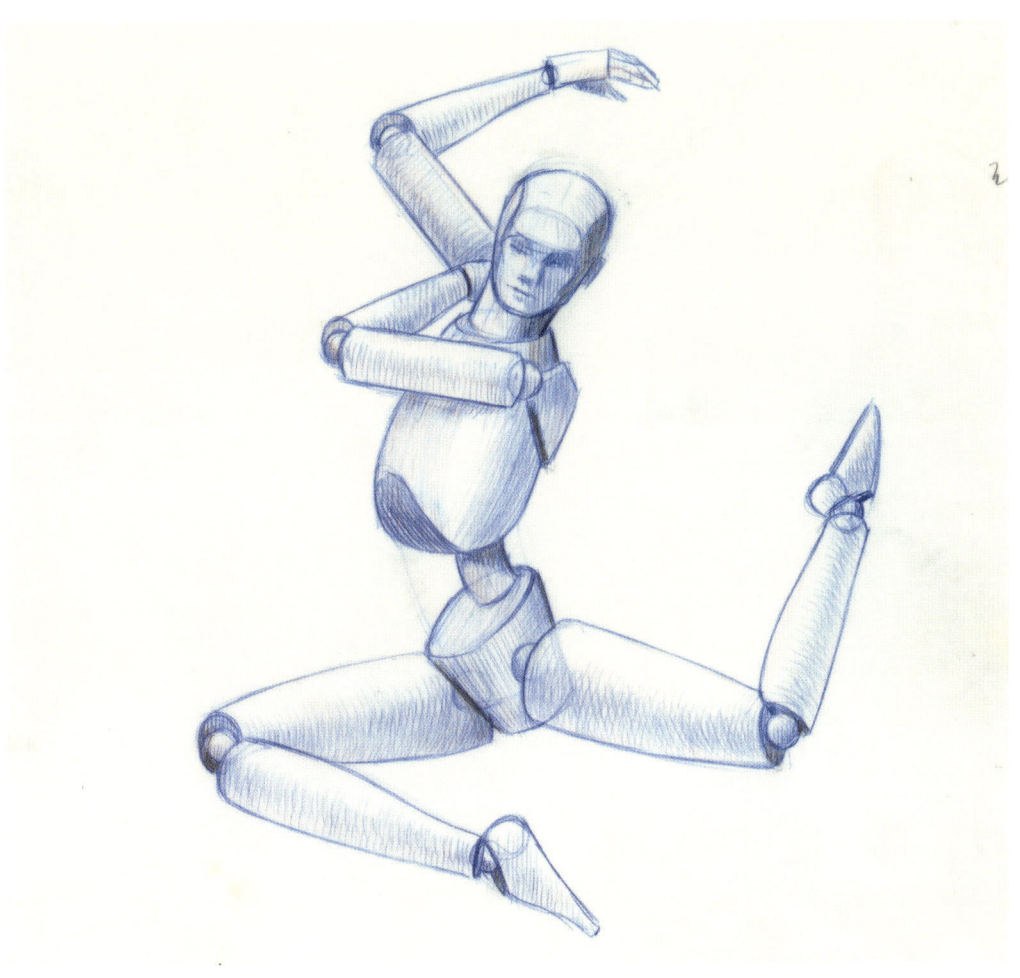

"PINWHEEL" OR SPIRALING
LINES OF ACTION ON
DYNAMIC FIGURE

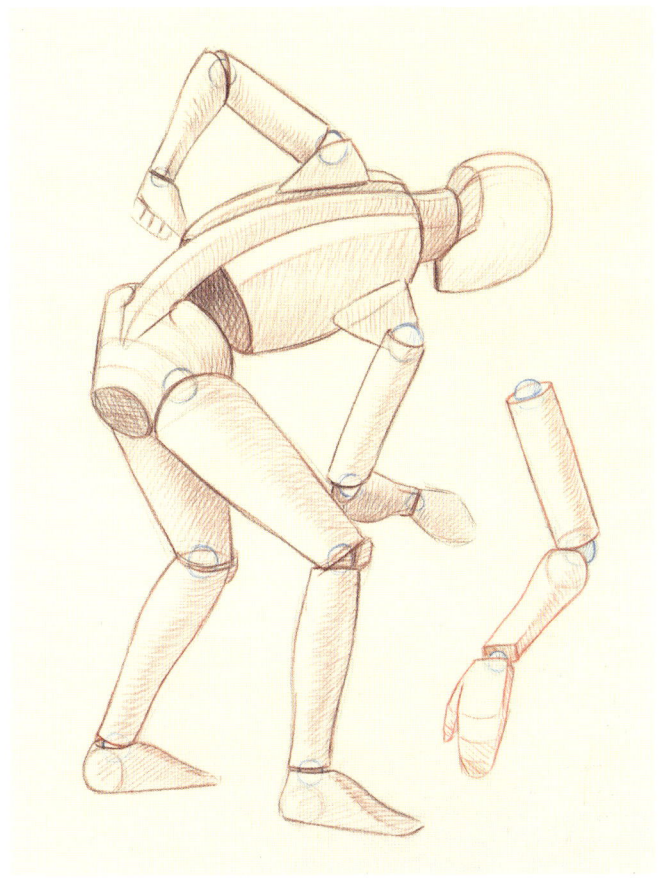

COMBINATION OF SPIRALING LINES OF ACTION AND ZIGZAG PATTERN
IN DYNAMIC POSE

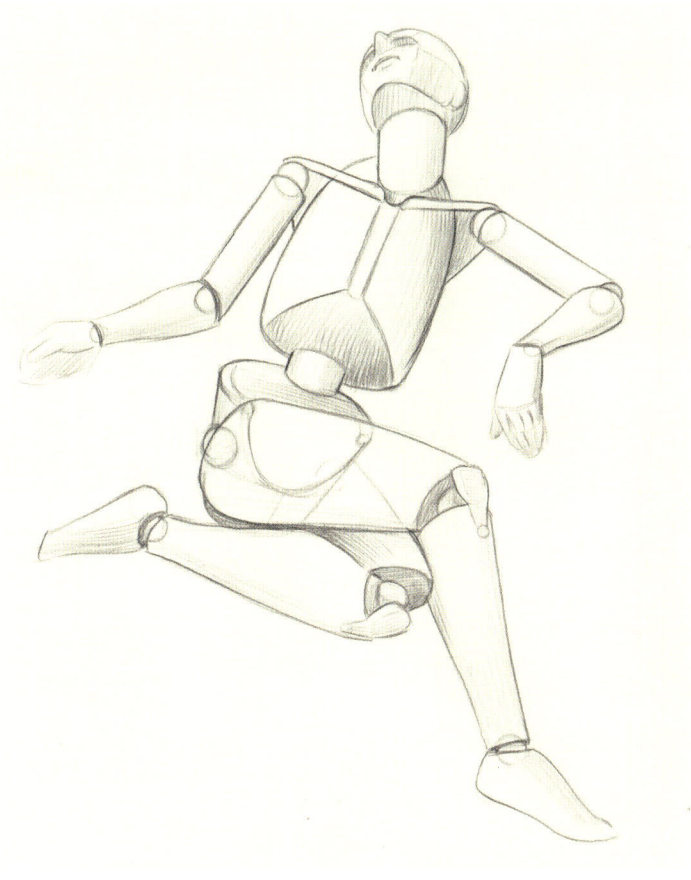

"PINWHEEL" OR SPIRALING ARRANGEMENT OF STATIC POSE

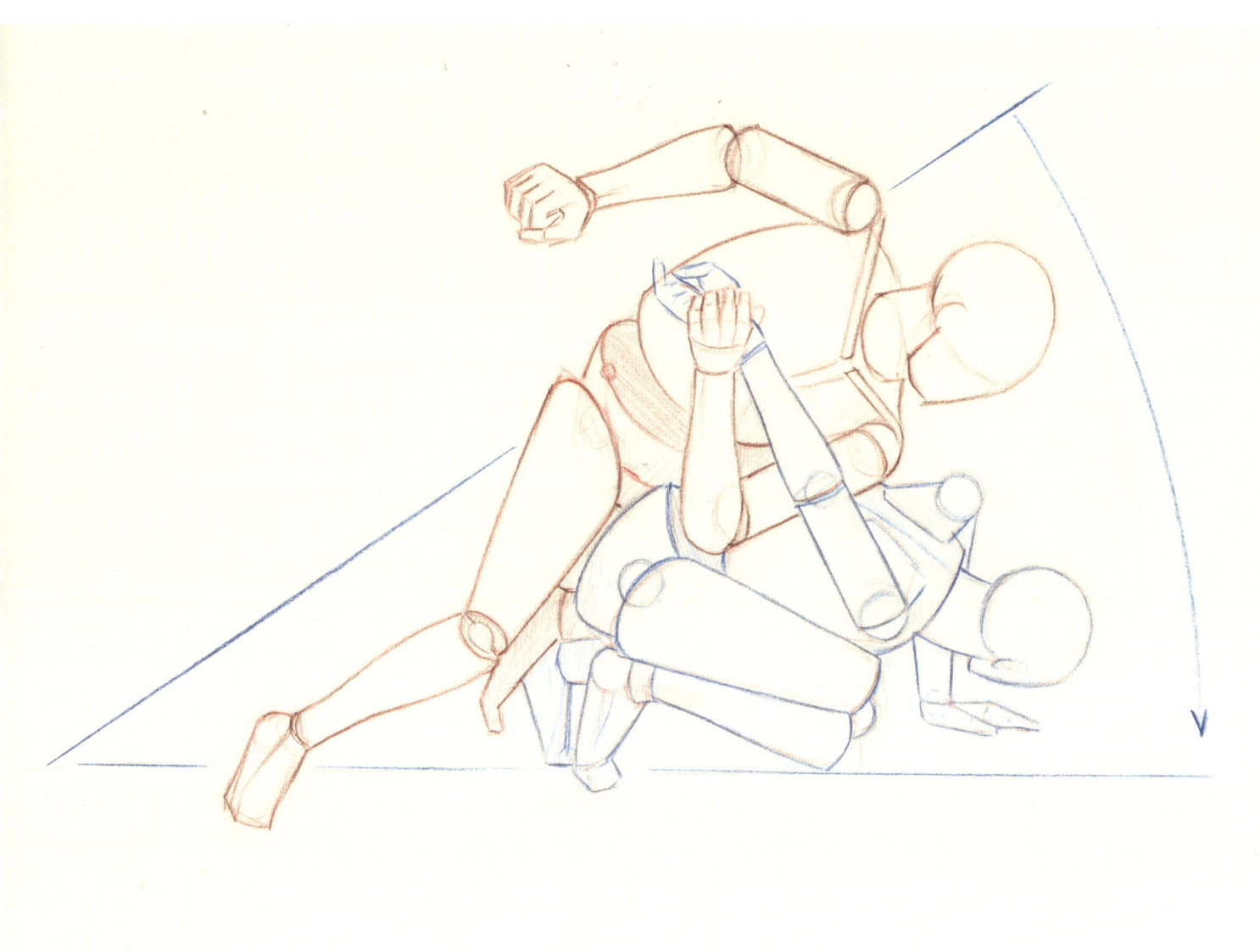

DOWNWARD LINE OF ACTION

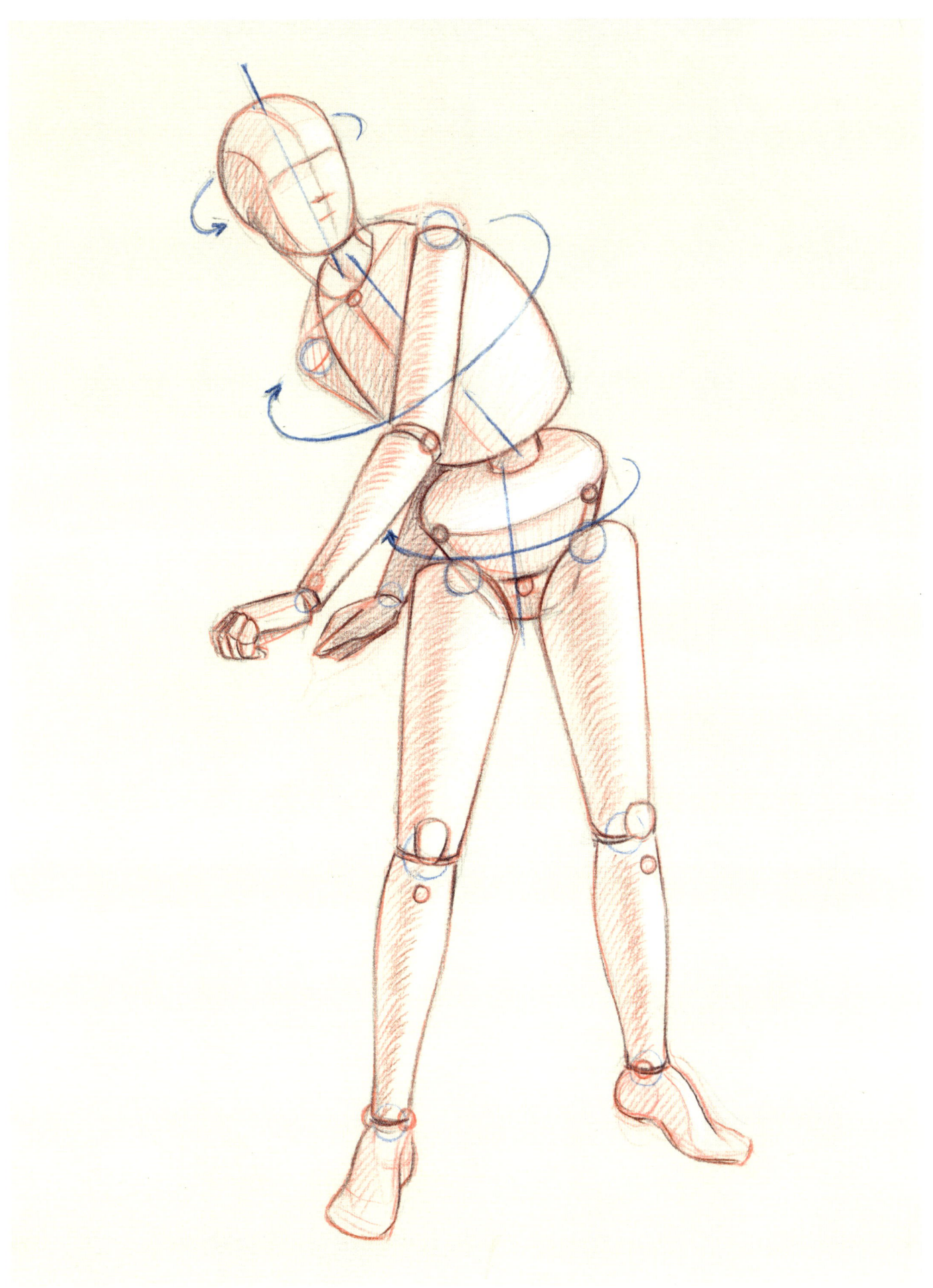

TWISTING/COILING LINES OF ACTION ON FIGURE'S AXIS

LEVEL 4

THE FORESHORTENED FIGURE

Stereometry is very useful in unlocking the complexity of a strongly *foreshortened* pose. Foreshortening occurs when a figure is seen from an extreme angle, with the consequent compression of the body's planes and the overlapping of its volumes. When working with such a pose, it is always a good idea to prepare a few preliminary sketches before starting to draw it, as the image below demonstrates. A stereometric study can reveal angles, the overlapping of the forms, and the patterns of light and shadow. It can also give you a more accurate idea of the measurements of the body's various forms, allowing you to bypass your assumptions of what the pose "should" look like and giving you more objective information instead.

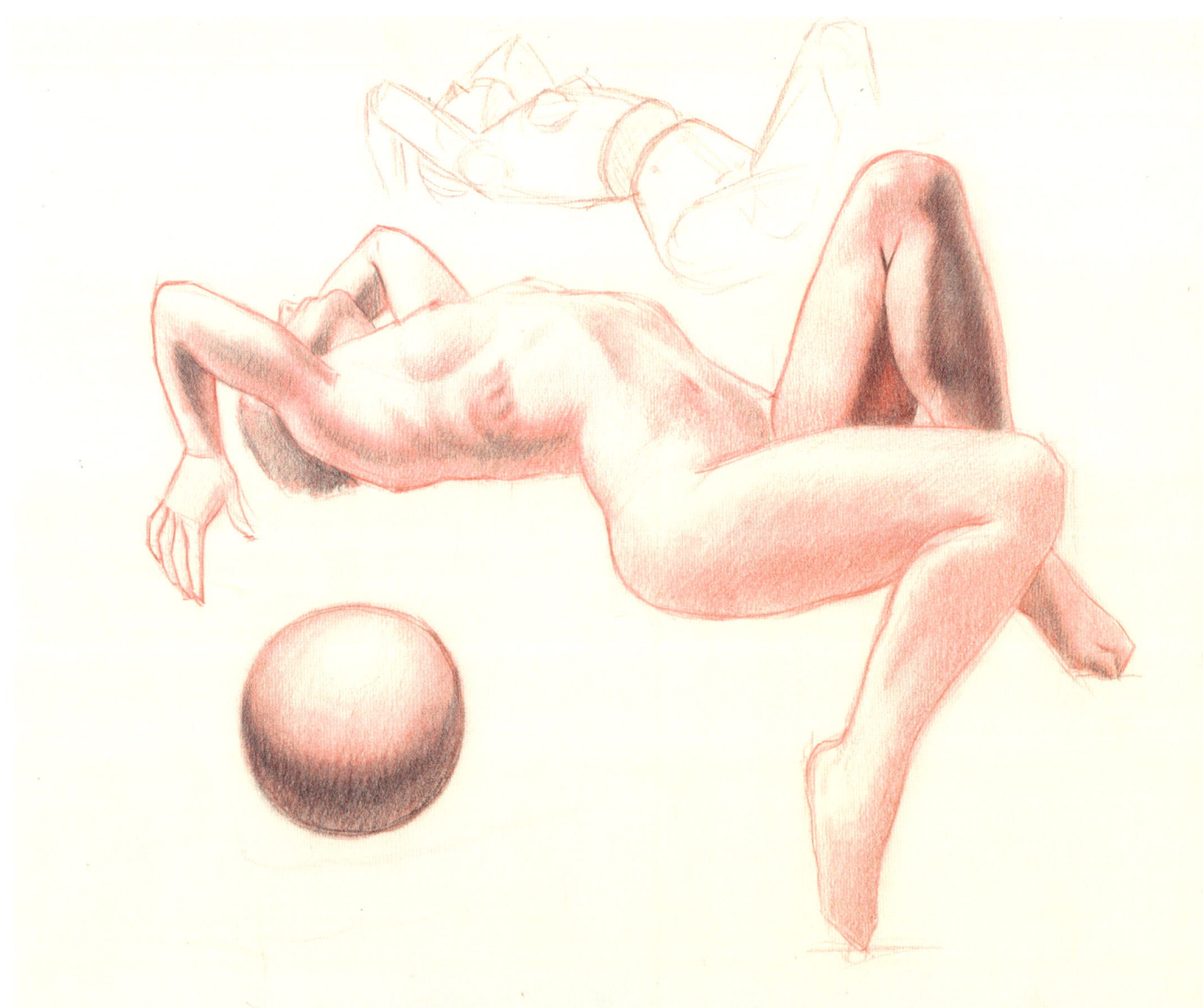

PUTTING THE BODY IN FORESHORTENED PERSPECTIVE

This exercise, inspired by images created by Renaissance artists Piero della Francesca and Albrecht Dürer, explains how to measure the body to draw it in a foreshortened pose.

Draw a figure (male or female) in side and front views, following the drawing at right and using a grid to ensure that the figures have the same measurements in both views.

Now draw the side view of the same figure leaning backward at an angle of about 45 degrees.

Using a ruler and a triangle, then draw horizontal parallel lines, starting from the top and bottom of each segment of the leaning figure and going all the way to the right edge of the page. These lines reveal the height of the segments as affected by the foreshortening.

Now, again using a ruler and a triangle, draw vertical lines that start from each side of the various segments of the figure on the top right. These lines give you the width of each segment of the foreshortened figure that you are about to draw.

Using a colored pencil, indicate the various points of intersection of width and height (the vertical and horizontal lines). These show you the height of each volume of the figure as affected by the foreshortening.

Then repeat the exercise by leaning the same figure backward at a more extreme angle, as shown in the reference images at the bottom of the drawing.

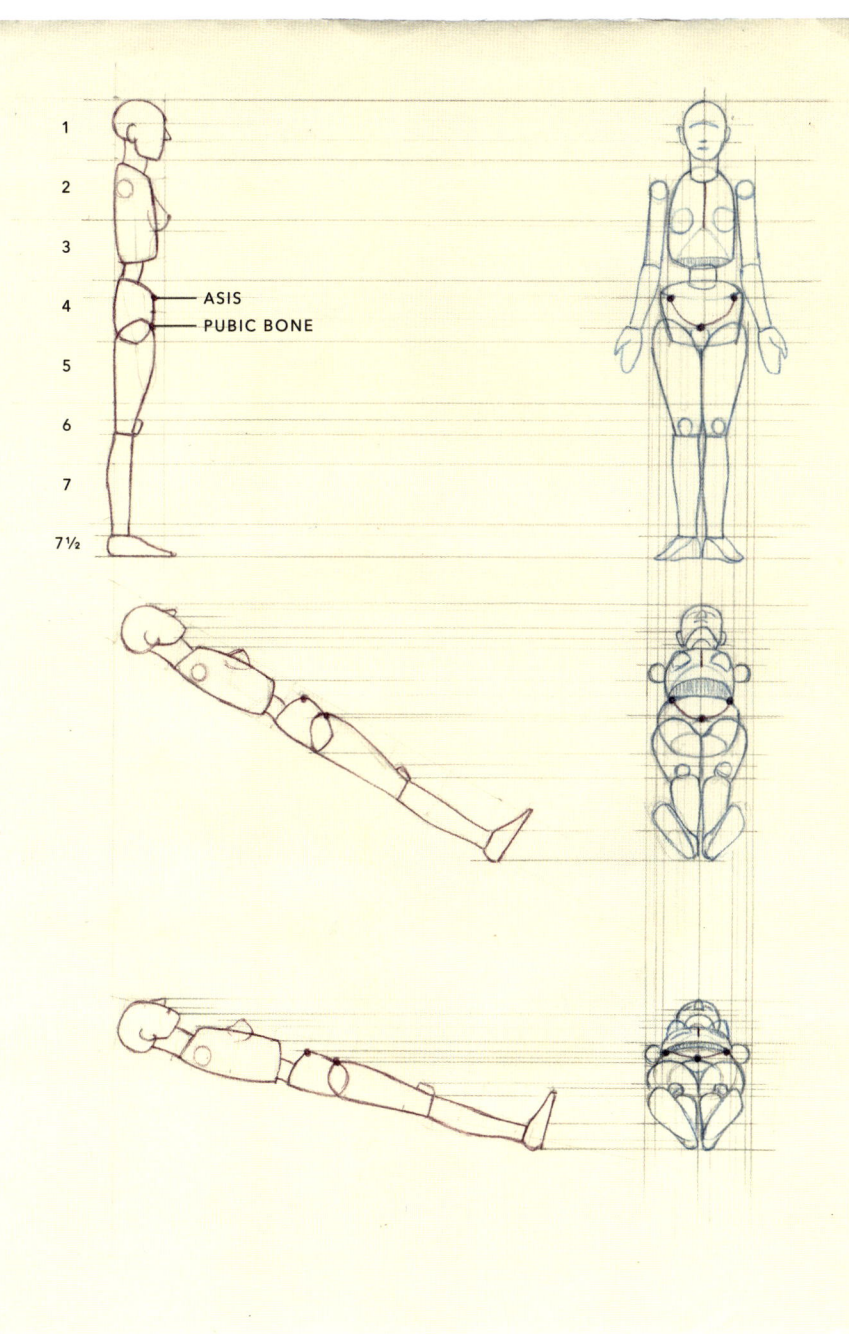

EXERCISE 1.19
THINK FORM, NOT SHAPE

Copy the drawing below, considering these concepts:

- Whether you work from imagination or from life, what you know about your subject will influence the resulting drawing. Observation alone is usually not sufficient to let you "see" all the many details—structural, anatomical, tonal—the subject might present.

- Use an "informed line." We draw what we know, and the more we know about a subject, the more things we see. This will become even more evident as we explore the body in more depth in later chapters.

- When drawing the figure in any pose—but especially a foreshortened pose—it is important to think *form* instead of mere shape. Drawing a subject as a shape, using an outline, will create a flat, two-dimensional drawing. But if you think of form—of three dimensions instead of just an outline—the resulting drawing will be remarkably different.

- The way you think about a subject will inform your drawing. Drawing is, or should be, the visualization of a thinking process.

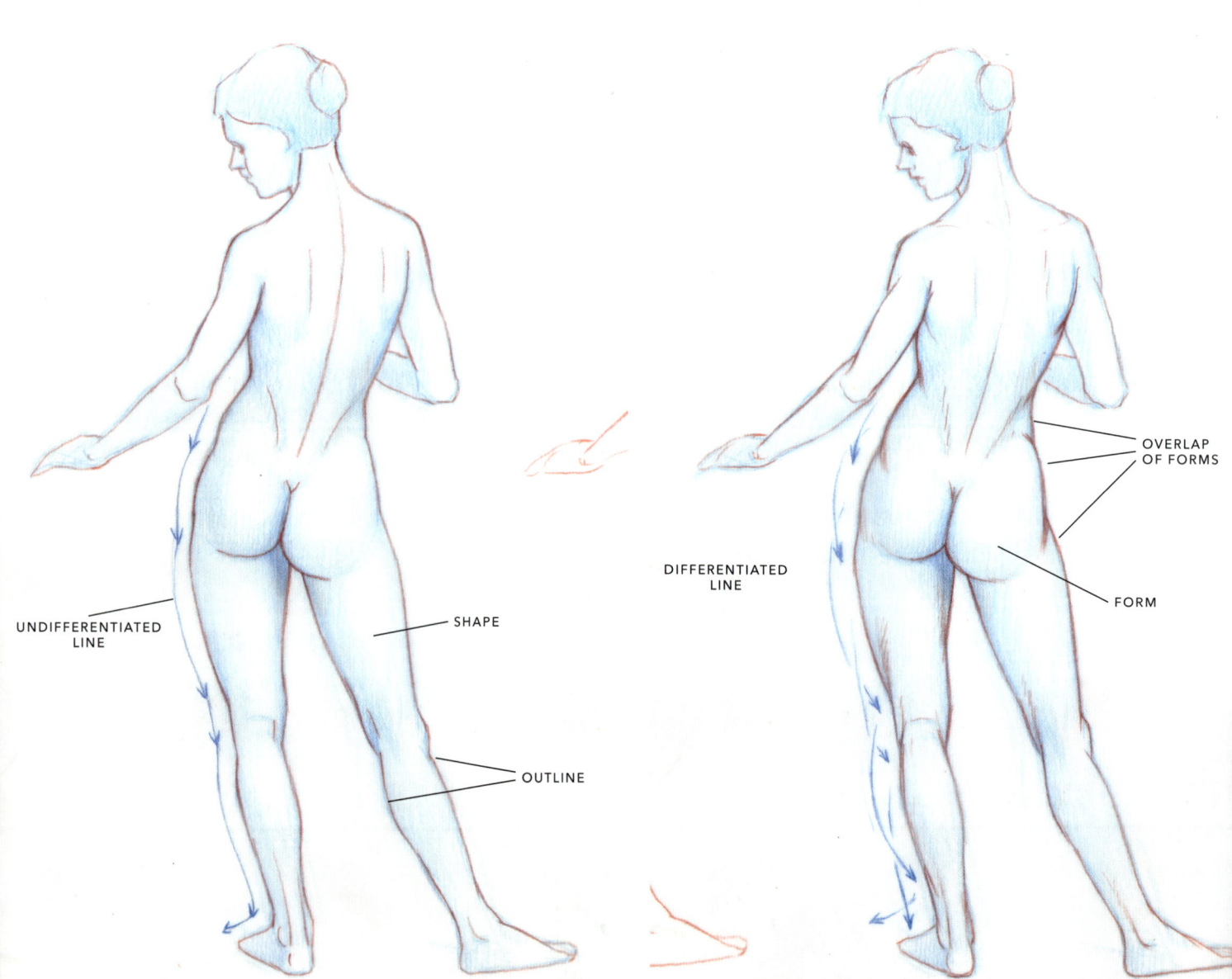

UNDIFFERENTIATED LINE

SHAPE

OUTLINE

DIFFERENTIATED LINE

OVERLAP OF FORMS

FORM

THREE-DIMENSIONAL VOLUMES

When drawing the forms of the body, think of them as distinct three-dimensional volumes that you connect, align, and overlap properly and with the correct proportional relationships. Copying the drawings below—which treat body segments as if they were beads on a string—will help you to practice this concept.

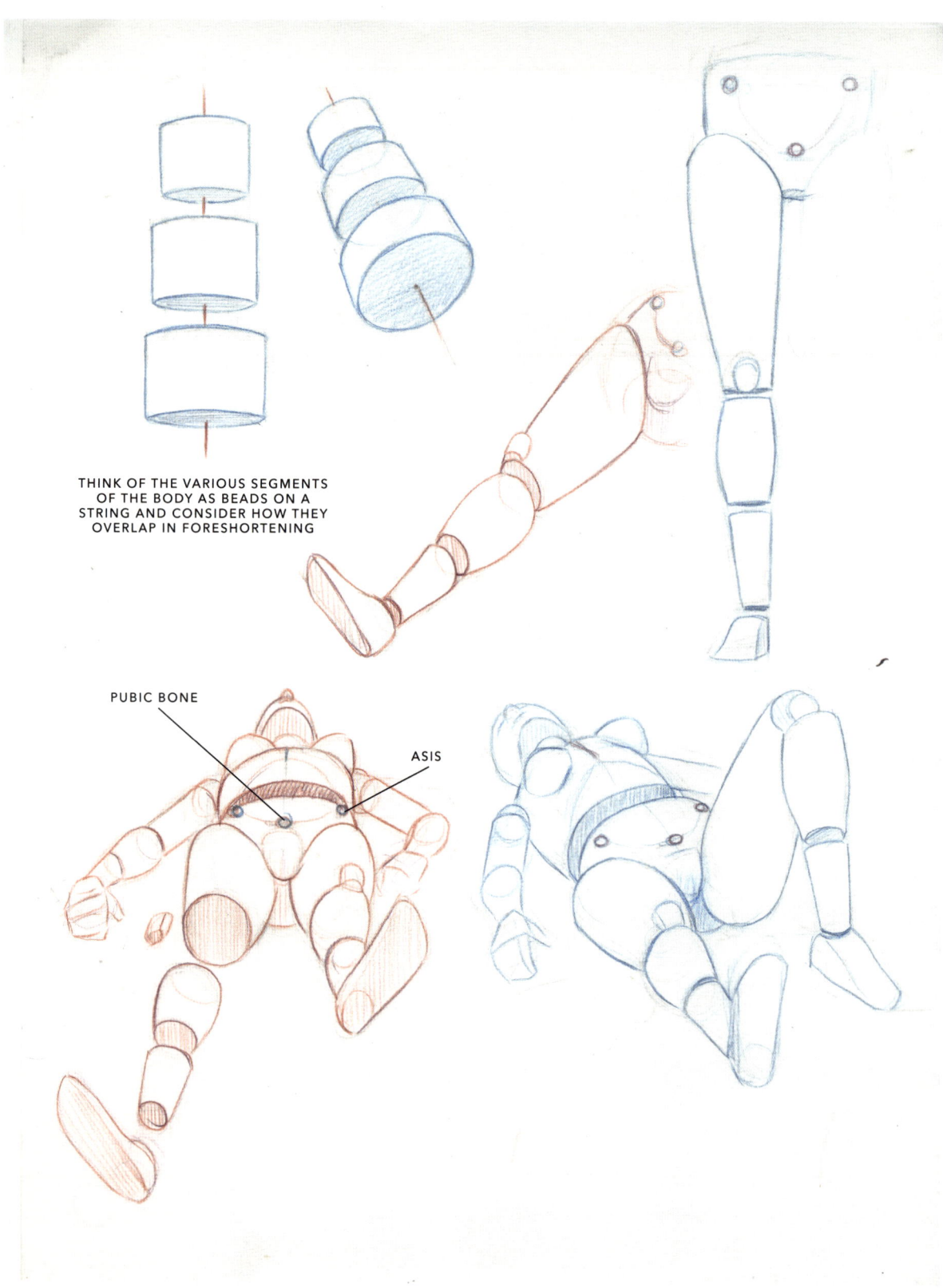

THINK OF THE VARIOUS SEGMENTS
OF THE BODY AS BEADS ON A
STRING AND CONSIDER HOW THEY
OVERLAP IN FORESHORTENING

PUBIC BONE

ASIS

EXERCISE 1.21

MEASURING: PROPORTIONAL RELATIONSHIPS AND ALIGNMENTS

The proportional relationships method involves comparing the measurements of the various segments of the figure to each other. The method typically uses the head as the basic unit of measure and relates it proportionally to all the other parts of the figure. But you can also compare any part of the figure to any other part, even when the figure is in a foreshortened pose.

The illustration below shows a quick three-step demonstration of the method. In step 1, I used the thigh as the basic unit of measure, simply because in this pose it is the most obvious part of the body for this purpose. As you can see, the thigh serves as a ruler for finding the positions of the pelvis, ribcage, and head.

Step 2 shows how vertical and horizontal alignments are used to find the positions of all the parts of the figure. And the third step shows the finished stereometric figure, which I also used to study the effect of the light on its forms.

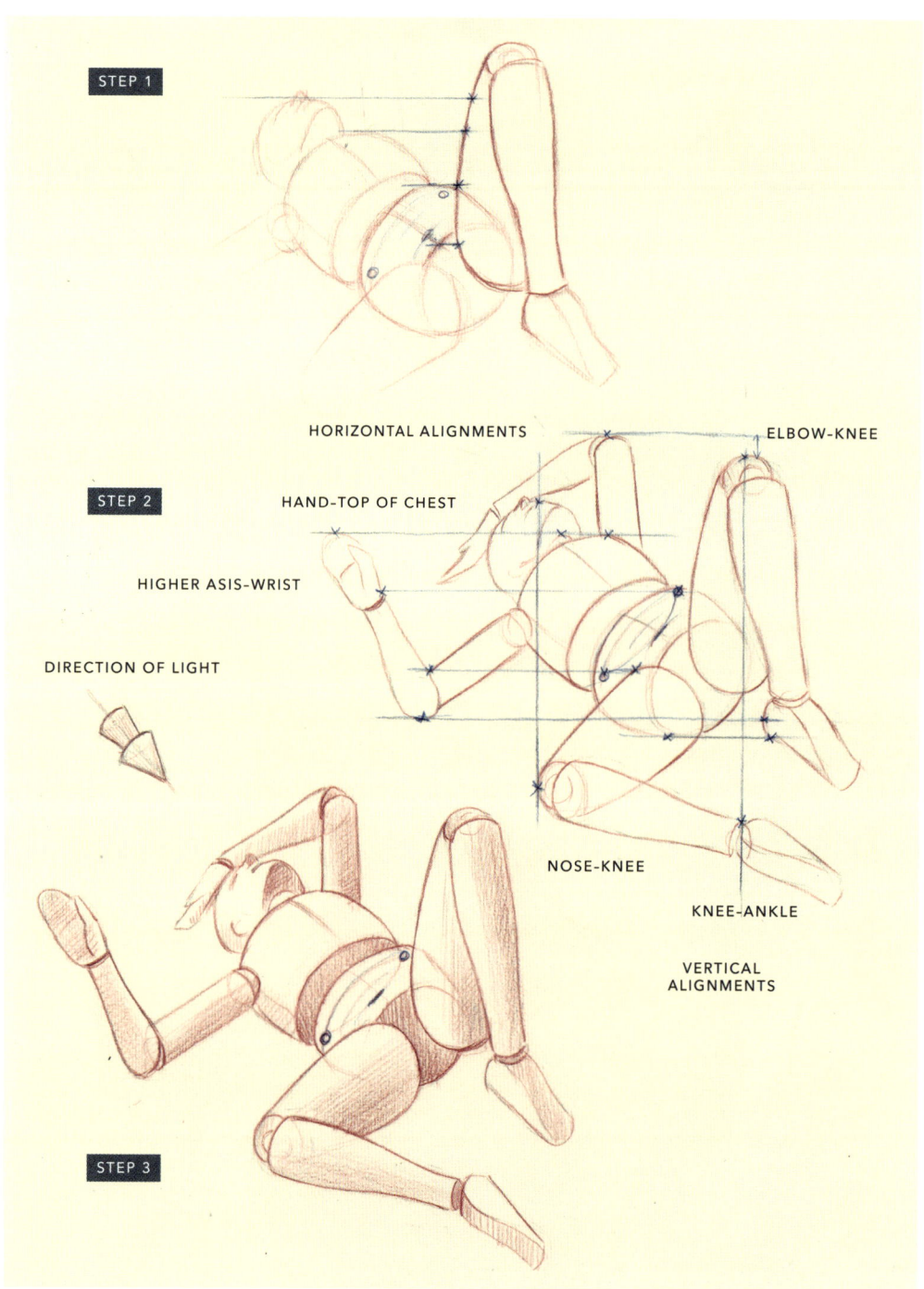

STEP 1

HORIZONTAL ALIGNMENTS

ELBOW-KNEE

STEP 2

HAND-TOP OF CHEST

HIGHER ASIS-WRIST

DIRECTION OF LIGHT

NOSE-KNEE

KNEE-ANKLE

VERTICAL
ALIGNMENTS

STEP 3

EXERCISE 1.22
PRELIMINARY STUDIES

The sketches here show how stereometry can be used to do preliminary studies of different poses and from different angles of view, changing the position of the arms, head, legs, torso, and hips before finally settling on one pose. For this exercise, create sketches in which you move body segments to create various foreshortened poses. It is a good habit to start a drawing session like this by sketching a standing stereometric figure to remind yourself of its forms and proportions.

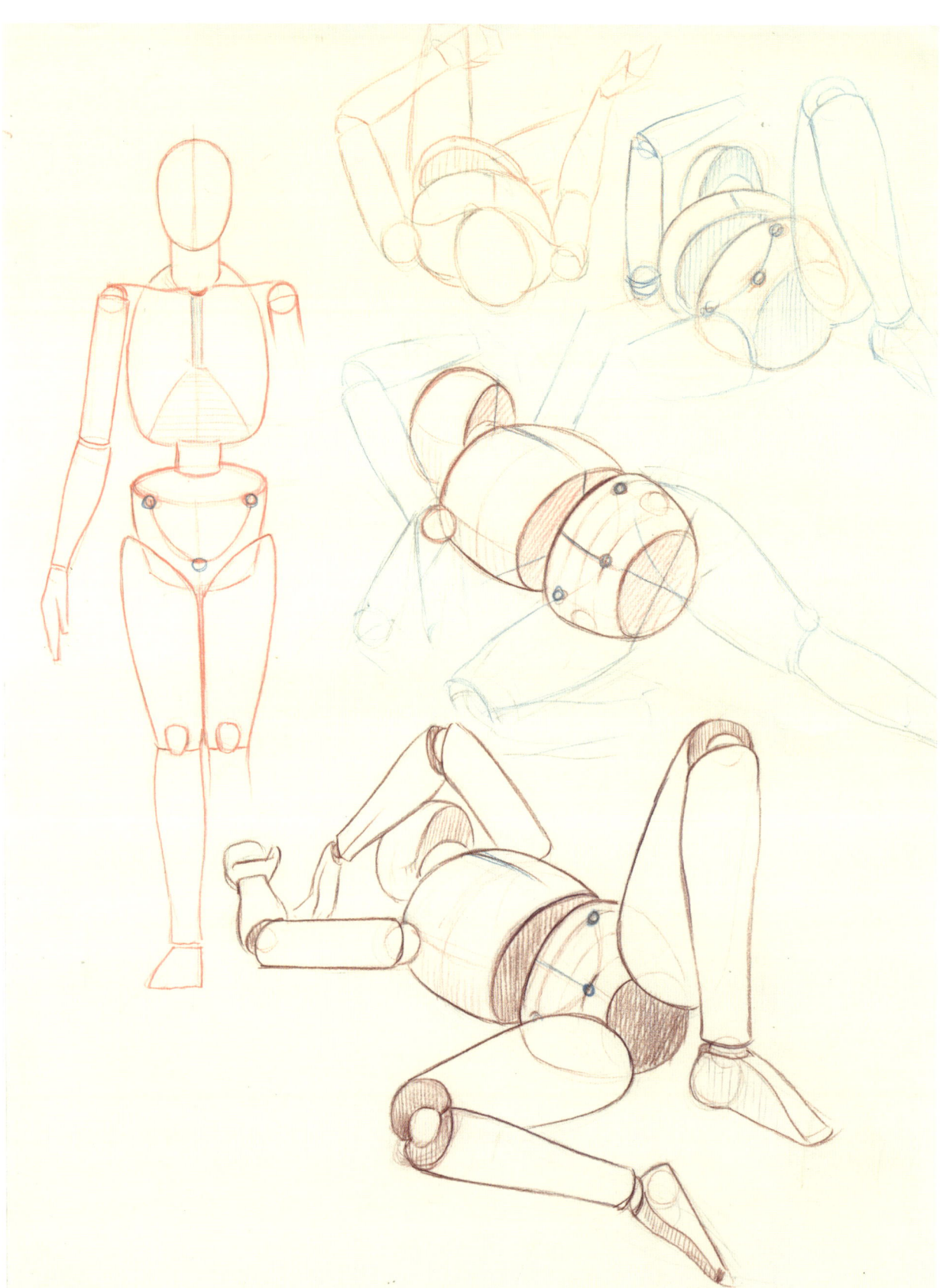

EXERCISE 1.23

THE "STRUCTURAL GHOST"

So far, we have drawn stereometric figures with a fair degree of precision and a relatively high amount of detail. This approach, exemplified in the drawing below, is very useful for didactic purposes—to learn the method, check alignments, measure segments, and become familiar with the positions of the landmarks and the volumes of the body. This is the background—the thinking behind—any figure drawing rooted in the stereometric method.

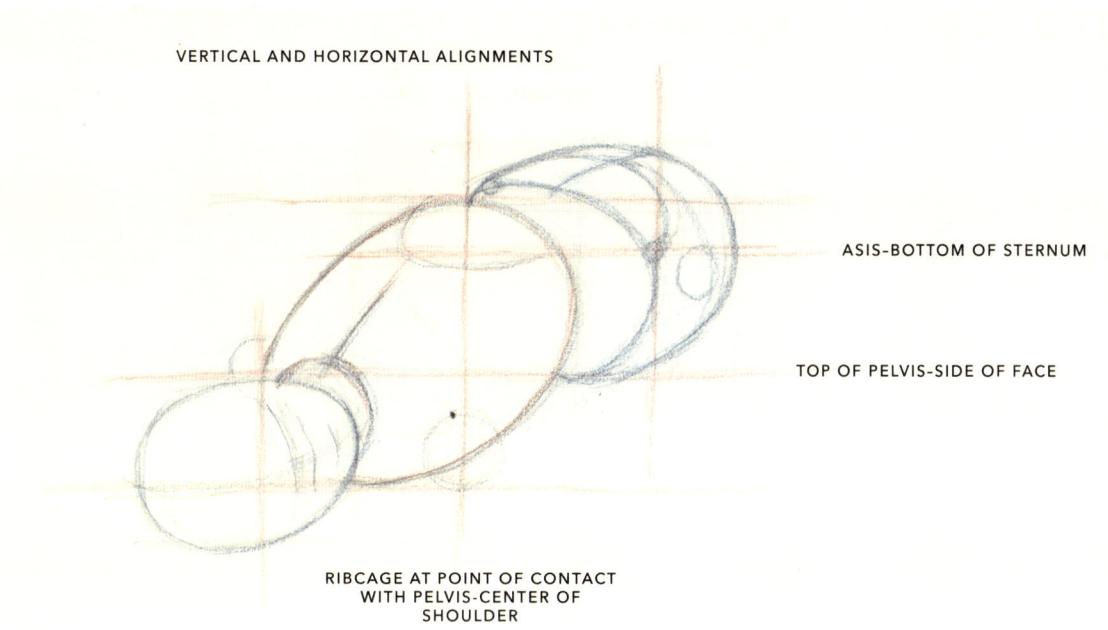

VERTICAL AND HORIZONTAL ALIGNMENTS

ASIS-BOTTOM OF STERNUM

TOP OF PELVIS-SIDE OF FACE

RIBCAGE AT POINT OF CONTACT
WITH PELVIS-CENTER OF
SHOULDER

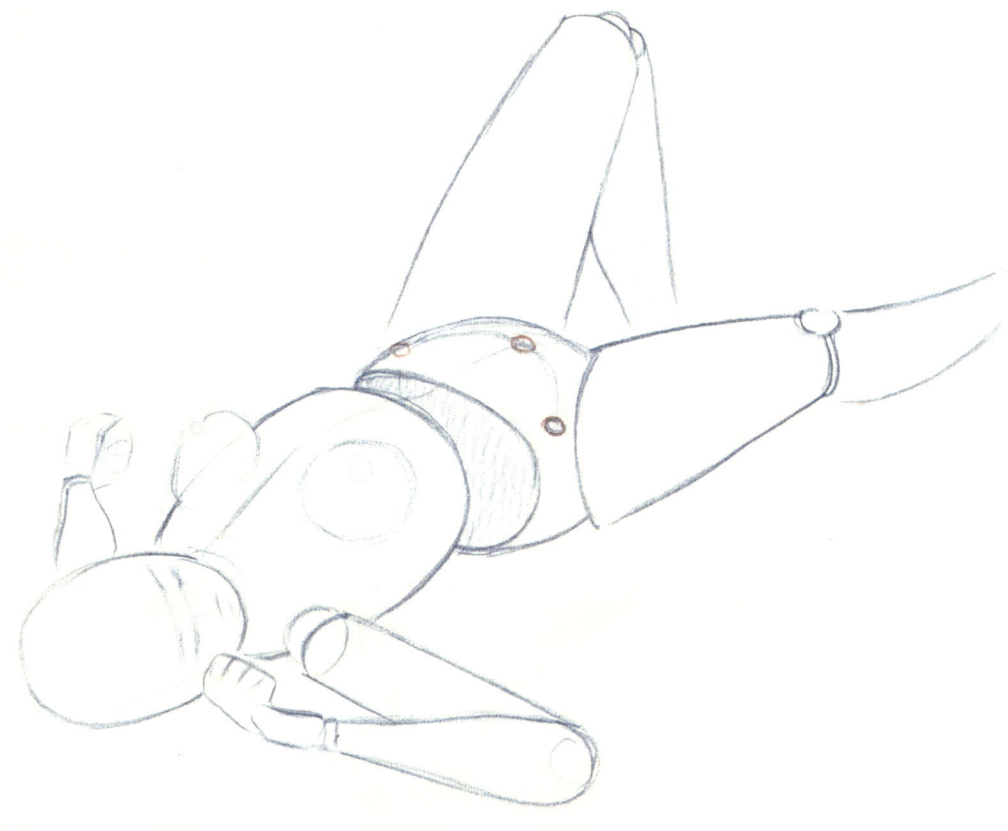

When you actually draw the figure from life, however, you can't go through an elaborate, exacting procedure. Instead, you need to draw just a few thin, barely visible lines of reference for the stereometric volumes and measurements and then to superimpose the organic forms of the figure on this delicate initial scaffolding (which I call the *structural ghost*). The three-step sequence anticipates the material discussed in the following chapters, showing how to gradually proceed from an initial stereometric visualization of the figure to a realistic and fully rendered artwork.

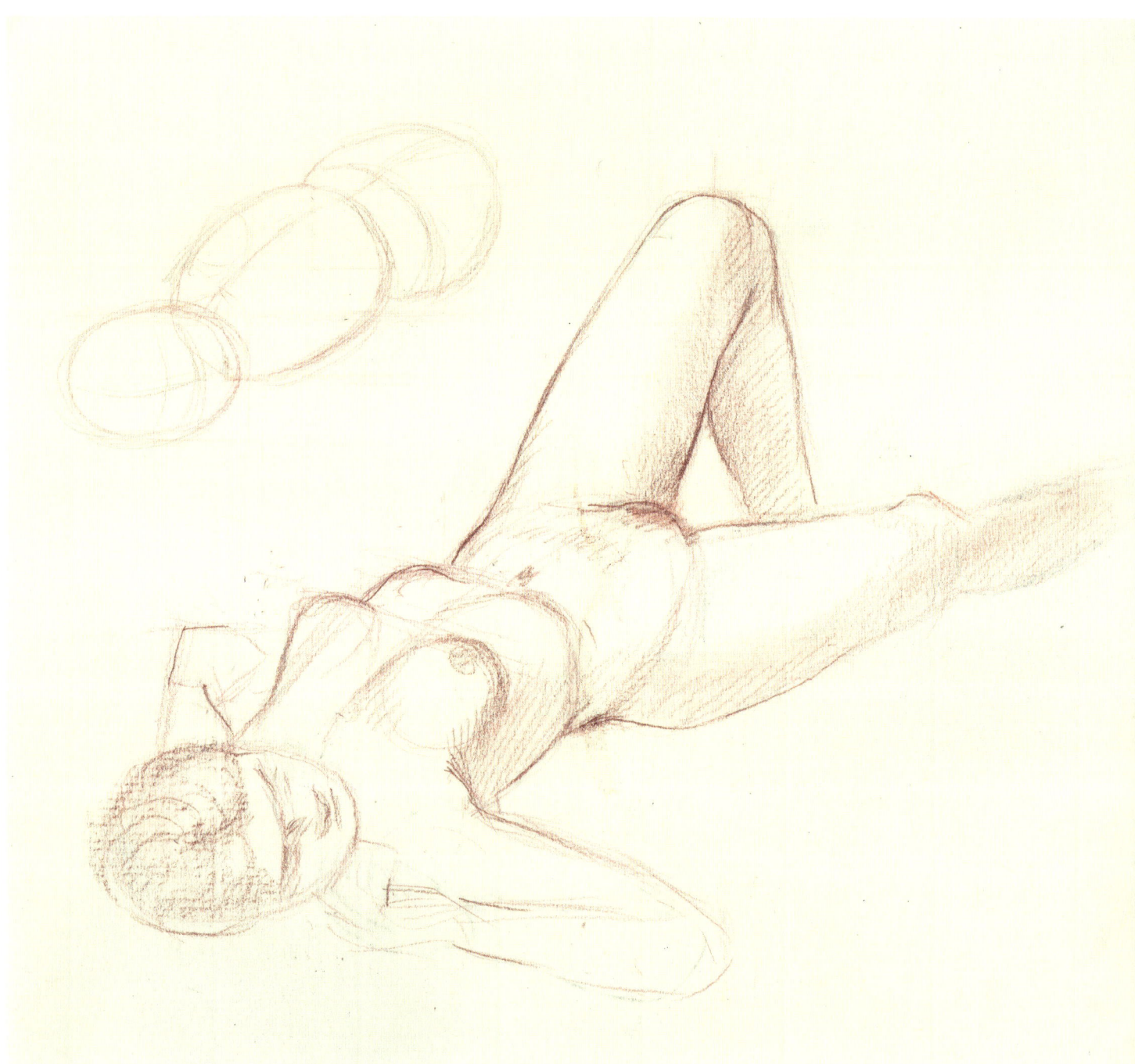

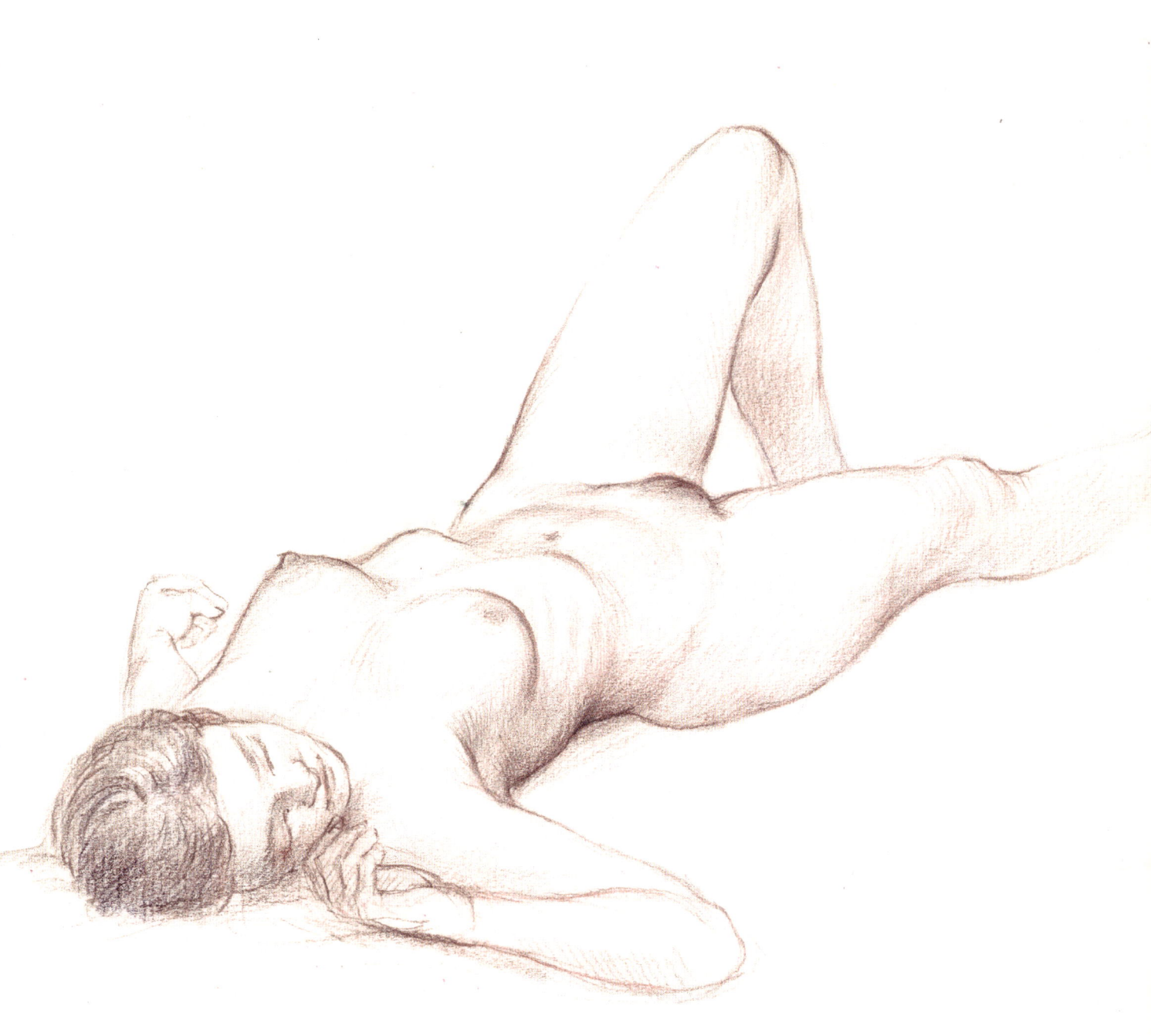

EXERCISE 1.24
QUICK SKETCHES PRACTICE

To review and practice stereometry, copy the figures on the next few pages and then create more on your own from other reference images or imagination. The more you practice, the more your technical skill will improve and the more fluent you'll become with the method.

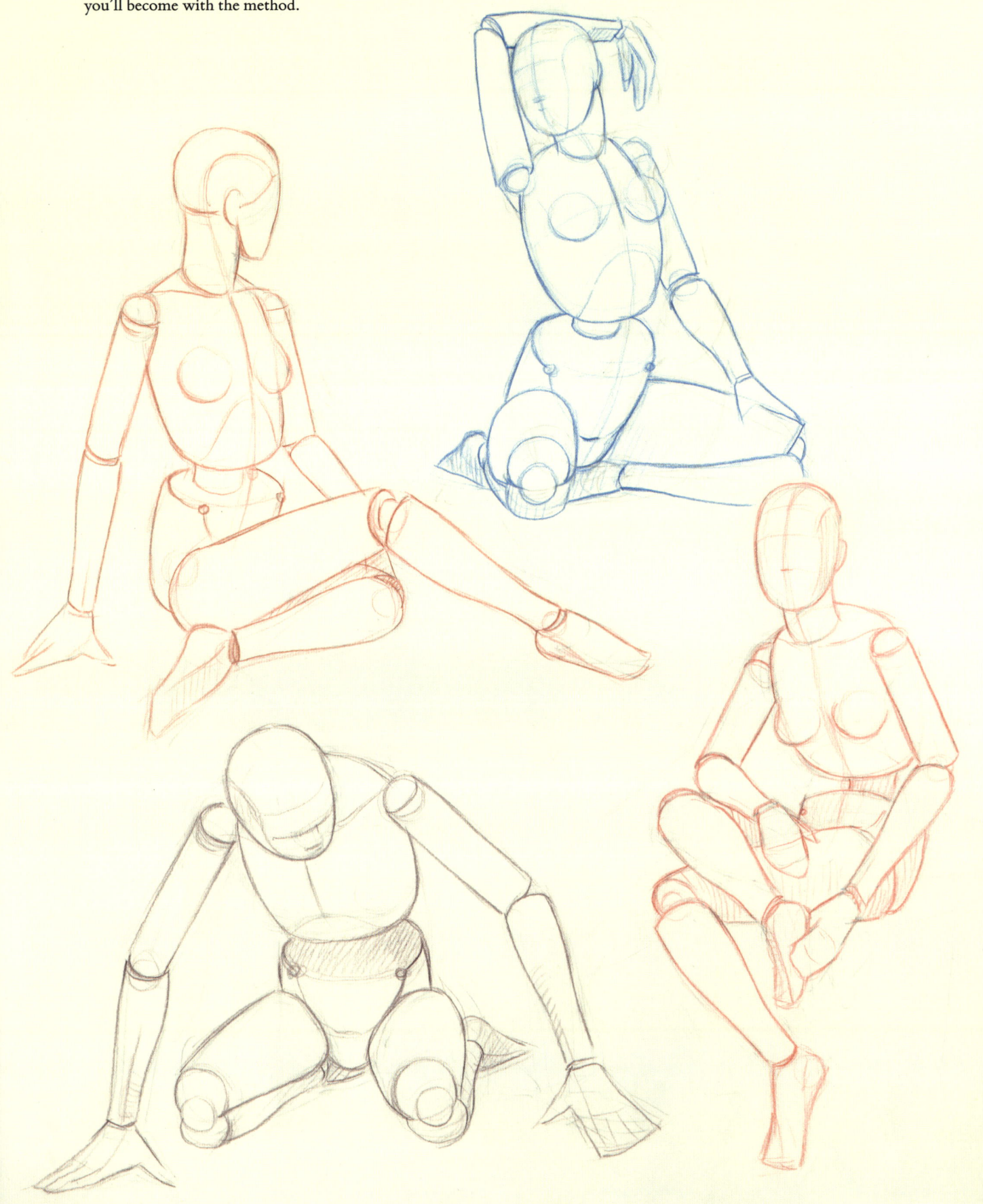

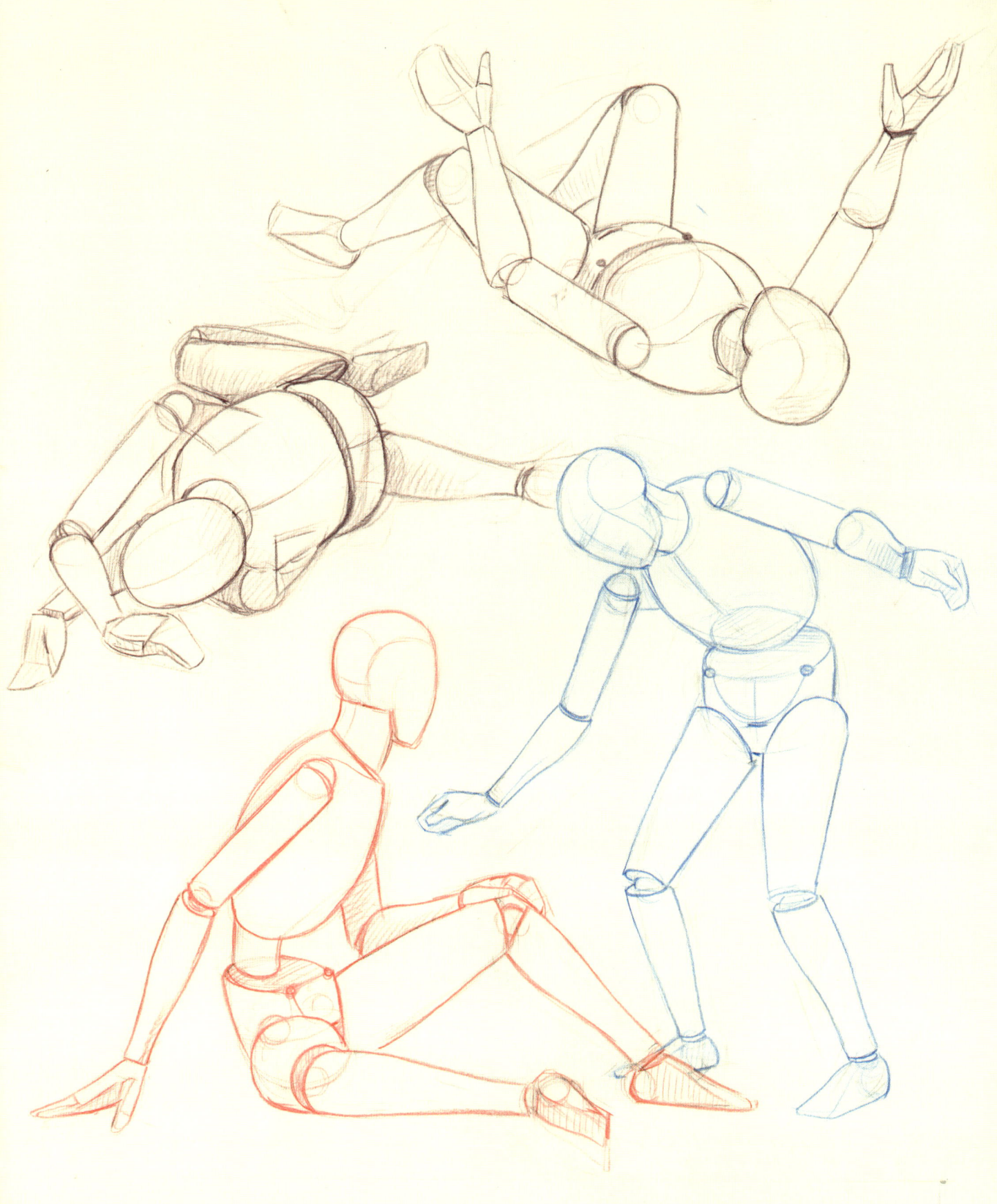

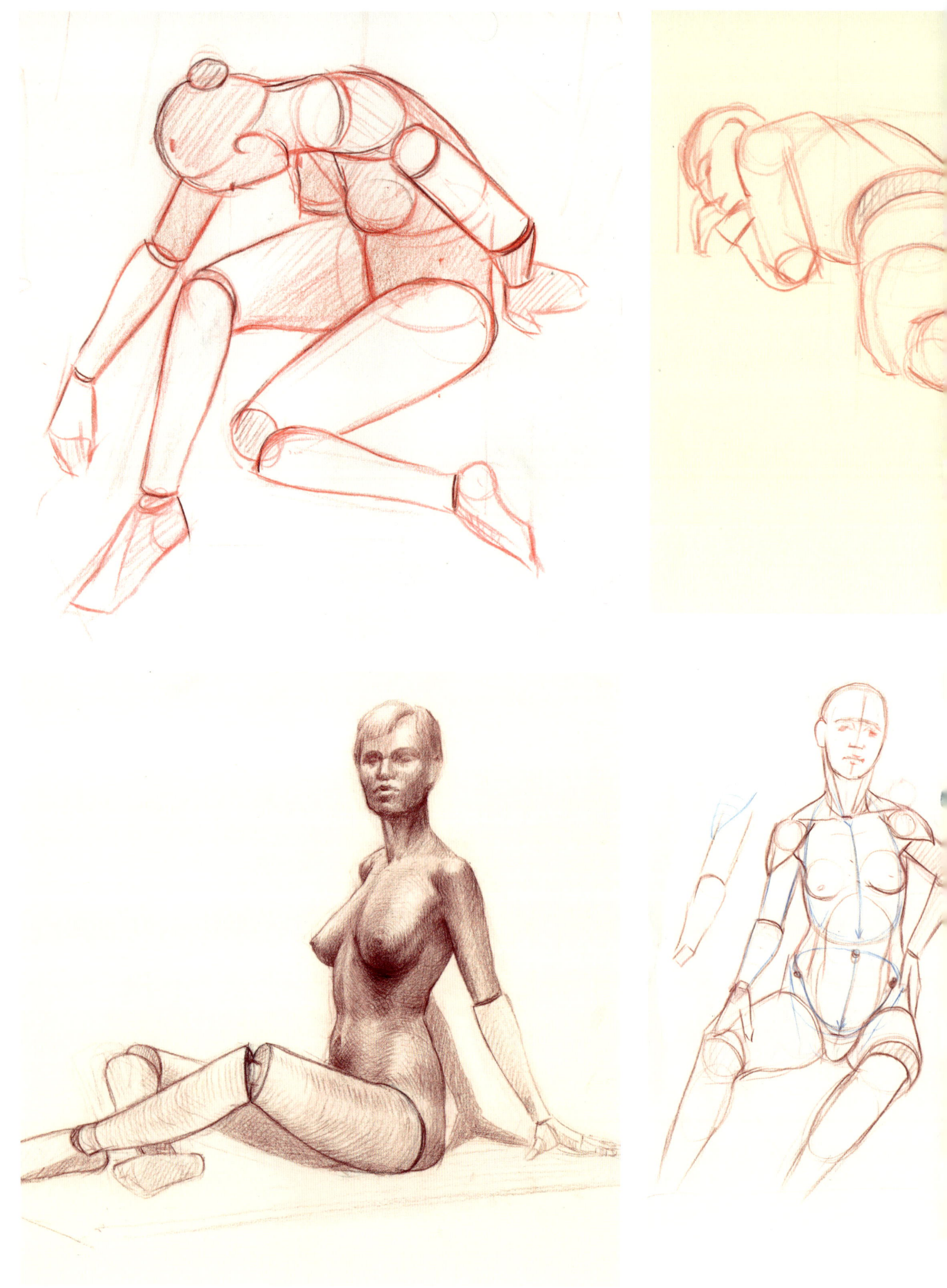

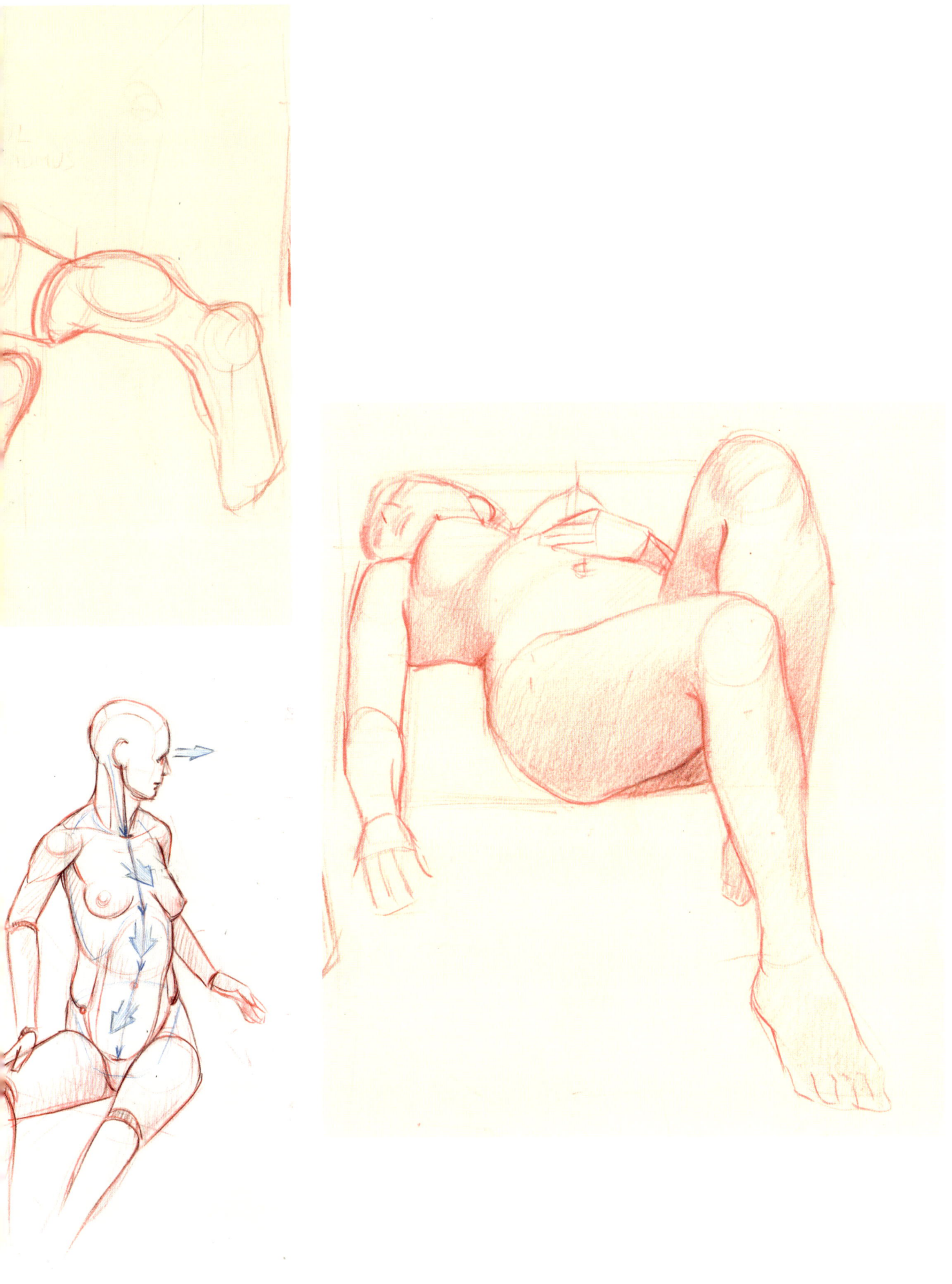

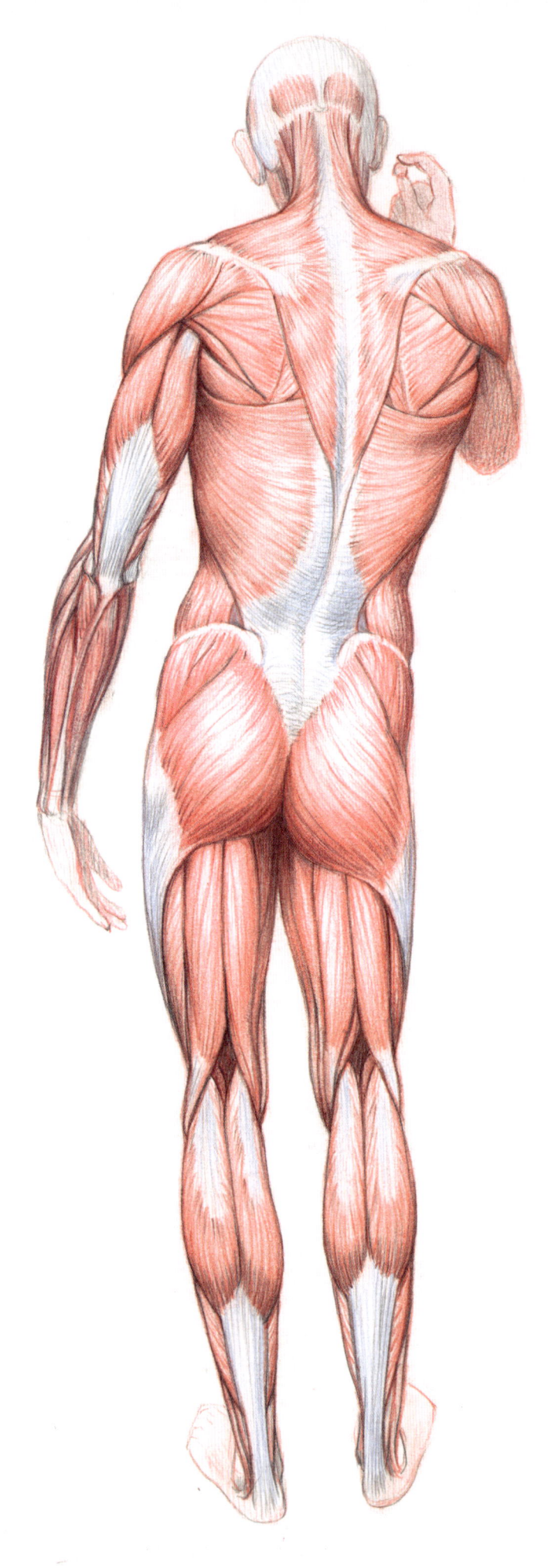

CHAPTER 2

IDENTIFYING SKELETAL AND MUSCULAR STRUCTURES

In my experience, one of the main problems encountered by anatomy and figure drawing students involves applying the knowledge acquired in anatomy courses to the actual practice of figure drawing. This chapter is designed to facilitate the transition from the typical representation of the human body in anatomical charts to the specific forms of living models.

FROM TYPICAL REPRESENTATION TO SPECIFIC FORMS

This chapter is divided into two levels, which guide you through the transition from the typical proportions of anatomical charts to the idealized forms of sculpture. (It's in the following chapter that we'll deal with the specific forms of individual models' bodies.) The exercises in level 1 help you achieve basic knowledge of the skeletal and muscular systems; in the exercises in level 2, you practice positioning the main muscles on stereometric figures aided by the skeletal landmarks.

LEVEL 1

SKELETAL AND SUPERFICIAL MUSCULAR STRUCTURE OF THE HUMAN BODY

The exercises and anatomical reference charts in this first level are dedicated to the skeletal and superficial muscular structures of the male and female bodies. (The body possesses several layers of muscles; the superficial muscles are those closest to the skin.)

The first eight exercises subdivide the human body into segments: head, torso, upper limbs, pelvis, and lower limbs in anterior and posterior views of male and female figures. The last two exercises in level 1 show the full male and female figures in side view. The illustrations for these ten exercises also double as reference charts.

All these exercises show the skeleton and superficial muscles side by side to illustrate the connections between the deep structure (skeleton) and superficial forms (superficial muscles) of the body. They also compare the male and female skeletal structures and their effect on the body's external morphology.

At the end of level 1 are six reference charts showing the external forms, skeleton, and superficial muscles; these can also be copied as a way of reviewing the material you've studied up to this point.

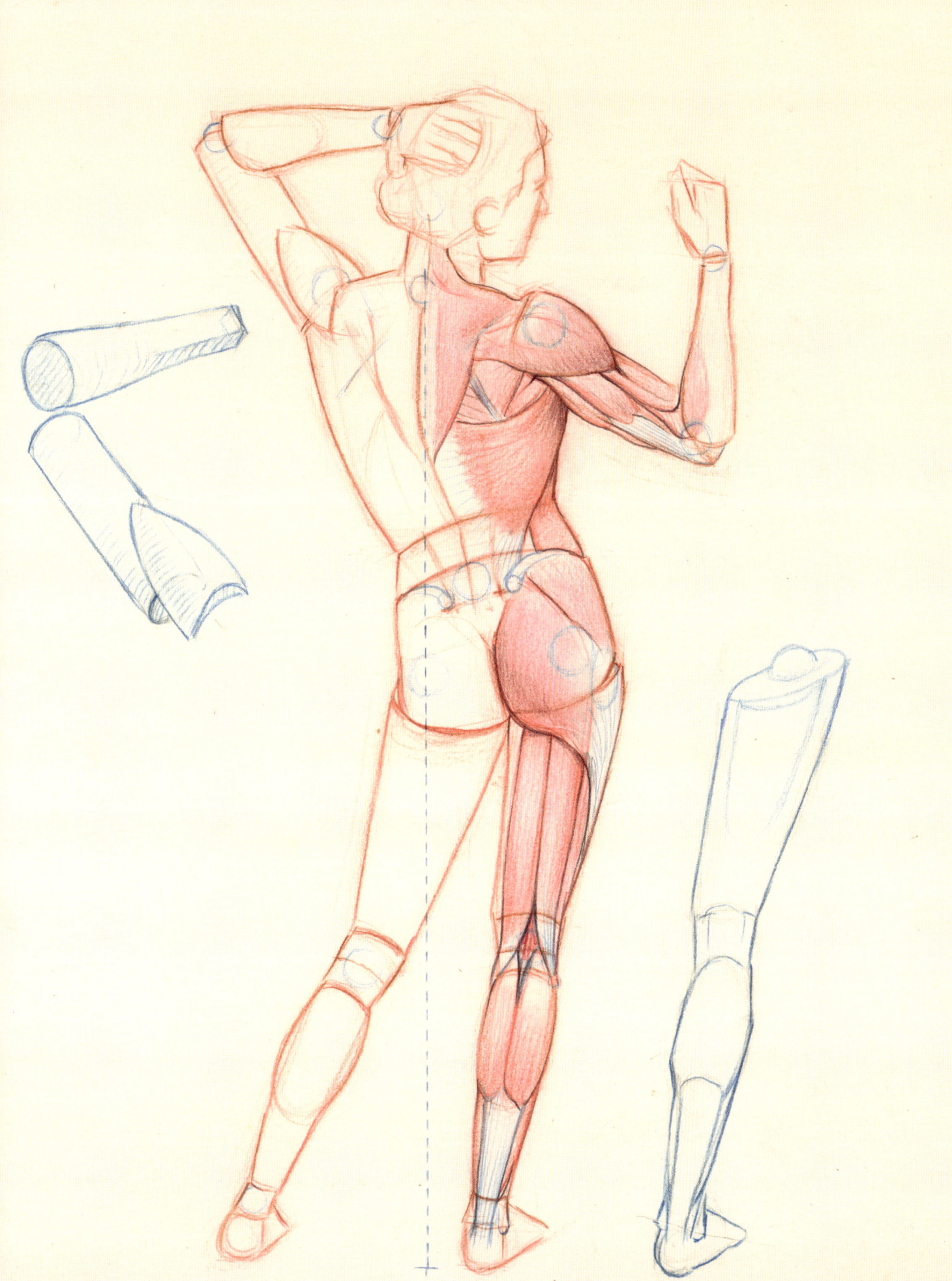

THE SKELETON AND SUPERFICIAL MUSCLES OF THE TORSO (MALE, FRONT VIEW)

Place a piece of tracing paper over the gridded page opposite, and copy the image below using the grid as a guide. Perform the exercise as many times as you want, using a new sheet of tracing paper each time. Once you feel you've had enough practice, try drawing the image from memory and without using the gridded page.

In this and the following exercise, compare the ribcage and pelvis widths of men and women. In men, the ribcage and pelvis have the same width, producing the male torso's straight profile. In women, the ribcage is a bit narrower than the pelvis, producing the female torso's characteristic hourglass profile.

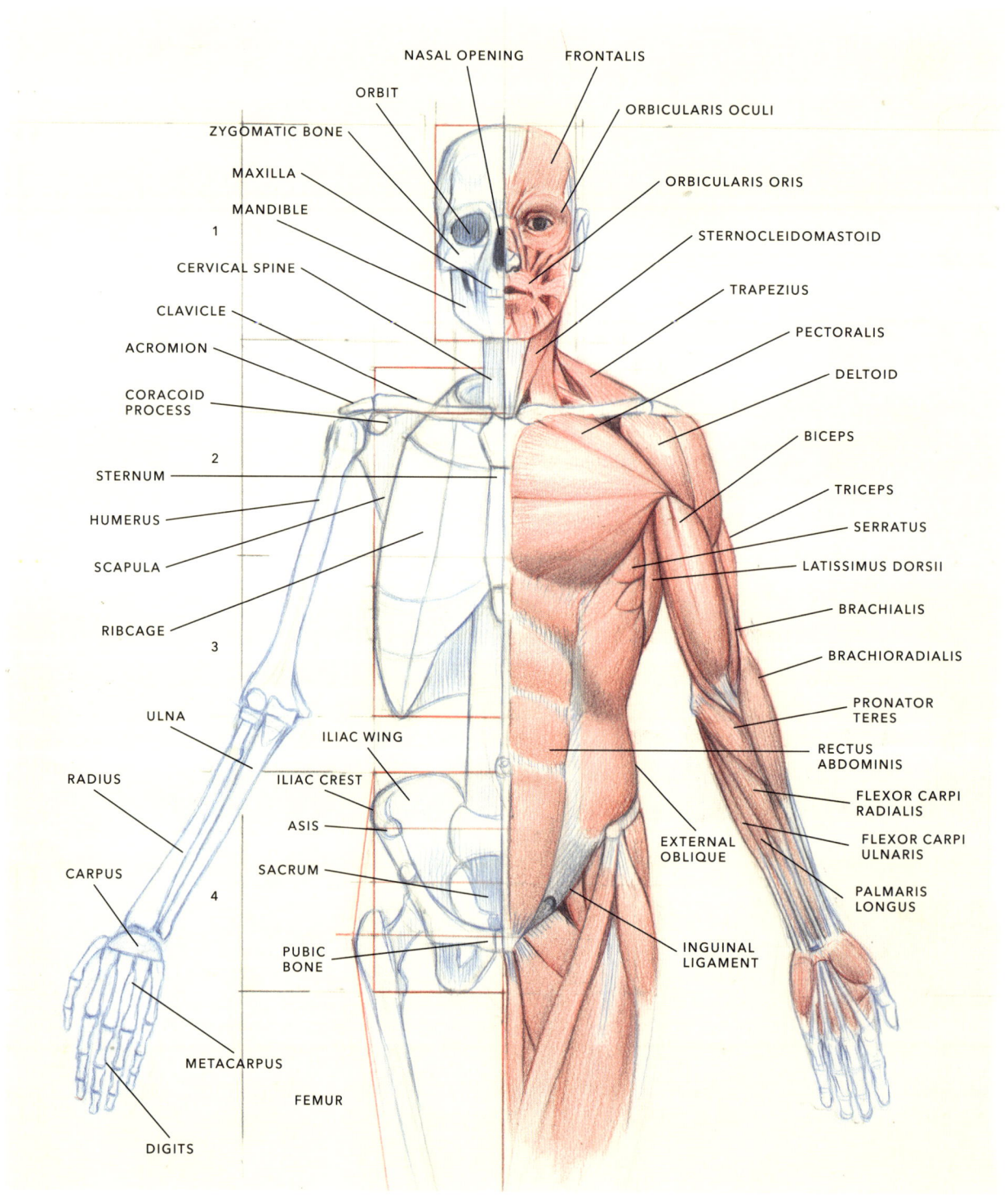

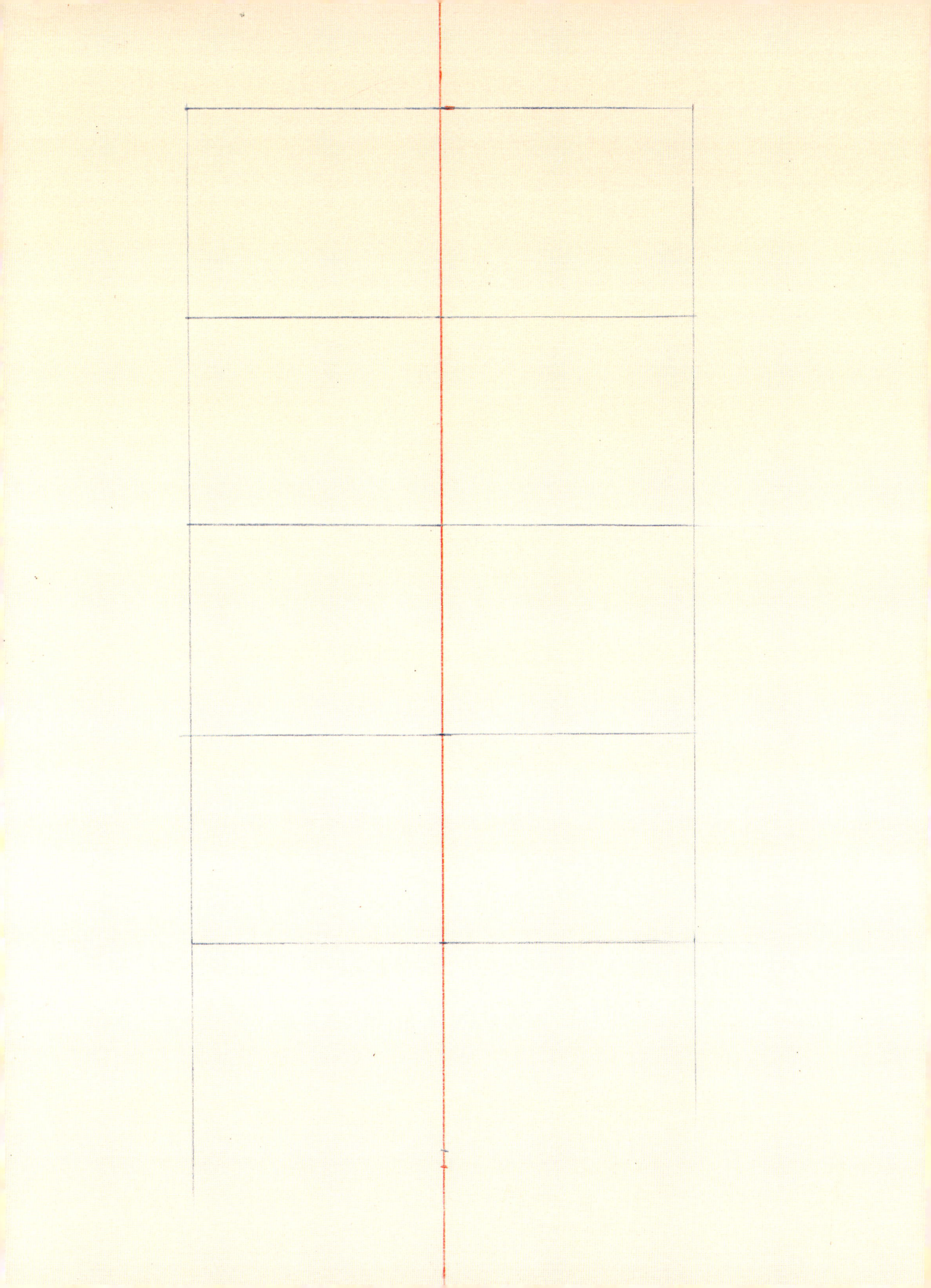

THE SKELETON AND SUPERFICIAL MUSCLES OF THE TORSO (FEMALE, FRONT VIEW)

Place a piece of tracing paper over the gridded page to the right of the image below, and copy the image using the grid as a guide. Perform the exercise as many times as you want, using a new sheet of tracing paper each time. Once you feel you've had enough practice, try drawing the image from memory and without using the gridded page.

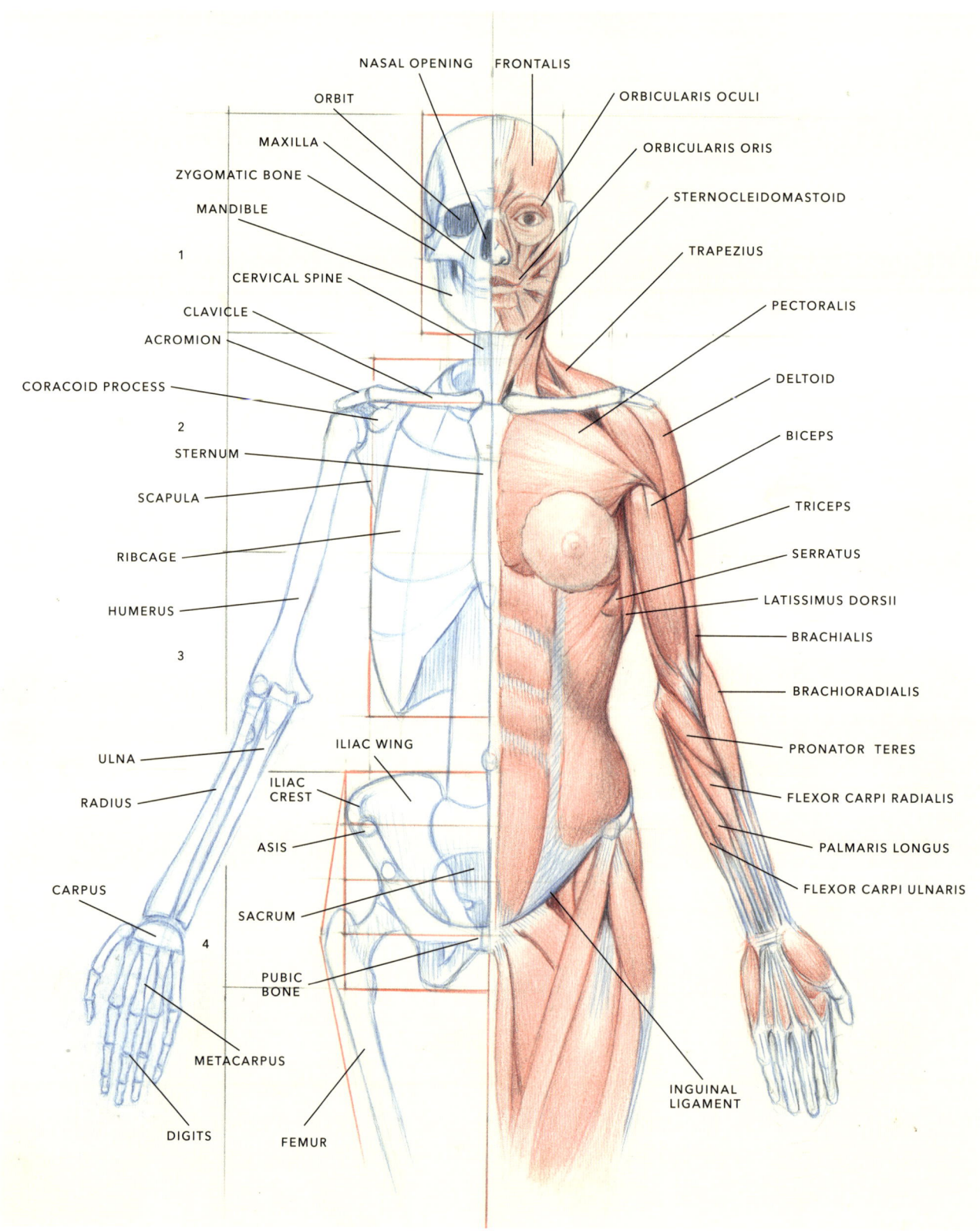

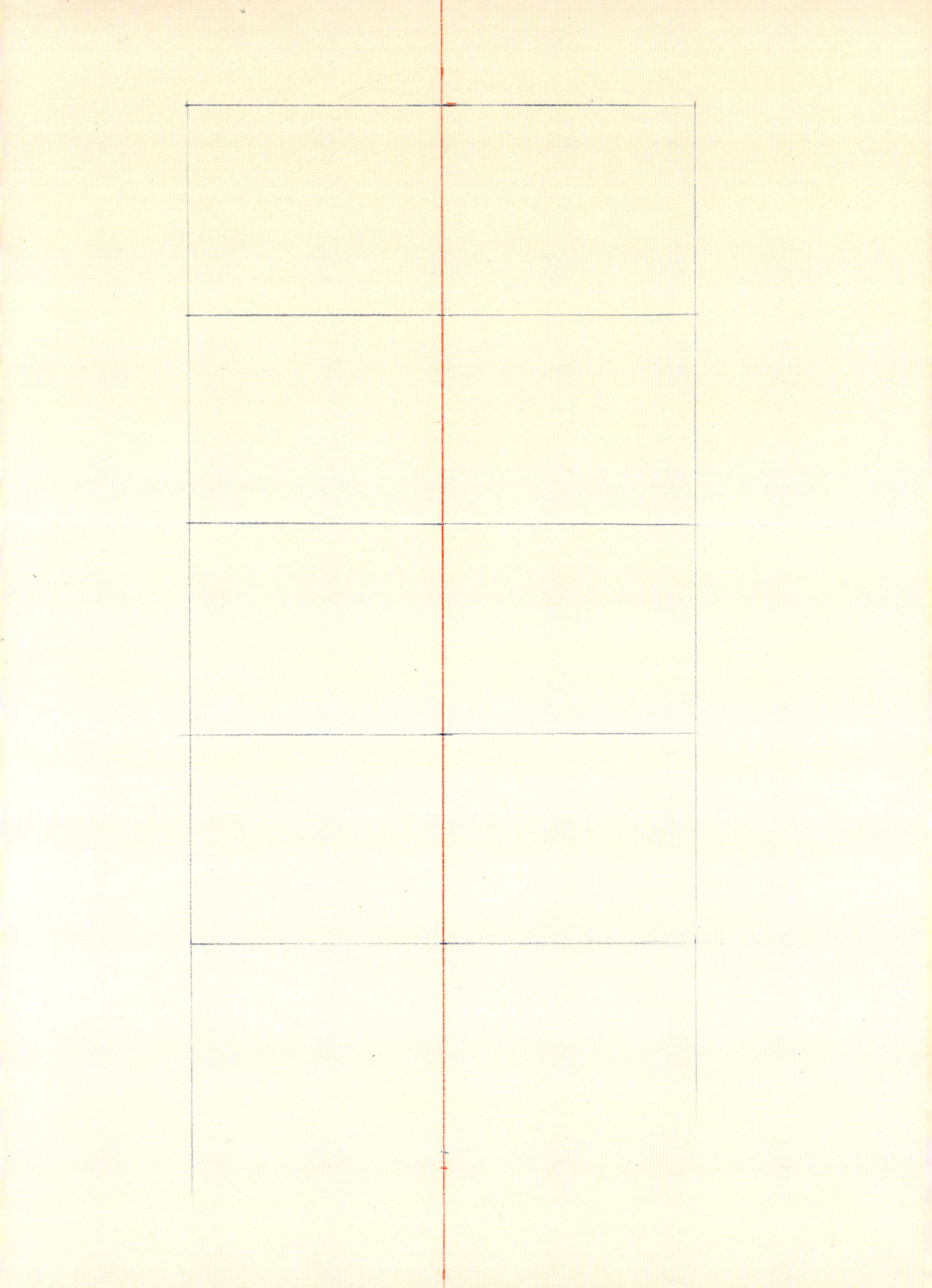

EXERCISE 2.3
THE SKELETON AND SUPERFICIAL MUSCLES OF THE TORSO (MALE, BACK VIEW)

Place a piece of tracing paper over the gridded page beginning on the previous page and continuing below and opposite and copy the image using the grid as a guide. Perform the exercise as many times as you want, using a new sheet of tracing paper each time. Once you feel you've had enough practice, try drawing the image from memory and without using the gridded page.

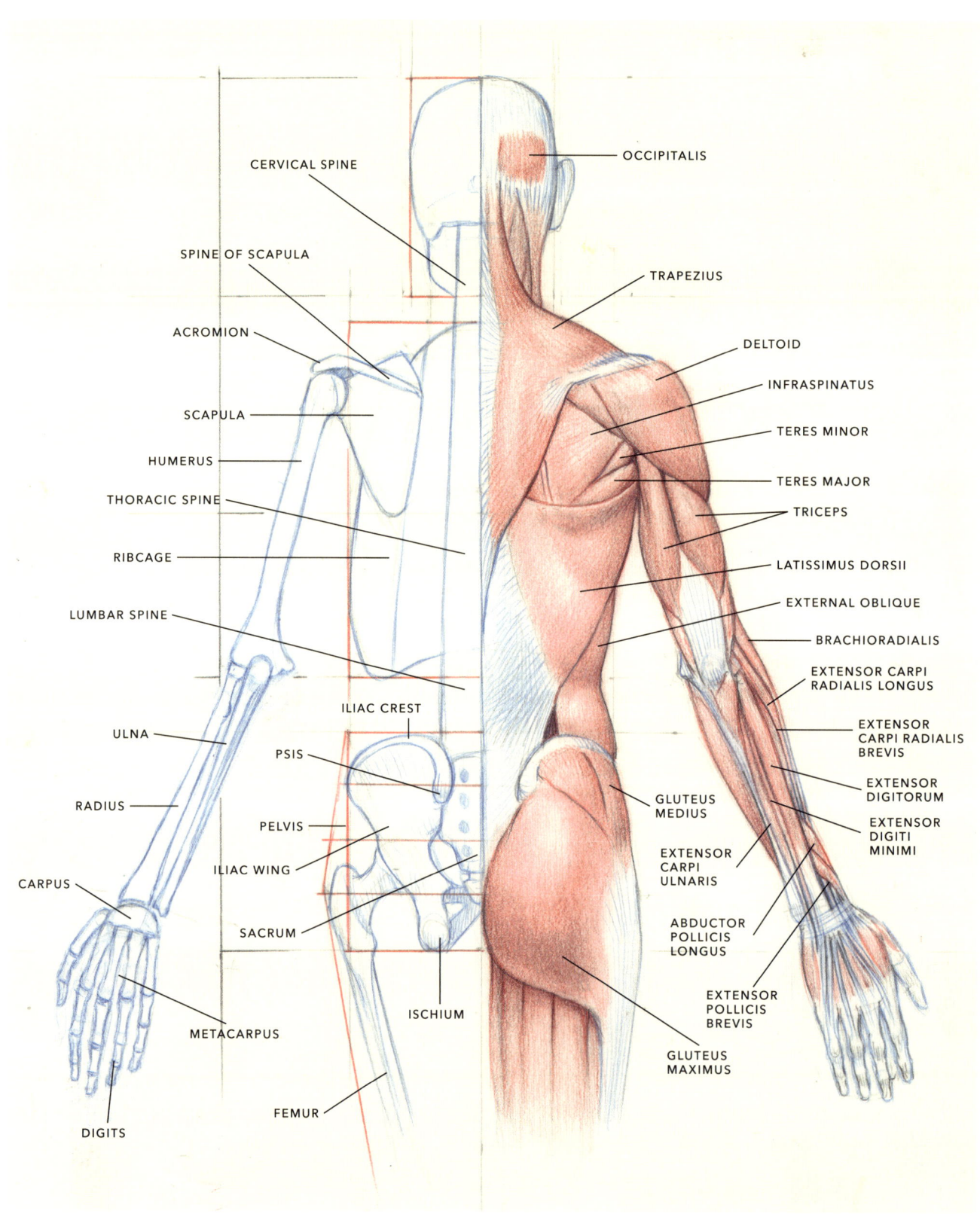

CERVICAL SPINE

SPINE OF SCAPULA

ACROMION

SCAPULA

HUMERUS

THORACIC SPINE

RIBCAGE

LUMBAR SPINE

ULNA

RADIUS

CARPUS

METACARPUS

DIGITS

ILIAC CREST

PSIS

PELVIS

ILIAC WING

SACRUM

ISCHIUM

FEMUR

OCCIPITALIS

TRAPEZIUS

DELTOID

INFRASPINATUS

TERES MINOR

TERES MAJOR

TRICEPS

LATISSIMUS DORSII

EXTERNAL OBLIQUE

BRACHIORADIALIS

EXTENSOR CARPI RADIALIS LONGUS

EXTENSOR CARPI RADIALIS BREVIS

EXTENSOR DIGITORUM

EXTENSOR DIGITI MINIMI

GLUTEUS MEDIUS

EXTENSOR CARPI ULNARIS

ABDUCTOR POLLICIS LONGUS

EXTENSOR POLLICIS BREVIS

GLUTEUS MAXIMUS

THE SKELETON AND SUPERFICIAL MUSCLES OF THE TORSO (FEMALE, BACK VIEW)

Place a piece of tracing paper over the gridded page opposite, and copy the image below using the grid as a guide. Perform the exercise as many times as you want, using a new sheet of tracing paper each time. Once you feel you've had enough practice, try drawing the image from memory and without using the gridded page.

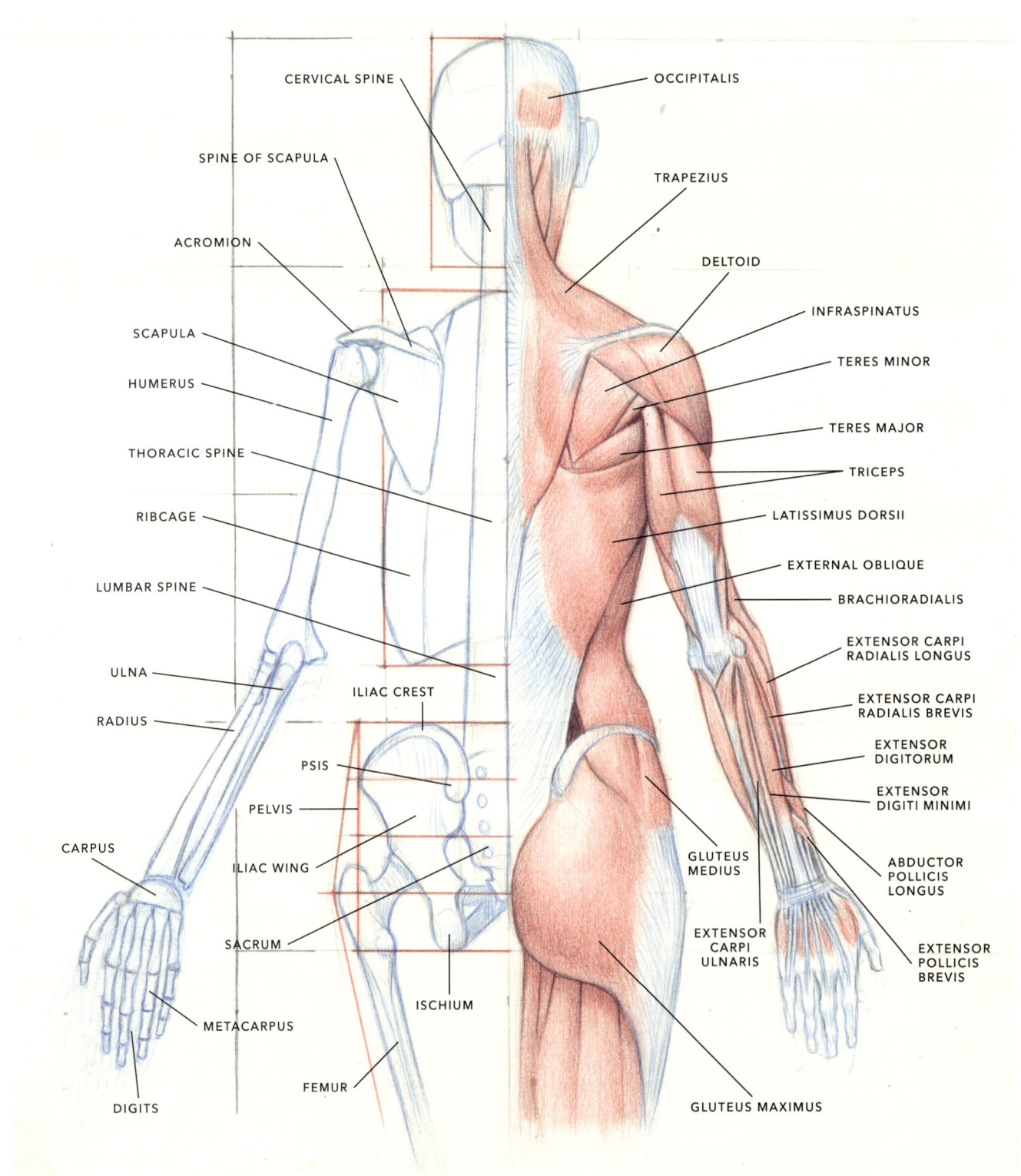

CERVICAL SPINE

OCCIPITALIS

SPINE OF SCAPULA

TRAPEZIUS

ACROMION

DELTOID

INFRASPINATUS

SCAPULA

TERES MINOR

HUMERUS

TERES MAJOR

THORACIC SPINE

TRICEPS

RIBCAGE

LATISSIMUS DORSII

LUMBAR SPINE

EXTERNAL OBLIQUE

BRACHIORADIALIS

EXTENSOR CARPI
RADIALIS LONGUS

ULNA

EXTENSOR CARPI
RADIALIS BREVIS

RADIUS

ILIAC CREST

EXTENSOR
DIGITORUM

PSIS

EXTENSOR
DIGITI MINIMI

PELVIS

CARPUS

ILIAC WING

GLUTEUS
MEDIUS

ABDUCTOR
POLLICIS
LONGUS

SACRUM

EXTENSOR
CARPI
ULNARIS

EXTENSOR
POLLICIS
BREVIS

METACARPUS

ISCHIUM

FEMUR

DIGITS

GLUTEUS MAXIMUS

THE SKELETON AND SUPERFICIAL MUSCLES OF THE LEGS (MALE, FRONT VIEW)

Place a piece of tracing paper over the gridded page opposite, and copy the image below using the grid as a guide. Perform the exercise as many times as you want, using a new sheet of tracing paper each time. Once you feel you've had enough practice, try drawing the image from memory and without using the gridded page.

In this and the following exercise, compare how the difference in pelvis width affects the male and female profiles at the level of the legs. The female pelvis is proportionally wider than the male's; because of this, women's hip joints are a little bit farther apart. This affects the angle of the femur's axis—the *Q angle*—which in men is narrower (about 12 degrees) and in women wider (about 16 degrees), resulting in the typical difference in profile between men and women at the level of hips and legs.

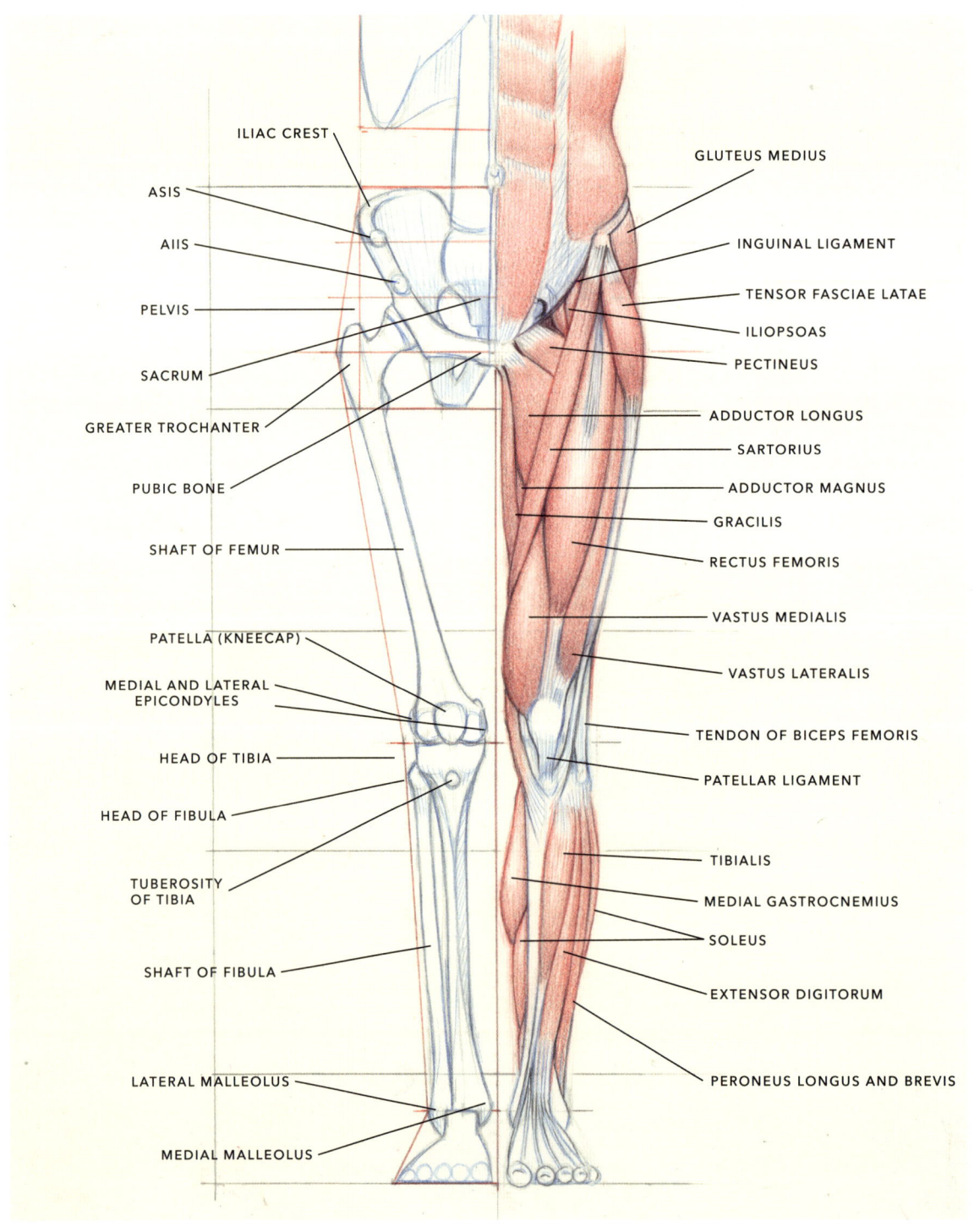

ILIAC CREST

ASIS

AIIS

PELVIS

SACRUM

GREATER TROCHANTER

PUBIC BONE

SHAFT OF FEMUR

PATELLA (KNEECAP)

MEDIAL AND LATERAL EPICONDYLES

HEAD OF TIBIA

HEAD OF FIBULA

TUBEROSITY OF TIBIA

SHAFT OF FIBULA

LATERAL MALLEOLUS

MEDIAL MALLEOLUS

GLUTEUS MEDIUS

INGUINAL LIGAMENT

TENSOR FASCIAE LATAE

ILIOPSOAS

PECTINEUS

ADDUCTOR LONGUS

SARTORIUS

ADDUCTOR MAGNUS

GRACILIS

RECTUS FEMORIS

VASTUS MEDIALIS

VASTUS LATERALIS

TENDON OF BICEPS FEMORIS

PATELLAR LIGAMENT

TIBIALIS

MEDIAL GASTROCNEMIUS

SOLEUS

EXTENSOR DIGITORUM

PERONEUS LONGUS AND BREVIS

THE SKELETON AND SUPERFICIAL MUSCLES OF THE LEGS (FEMALE, FRONT VIEW)

Place a piece of tracing paper over the gridded page opposite, and copy the image using the grid as a guide. Perform the exercise as many times as you want, using a new sheet of tracing paper each time. Once you feel you've had enough practice, try drawing the image from memory and without using the gridded page.

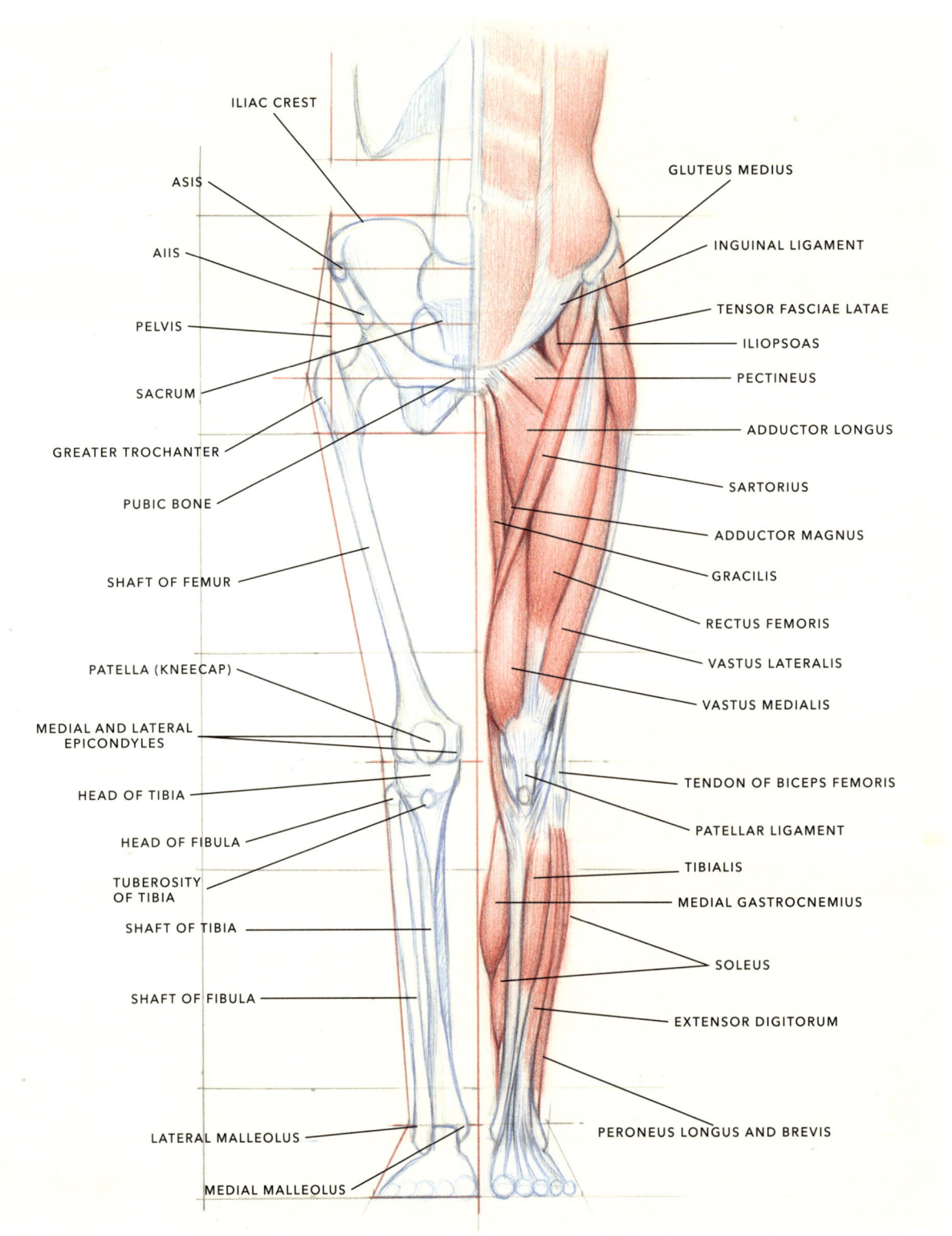

ILIAC CREST

ASIS

AIIS

PELVIS

SACRUM

GREATER TROCHANTER

PUBIC BONE

SHAFT OF FEMUR

PATELLA (KNEECAP)

MEDIAL AND LATERAL EPICONDYLES

HEAD OF TIBIA

HEAD OF FIBULA

TUBEROSITY OF TIBIA

SHAFT OF TIBIA

SHAFT OF FIBULA

LATERAL MALLEOLUS

MEDIAL MALLEOLUS

GLUTEUS MEDIUS

INGUINAL LIGAMENT

TENSOR FASCIAE LATAE

ILIOPSOAS

PECTINEUS

ADDUCTOR LONGUS

SARTORIUS

ADDUCTOR MAGNUS

GRACILIS

RECTUS FEMORIS

VASTUS LATERALIS

VASTUS MEDIALIS

TENDON OF BICEPS FEMORIS

PATELLAR LIGAMENT

TIBIALIS

MEDIAL GASTROCNEMIUS

SOLEUS

EXTENSOR DIGITORUM

PERONEUS LONGUS AND BREVIS

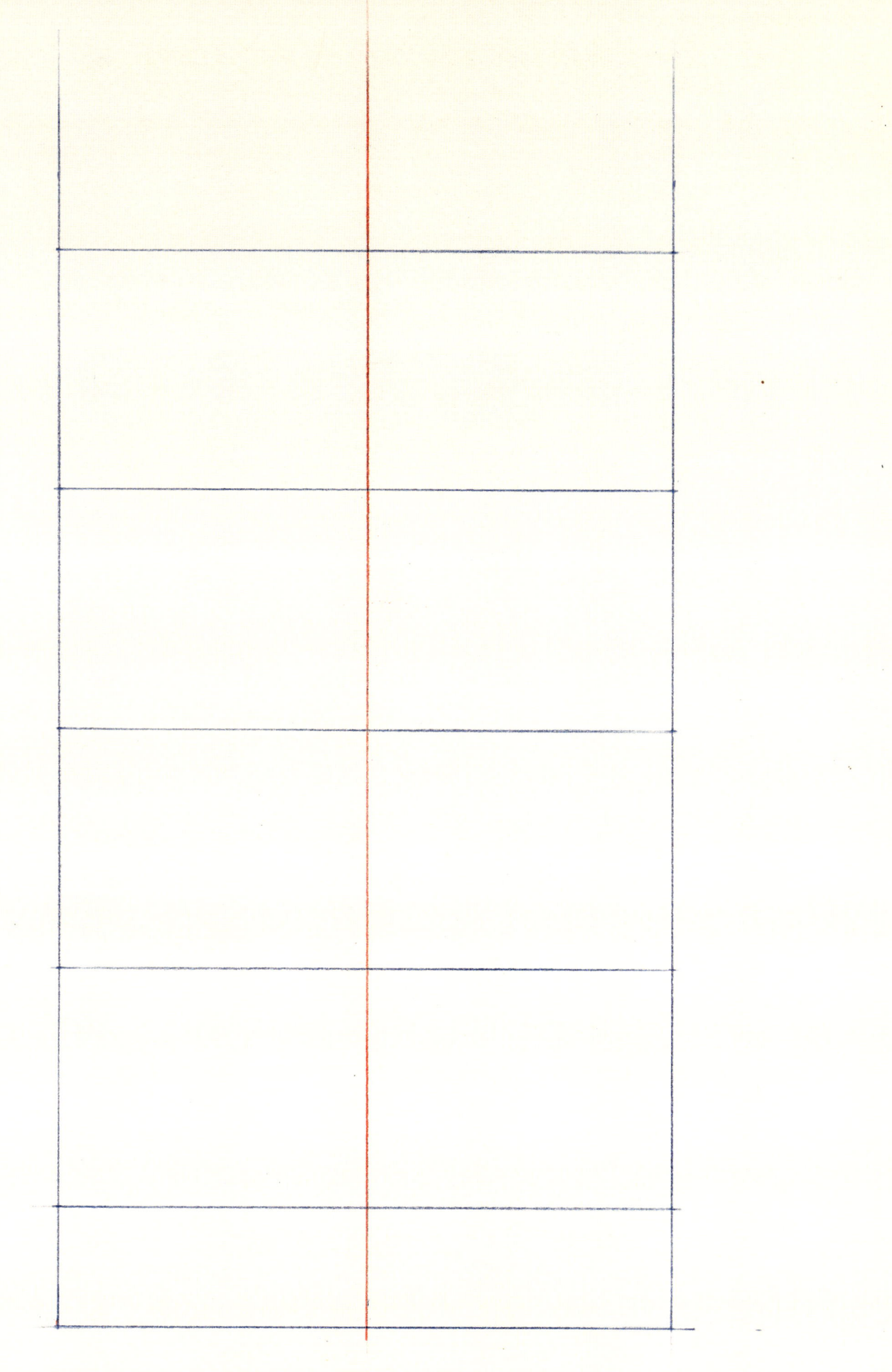

THE SKELETON AND SUPERFICIAL MUSCLES OF THE LEGS (MALE, BACK VIEW)

Place a piece of tracing paper over the gridded page opposite, and copy the image below using the grid as a guide. Perform the exercise as many times as you want, using a new sheet of tracing paper each time. Once you feel you've had enough practice, try drawing the image from memory and without using the gridded page.

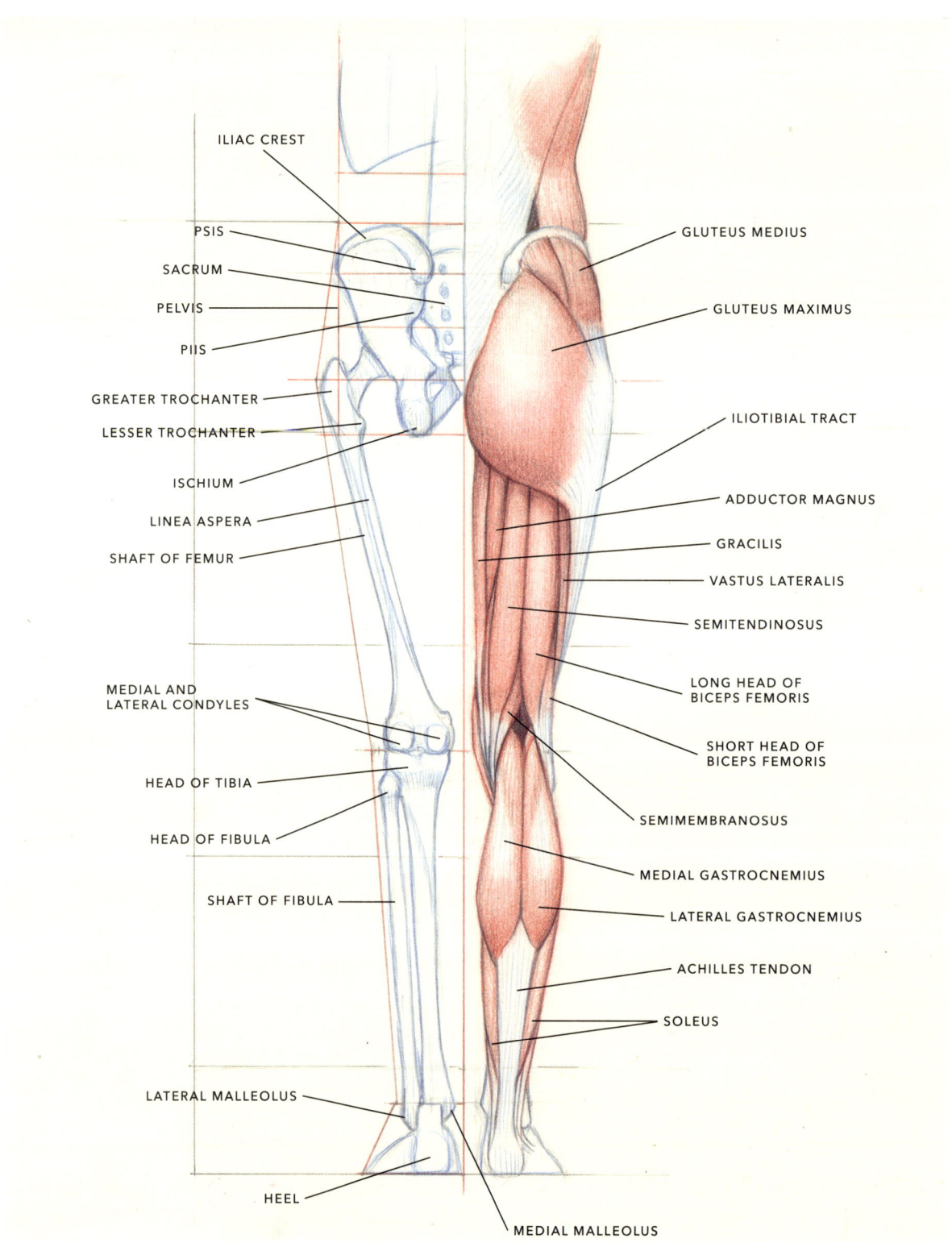

ILIAC CREST

PSIS

SACRUM

PELVIS

PIIS

GREATER TROCHANTER

LESSER TROCHANTER

ISCHIUM

LINEA ASPERA

SHAFT OF FEMUR

MEDIAL AND
LATERAL CONDYLES

HEAD OF TIBIA

HEAD OF FIBULA

SHAFT OF FIBULA

LATERAL MALLEOLUS

HEEL

MEDIAL MALLEOLUS

GLUTEUS MEDIUS

GLUTEUS MAXIMUS

ILIOTIBIAL TRACT

ADDUCTOR MAGNUS

GRACILIS

VASTUS LATERALIS

SEMITENDINOSUS

LONG HEAD OF
BICEPS FEMORIS

SHORT HEAD OF
BICEPS FEMORIS

SEMIMEMBRANOSUS

MEDIAL GASTROCNEMIUS

LATERAL GASTROCNEMIUS

ACHILLES TENDON

SOLEUS

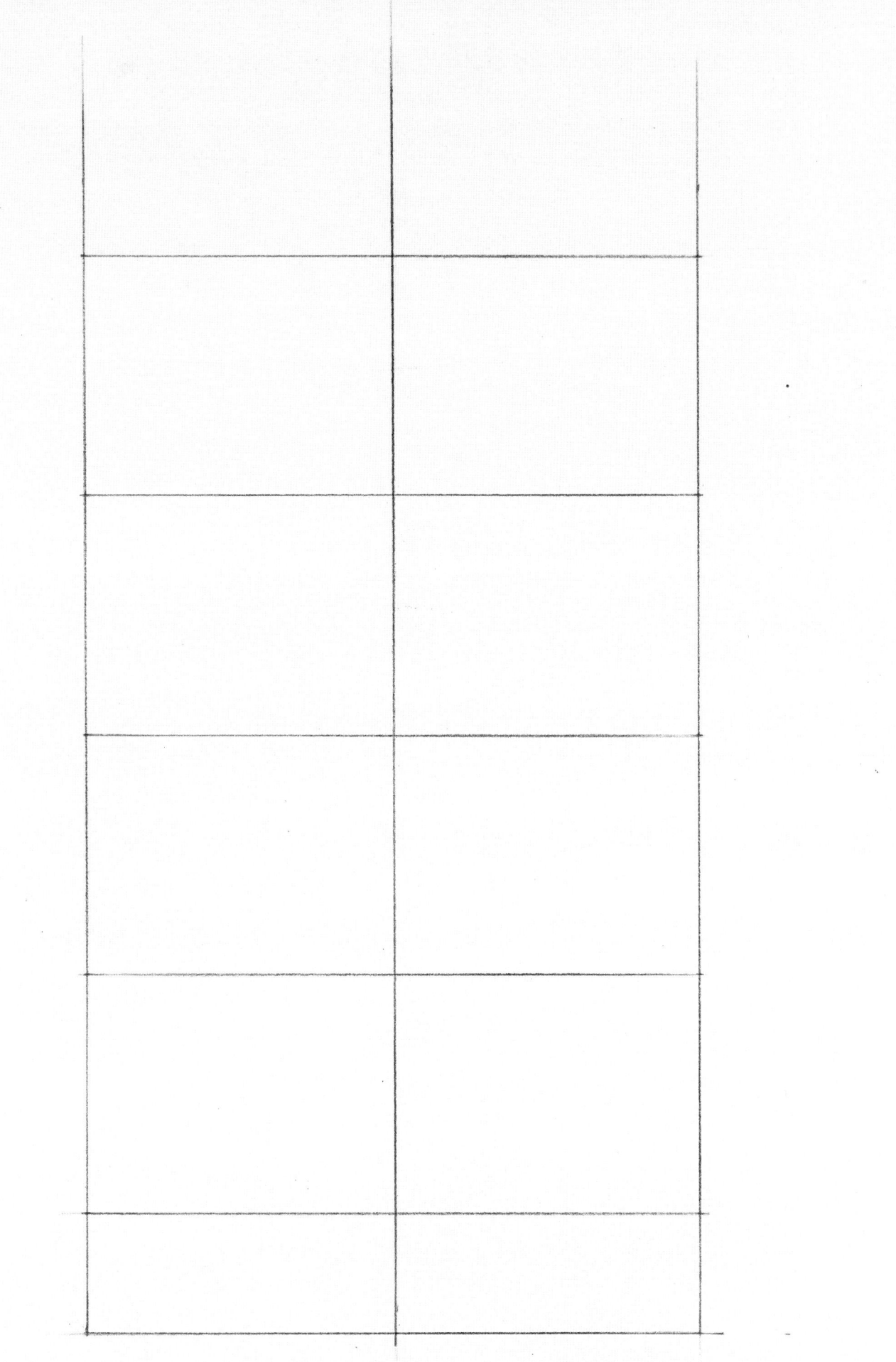

THE SKELETON AND SUPERFICIAL MUSCLES OF THE LEGS (FEMALE, BACK VIEW)

Place a piece of tracing paper over the gridded page opposite, and copy the image below using the grid as a guide. Perform the exercise as many times as you want, using a new sheet of tracing paper each time. Once you feel you've had enough practice, try drawing the image from memory and without using the gridded page.

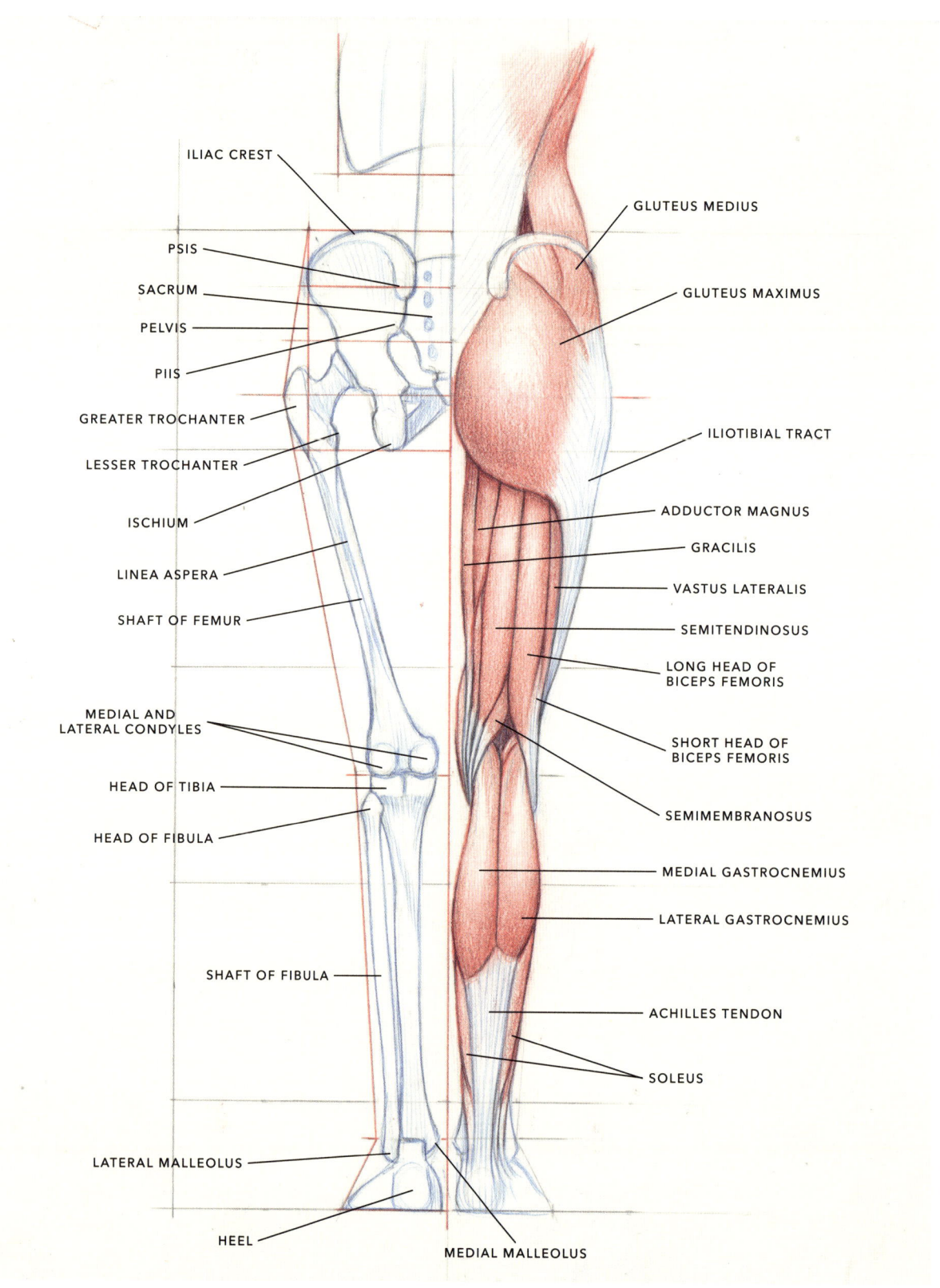

ILIAC CREST

PSIS

SACRUM

PELVIS

PIIS

GREATER TROCHANTER

LESSER TROCHANTER

ISCHIUM

LINEA ASPERA

SHAFT OF FEMUR

MEDIAL AND
LATERAL CONDYLES

HEAD OF TIBIA

HEAD OF FIBULA

SHAFT OF FIBULA

LATERAL MALLEOLUS

HEEL

MEDIAL MALLEOLUS

GLUTEUS MEDIUS

GLUTEUS MAXIMUS

ILIOTIBIAL TRACT

ADDUCTOR MAGNUS

GRACILIS

VASTUS LATERALIS

SEMITENDINOSUS

LONG HEAD OF
BICEPS FEMORIS

SHORT HEAD OF
BICEPS FEMORIS

SEMIMEMBRANOSUS

MEDIAL GASTROCNEMIUS

LATERAL GASTROCNEMIUS

ACHILLES TENDON

SOLEUS

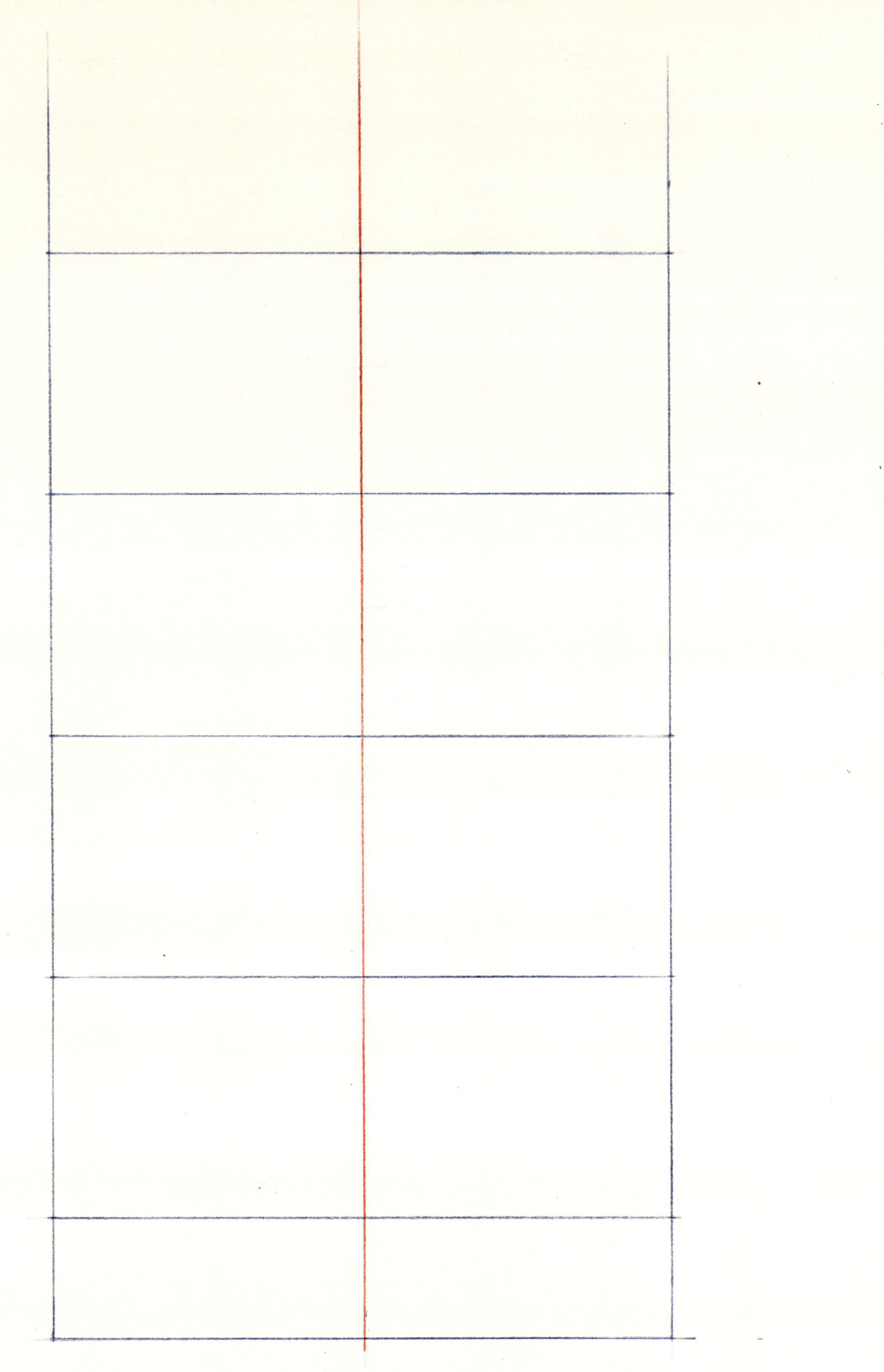

EXERCISE 2.9

THE SKELETON AND SUPERFICIAL MUSCLES OF THE MALE FIGURE, SIDE VIEW

Place a piece of tracing paper over the gridded page opposite, and copy the image belowusing the grid as a guide. Perform the exercise as many times as you want, using a new sheet of tracing paper each time. Once you feel you've had enough practice, try drawing the image from memory and without using the gridded page.

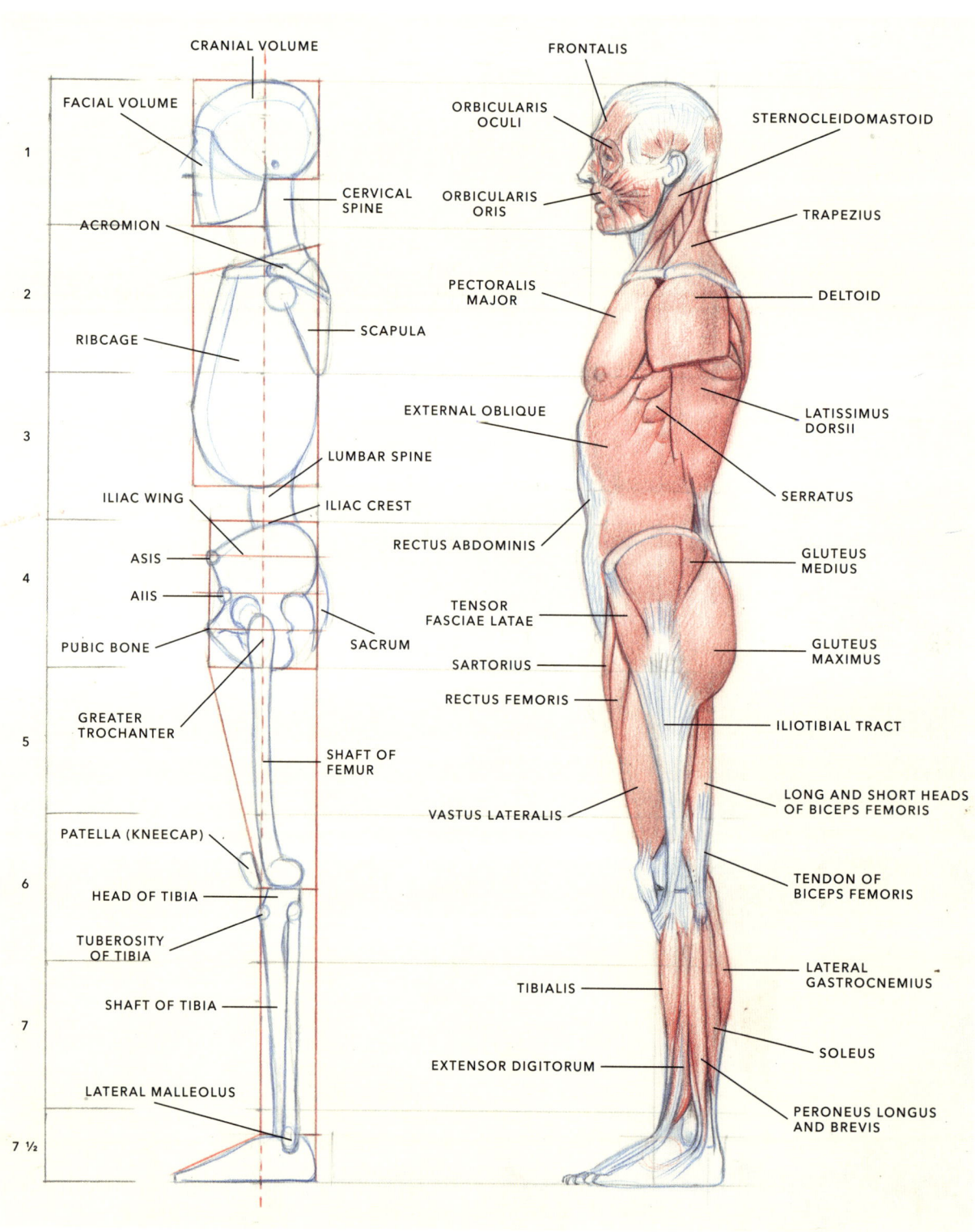

THE SKELETON AND SUPERFICIAL MUSCLES OF THE FEMALE FIGURE, SIDE VIEW

Place a piece of tracing paper over the gridded page opposite, and copy the image below using the grid as a guide. Perform the exercise as many times as you want, using a new sheet of tracing paper each time. Once you feel you've had enough practice, try drawing the image from memory and without using the gridded page.

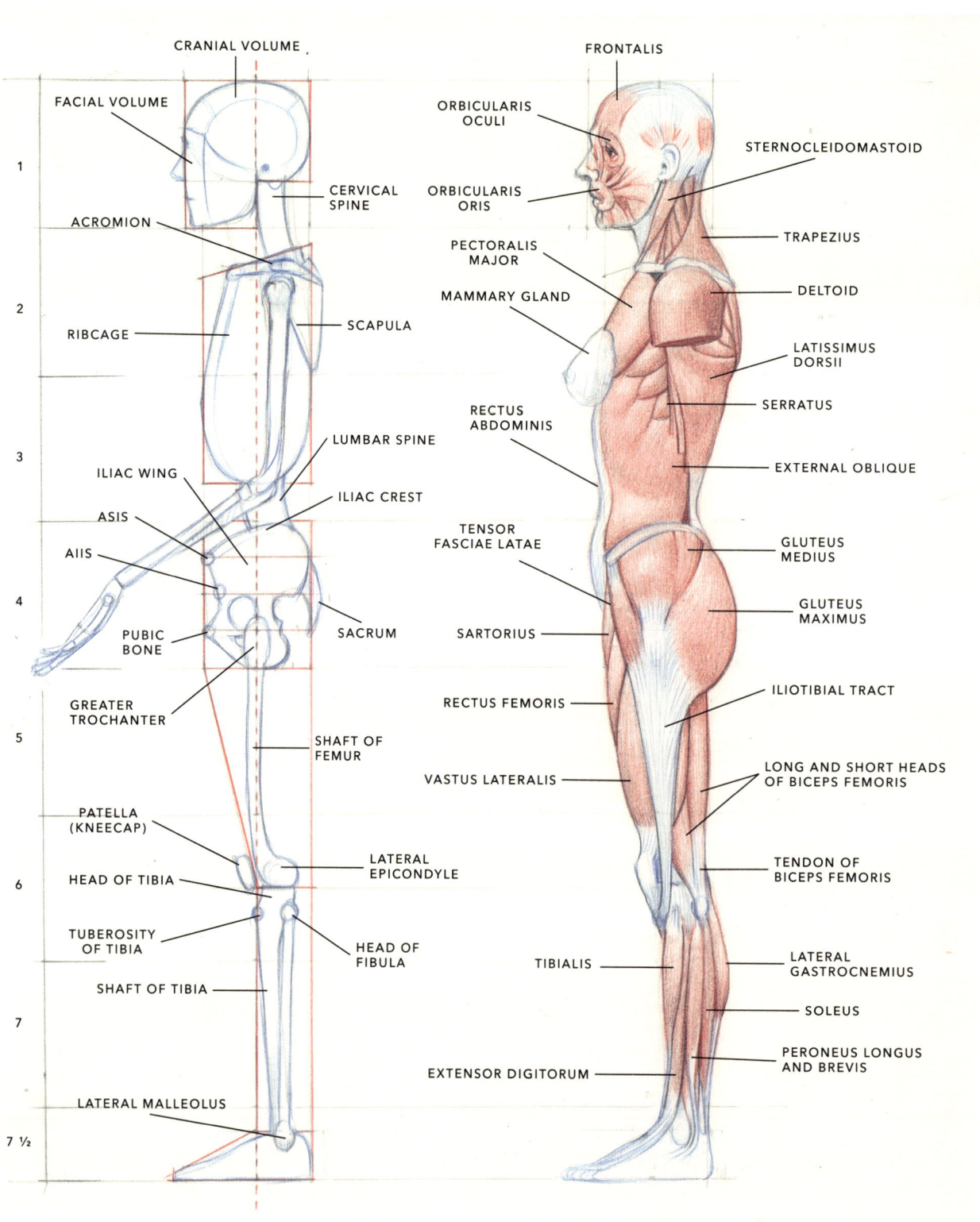

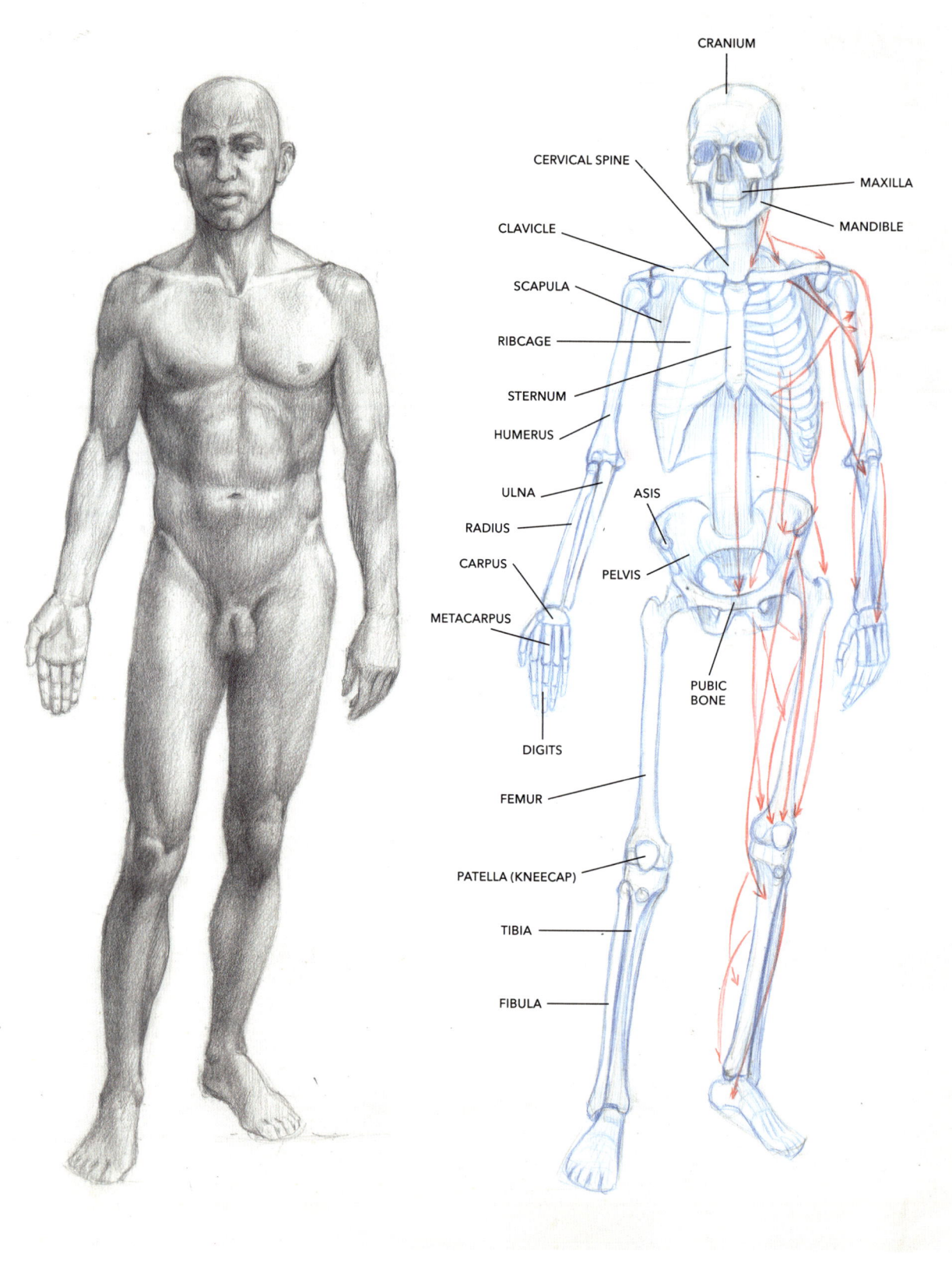

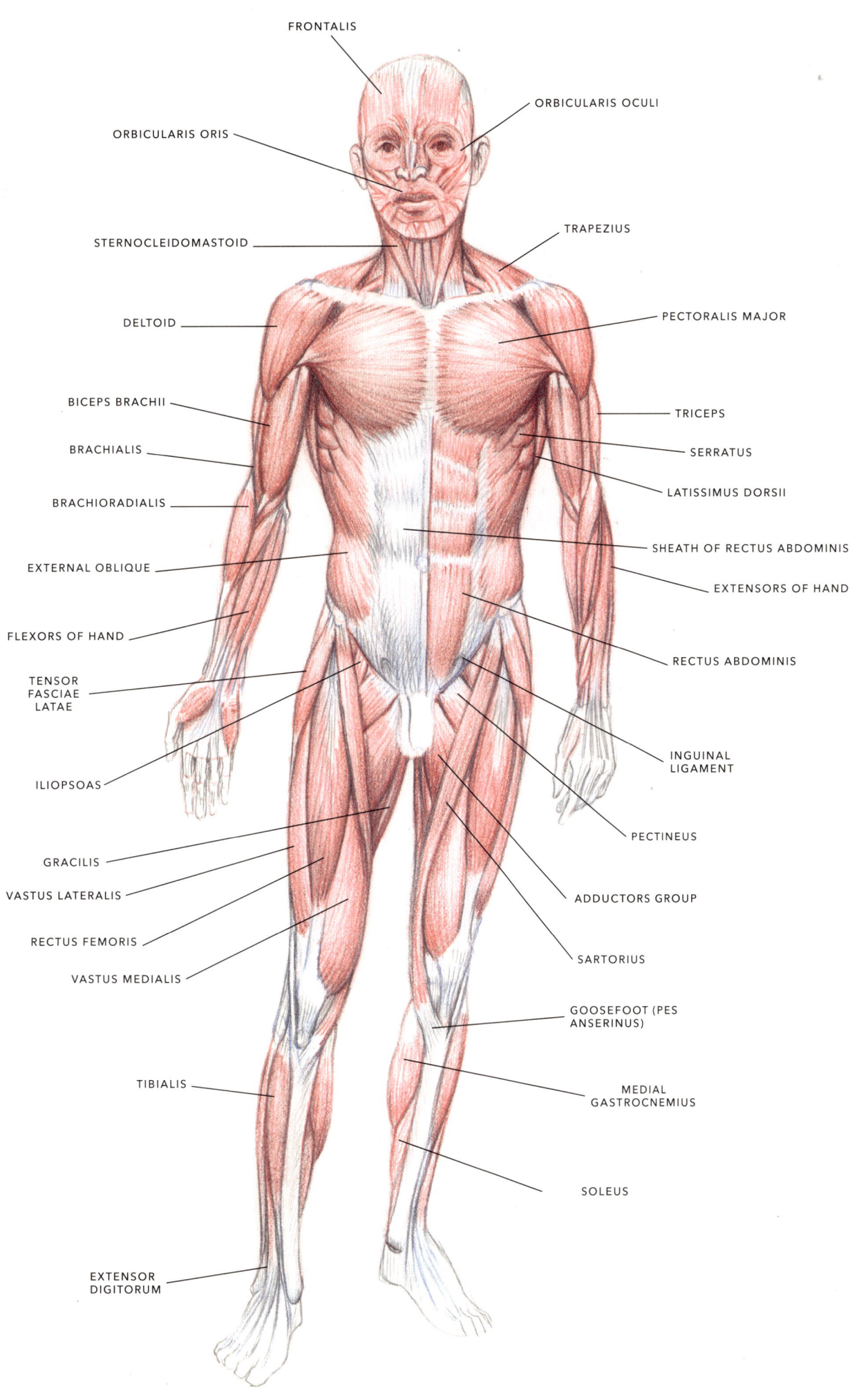

FRONTALIS

ORBICULARIS OCULI

ORBICULARIS ORIS

TRAPEZIUS

STERNOCLEIDOMASTOID

DELTOID

PECTORALIS MAJOR

BICEPS BRACHII

TRICEPS

BRACHIALIS

SERRATUS

BRACHIORADIALIS

LATISSIMUS DORSII

SHEATH OF RECTUS ABDOMINIS

EXTERNAL OBLIQUE

EXTENSORS OF HAND

FLEXORS OF HAND

RECTUS ABDOMINIS

TENSOR
FASCIAE
LATAE

INGUINAL
LIGAMENT

ILIOPSOAS

PECTINEUS

GRACILIS

ADDUCTORS GROUP

VASTUS LATERALIS

RECTUS FEMORIS

SARTORIUS

VASTUS MEDIALIS

GOOSEFOOT (PES
ANSERINUS)

TIBIALIS

MEDIAL
GASTROCNEMIUS

SOLEUS

EXTENSOR
DIGITORUM

CERVICAL SPINE

SPINE OF SCAPULA

ACROMION

SCAPULA

HUMERUS

THORACIC SPINE

RIBCAGE

RADIUS

LUMBAR SPINE

ULNA

PELVIS

PSIS

ILIAC WING

SACRUM

ISCHIUM

GREATER TROCHANTER

FEMUR

FIBULA

TIBIA

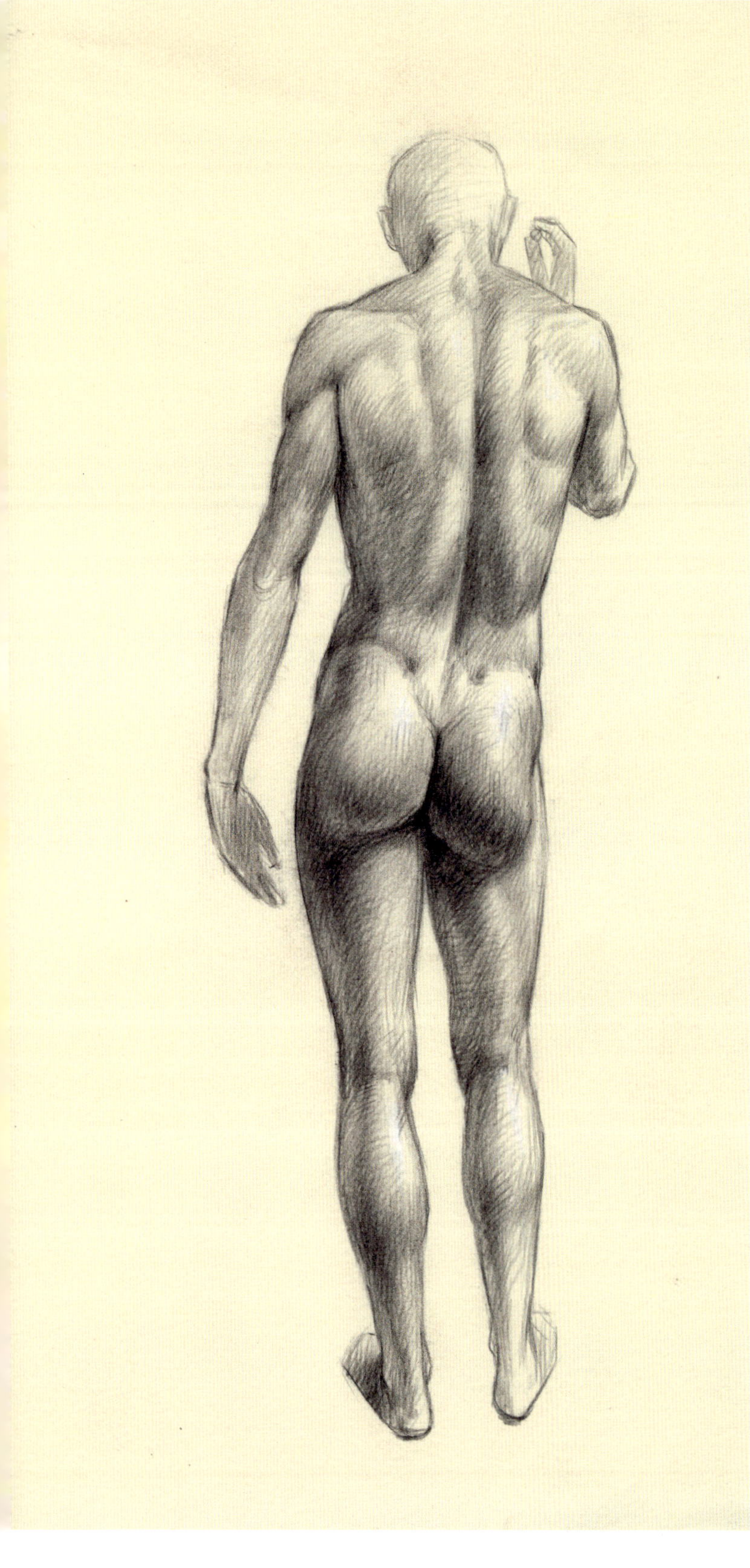

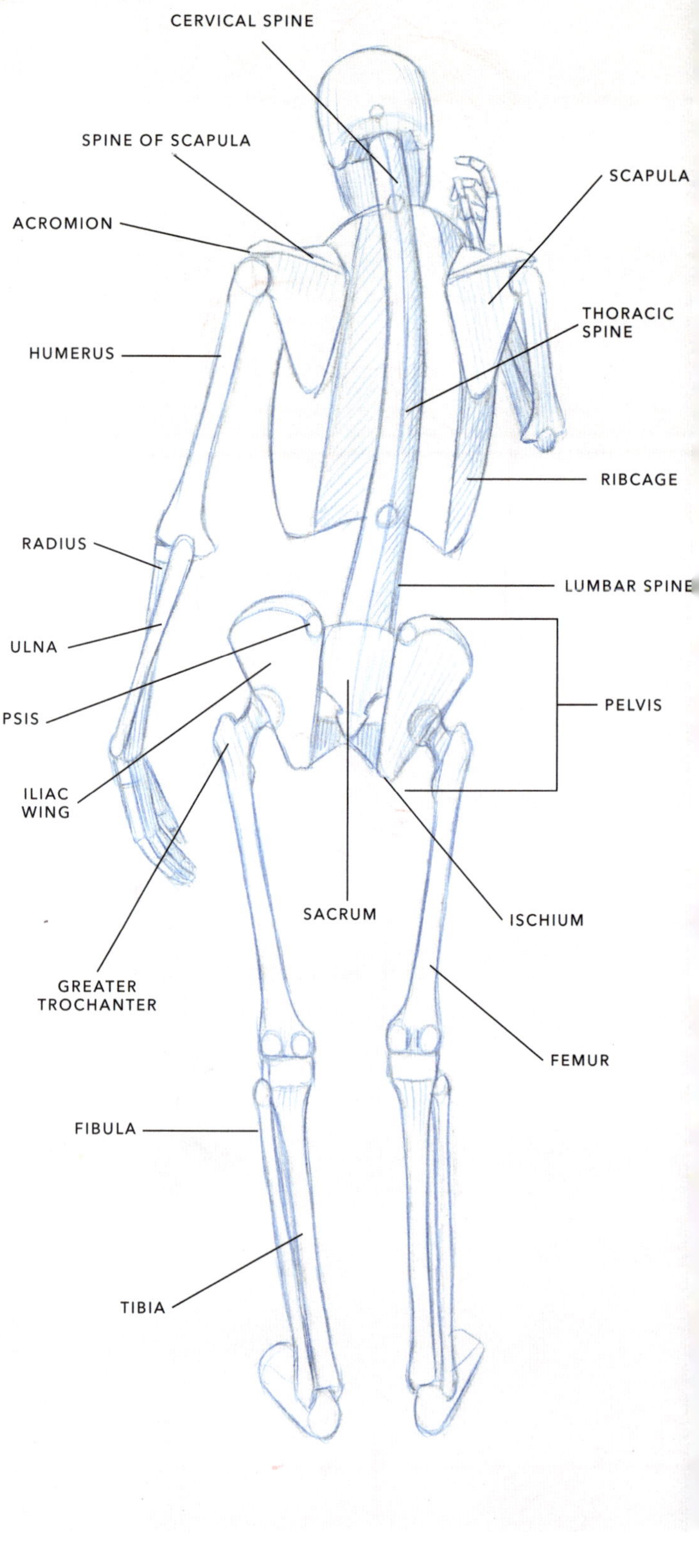

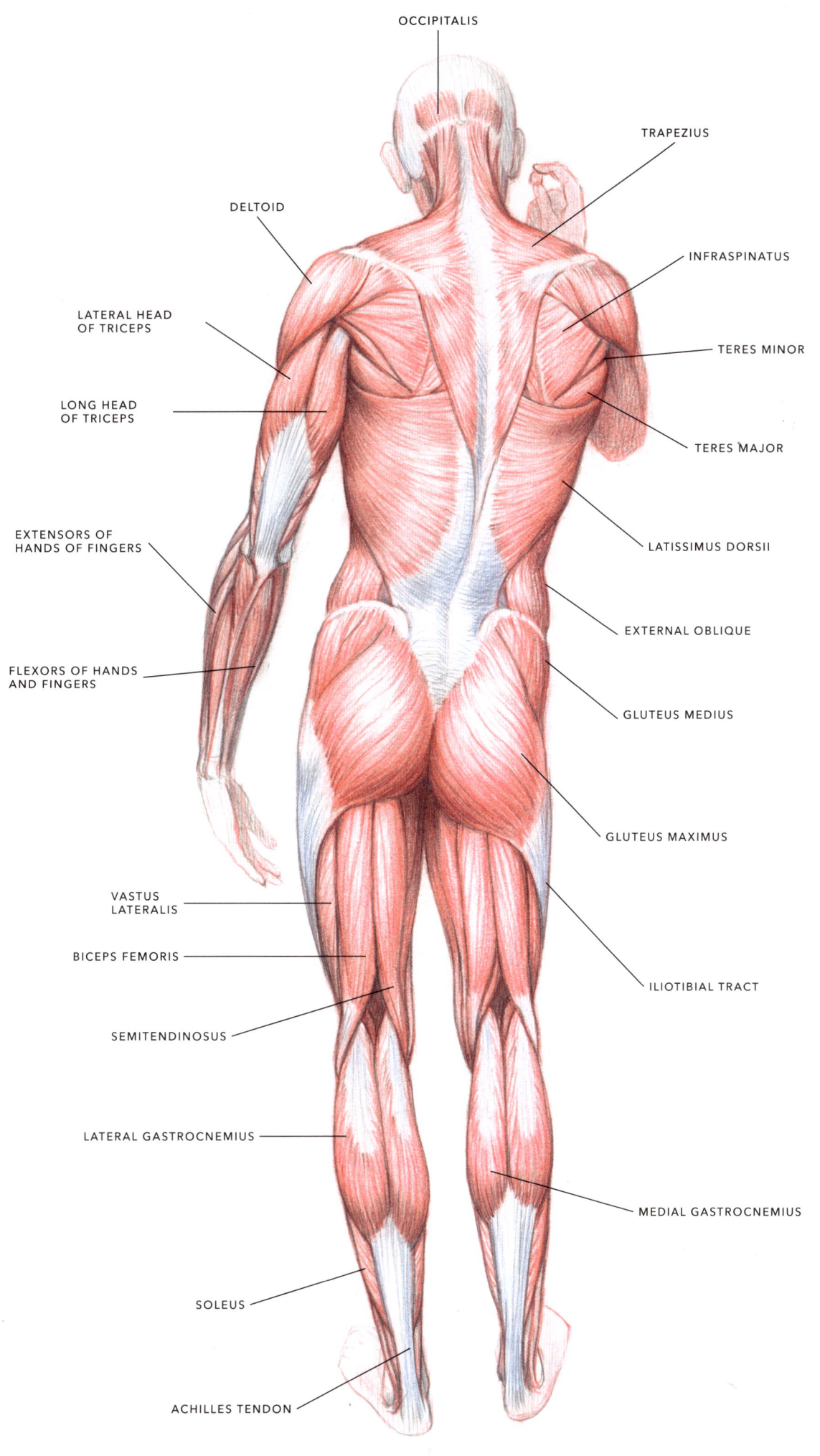

OCCIPITALIS

TRAPEZIUS

DELTOID

INFRASPINATUS

LATERAL HEAD
OF TRICEPS

TERES MINOR

LONG HEAD
OF TRICEPS

TERES MAJOR

LATISSIMUS DORSII

EXTENSORS OF
HANDS OF FINGERS

EXTERNAL OBLIQUE

FLEXORS OF HANDS
AND FINGERS

GLUTEUS MEDIUS

GLUTEUS MAXIMUS

VASTUS
LATERALIS

BICEPS FEMORIS

SEMITENDINOSUS

ILIOTIBIAL TRACT

LATERAL GASTROCNEMIUS

MEDIAL GASTROCNEMIUS

SOLEUS

ACHILLES TENDON

LEVEL 2

IDENTIFYING SKELETAL LANDMARKS AND SUPERFICIAL MUSCLE VOLUMES

Drawing from statues or from plaster casts of statues (known as *cast drawing*) has been an invaluable pedagogical tool in art schools for centuries. Copying the idealized forms of a cast or sculpture helps student artists identify the body's anatomical structures. For this reason, the reference images for several exercises of level 2 are photos of sculptures, facilitating your transition from the anatomical charts of section 1 to the photos of live models in chapter 3.

EXERCISE 2.11

POLYKLEITOS' *DORYPHOROS* (SPEAR BEARER)

This is the sculpture that, in a sense, started it all. Polykleitos' *Doryphoros,* also known as the Spear Bearer, has defined the Western method of sculpting, painting, and drawing the human figure for millennia. This work, created at the height of classical Greek civilization in the 5th century BCE, illustrates the ideal human figure as described in Polykleitos' Canon, his text on proportion. That text, discussed by several ancient authors, no longer exists. Nor does the bronze original of the *Doryphoros,* which survives in several Roman marble copies, including the one depicted here.

Start this exercise by copying the photo, trying to identify the landmarks, muscles, tendons, and all the other anatomical details you find labeled in the drawing on page 119. Take care to mark the skeletal landmarks on your drawing. You can use those when recreating the Spear Bearer's skeleton, as shown on page 118, by positioning a piece of tracing paper over your finished drawing of the sculpture.

RIGHT: Anonymous, Doryphorus from Pompeii, 1st century, BC, Carrara marble, 78.7 inches (200 cm). Naples National Archaeological Museum.

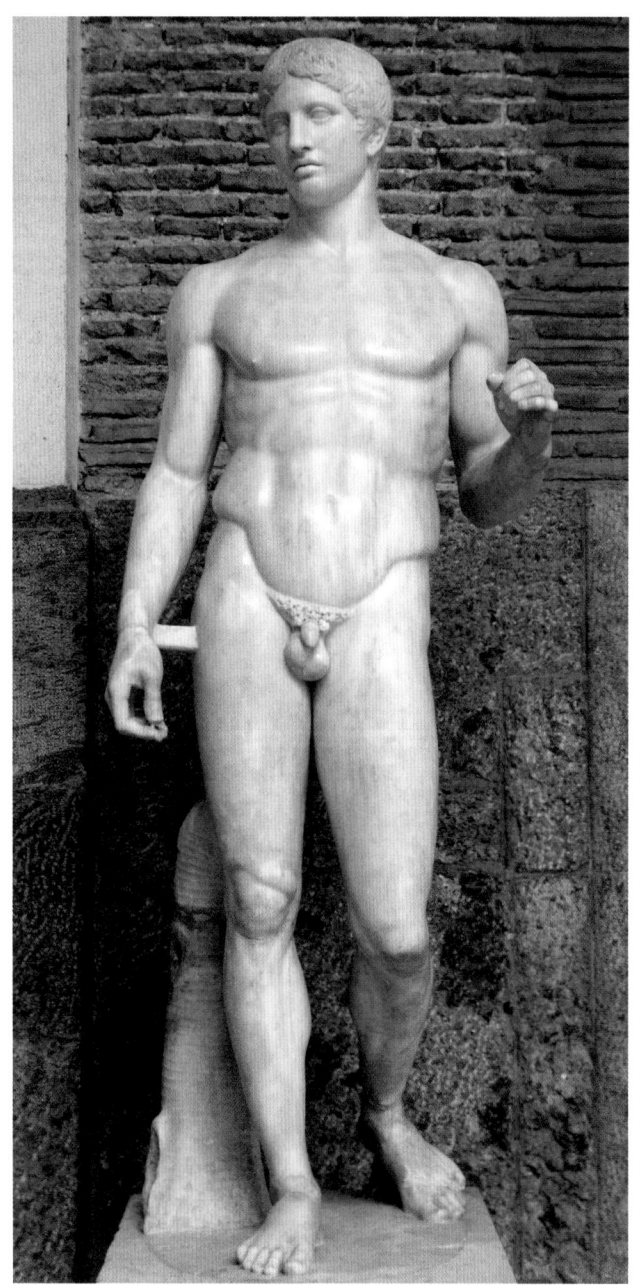

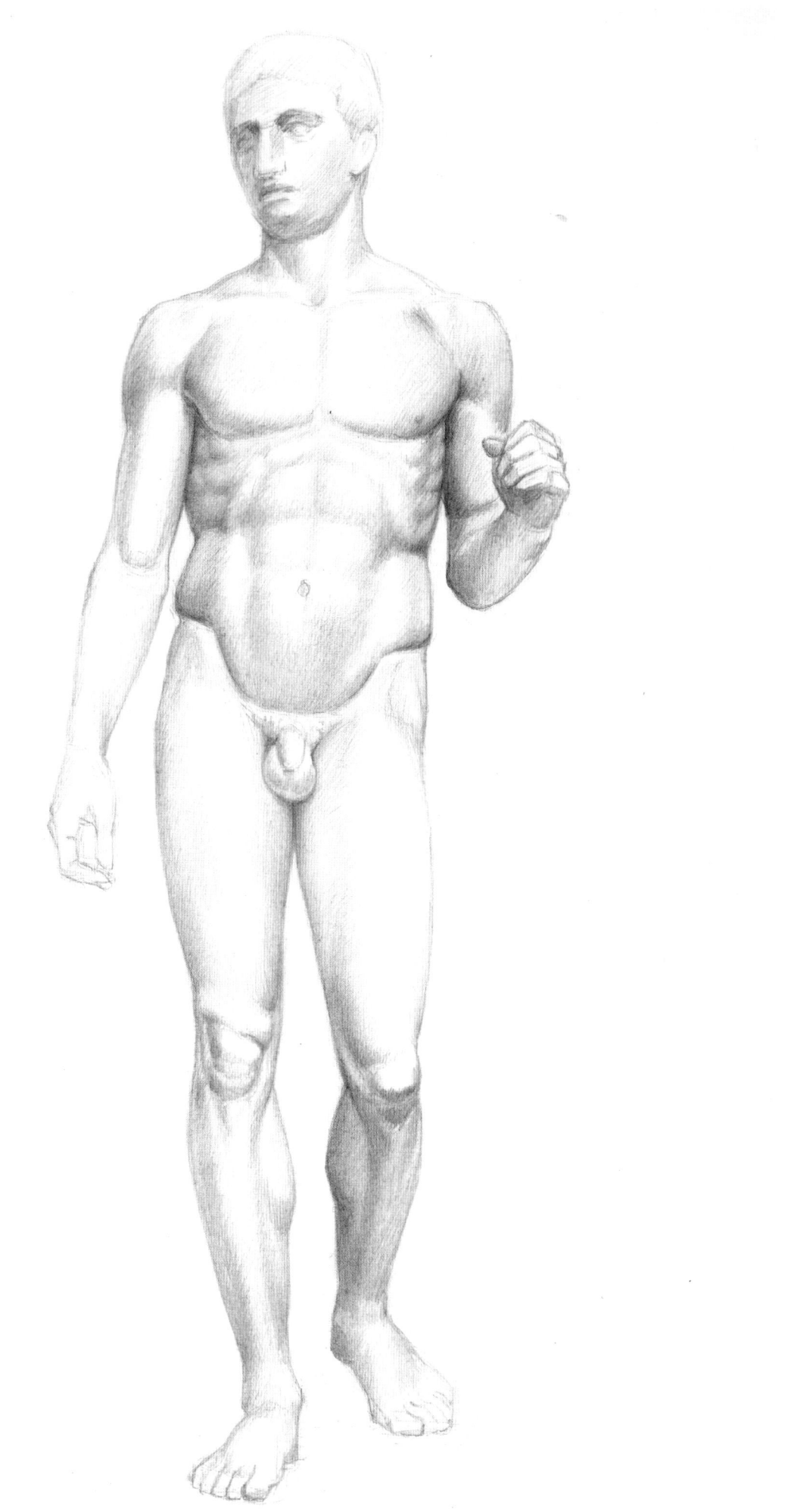

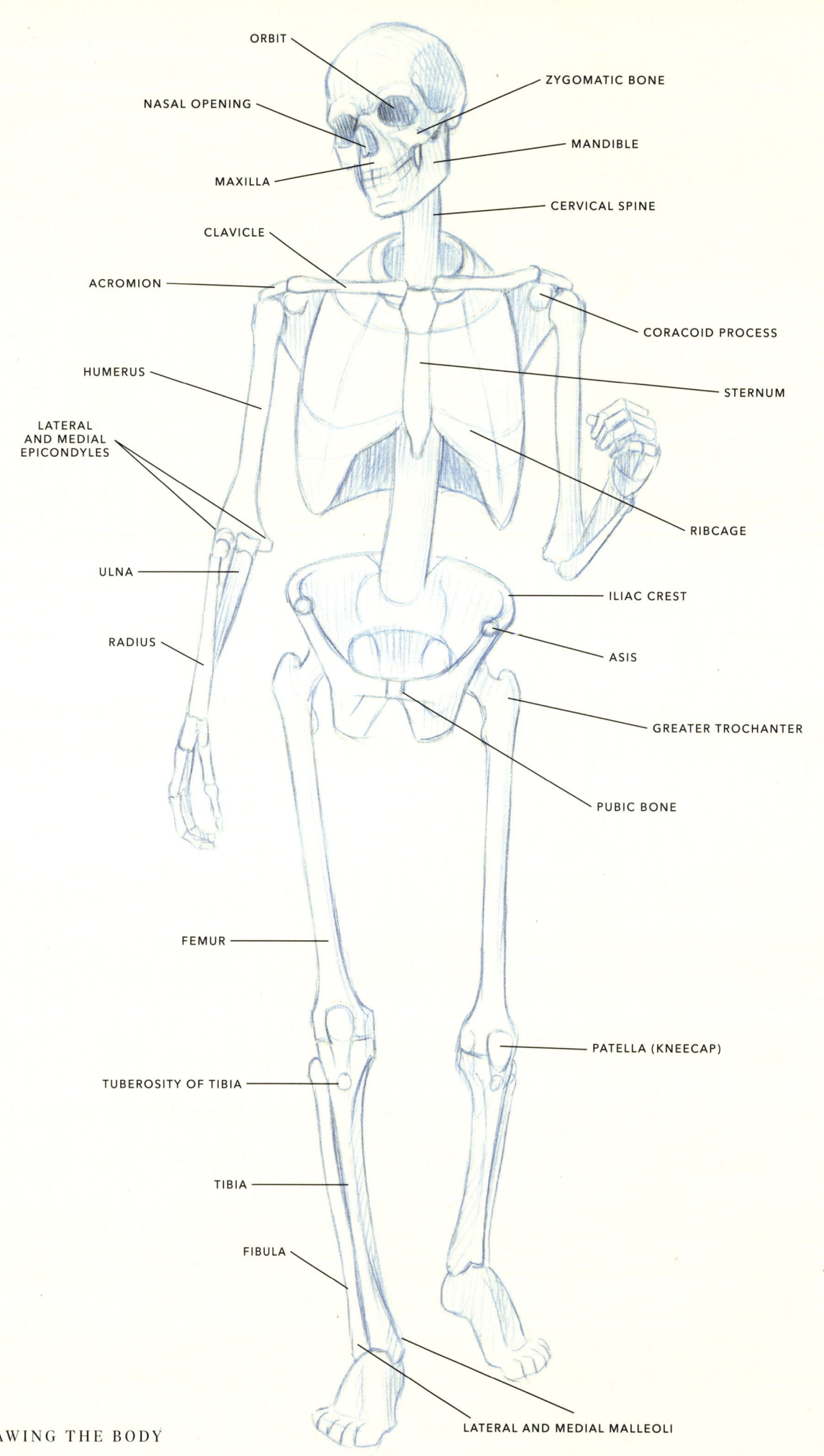

ORBIT

ZYGOMATIC BONE

NASAL OPENING

MANDIBLE

MAXILLA

CERVICAL SPINE

CLAVICLE

ACROMION

CORACOID PROCESS

HUMERUS

STERNUM

LATERAL
AND MEDIAL
EPICONDYLES

ULNA

RIBCAGE

RADIUS

ILIAC CREST

ASIS

GREATER TROCHANTER

PUBIC BONE

FEMUR

PATELLA (KNEECAP)

TUBEROSITY OF TIBIA

TIBIA

FIBULA

LATERAL AND MEDIAL MALLEOLI

When the skeleton is completed, you can place another piece of tracing paper over it and draw the muscles over the skeleton, using the image below as a reference. If you feel up to it, you can perform this exercise without using tracing paper, by drawing each stage freehand.

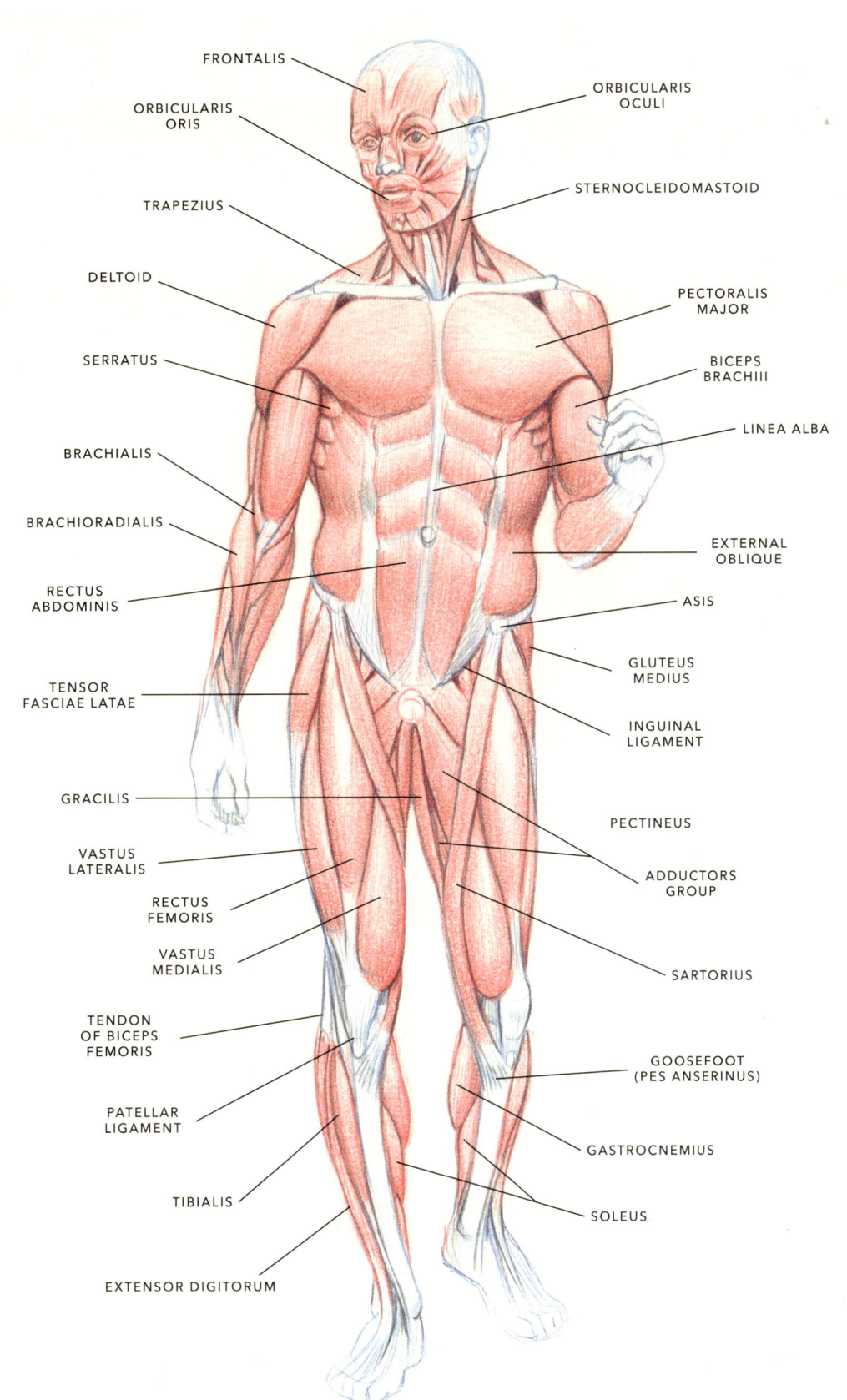

FRONTALIS

ORBICULARIS ORIS

ORBICULARIS OCULI

TRAPEZIUS

STERNOCLEIDOMASTOID

DELTOID

PECTORALIS MAJOR

SERRATUS

BICEPS BRACHIII

BRACHIALIS

LINEA ALBA

BRACHIORADIALIS

EXTERNAL OBLIQUE

RECTUS ABDOMINIS

ASIS

GLUTEUS MEDIUS

TENSOR FASCIAE LATAE

INGUINAL LIGAMENT

GRACILIS

PECTINEUS

VASTUS LATERALIS

ADDUCTORS GROUP

RECTUS FEMORIS

VASTUS MEDIALIS

SARTORIUS

TENDON OF BICEPS FEMORIS

GOOSEFOOT (PES ANSERINUS)

PATELLAR LIGAMENT

GASTROCNEMIUS

TIBIALIS

SOLEUS

EXTENSOR DIGITORUM

EXERCISES 2.12 TO 2.20

POSITIONING MUSCLES OVER STEREOMETRIC RENDERINGS

The following nine exercises are designed to help you position the superficial muscles over stereometric volumes, guided by the skeletal and soft landmarks. You'll practice transitioning from the stereometric scaffolding to a more organic rendering of the figure, in anticipation of the next chapter where, guided by the skeletal and soft landmarks, you will apply the muscles over a more realistic rendering of the skeleton. Most of the exercises here further develop images introduced in the previous chapter. To do the exercises, you may draw directly on drawings you've already made, or, if you'd prefer, lay tracing paper over those and draw on it instead.

EXERCISE 2.12

A STANDING MALE FIGURE, FROM STEREOMETRY TO SUPERFICIAL MUSCLES

Draw the muscle layers, gradually subdividing the main stereometric volumes into the major muscular groups. Label the muscles and landmarks to practice memorizing them.

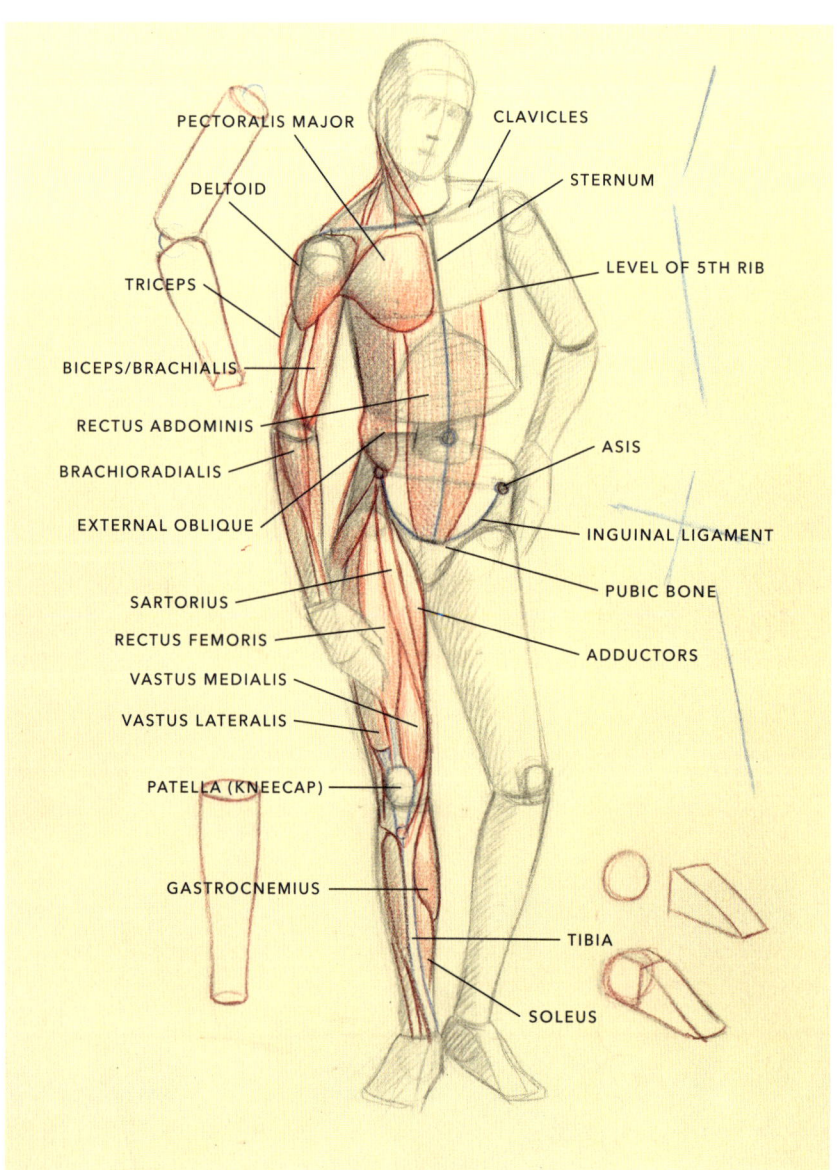

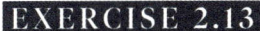

THE LEG, FROM STEREOMETRY TO SUPERFICIAL MUSCLES

Position the muscles on this stereometric figure, including guidelines you see in the reference image, to better visualize the volumetric characteristics of the muscles.

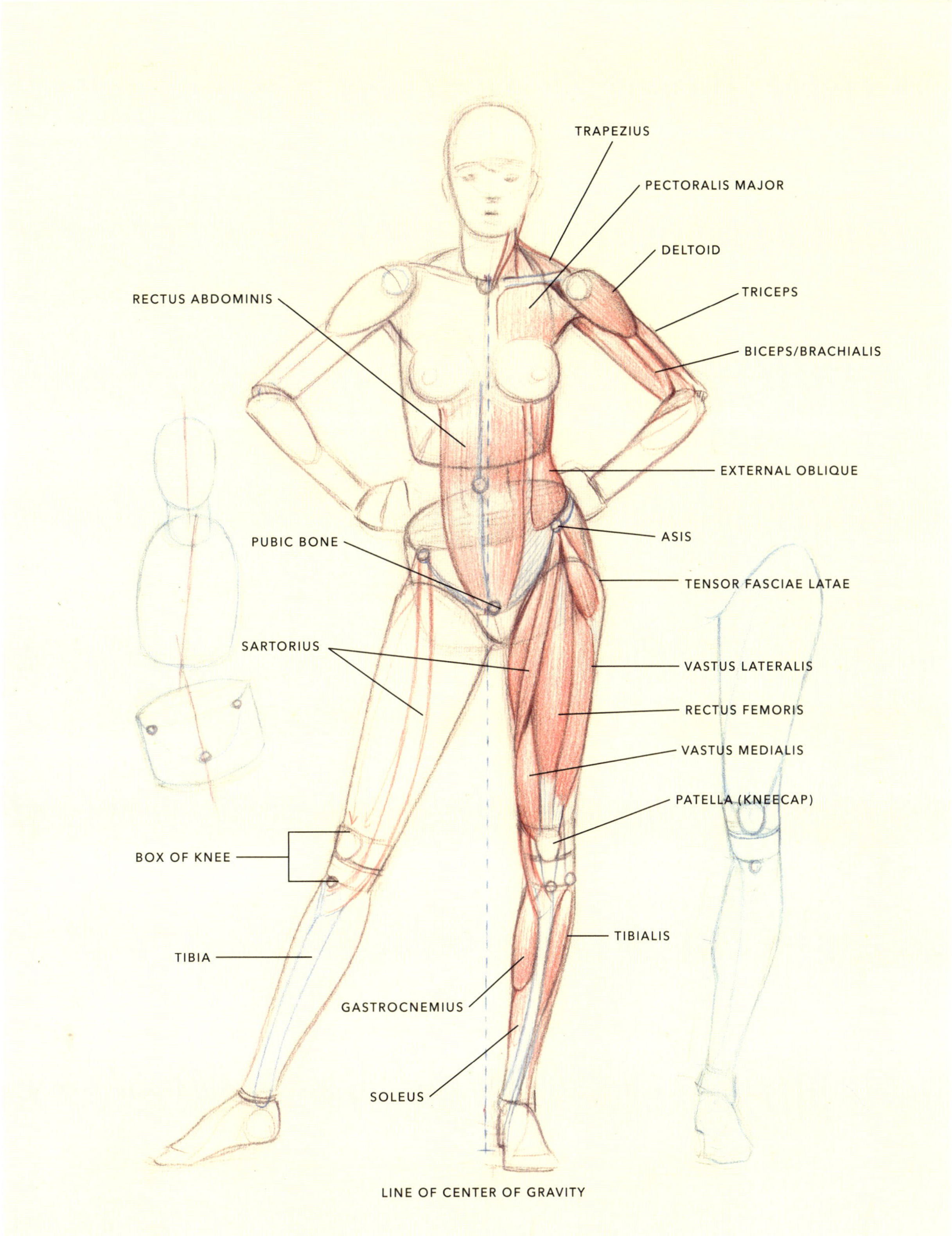

TRAPEZIUS

PECTORALIS MAJOR

DELTOID

TRICEPS

RECTUS ABDOMINIS

BICEPS/BRACHIALIS

EXTERNAL OBLIQUE

PUBIC BONE

ASIS

TENSOR FASCIAE LATAE

SARTORIUS

VASTUS LATERALIS

RECTUS FEMORIS

VASTUS MEDIALIS

PATELLA (KNEECAP)

BOX OF KNEE

TIBIALIS

TIBIA

GASTROCNEMIUS

SOLEUS

LINE OF CENTER OF GRAVITY

WRAPPING THE MUSCLE VOLUMES

Position the muscles on this stereometric figure, paying particular attention to how the muscles wrap over other muscles or bones. Doing so will help you achieve a more convincing sense of three-dimensionality.

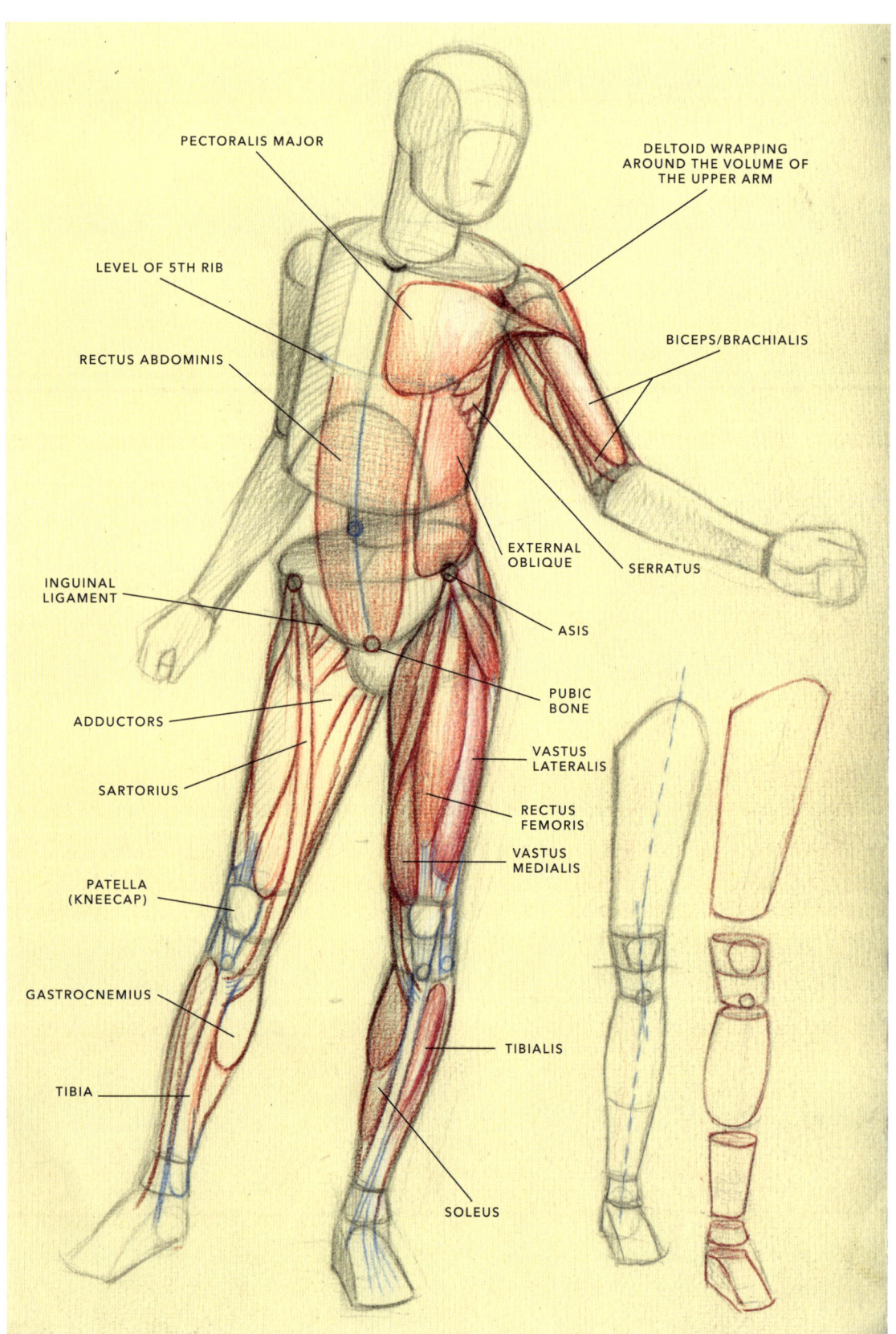

ADDING MUSCULAR DETAIL

Apply the muscles on the figure and draw cross-section lines over them to visualize their volume more clearly. Add an extra level of detail by subdividing the deltoid, rectus abdominis, and serratus into their main segments.

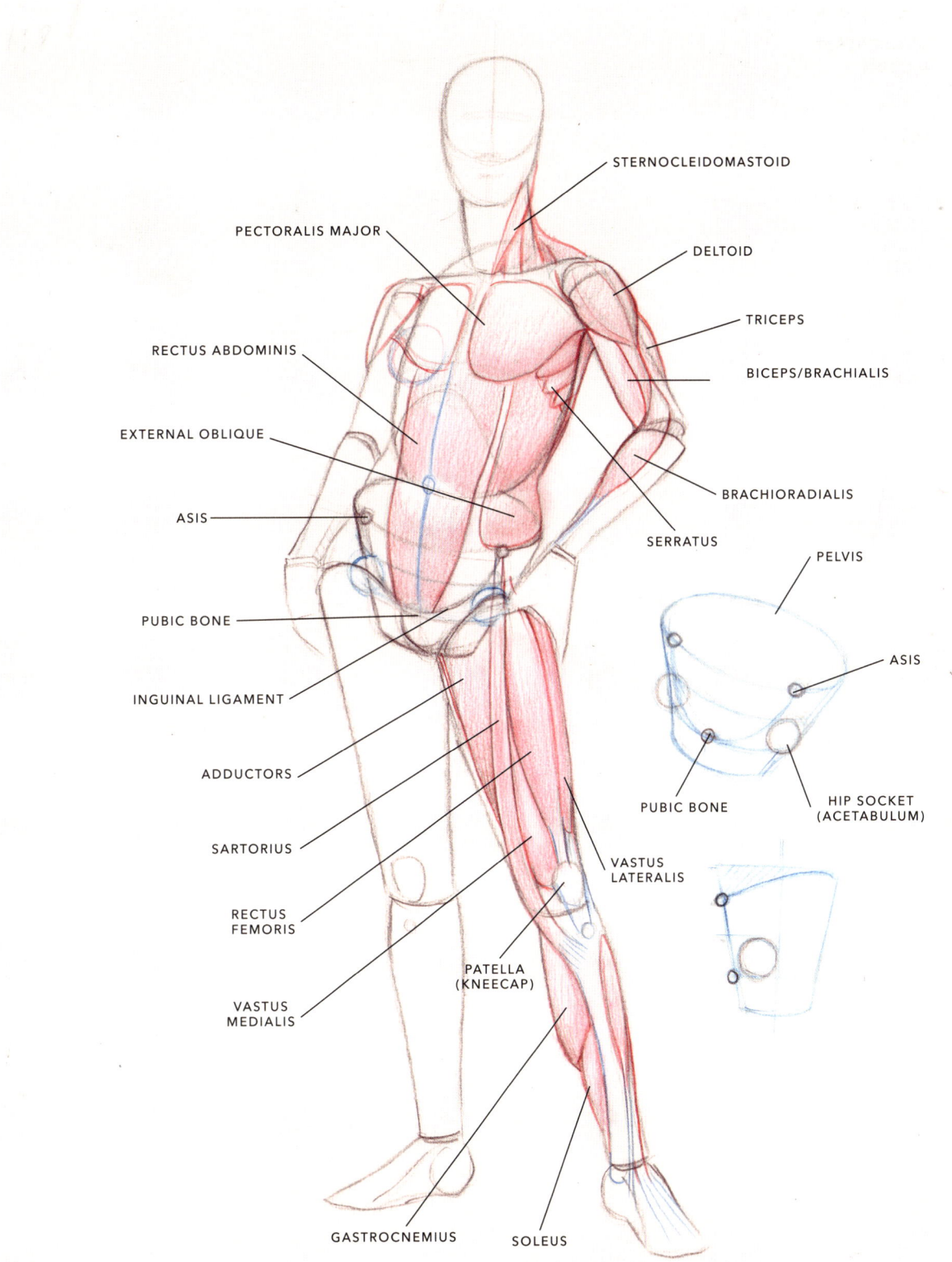

STERNOCLEIDOMASTOID

PECTORALIS MAJOR

DELTOID

TRICEPS

BICEPS/BRACHIALIS

RECTUS ABDOMINIS

EXTERNAL OBLIQUE

BRACHIORADIALIS

ASIS

SERRATUS

PELVIS

ASIS

PUBIC BONE

INGUINAL LIGAMENT

HIP SOCKET
(ACETABULUM)

PUBIC BONE

ADDUCTORS

SARTORIUS

VASTUS
LATERALIS

RECTUS
FEMORIS

PATELLA
(KNEECAP)

VASTUS
MEDIALIS

GASTROCNEMIUS

SOLEUS

EXERCISE 2.16
SUBDIVIDING MUSCULAR VOLUMES

The two-step sequence on the left of the image shows how to draw the muscles of the thigh by gradually subdividing its overall volume into smaller muscular groups. The leg on the right side of the image shows a more realistic rendering of the muscles.

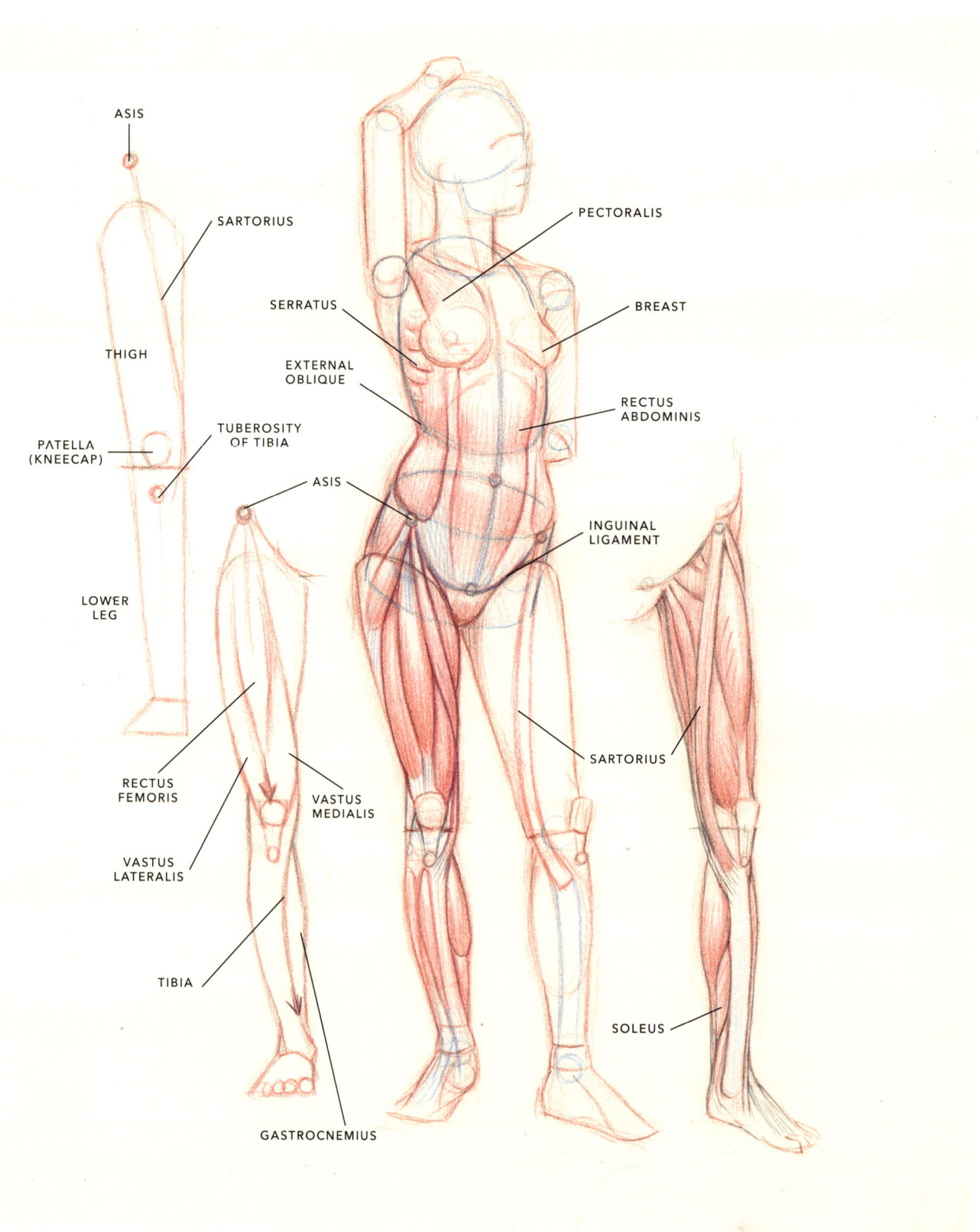

ASIS

SARTORIUS

PECTORALIS

THIGH

SERRATUS

BREAST

EXTERNAL OBLIQUE

TUBEROSITY OF TIBIA

RECTUS ABDOMINIS

PATELLA (KNEECAP)

ASIS

LOWER LEG

INGUINAL LIGAMENT

RECTUS FEMORIS

VASTUS MEDIALIS

VASTUS LATERALIS

SARTORIUS

TIBIA

SOLEUS

GASTROCNEMIUS

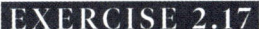

EXERCISE 2.17
POSITIONING MUSCLE GROUPS

Practice positioning the main muscular groups of the back of the torso and legs over the stereometric scaffolding. Notice how the stereometric legs are subdivided in smaller volumes—thigh, box of knee, lower leg, ankles, foot—and how these volumes are all oriented at specific angles in relation to each other.

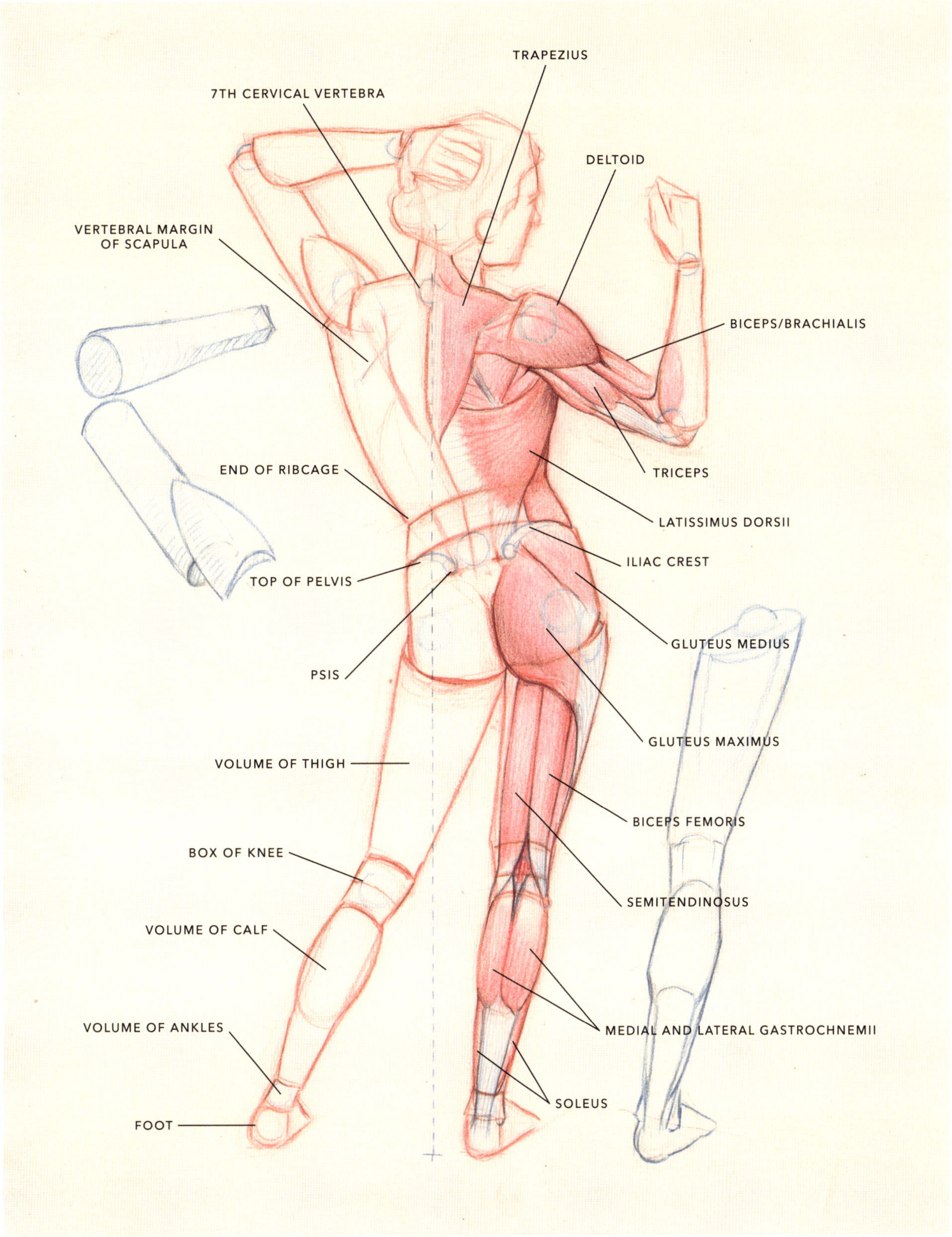

TRAPEZIUS

7TH CERVICAL VERTEBRA

DELTOID

VERTEBRAL MARGIN OF SCAPULA

BICEPS/BRACHIALIS

END OF RIBCAGE

TRICEPS

LATISSIMUS DORSII

ILIAC CREST

TOP OF PELVIS

GLUTEUS MEDIUS

PSIS

GLUTEUS MAXIMUS

VOLUME OF THIGH

BICEPS FEMORIS

BOX OF KNEE

SEMITENDINOSUS

VOLUME OF CALF

VOLUME OF ANKLES

MEDIAL AND LATERAL GASTROCHNEMII

FOOT

SOLEUS

POSITIONING MUSCLES, FEMALE, BACK VIEW

Practice positioning the main muscular groups of the back of the torso over the stereometric scaffolding. Note how the stereometric volumes of the torso of the female figure can be conceptualized as three volumes—ribcage, waist, and pelvis—as shown in detail *A* on the right side of the image. Alternately, they can be reduced to only two main volumes—the ribcage and the waist and pelvis grouped together—as shown in detail *B* on the upper left. In women, these two volumes are similar in height, and knowing this makes it easier to quickly block in the main volumes of the torso in the correct proportional relationship.

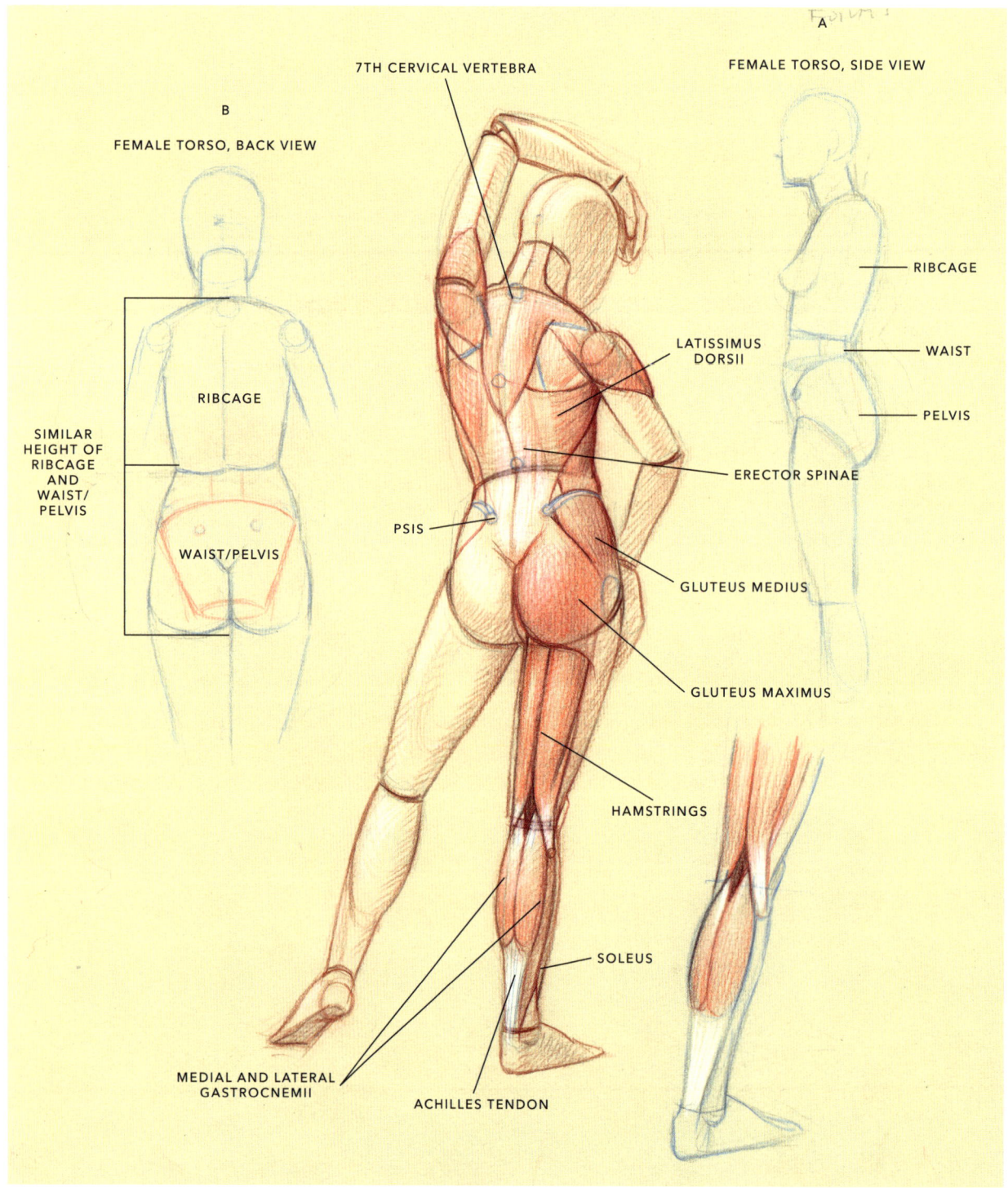

B

FEMALE TORSO, BACK VIEW

RIBCAGE

SIMILAR HEIGHT OF RIBCAGE AND WAIST/PELVIS

WAIST/PELVIS

7TH CERVICAL VERTEBRA

FEMALE TORSO, SIDE VIEW

RIBCAGE

WAIST

PELVIS

LATISSIMUS DORSII

ERECTOR SPINAE

PSIS

GLUTEUS MEDIUS

GLUTEUS MAXIMUS

HAMSTRINGS

SOLEUS

MEDIAL AND LATERAL GASTROCNEMII

ACHILLES TENDON

POSITIONING MUSCLES, MALE, SIDE VIEW

This exercise and the one that follows introduce poses in the side view that are more dynamic and challenging than those you've worked on previously. Again, practice positioning the muscles on the stereometric scaffolding.

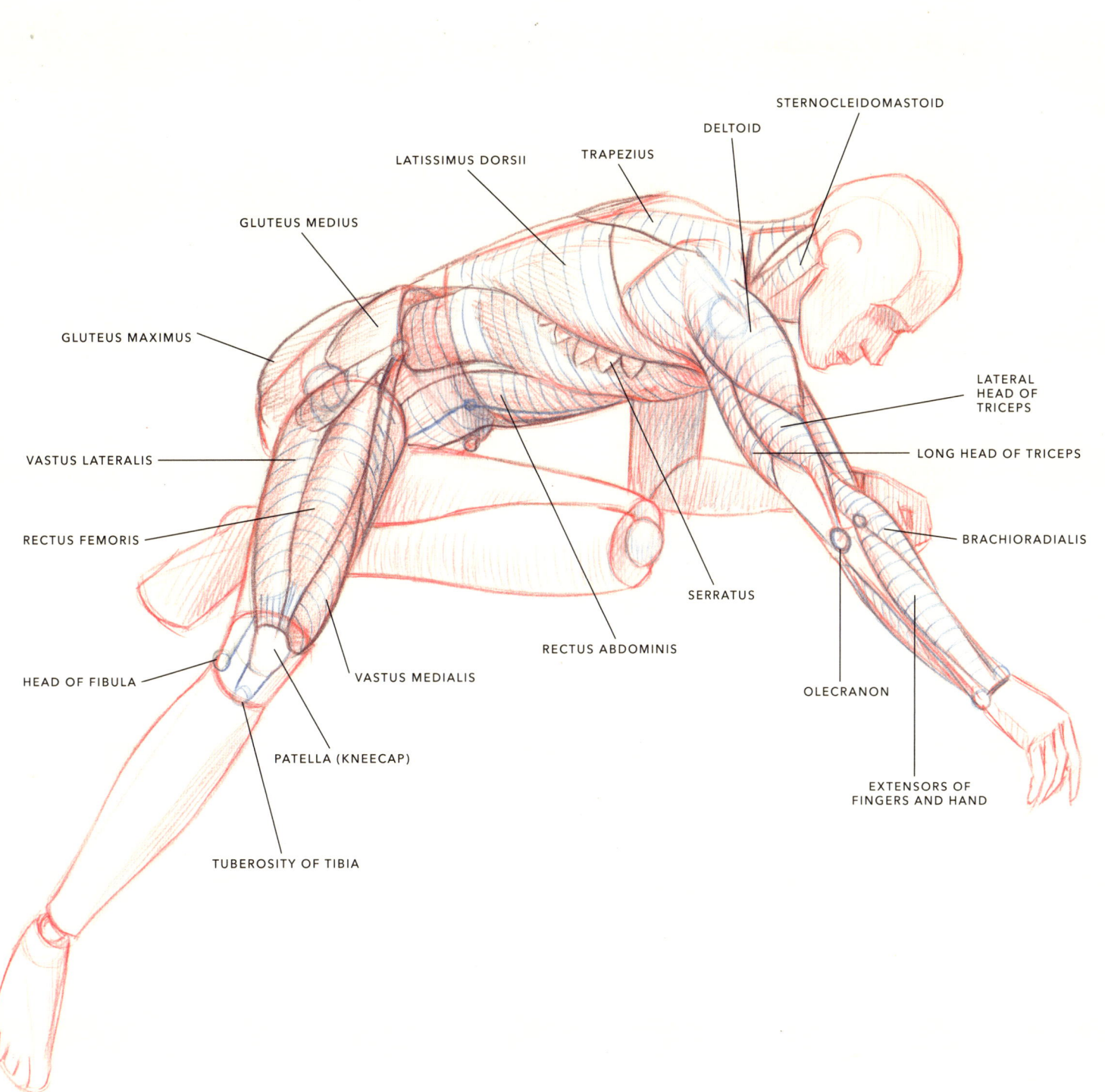

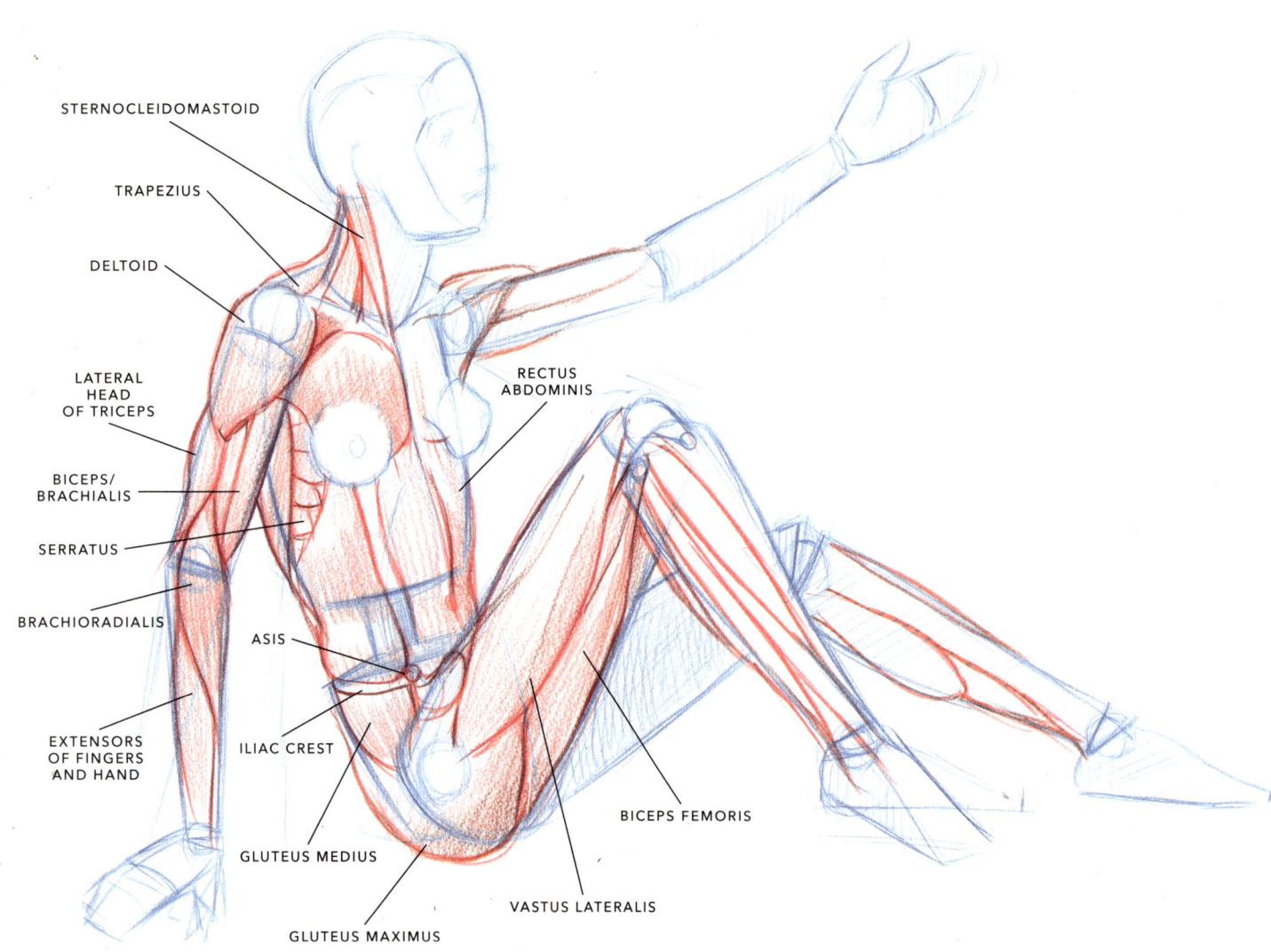

STERNOCLEIDOMASTOID

TRAPEZIUS

DELTOID

LATERAL HEAD OF TRICEPS

BICEPS/ BRACHIALIS

SERRATUS

BRACHIORADIALIS

EXTENSORS OF FINGERS AND HAND

RECTUS ABDOMINIS

ASIS

ILIAC CREST

GLUTEUS MEDIUS

GLUTEUS MAXIMUS

VASTUS LATERALIS

BICEPS FEMORIS

ADDITIONAL POSES

This chapter's two last poses—a front view and a back view—are here so that you can continue practicing positioning the muscles. But this time you'll do so *without* using reference images.

Copy the female figure at left, below and "carve" the main muscular groups out of the stereometric volumes. Label the muscles. After you've finished, check your work against the image on page 124. The pose of the figure at right is a little more challenging than the previous one. Position the main muscle groups on the stereometric figure and label them. Afterward, you can consult the images on page 115 to see how well you did.

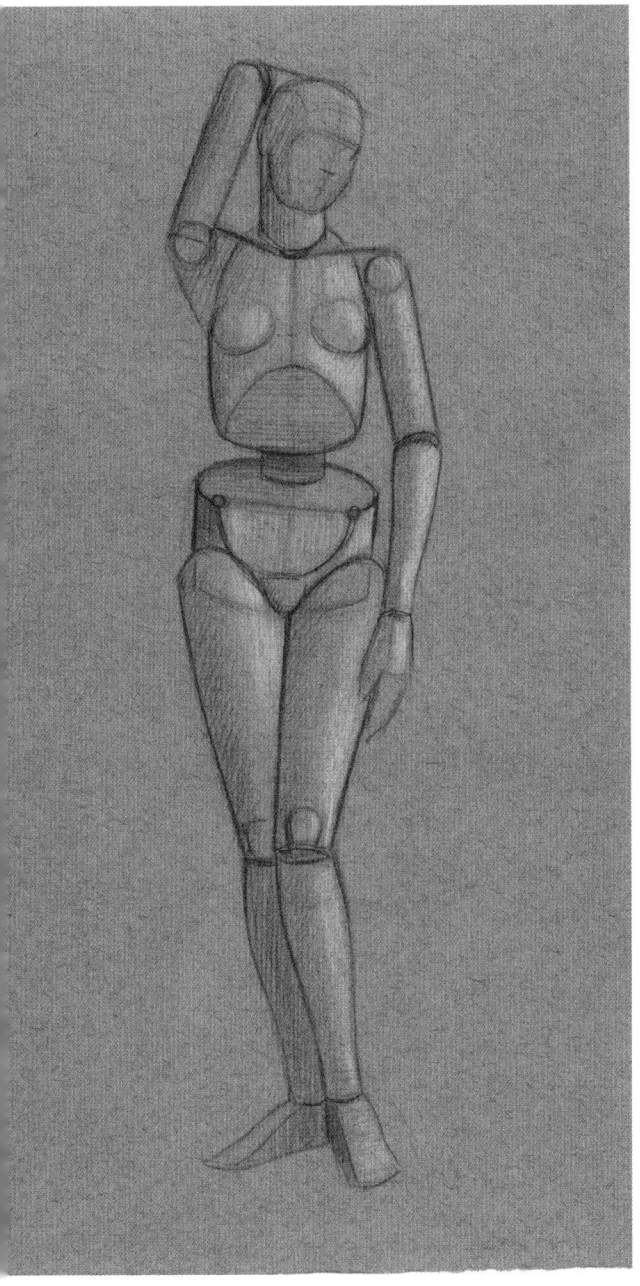
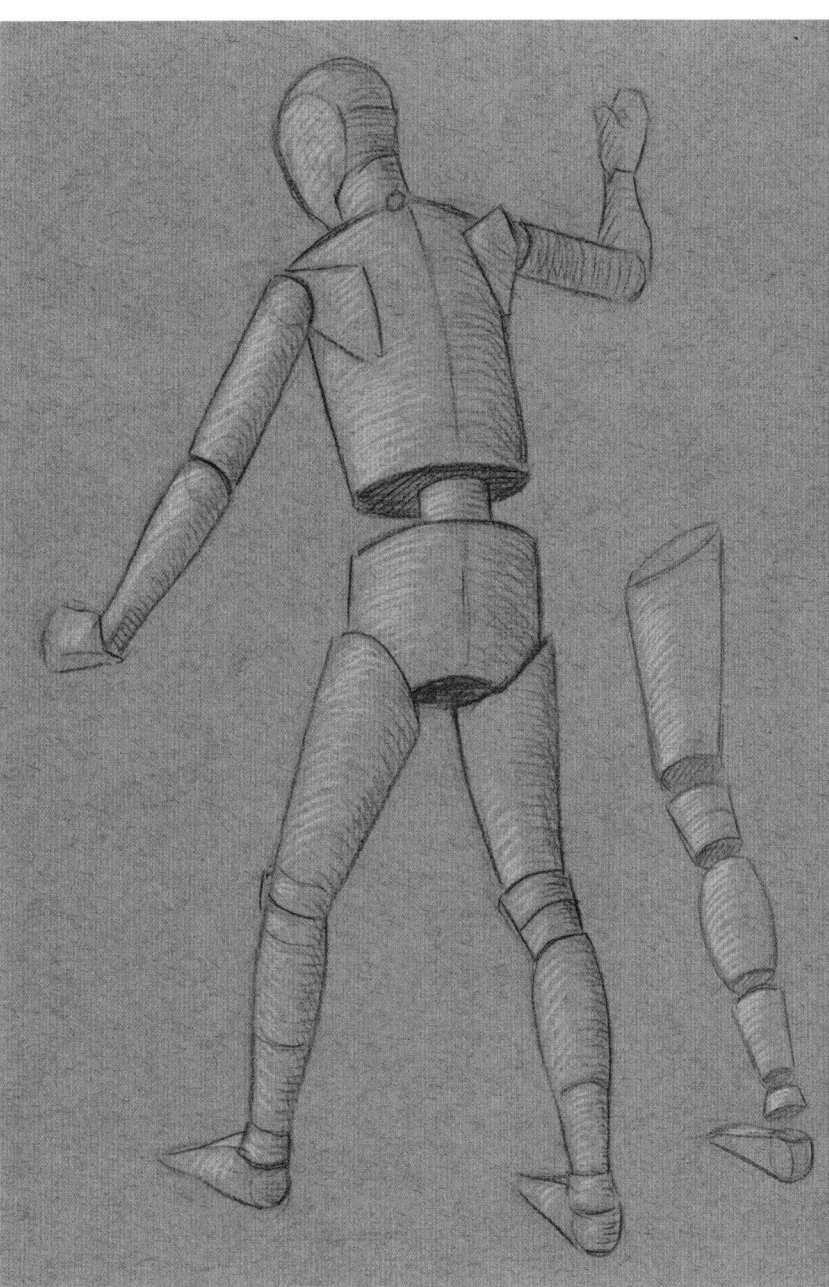

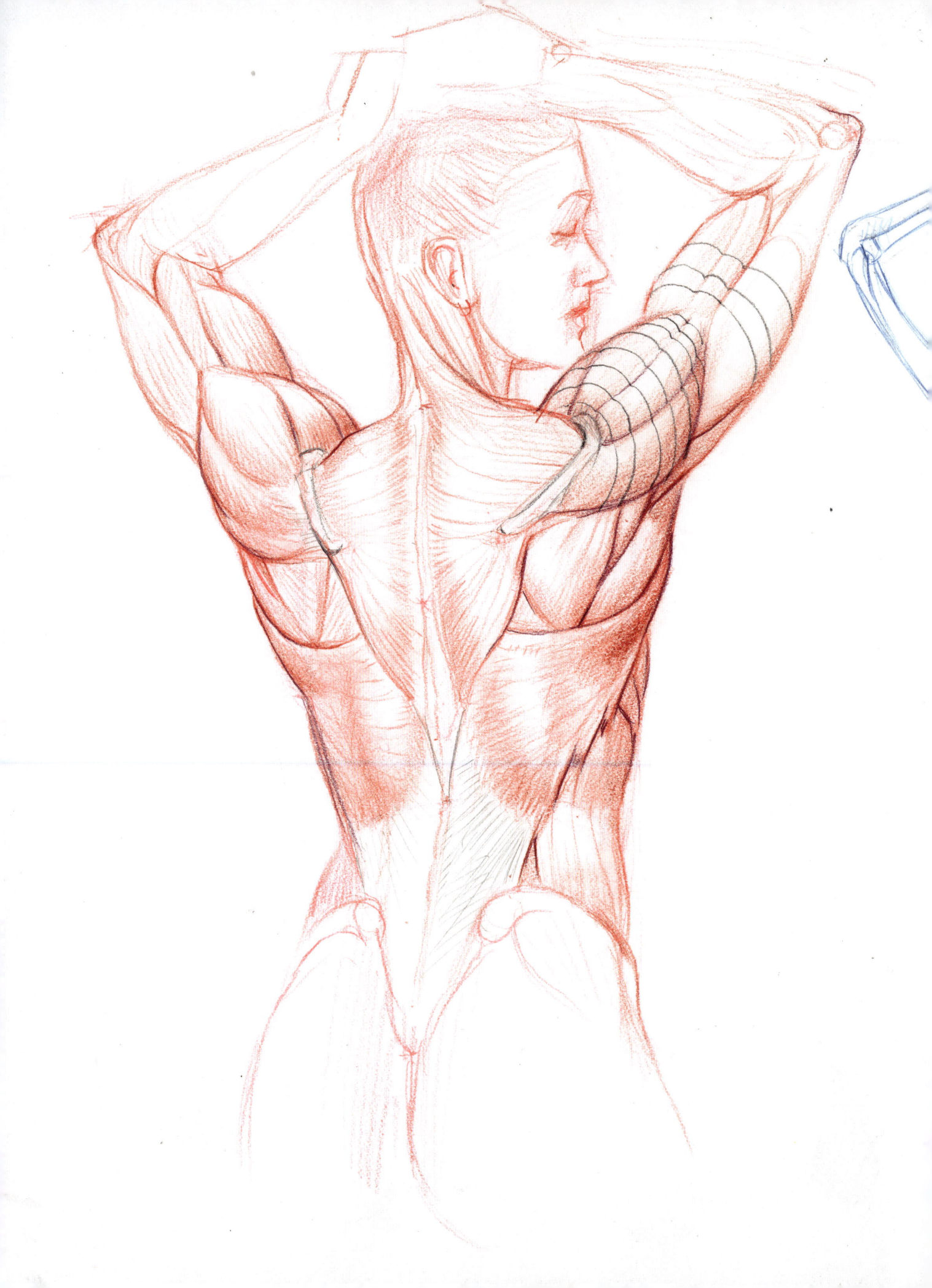

CHAPTER 3

WORKING FROM ART

In the exercises of chapters 1 and 2, we analytically "dissected" the body, separating out its various components; we acquired basic knowledge of the body's structural and proportional aspects with the aid of stereometry; and we studied the skeletal and muscular systems. We learned to recognize the skeletal and soft landmarks, to identify the muscles responsible for the main volumes of the external forms of the figure, and to properly position the muscles on the skeleton.

In this chapter, we will put all these separate parts back together and use them holistically to "read" the human figure, drawing it in a variety of complex poses, in movement, in foreshortening, in various light conditions. We'll also be progressing from copying artworks (both two-dimensional pieces and sculptures) to working from photos of real models, completing the transition from the anatomical charts of earlier chapters to actual human bodies.

TECHNICAL NOTE

The illustrations here show how I approach the task of layering the muscles over the skeleton. The drawing tool you use is very important. For this sequence, I used a mechanical pencil with blue lead for the skeleton and one with red lead for the muscles. The lead, manufactured by Pilot, is 0.5 mm in diameter, producing a sharp, precise line. If you like, you can draw the muscles directly on the drawing of the skeleton or use a sheet of tracing paper or frosted Mylar for the additions.

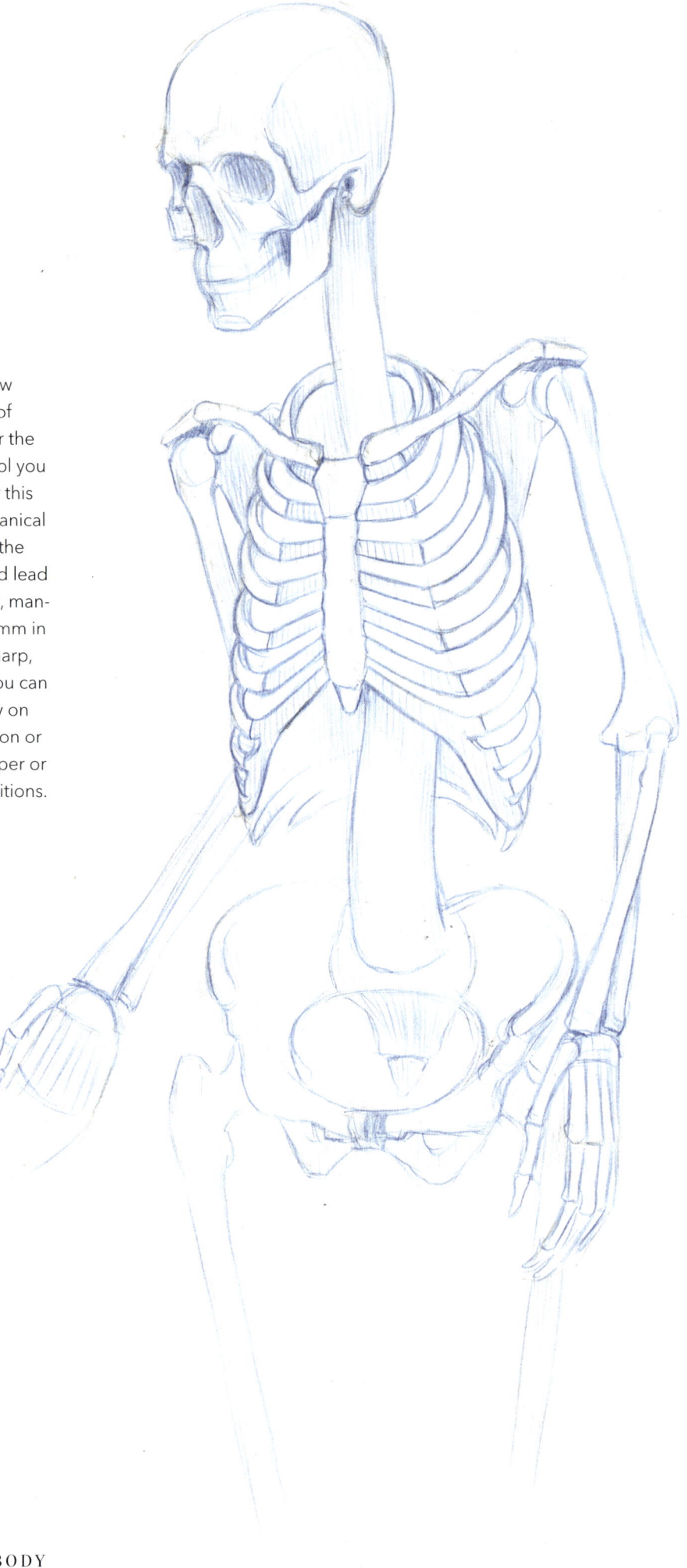

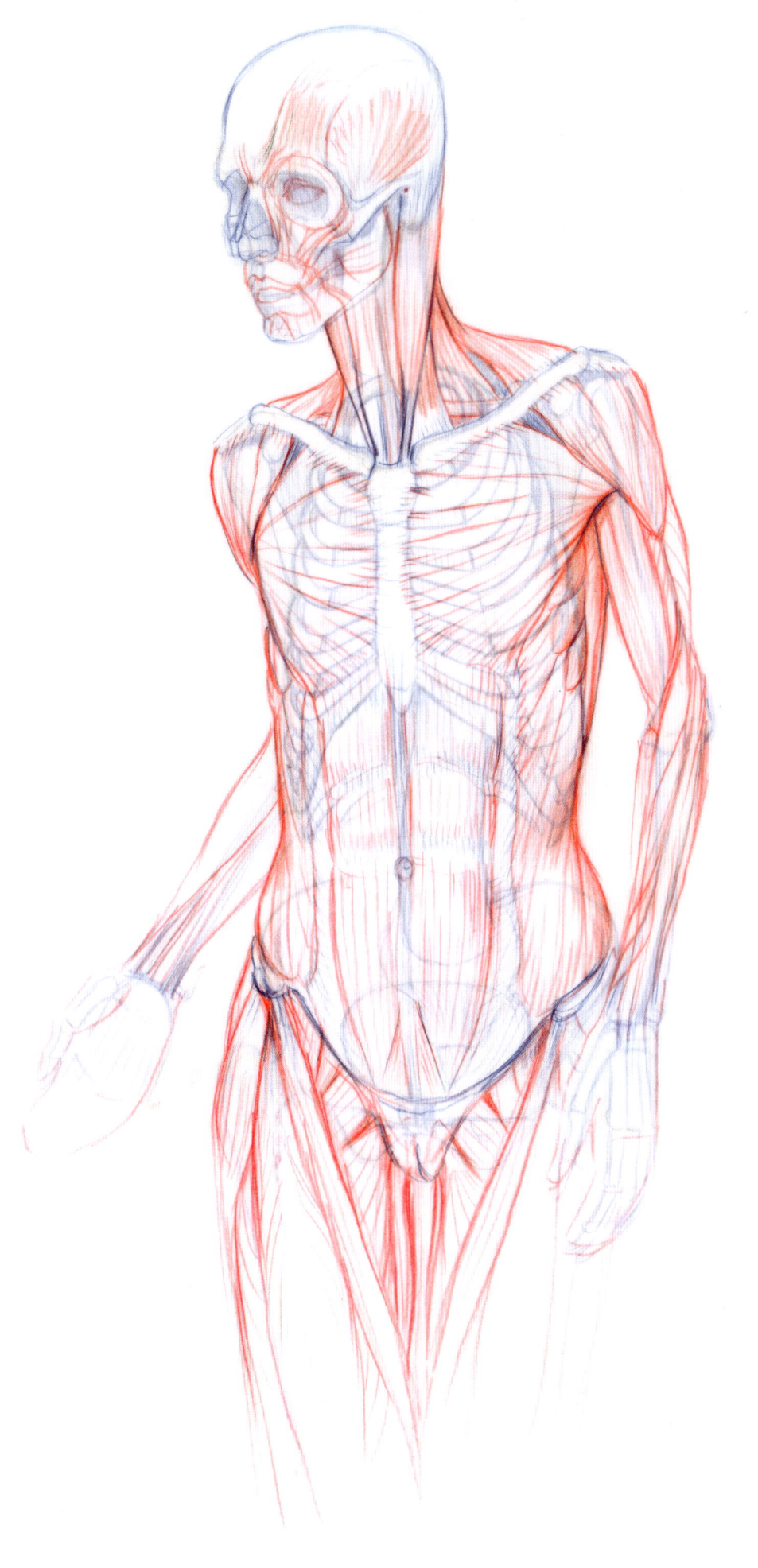

LEVEL 1

WORKING FROM DRAWINGS AND PAINTINGS

Copying the works of masters is an excellent exercise. By doing so, you can learn about the master's techniques and styles, appreciate their knowledge of anatomy, and delve into the conceptual, narrative and compositional aspects of their works. Spending time copying a master's works can also reveal details that you might not notice with ordinary observation. You may experience that sort of revelation when performing the first four exercises below, starting with a drawing by French master Pierre-Paul Prud'hon (1758–1823).

EXERCISE 3.1
A PIERRE-PAUL PRUD'HON DRAWING

Perform the following steps to practice reading the human form, to identify the skeletal landmarks, to use them to reconstruct the skeletal structure, and then to layer the muscles over the skeleton.

Please note that this sequence does not necessarily demonstrate Prud'hon's own drawing technique, but, by following these steps, you can nonetheless gain insight into his artistic approach to the figure and appreciate his knowledge of human anatomy.

STEP 1

IDENTIFY SKELETAL LANDMARKS AND MAIN MUSCULAR VOLUMES

Copy the image and identify the skeletal landmarks and main muscular volumes that you use will use to reconstruct the skeleton and muscular structures.

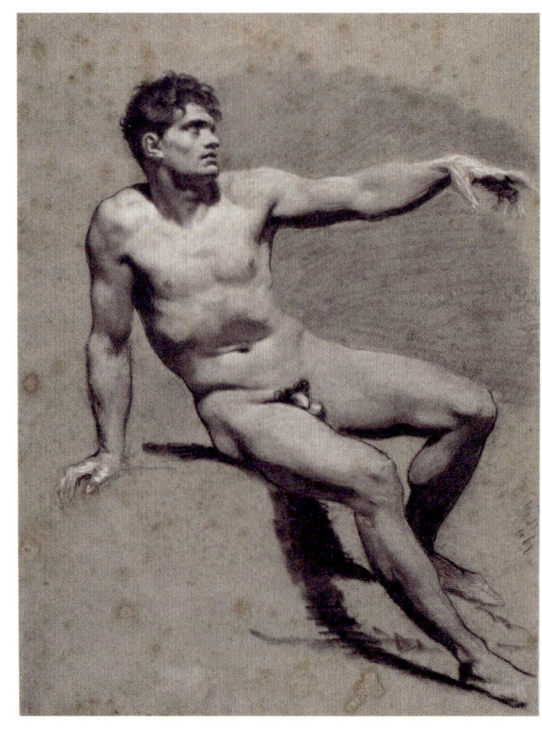

RIGHT: Pierre-Paul Prud'hon, *Seated Nude with Arm Extended*, n.d., black and white chalk on blue-tinted paper.

STEP 2
RECONSTRUCT THE SKELETON

Follow the skeletal landmarks you identified in the previous step to recreate the skeleton hiding beneath Prud'hon's beautifully rendered form.

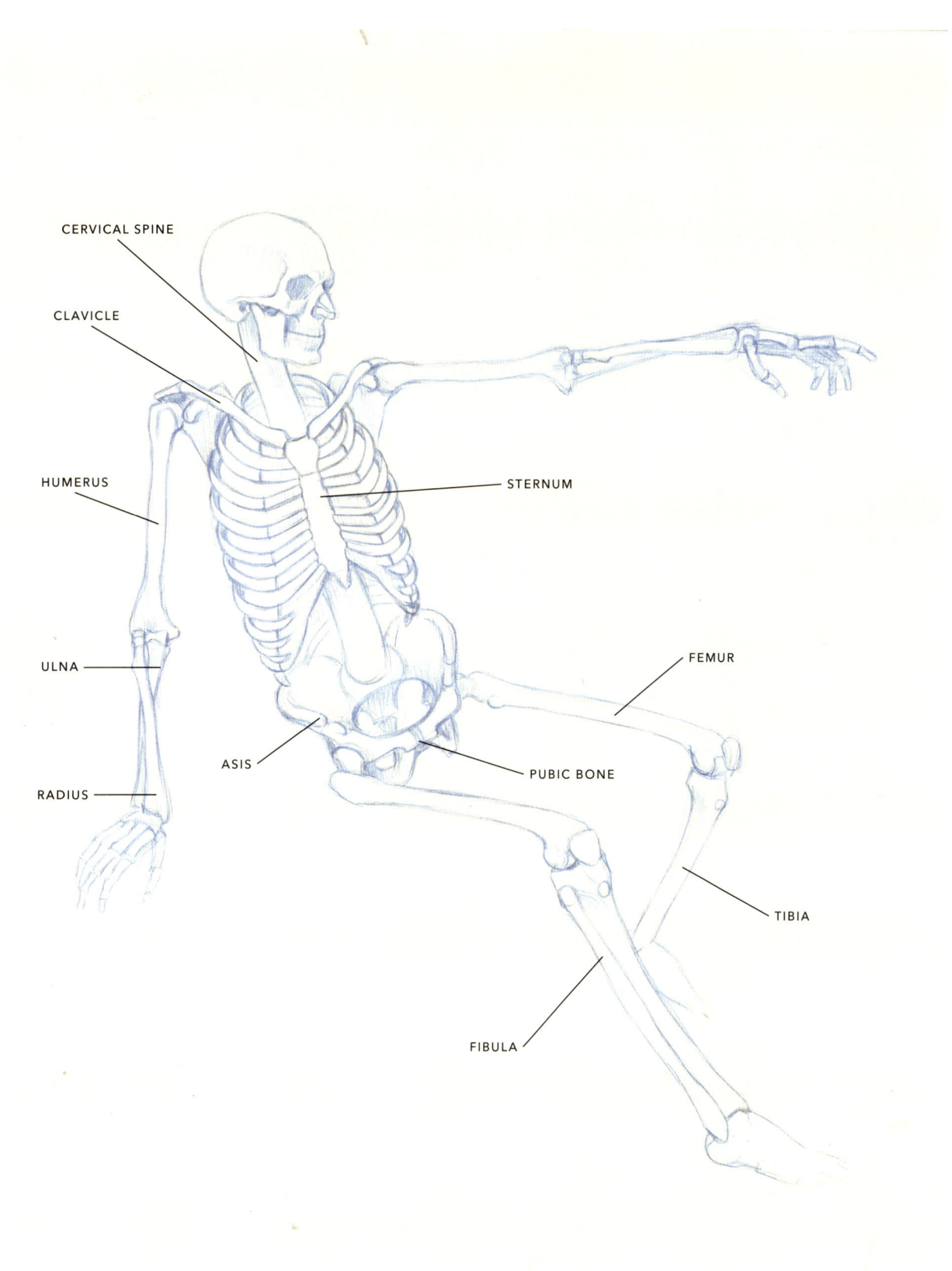

STEP 3

ADD THE MUSCLES

Layer the superficial muscular volumes over the skeleton. You may use tracing paper for this step.

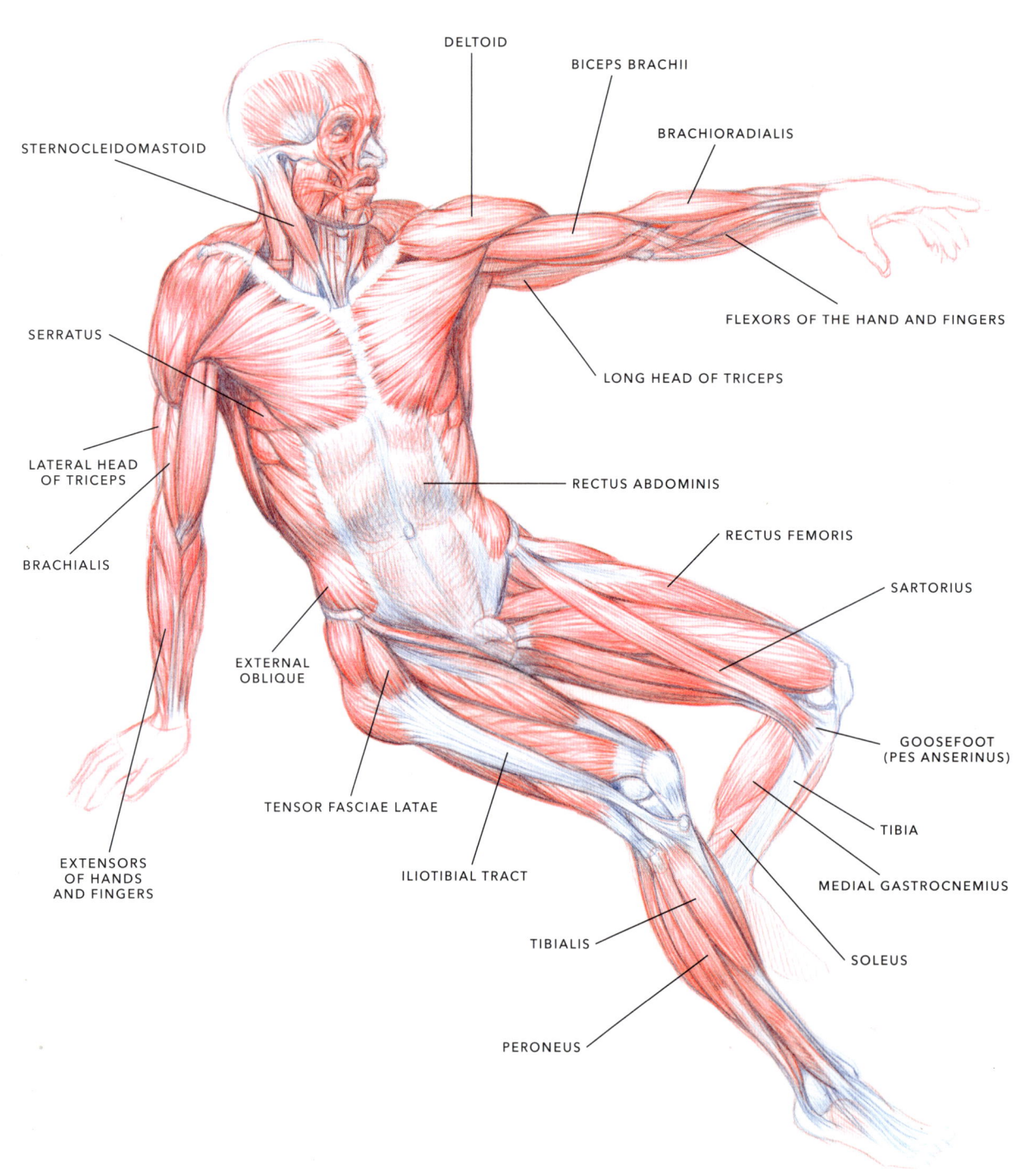

DELTOID

BICEPS BRACHII

BRACHIORADIALIS

STERNOCLEIDOMASTOID

FLEXORS OF THE HAND AND FINGERS

LONG HEAD OF TRICEPS

SERRATUS

LATERAL HEAD
OF TRICEPS

RECTUS ABDOMINIS

RECTUS FEMORIS

SARTORIUS

BRACHIALIS

EXTERNAL
OBLIQUE

GOOSEFOOT
(PES ANSERINUS)

TENSOR FASCIAE LATAE

TIBIA

ILIOTIBIAL TRACT

MEDIAL GASTROCNEMIUS

EXTENSORS
OF HANDS
AND FINGERS

TIBIALIS

SOLEUS

PERONEUS

EXERCISE 3.2
TITIAN'S *SAINT SEBASTIAN*

In the Pinacoteca di Bologna, the city museum of my Italian hometown, there hangs an unfinished oil painting by the great Venetian master Titian. In that picture, an arm gradually emerges from a dark brown ground; Titian does not seem to have followed any drawing here, depending instead on a few quickly sketched-in lines painted in an oil color that is slightly darker than the ground. What little is visible of the finished arm, is truly arresting: the colors, the convincing volumes of the muscles, the light—all create an incredible sense of life and realism, apparently obtained without starting from an accurate drawing.

It's likely that the figure of Sant Sebastian shown here, which Titian painted for the Alveroldi Altarpiece in Brescia, was also created starting with a few measuring lines but without a detailed preparatory drawing. This doesn't mean, however, that Titian was not paying much attention to anatomy when painting; on the contrary, anatomical knowledge was so deeply assimilated by Titian that he did not need an accurate preliminary drawing in order to paint a detailed and accurate human figure.

The study of anatomy was an important part of the training of young artists working at the botteghe (studios) of masters like Titian. That anatomical education is reflected in the fact that Jan Van Calcar, who prepared the anatomical illustrations for Andreas Vesalius's revolutionary work De Humani Corporis Fabrica ("On the Fabric of the Human Body," 1543), was one of Titian's pupils.

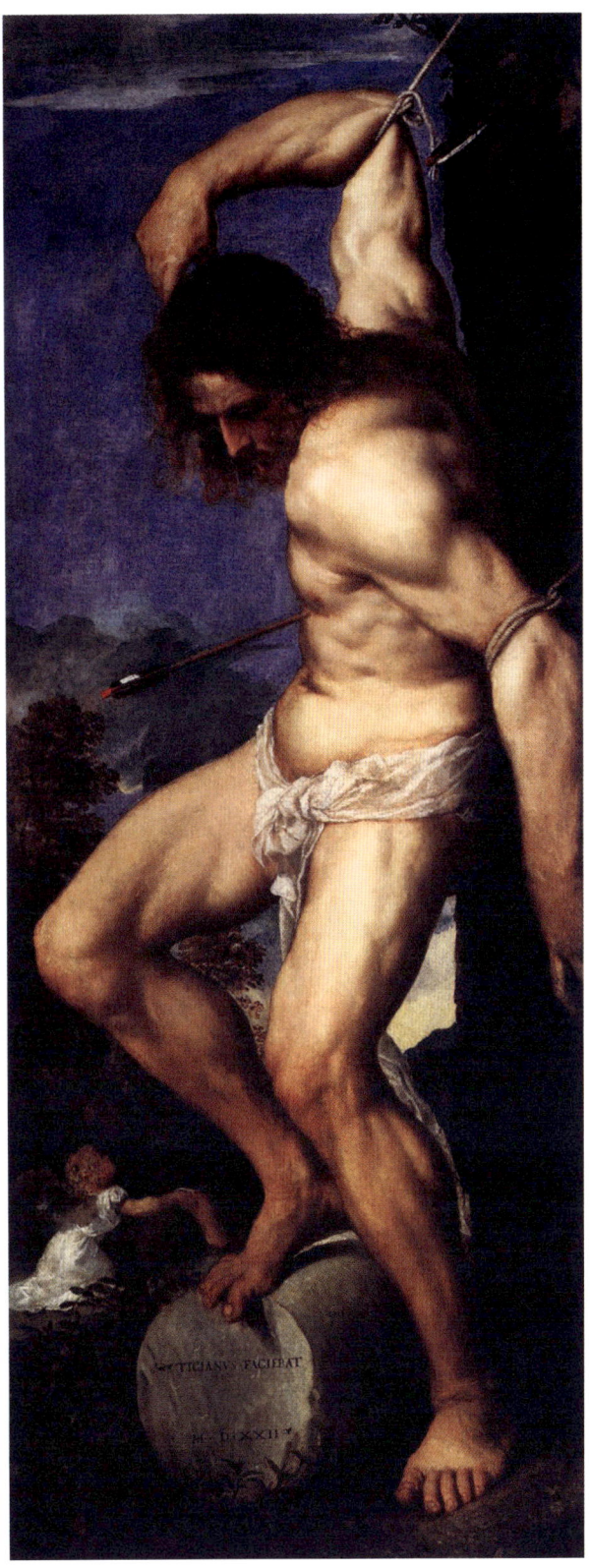

Titian (Tiziano Vecellio), *Saint Sebastian*, lower right-hand panel from the Averoldi Altarpiece, 1520–22, oil on panel, approx. 67 x 27 inches (170 x 65 cm). Church of Santi Nazaro e Celso, Brescia, Italy.

STEP 1

COPY THE REFERENCE IMAGE

Copying the reference image is a way to explore in detail the structural and anatomical aspect of the figure and to help you to identify the skeletal landmarks and muscular volumes—necessary information for performing steps 2 and 3. For my drawing, I used the *trois crayons* technique discussed on page 196.

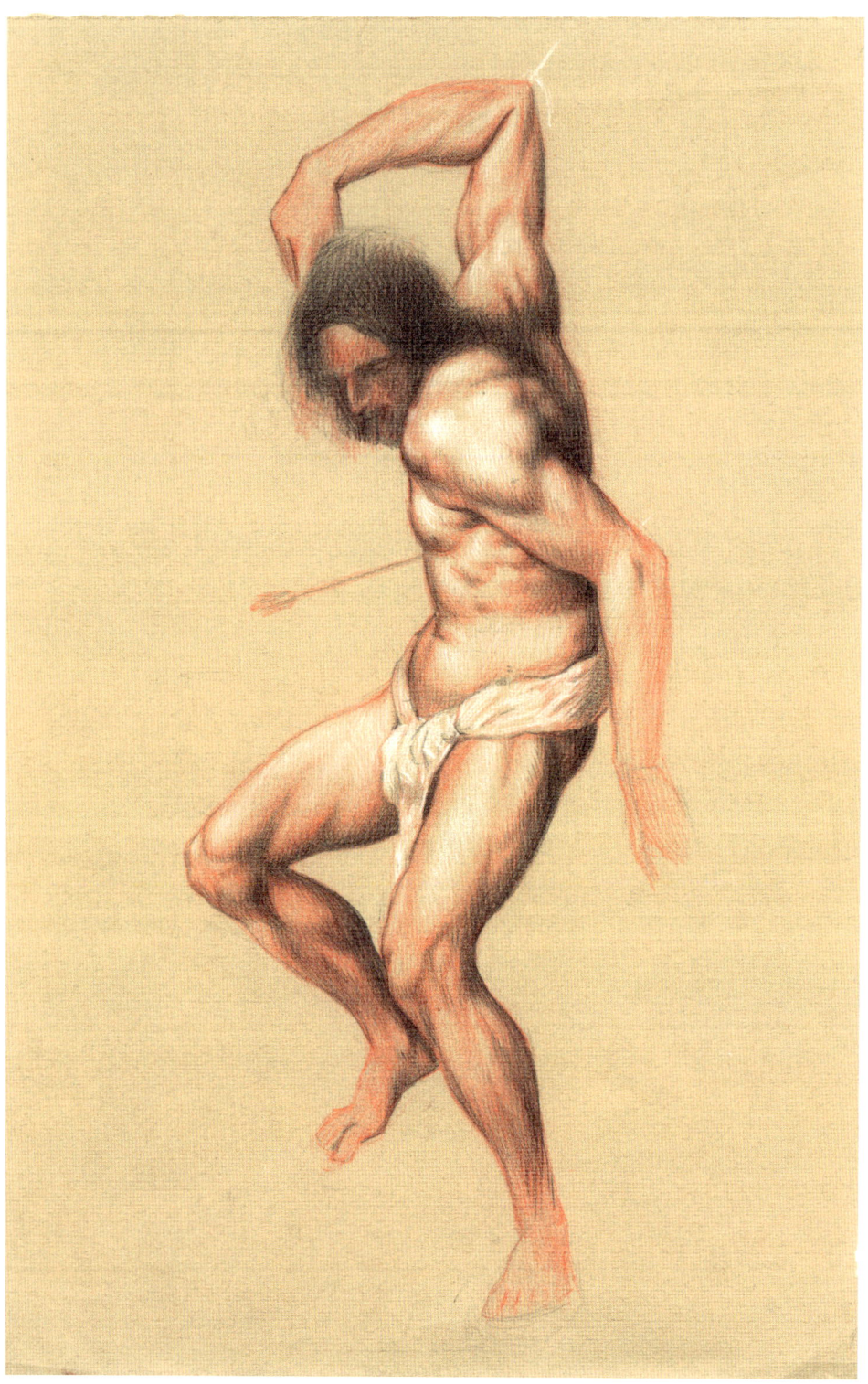

STEP 2

RECONSTRUCT THE SKELETON

Now reconstruct the skeleton using the skeletal landmarks you detected in step 1.

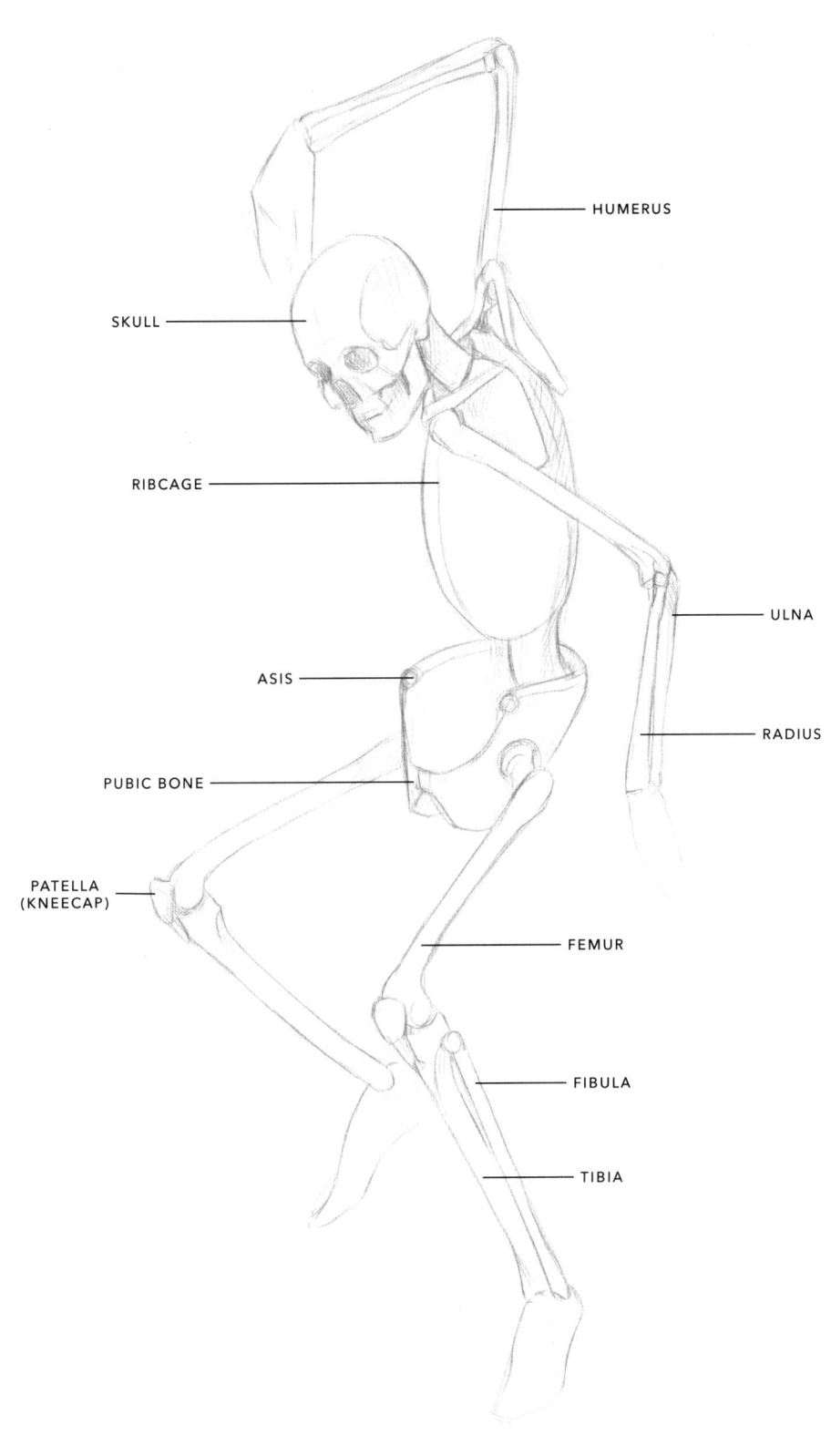

SKULL

HUMERUS

RIBCAGE

ULNA

ASIS

RADIUS

PUBIC BONE

PATELLA
(KNEECAP)

FEMUR

FIBULA

TIBIA

STEP 2

ADD THE MUSCLE VOLUMES

Positioning a sheet of tracing paper over the drawing of the skeleton, draw the muscle
volumes directly on top of it .

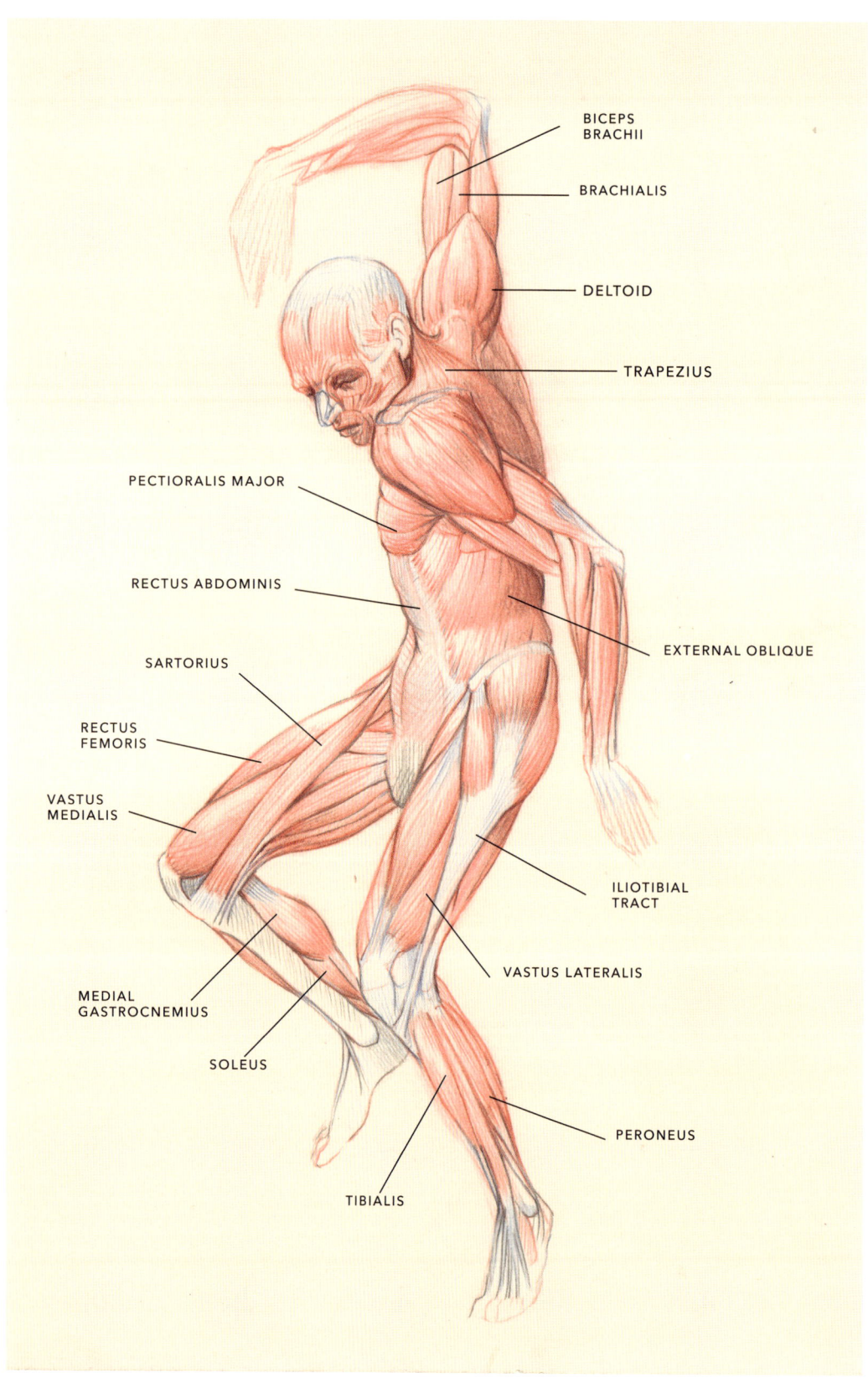

BICEPS
BRACHII

BRACHIALIS

DELTOID

TRAPEZIUS

PECTIORALIS MAJOR

RECTUS ABDOMINIS

EXTERNAL OBLIQUE

SARTORIUS

RECTUS
FEMORIS

VASTUS
MEDIALIS

ILIOTIBIAL
TRACT

MEDIAL
GASTROCNEMIUS

VASTUS LATERALIS

SOLEUS

PERONEUS

TIBIALIS

EXERCISE 3.3
RAPHAEL'S *FIGHTING MEN*

The drawing by Raphael shown here is a great example of what is referred to as the *Florentine Structural System*, a drawing technique that considers the human body's volumetric characteristics and views the body as a structure constituted of various parts assembled together. Raphael used structural, or framing, lines, which are particularly efficient in describing the volumetric development of the forms of the body. The flawlessly constructed, solid, volumetric, and convincingly dynamic figures in Raphael's drawing show the advantages of utilizing anatomical knowledge when drawing, painting, or sculpting.

With this exercise, you will practice composition and narrative, the structural construction and dynamism of the figure, and how to position the muscles over figures in action. And you'll also practice using the hatching lines that so clearly describe the figures' bodies, emphasizing their volumes.

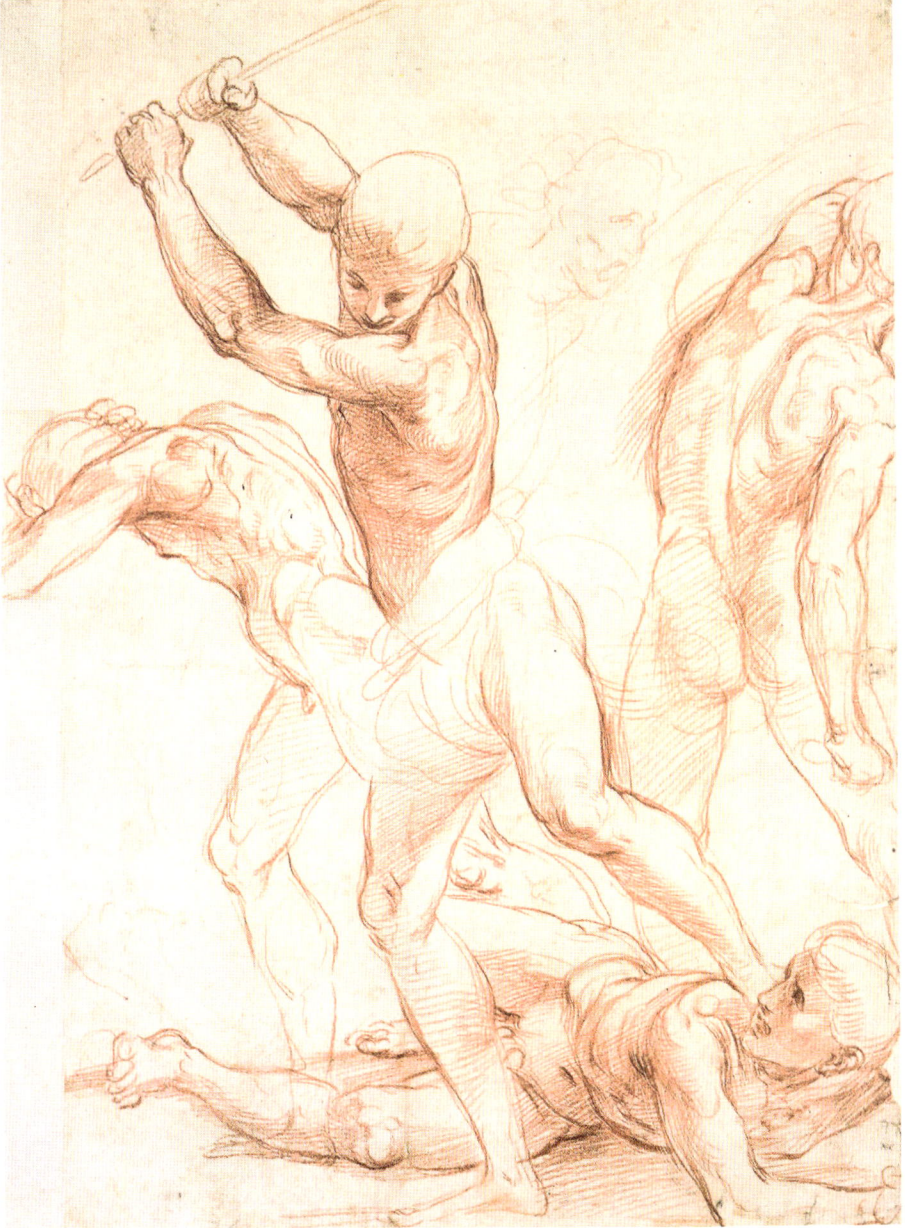

Raphael, *Fighting Men,* 1510–11, red chalk over lead point on paper, 15 x 11 ⅛ inches. Ashmolean Museum, London.

STEP 1

RENDER STEREOMETRIC VOLUMES

Begin by rendering the figures in Raphael's drawing as stereometric volumes to better visualize their movements individually and as a group. The action lines you see in the image here will help in this task. The stereometric representations of the figures also make it easier to appreciate the dynamism of each segment of the body.

Aspects of the composition can be better appreciated when the figures are reduced to stereometric volumes. For example, the actors in this drawing can be divided in two groups, one focal and one accessory. The two figures in the foreground, organized as an upside-down *T*, are clearly the focus. They are opposites in just about every way: one is standing and vertical, the other lying down and horizontal; one is active, the other passive; one is reaching upward, the other is scrambling away; one is giving, the other receiving; one expresses rage, the other terror. The gaze they exchange connects them and anticipates the direction of the blow that will soon follow.

Meanwhile, the two accessory figures in the background reinforce the action of the main actors: they are organized in a *V* that frames the foreground figures, and even though their lines of action diverge, moving away from the blow being delivered by the main standing figure, their bodies create a funnel that amplifies the energy of that blow.

Copy this work, considering these compositional devices and paying particular attention to the various stereometric segments of the figures to maintain their proportions and capture their movement.

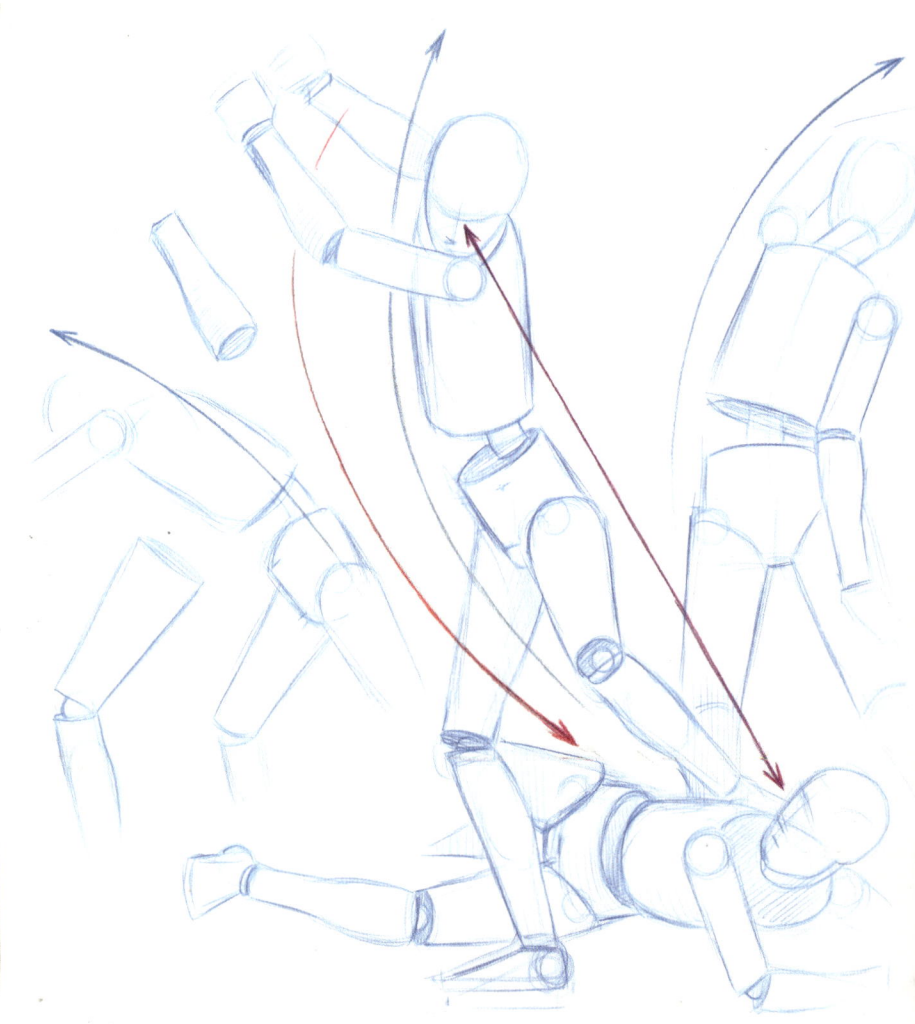

STEP 2

FOCUS ON ORGANIC ASPECTS

The previous step analyzed the compositional, narrative, and dynamic aspects of
Raphael's drawing. In this step, focus on the organic aspects of the figures: skeleton,
muscles, and external forms.

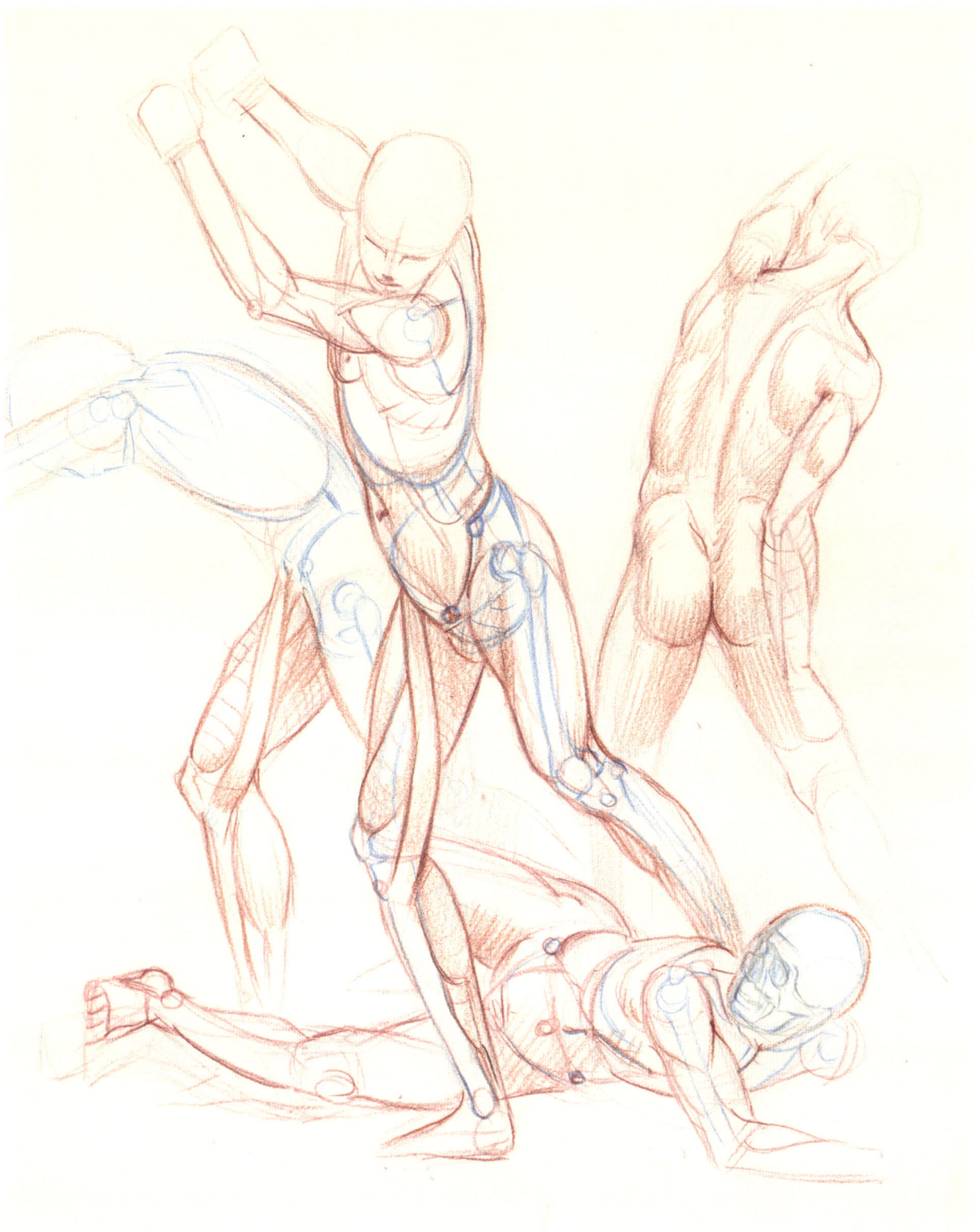

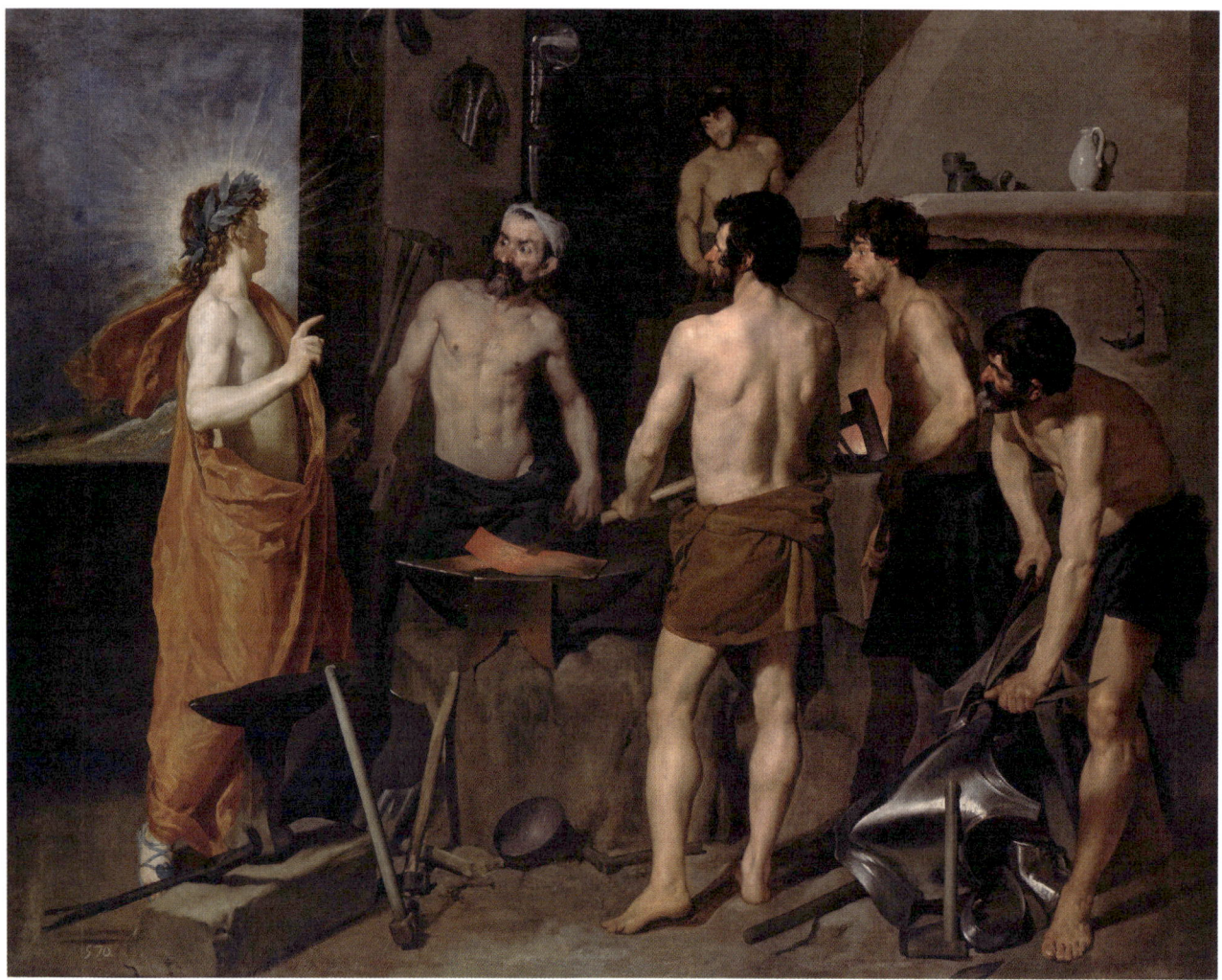

EXERCISE 3.4

VELÁZQUEZ'S *APOLLO IN THE FORGE OF VULCAN*

Apollo in the Forge of Vulcan is one of my favorite Velázquez paintings. The light and composition are impeccable, as is the anatomical accuracy of the figures, and the painting technique is simply sublime.

This work is also very witty: the narrative disguised behind the solemn façade is somewhat comical: Apollo is delivering to Vulcan the news that his wife, Venus, is having an affair with Mars. The shocked and embarrassed facial expressions of Vulcan and his attendants are rendered masterfully, getting us involved in this "OMG!" moment.

Diego Velázquez, *Apollo in the Forge of Vulcan*, 1630, oil on canvas, 87 ¾ × 114 ⅛ inches (223 × 290 cm). Museo del Prado, Madrid, Spain.

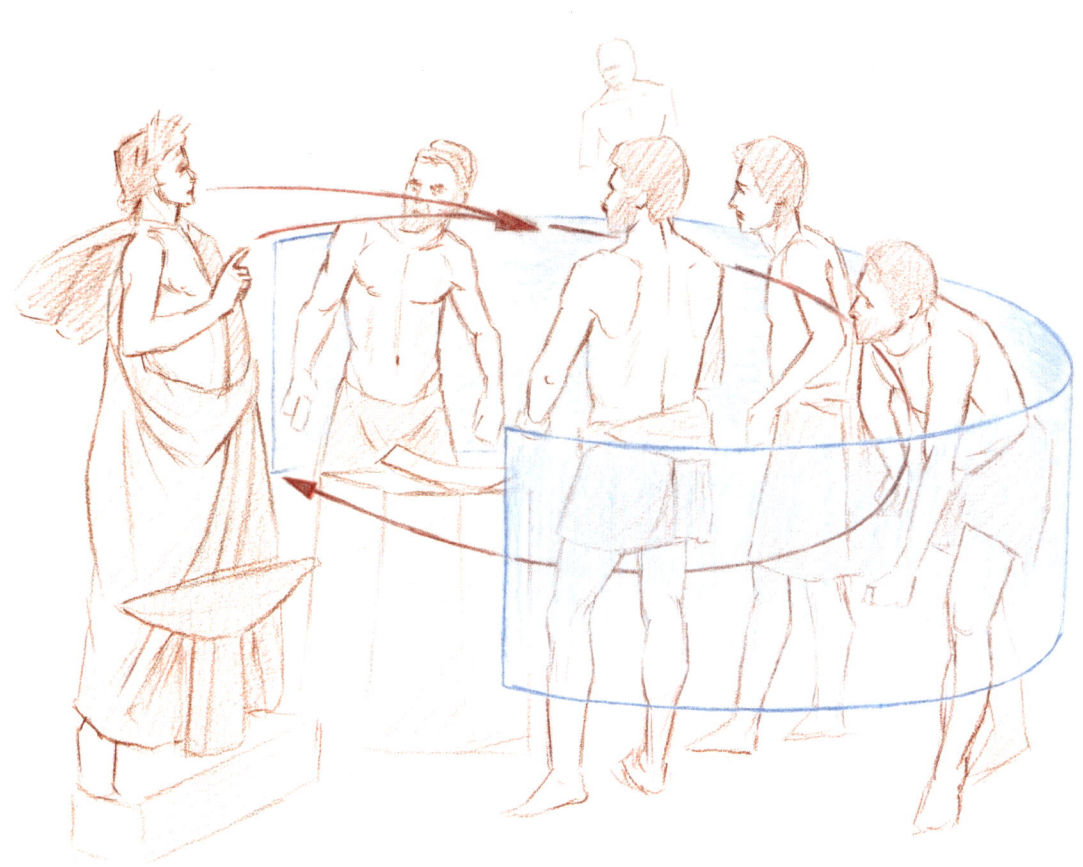

STEP 1

STUDY THE COMPOSITION

Let's start this exercise studying the compositional structure. Apollo's peremptory presence demands the attention of all the actors in the scene, who, frozen in their poses, immediately turn their gazes on him.

Apollo's stance, gaze, gesture, and word propel the action from left to right. This powerful movement would go right through the right side of the painting if it were not for the last two assistants bending slightly, a clever compositional device that redirects the trajectory of Apollo's announcement with a curved line that leads back to him, keeping the energy of his action—a perpetual circular movement—within the frame.

The assistants are arranged in a horseshoe pattern or that of a vessel that catches Apollo's message. This *U*-shaped formation also creates a barrier between us and them: we are not supposed to know or hear about the gods' private, adulterous business. I find an affinity between this composition and Caravaggio's composition for *The Calling of Saint Matthew* (1599–1600), where the actors are similarly organized in a group pose that mirrors that of the Velázquez painting.

STEP 2

RECREATE THE SKELETAL STRUCTURE

This step focuses on the skeletons of the two figures closest to Apollo. Identify the skeletal landmarks on the surface of these figures and recreate the skeletal structures as shown in the image here. Note that the loincloth of the figure on the right makes it a bit more challenging to identify the position of the pelvis.

STEP 3

DRAW THE MUSCULAR VOLUMES AND EXTERNAL FORMS

Working with the same two figures, now draw the superficial muscles (figure on the left) and the external forms (figure on the right).

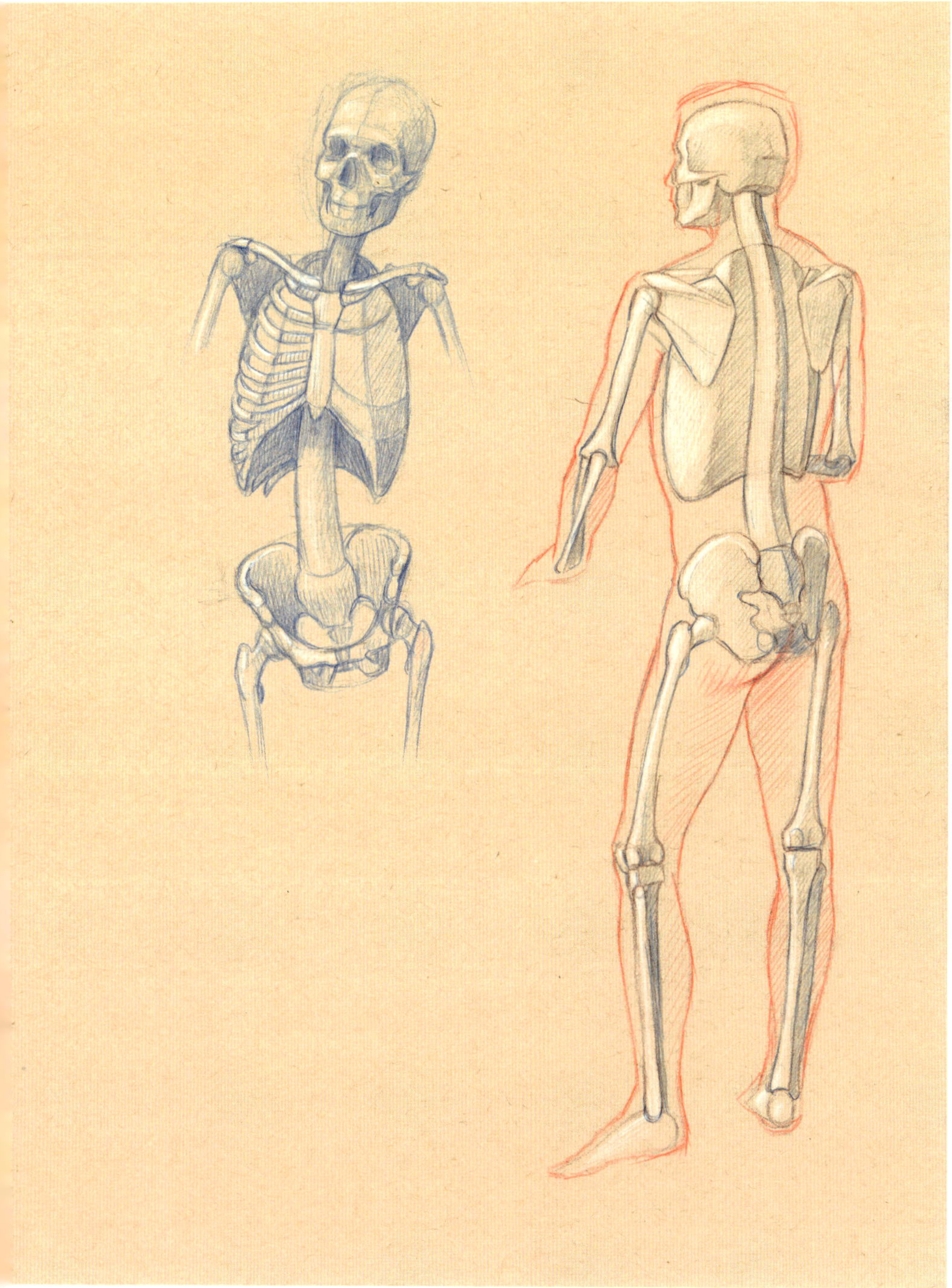

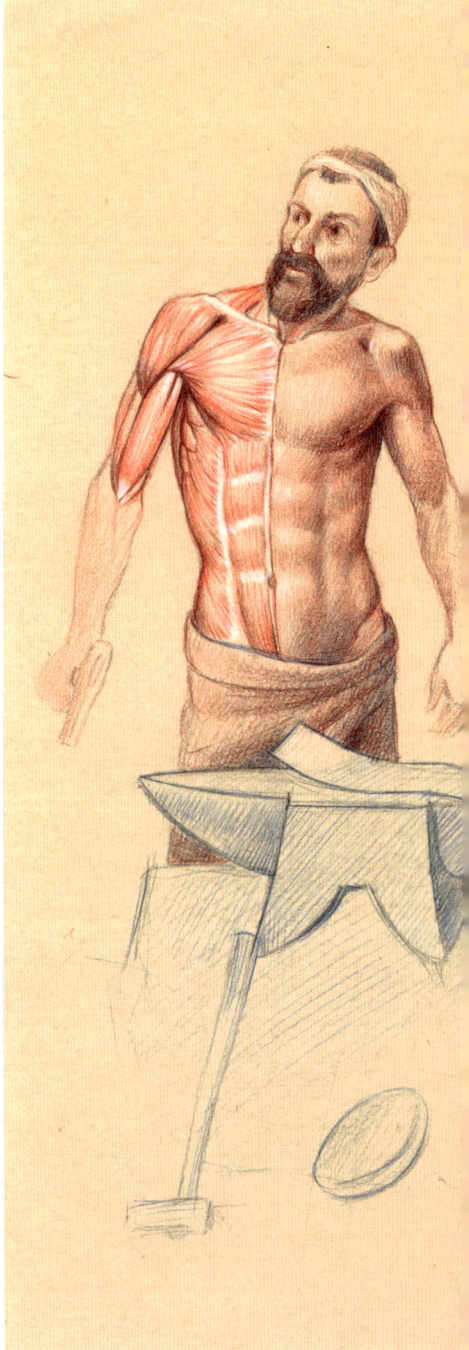

STEP 4

A FLEXED FIGURE

Finally, try your hand at a more dynamic pose—that of the slightly flexed figure at the painting's far right. Focus on the overlapping of the axial skeleton segments, the muscles of the arm and leg, and the external forms where visible.

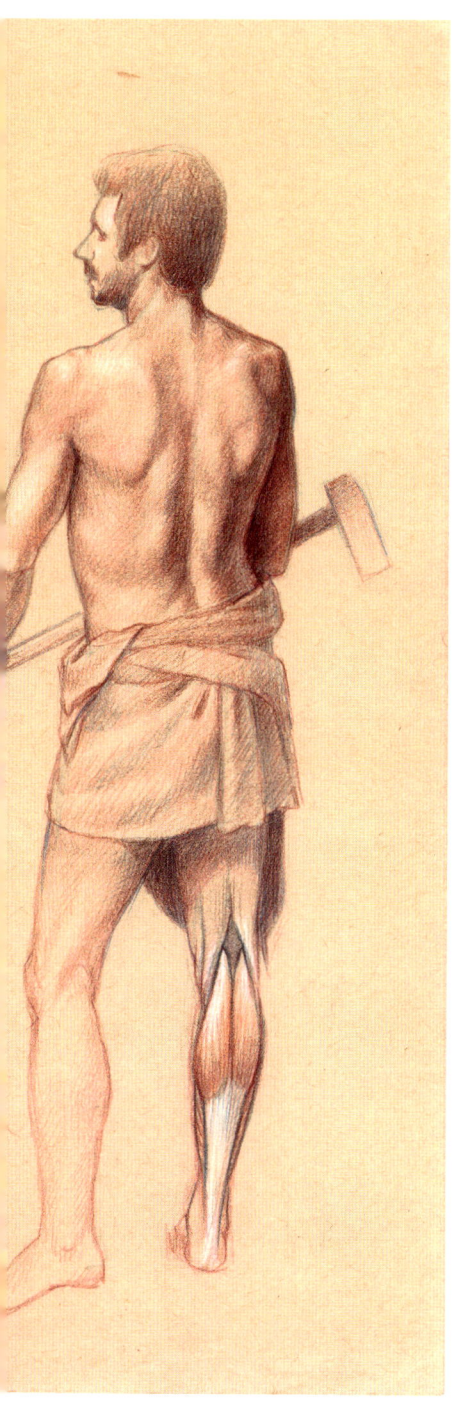

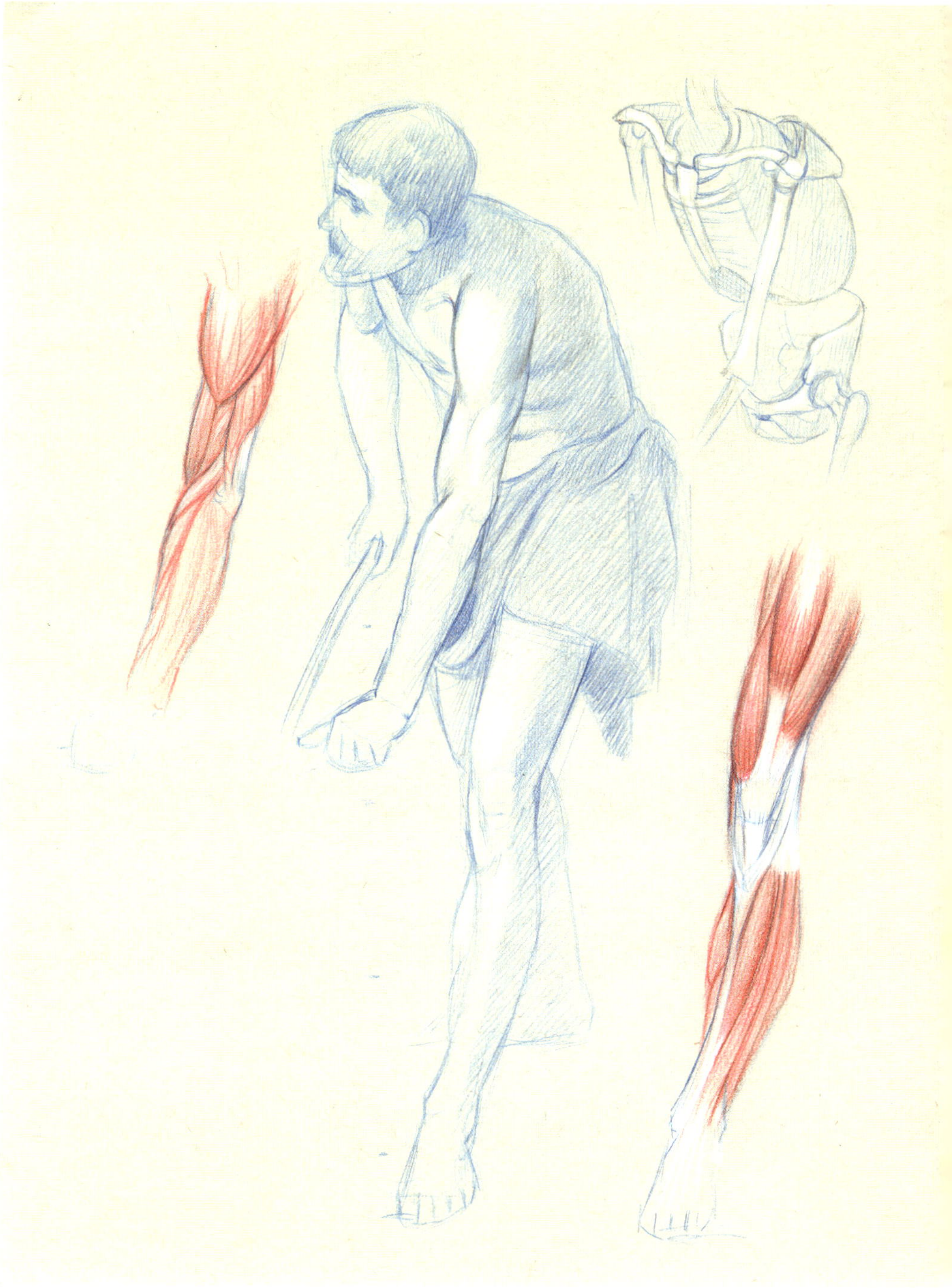

LEVEL 2

WORKING FROM SCULPTURES

This second level of chapter 3 increases the level of difficulty, asking you to identify the landmarks and muscle volumes in sculptures instead of drawings and paintings. The sculptures I chose for these exercises show a degree of idealization, making it easier to find the landmarks and muscular volumes, while at the same time the works' three-dimensional forms bring you a step closer to the great variety of specific forms that a real human body can exhibit.

EXERCISE 3.5
BRIAN BOOTH CRAIG'S *EXECUTIONER*

This exercise focuses on the *Executioner,* a sculpture by my friend Brian Booth Craig. The proportions of this figure are not nearly as idealized as those of Polykleitos' *Doryphoros* (page 116), bringing us closer to a real human being. The exercise asks you to build up the figure by first establishing the skeletal structure, then layering it with muscles and eventually with the skin.

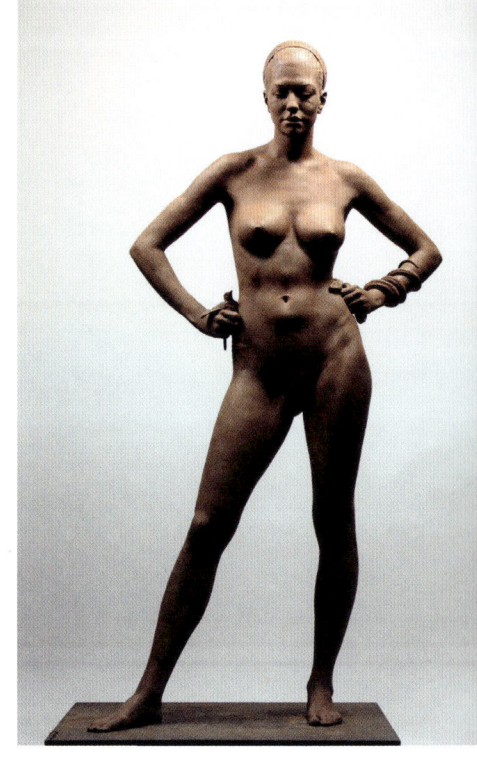

Brian Booth Craig, *Executioner*. Courtesy of the artist.

STEP 1

RECREATE THE SKELETON

Using the photo of the sculpture as your reference, identify the skeletal landmarks and use them to recreate the skeletal structure of *Executioner*.

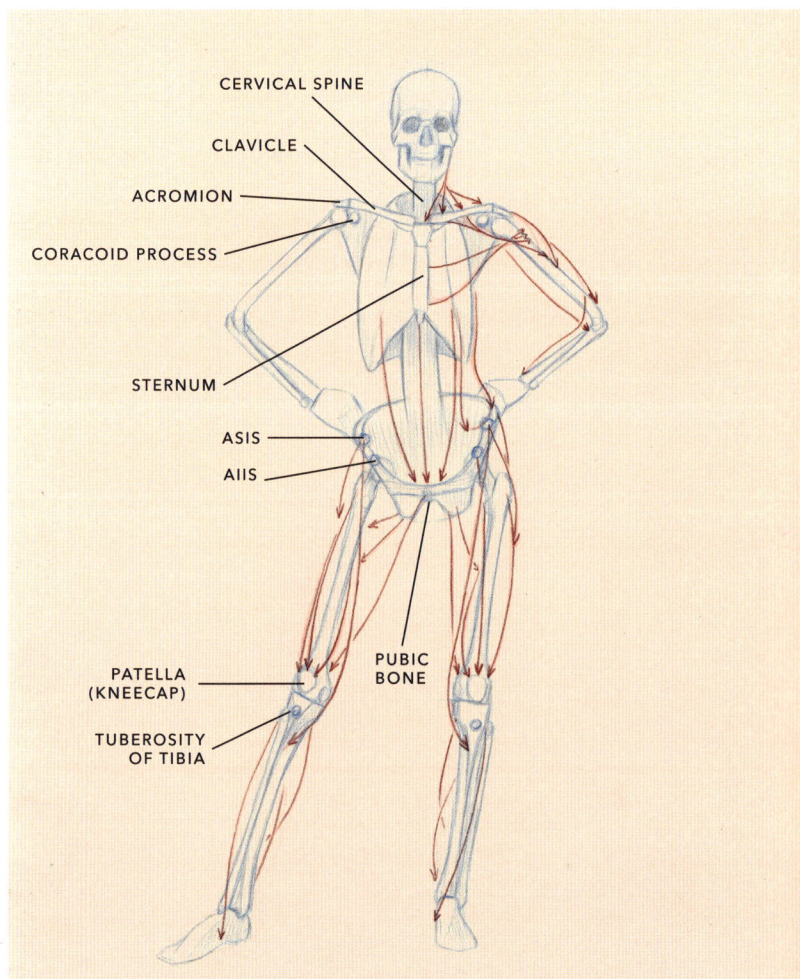

STEP 2

ADD THE MUSCLES

Apply the superficial muscles over the skeletal structure, and label the muscles.

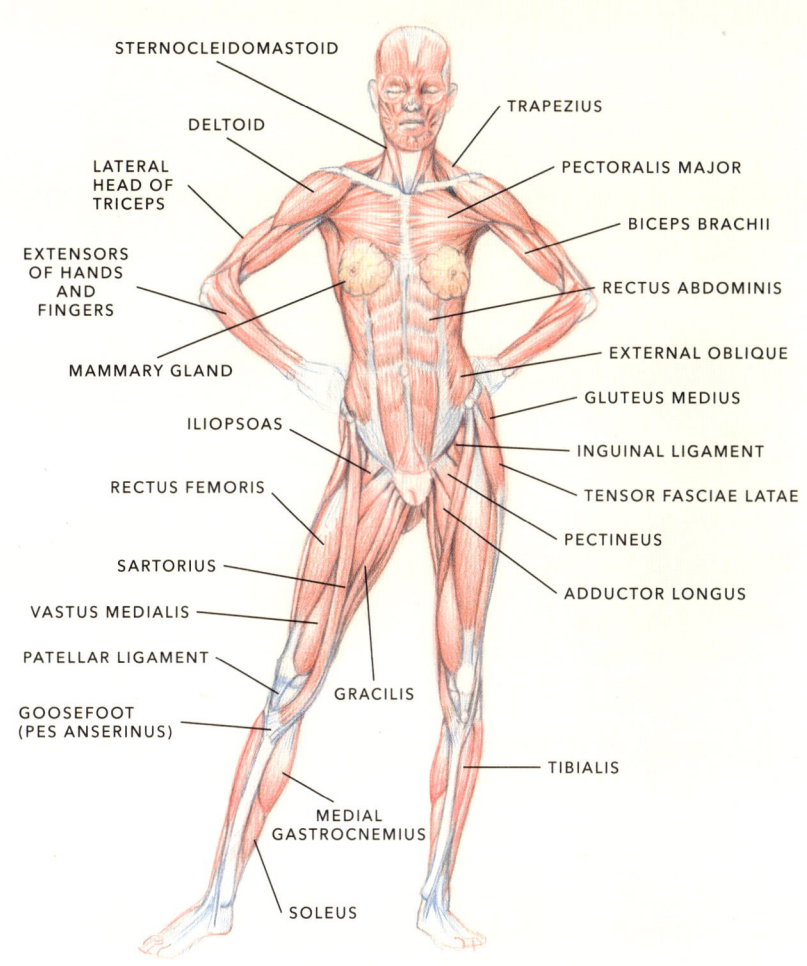

STERNOCLEIDOMASTOID

TRAPEZIUS

DELTOID

LATERAL HEAD OF TRICEPS

PECTORALIS MAJOR

BICEPS BRACHII

EXTENSORS OF HANDS AND FINGERS

RECTUS ABDOMINIS

EXTERNAL OBLIQUE

MAMMARY GLAND

GLUTEUS MEDIUS

ILIOPSOAS

INGUINAL LIGAMENT

TENSOR FASCIAE LATAE

RECTUS FEMORIS

PECTINEUS

SARTORIUS

ADDUCTOR LONGUS

VASTUS MEDIALIS

PATELLAR LIGAMENT

GRACILIS

GOOSEFOOT (PES ANSERINUS)

TIBIALIS

MEDIAL GASTROCNEMIUS

SOLEUS

STEP 3

APPLY THE OUTER FORM

Now draw the sculpture, guided by the reference photo but also trying to use the skeletal and soft landmarks and the main muscular volumes to inform your drawing.

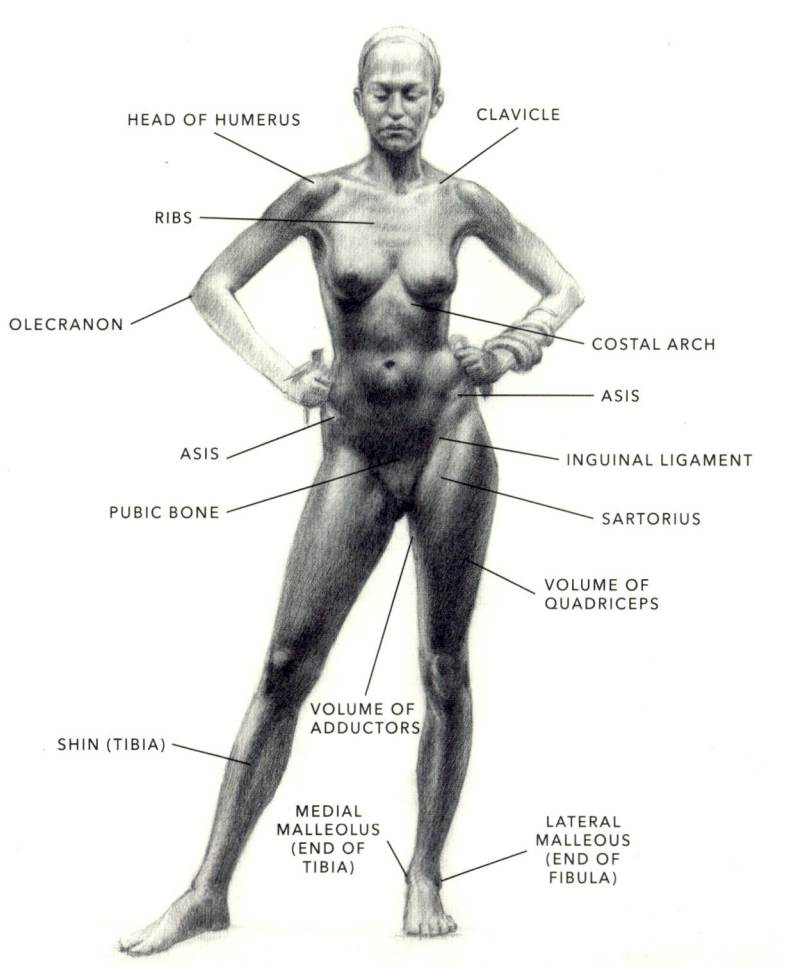

HEAD OF HUMERUS

CLAVICLE

RIBS

OLECRANON

COSTAL ARCH

ASIS

ASIS

INGUINAL LIGAMENT

PUBIC BONE

SARTORIUS

VOLUME OF QUADRICEPS

VOLUME OF ADDUCTORS

SHIN (TIBIA)

MEDIAL MALLEOLUS (END OF TIBIA)

LATERAL MALLEOUS (END OF FIBULA)

BRIAN BOOTH CRAIG'S *FLAVIA*

Brian Booth Craig's *Flavia* exhibits fuller forms than his *Executioner*, meaning that the landmarks will be slightly more difficult to identify because they're covered by thicker layer of subcutaneous fat than in the previous, leaner figure.

STEP 1

RECREATE THE SKELETON

Based on the skeletal and soft landmarks you find in the reference photo, recreate the skeletal structure of *Flavia*. And label the bones.

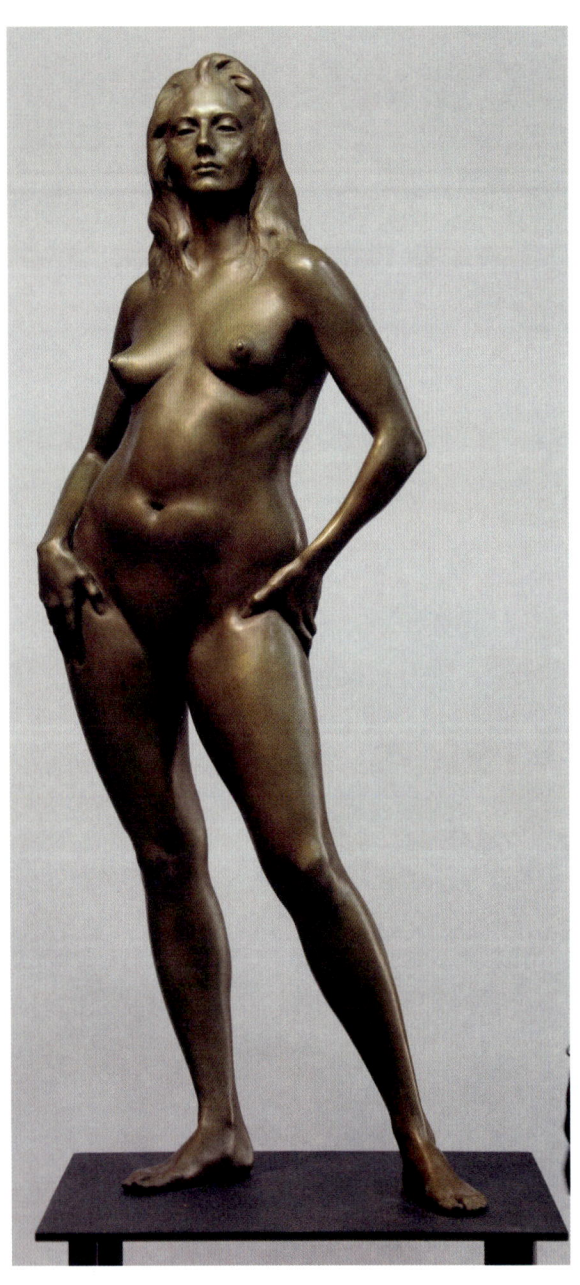

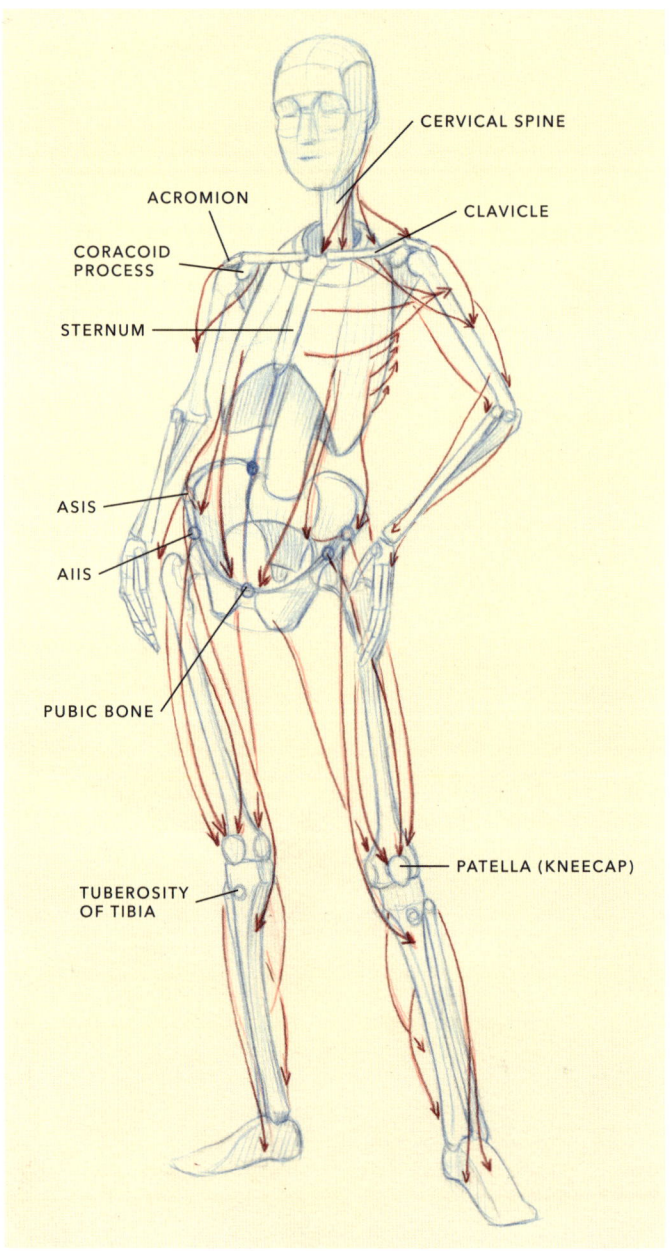

Brian Booth Craig, *Flavia,* 2019, bronze, 36 x 9 x 5 inches (91.4 x 22.9 x 12.7 cm). Courtesy of the artist.

STEP 2

APPLY SUPERFICIAL MUSCLES

As you did in the previous exercises, apply the superficial muscle layer over the skeletal structure and label the muscles.

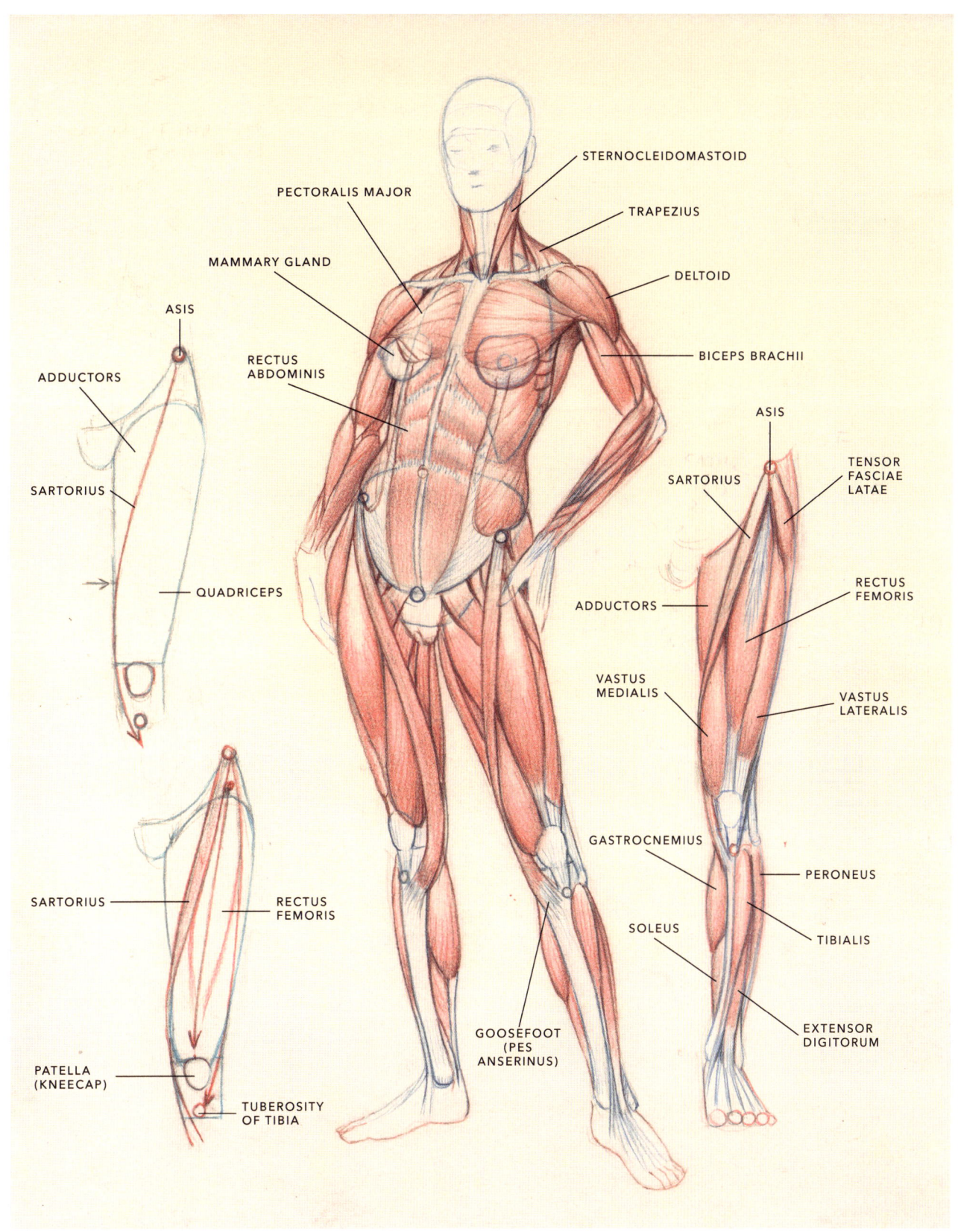

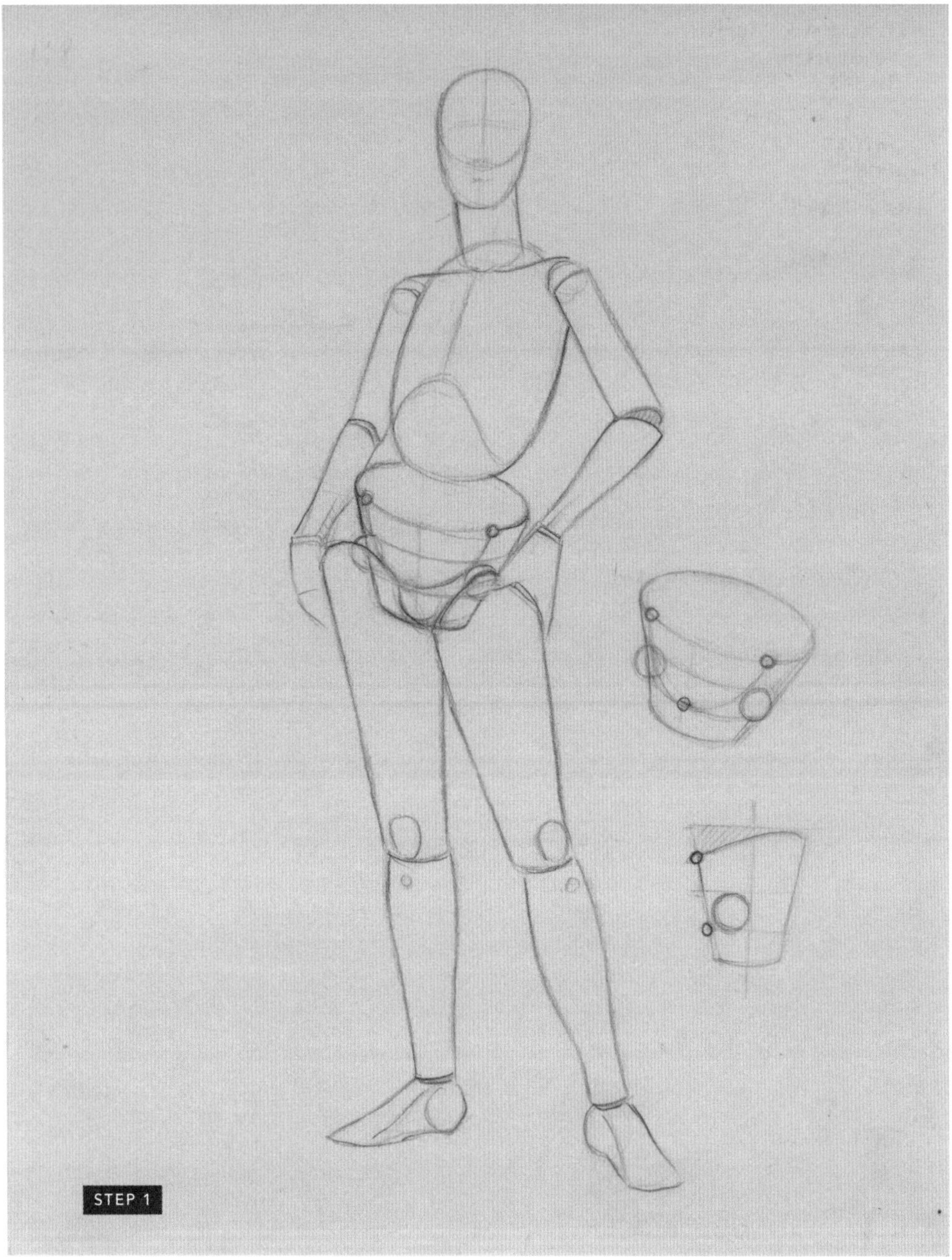

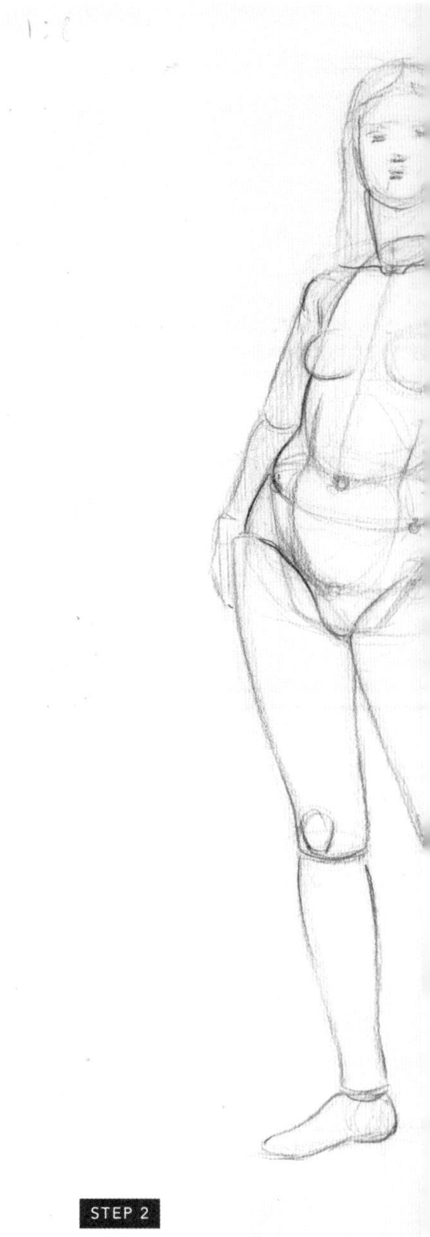

EXERCISE 3.7

LAYERING VOLUMES OVER A STEREOMETRIC RENDERING

In this exercise you start from the external forms rendered as stereometric volumes instead of from the skeletal structure.

STEP 1

RENDER THE FIGURE IN STEREOMETRIC VOLUMES

Start this sequence by drawing the stereometric rendering of the figure. This will be the scaffolding on which you'll gradually build a more organic rendering.

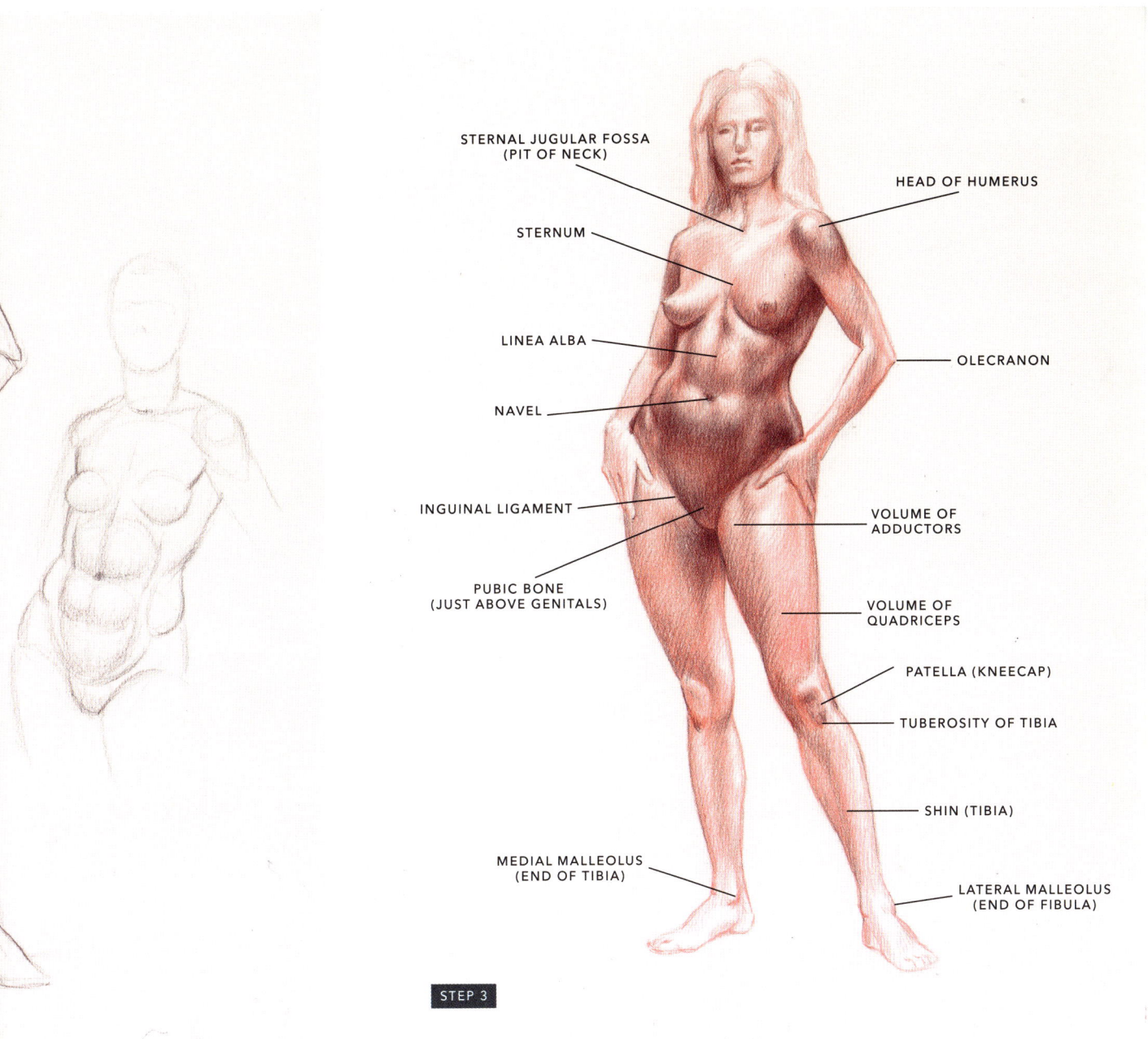

STERNAL JUGULAR FOSSA
(PIT OF NECK)

HEAD OF HUMERUS

STERNUM

LINEA ALBA

OLECRANON

NAVEL

INGUINAL LIGAMENT

VOLUME OF
ADDUCTORS

PUBIC BONE
(JUST ABOVE GENITALS)

VOLUME OF
QUADRICEPS

PATELLA (KNEECAP)

TUBEROSITY OF TIBIA

SHIN (TIBIA)

MEDIAL MALLEOLUS
(END OF TIBIA)

LATERAL MALLEOLUS
(END OF FIBULA)

STEP 3

STEP 2

APPLY GEOMETRIC VOLUMES

To the stereometric scaffolding, apply the external forms of the body—shoulders, breasts, abdomen, external obliques, and so on—rendered as geometric volumes. With this exercise, learn to look past the distracting details of the organic forms, concentrating instead on their overall volumetric qualities to create a convincing three-dimensional effect.

STEP 3

RENDER THE FIGURE REALISTICALLY

Now add the details over the volumetric study you created in the previous step.

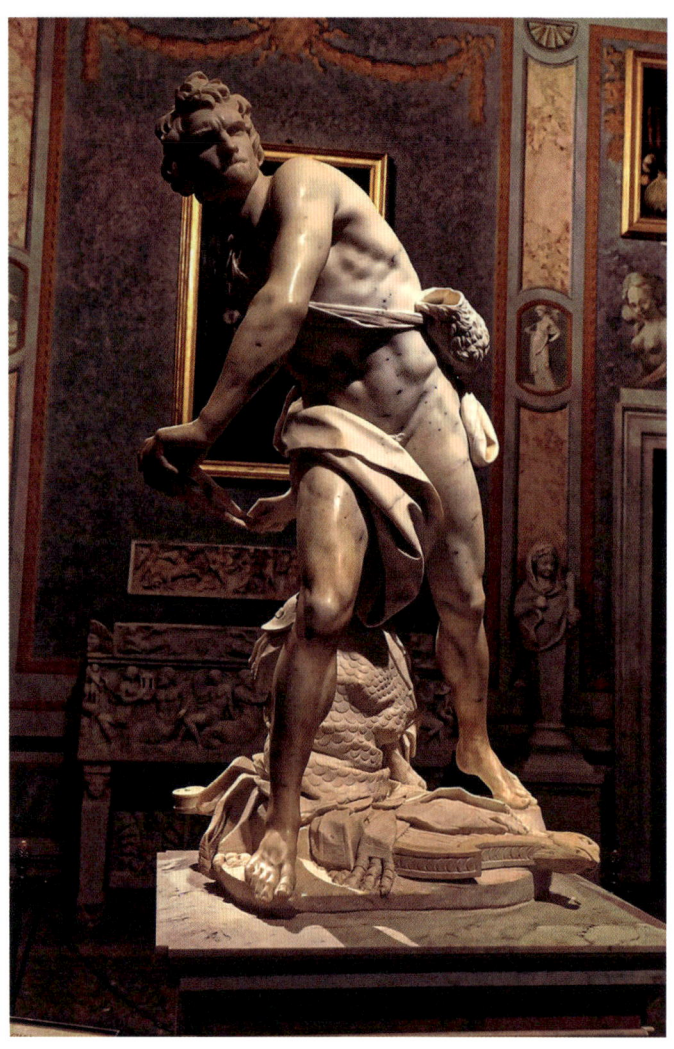

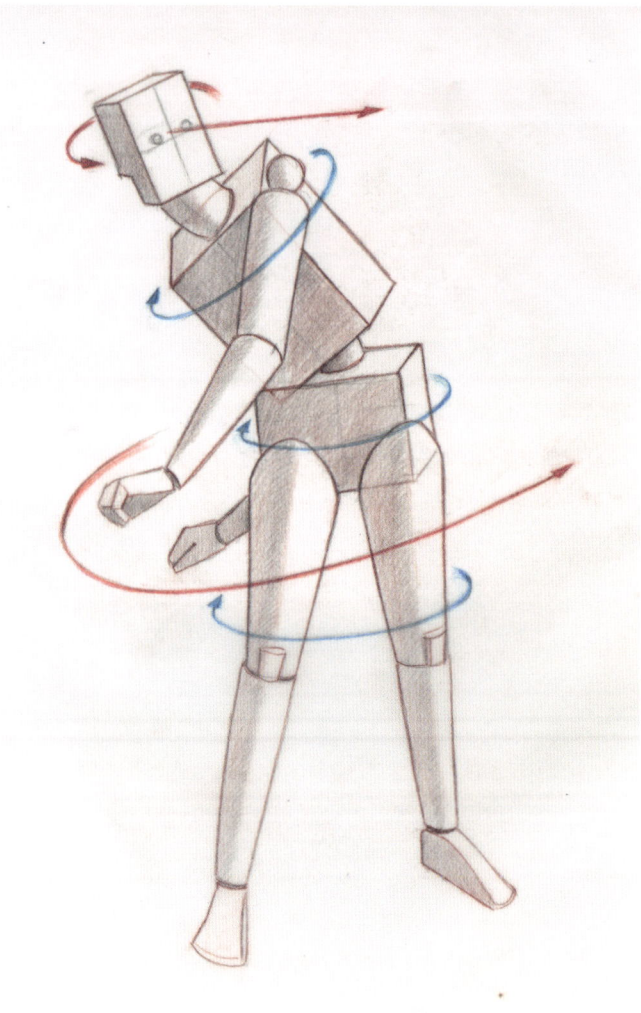

EXERCISE 3.8
BERNINI'S *DAVID*

This masterpiece by the Baroque master Gian Lorenzo Bernini is the subject of the folllowing exercise. Creating the figure–skeleton–muscles sequence will be a bit harder with this subject because the figure is partly covered by cloth, but that means you'll have to sharpen your observational skills.

STEP 1

RENDER THE FIGURE STEREOMETRICALLY

The first step of this exercise asks you to render the figure stereometrically. This will enable you to more clearly visualize the orientation and positioning of the figure's segments in relation to each other. The arrows shown in this drawing above right describe the dynamism of Bernini's masterpiece. The blue arrows represent the action that has already happened: the coiling of the body, charged like a spring and twisting away from the target. The red arrows represent the future action: the uncoiling of the body and the release of the stone, whose trajectory is foreseen by David's gaze. The subject is caught in the moment between past and future—an eternal present locked in marble.

Gian Lorenzo Bernini, *David*, 1623-24, marble, 67 inches (170 cm) tall. Galleria Borghese, Rome.

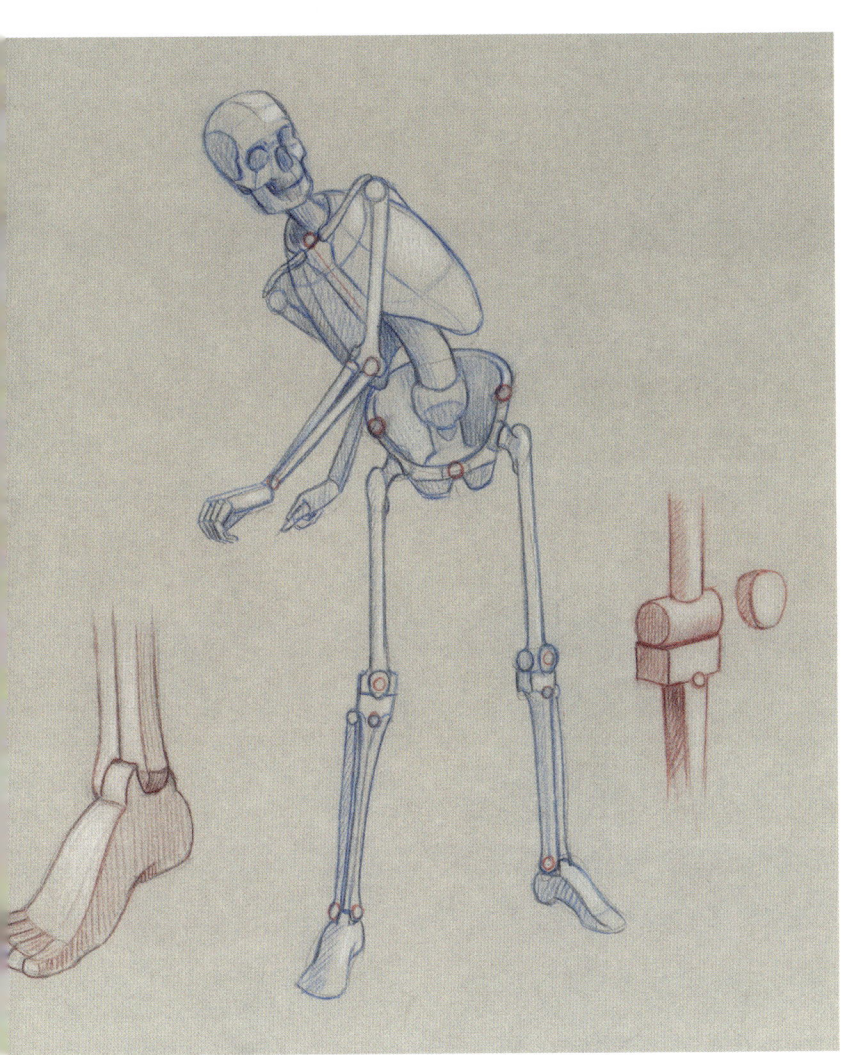

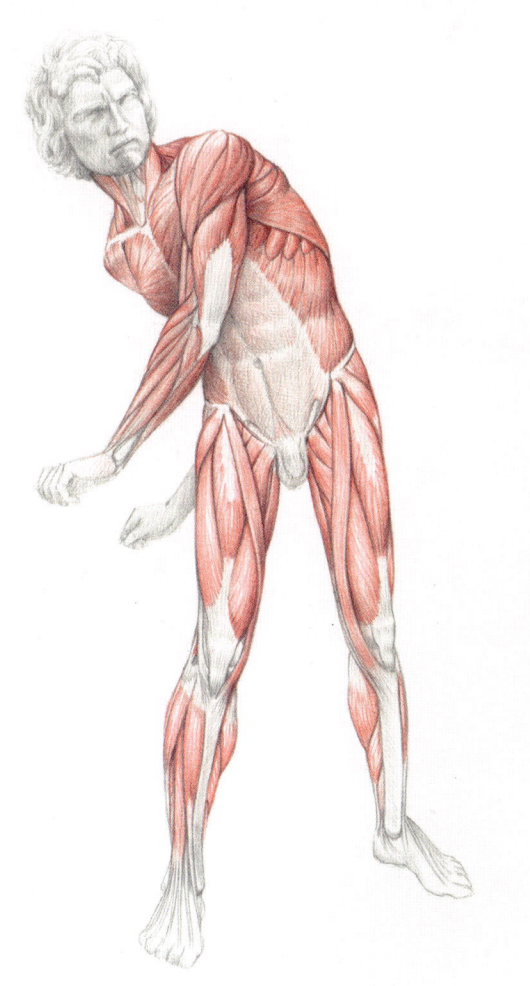

STEP 2

DRAW THE SKELETON

Draw the skeleton using clues from the stereometric rendering and from the photo of the sculpture. Also prepare also a few studies of the joints, like those in the image here, to better understand the connections between various parts of the body in movement.

STEP 3

APPLY THE MUSCLES

Positioning tracing paper over the skeleton or the stereometric volumes, layer on the muscles.

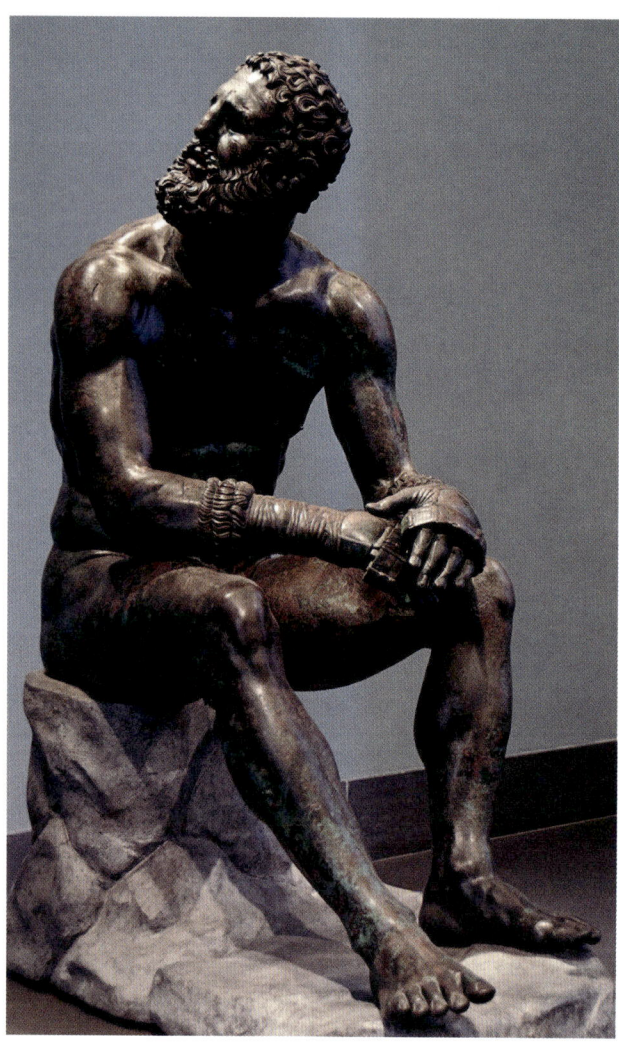

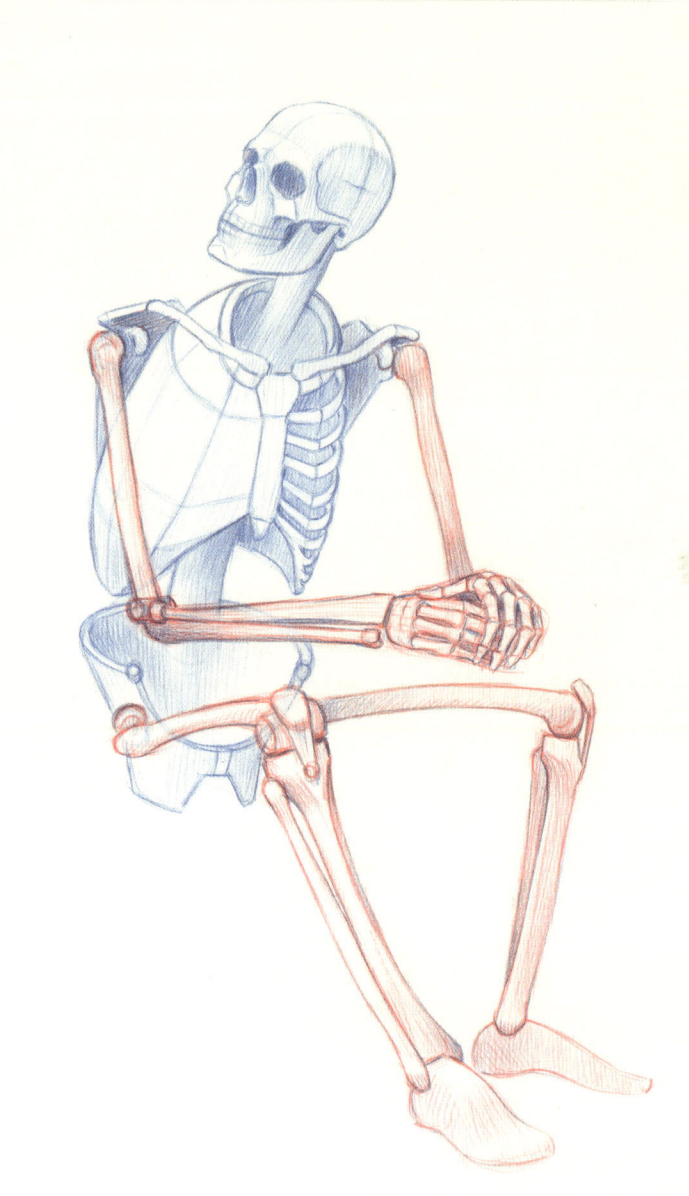

EXERCISE 3.9
THE QUIRINAL BOXER

This rare Hellenistic bronze was found intact in 1885 during construction work on the Quirinal Hill, one of Rome's seven hills. It had apparently been hidden in antiquity to protect it from being melted down, a common fate of many bronzes during the late Roman Empire.

For this exercise, perform our usual "reverse dissection." The boxer's sitting pose increases the challenge of reconstructing the skeletal and muscular structures.

ABOVE: *Quirinal Boxer* (*Boxer at Rest*), 330-50 BCE, bronze, 47 inches (119 cm) tall. Palazzo Massimo alle Terme, Rome, Italy.

STEP 1
RECONSTRUCT THE SKELETON

Find the skeletal landmarks in the reference photo and reconstruct the skeleton.

Although the skeleton in the drawing above is fairly detailed, it remains stylized, making it easier for you to focus on the essential volumes and helping you find structural details such as the positions of the hip joints and the orientation of the pelvis.

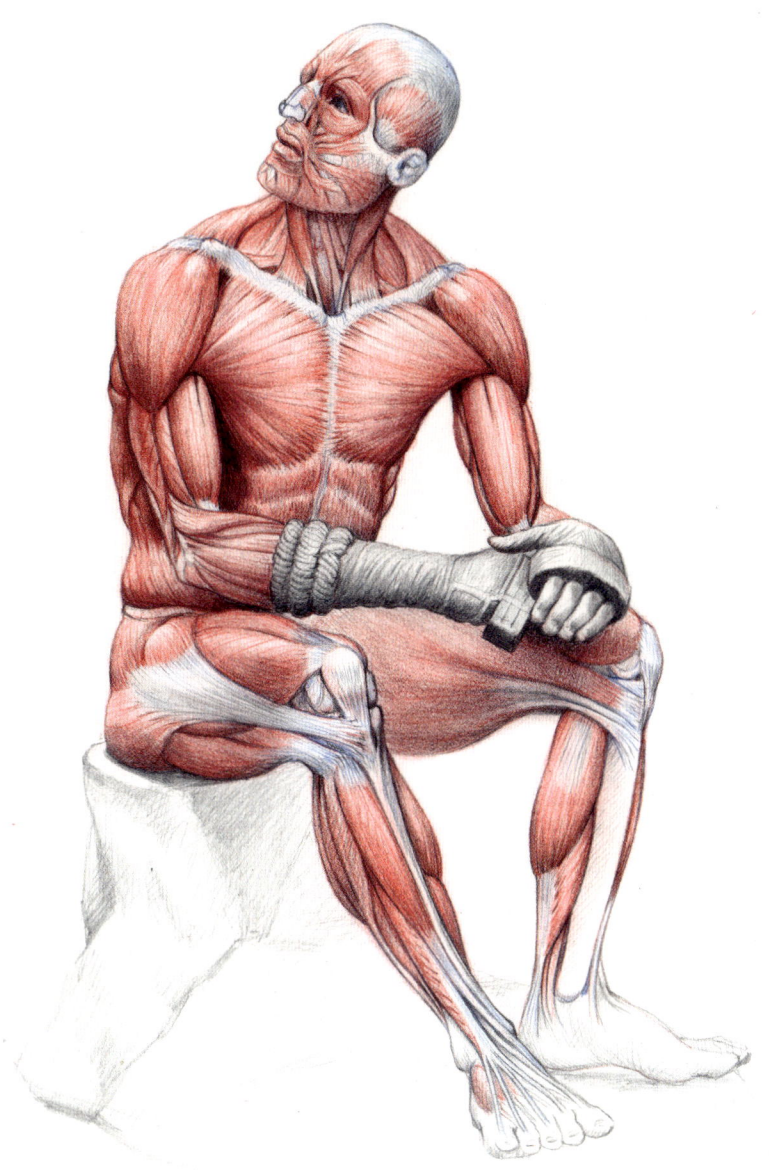

STEP 2

ADD THE MUSCLES

Now coat the skeleton with the muscles. For this step, you'll definitely want to draw on a sheet of tracing paper taped over the drawing of the skeleton. That way you can try several times without risking ruining your drawing of the skeleton.

This concludes Level 2. Congratulations! By now you have achieved a good knowledge of the body's landmarks, skeleton, and muscular structure, and of human anatomy in dynamic poses and at rest. You are now ready for Level 3!

LEVEL 3

WORKING FROM THE HUMAN FIGURE

In this level, you finally graduate to working from images of real models in a variety of poses and an increasing level of difficulty. The next six exercises all feature standing figures in plain front and back views, with the body landmarks and muscular volumes fairly easily identifiable. Performing these exercises will ease your transition from the sculptures of the previous level to the exercise at the end of the chapter showing a model in a more active, challenging pose.

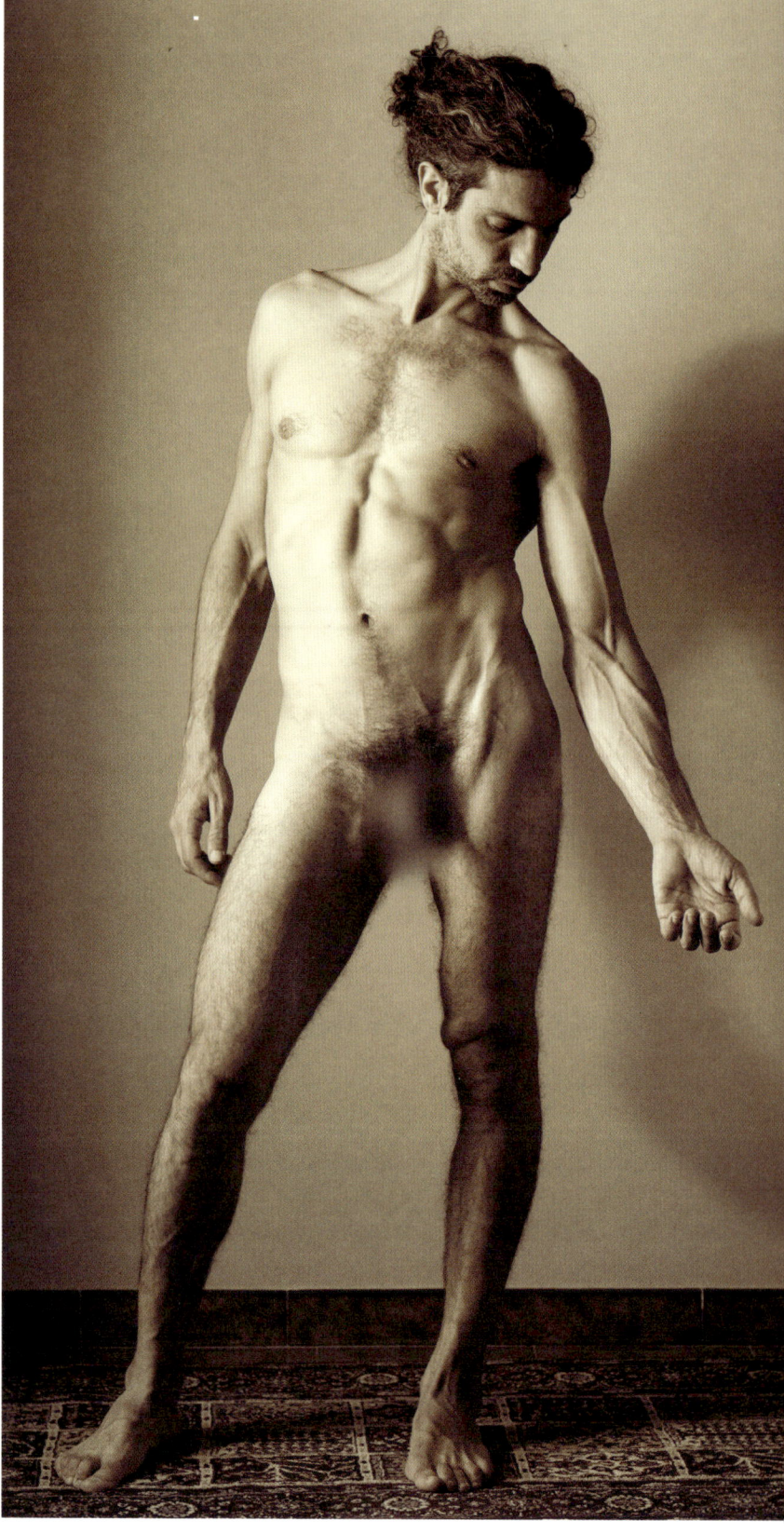

EXERCISE 3.10
MALE FIGURE, FRONT VIEW

The reference photo here is of Andrea Morani, an Italian model who is deeply dedicated to his profession and who works at various art schools and ateliers all over Europe and the United States. (You can also find him online, where he has both Instagram and Patreon sites.) I asked Andrea to create some poses for this book, a few inspired by Old Master artwork. This is his take on the figure of the executioner in Caravaggio's *Martyrdom of Saint Matthew*.

Execute this exercise following the same sequence as the exercises of Level 2: start with a figure drawing by copying the reference photo, mark the skeletal landmarks, then visualize the skeleton and, finally, add the superficial muscles.

STEP 1
COPY THE PHOTO

Copy the reference photo, identifying and labeling the skeletal landmarks and the external forms of the main muscular volumes.

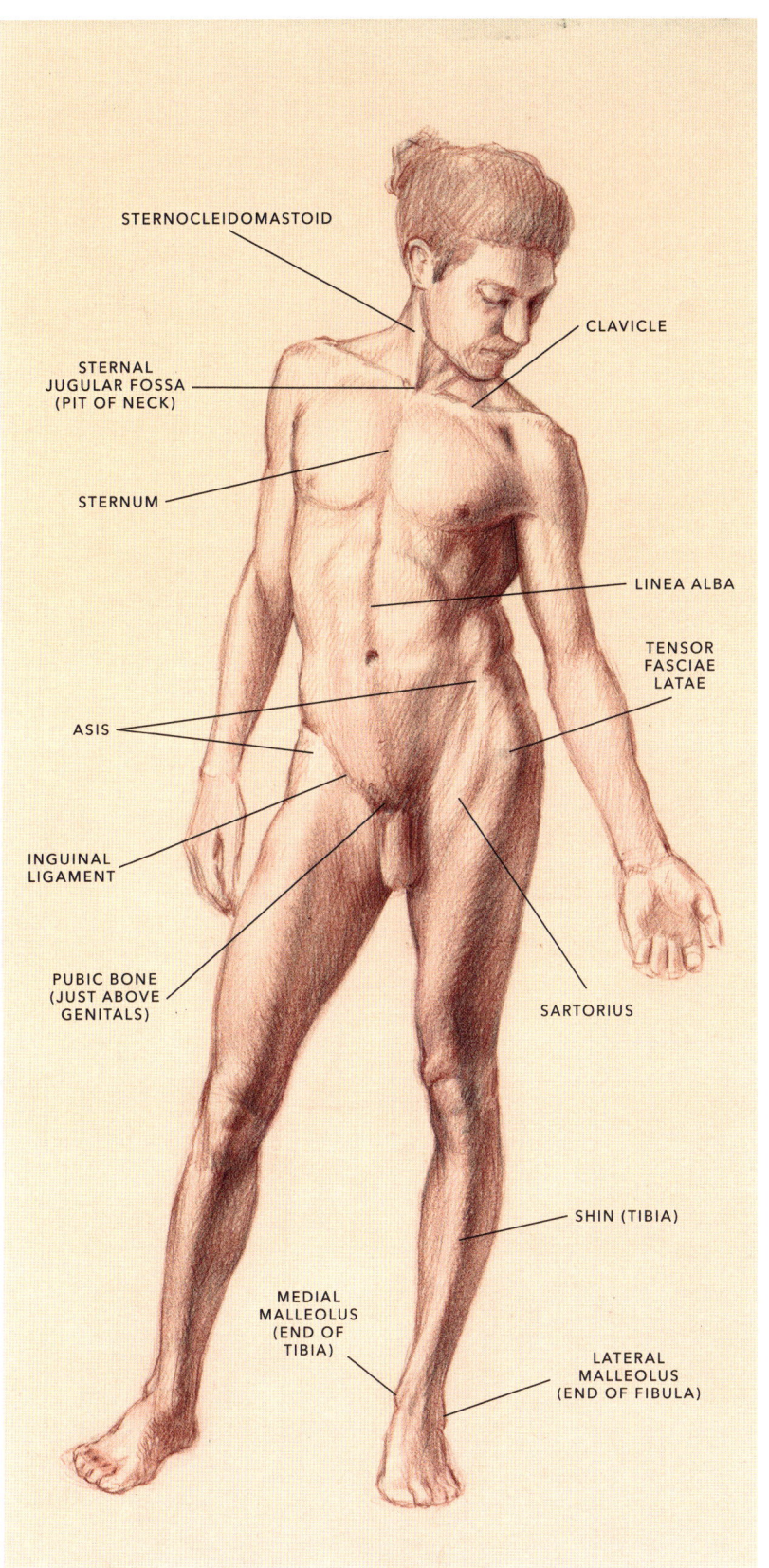

STEP 2

DRAW THE SKELETON

Guided by the skeletal landmarks, draw the skeleton. Also, add the arrows that show the direction of the muscular volumes.

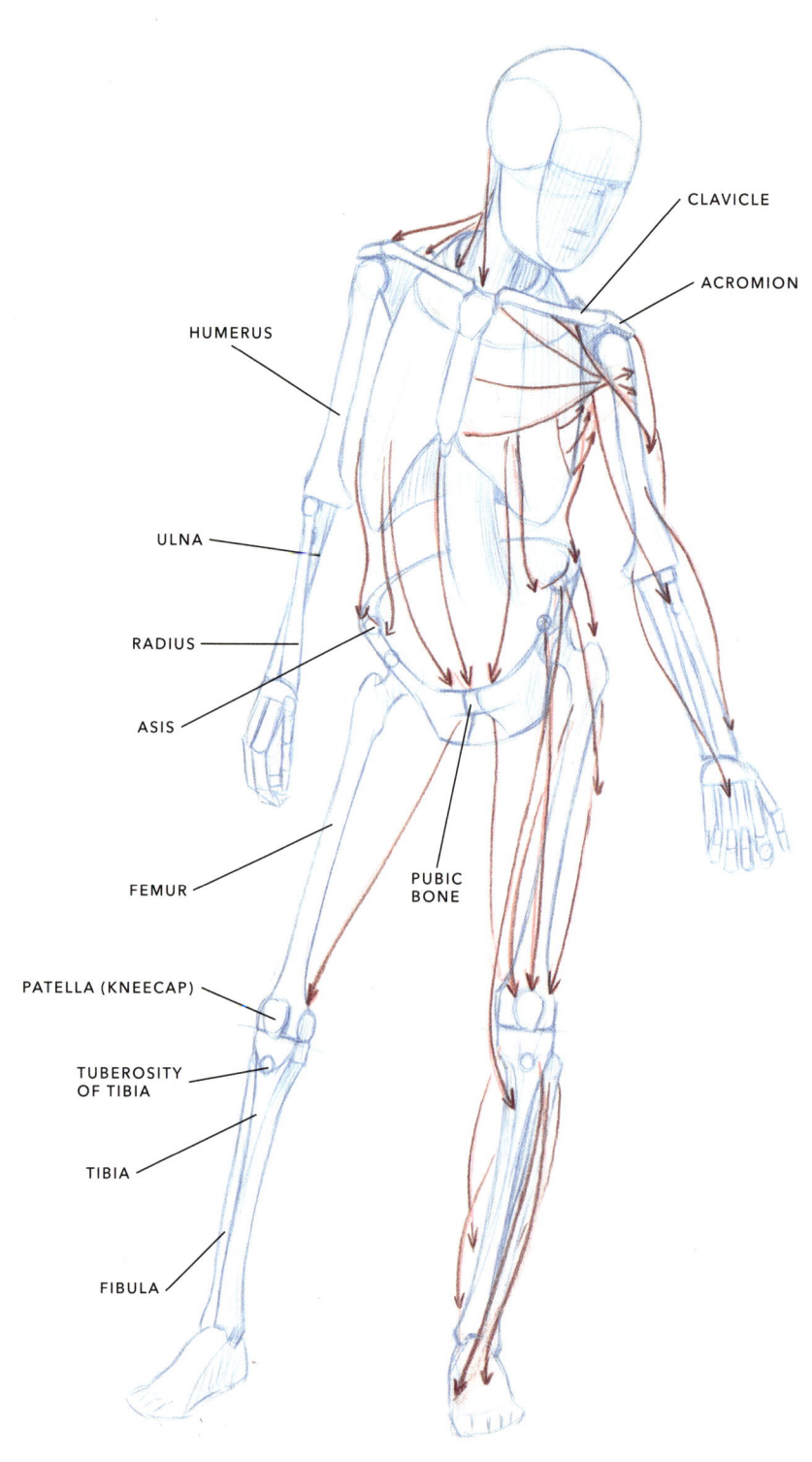

CLAVICLE

ACROMION

HUMERUS

ULNA

RADIUS

ASIS

FEMUR

PUBIC BONE

PATELLA (KNEECAP)

TUBEROSITY OF TIBIA

TIBIA

FIBULA

STEP 3

ADD THE MUSCLES

Layer the superficial muscles over the skeleton.

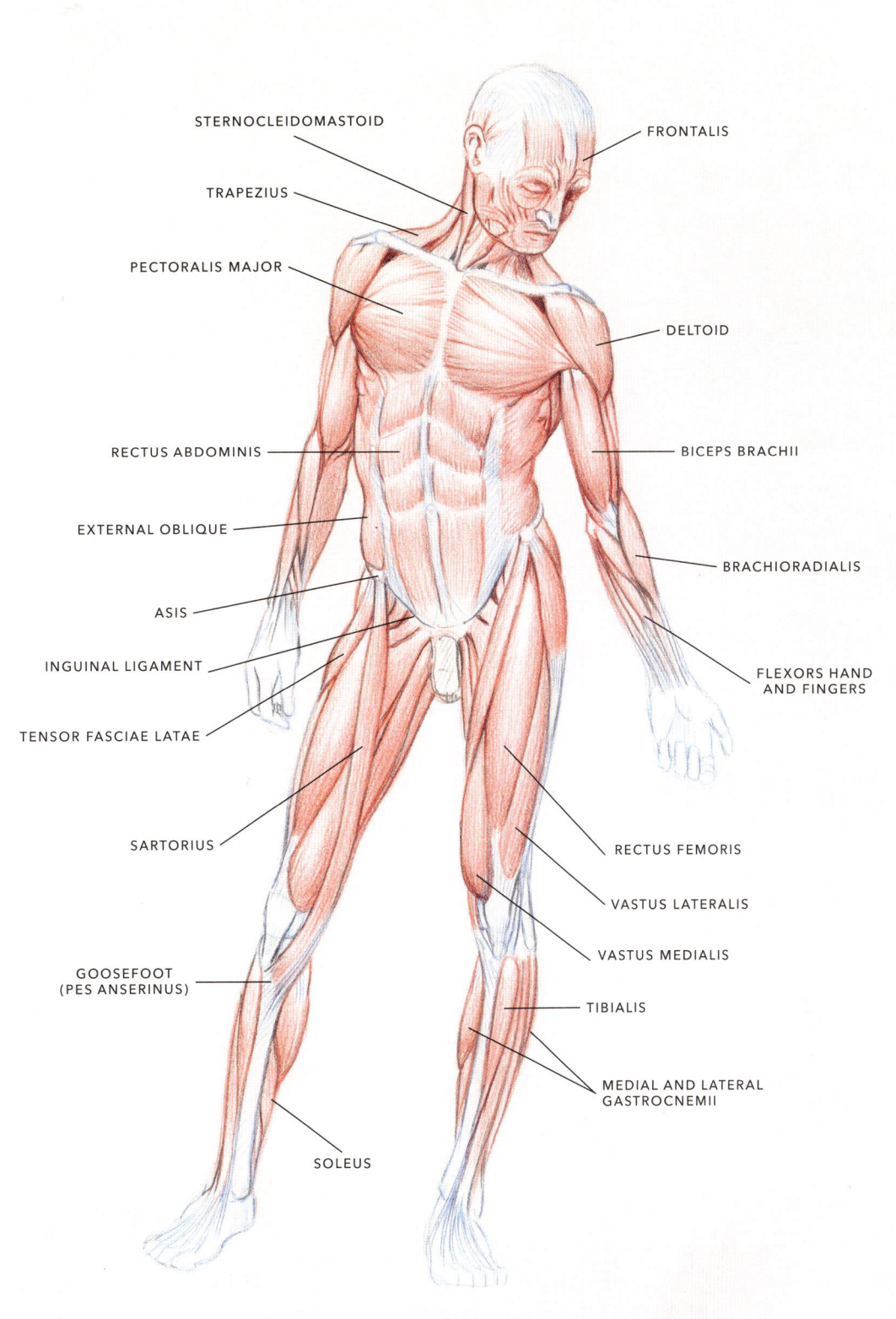

STERNOCLEIDOMASTOID

FRONTALIS

TRAPEZIUS

PECTORALIS MAJOR

DELTOID

RECTUS ABDOMINIS

BICEPS BRACHII

EXTERNAL OBLIQUE

BRACHIORADIALIS

ASIS

INGUINAL LIGAMENT

FLEXORS HAND
AND FINGERS

TENSOR FASCIAE LATAE

SARTORIUS

RECTUS FEMORIS

VASTUS LATERALIS

VASTUS MEDIALIS

GOOSEFOOT
(PES ANSERINUS)

TIBIALIS

MEDIAL AND LATERAL
GASTROCNEMII

SOLEUS

FEMALE FIGURE, FRONT VIEW

The poses of the Spanish model Vilidian Vilks are creative, dynamic, and often quite beautiful. Many are inspired by the works of artists like Egon Schiele, whom she freely interprets. Like Andrea, Vilidian also travels extensively for in-person posing sessions, and she, too, has online sites at both Instagram and Patreon.

For the following exercises, I asked Vilidian for some relatively tame poses. Follow the same steps as for the previous exercise to create the drawings for this sequence.

STEP 1

COPY THE PHOTO

Copy the reference image, identifying and using the landmarks and the main muscular groups to ensure your drawing's accuracy.

STEP 2

DRAW THE SKELETON

Reconstruct the skeletal structure and add the arrows showing the position and direction of the muscles.

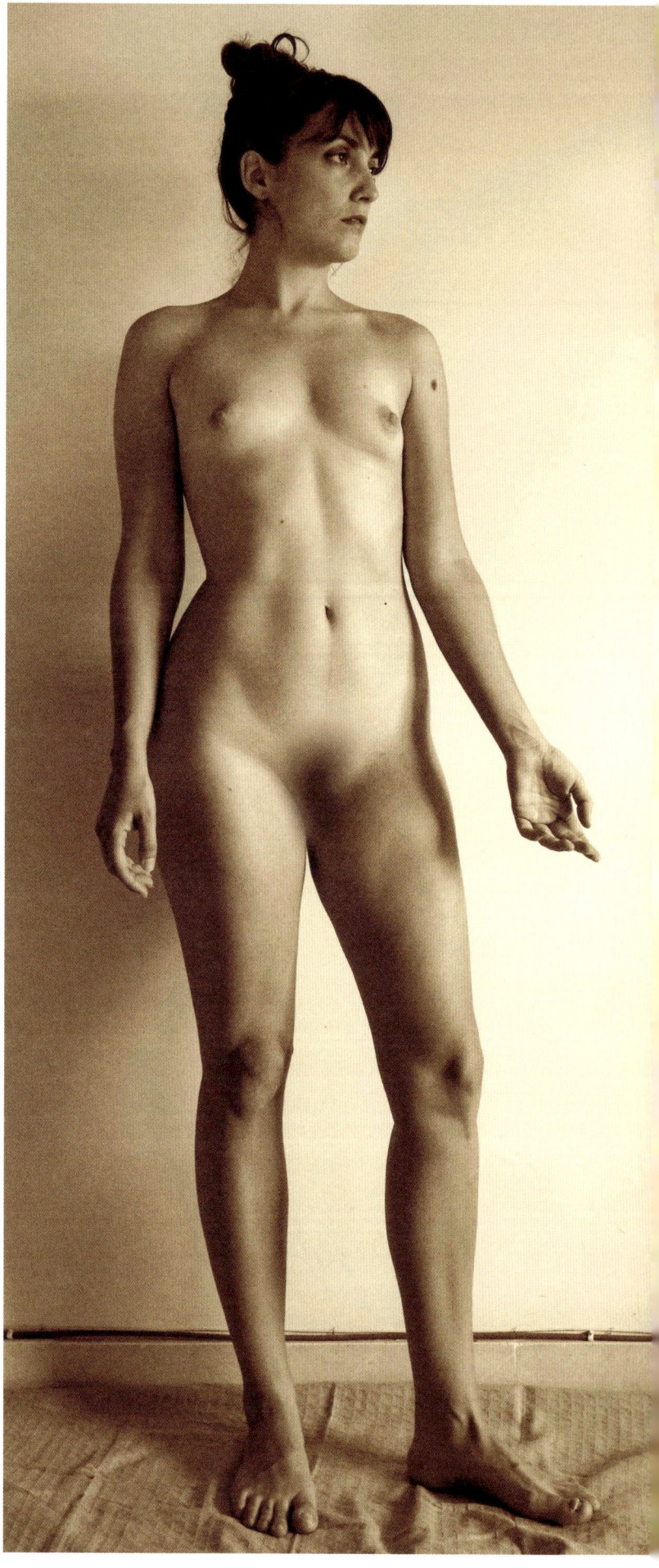

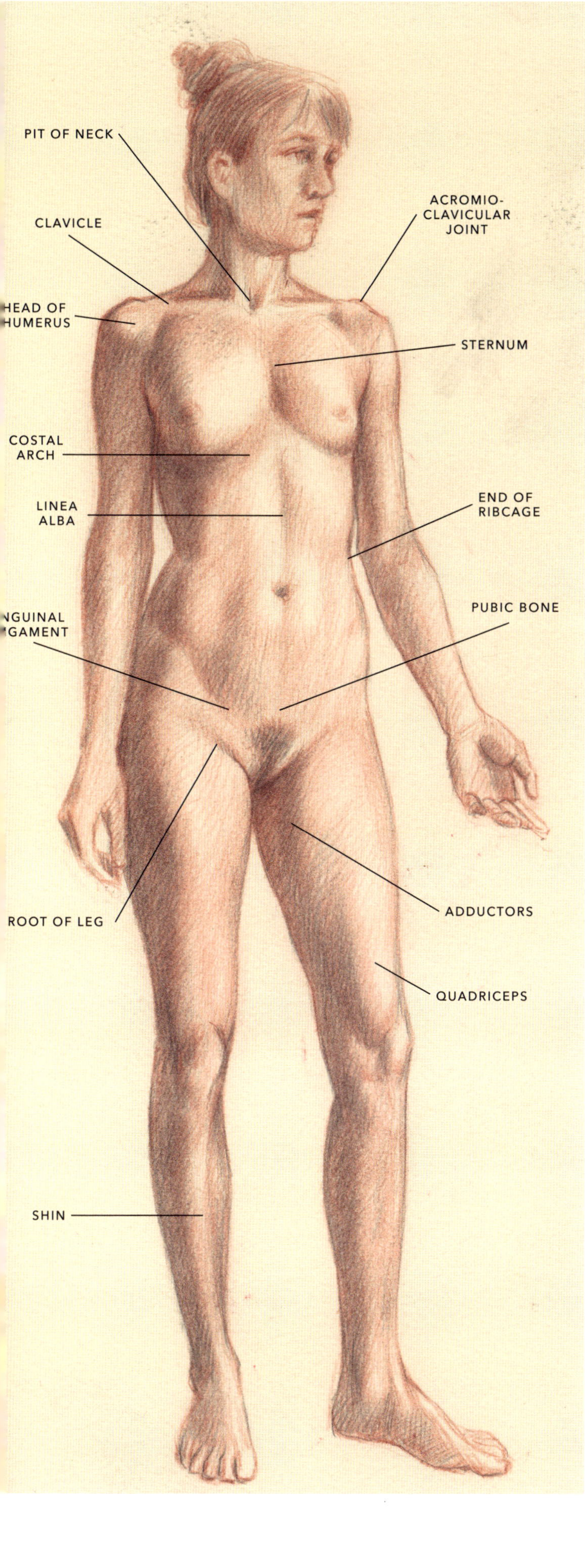

PIT OF NECK

CLAVICLE

HEAD OF
HUMERUS

COSTAL
ARCH

LINEA
ALBA

NGUINAL
GAMENT

ROOT OF LEG

SHIN

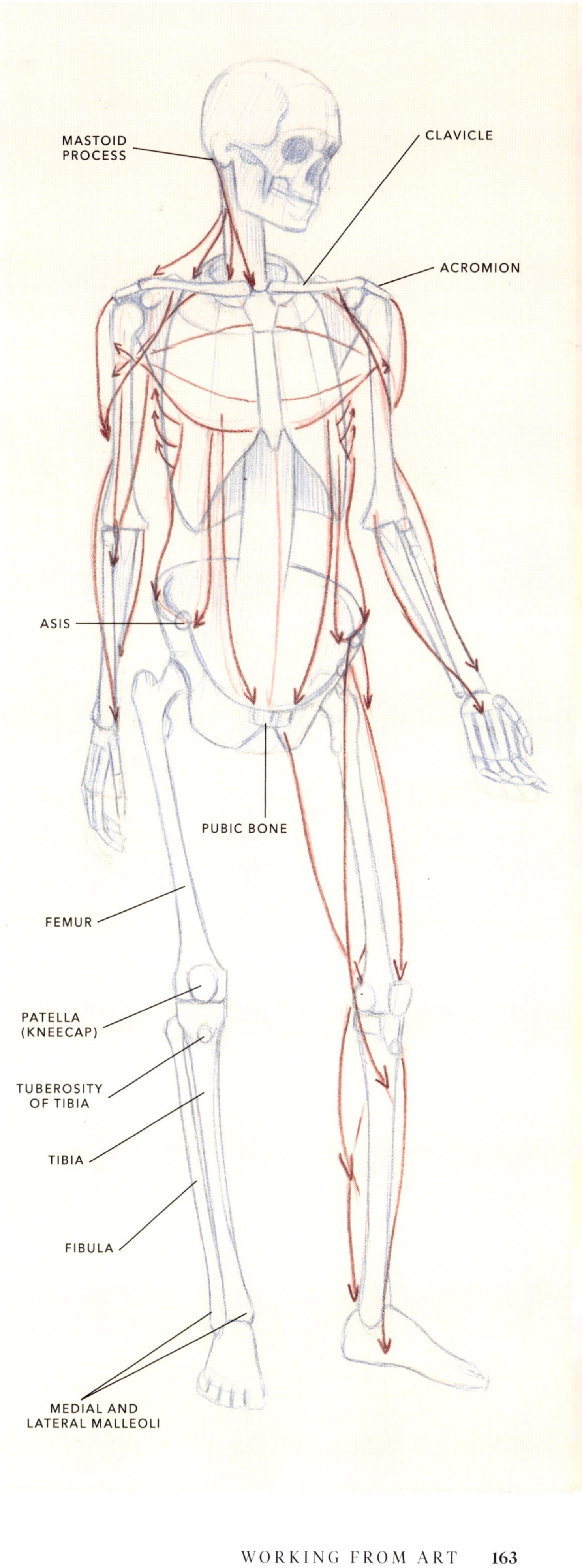

ACROMIO-
CLAVICULAR
JOINT

STERNUM

END OF
RIBCAGE

PUBIC BONE

ADDUCTORS

QUADRICEPS

MASTOID
PROCESS

ASIS

PUBIC BONE

FEMUR

PATELLA
(KNEECAP)

TUBEROSITY
OF TIBIA

TIBIA

FIBULA

MEDIAL AND
LATERAL MALLEOLI

CLAVICLE

ACROMION

STEP 3

ADD THE MUSCULAR VOLUMES

Informed by the previous step, where the directions of the muscles are shown, add the muscular volumes to this figure.

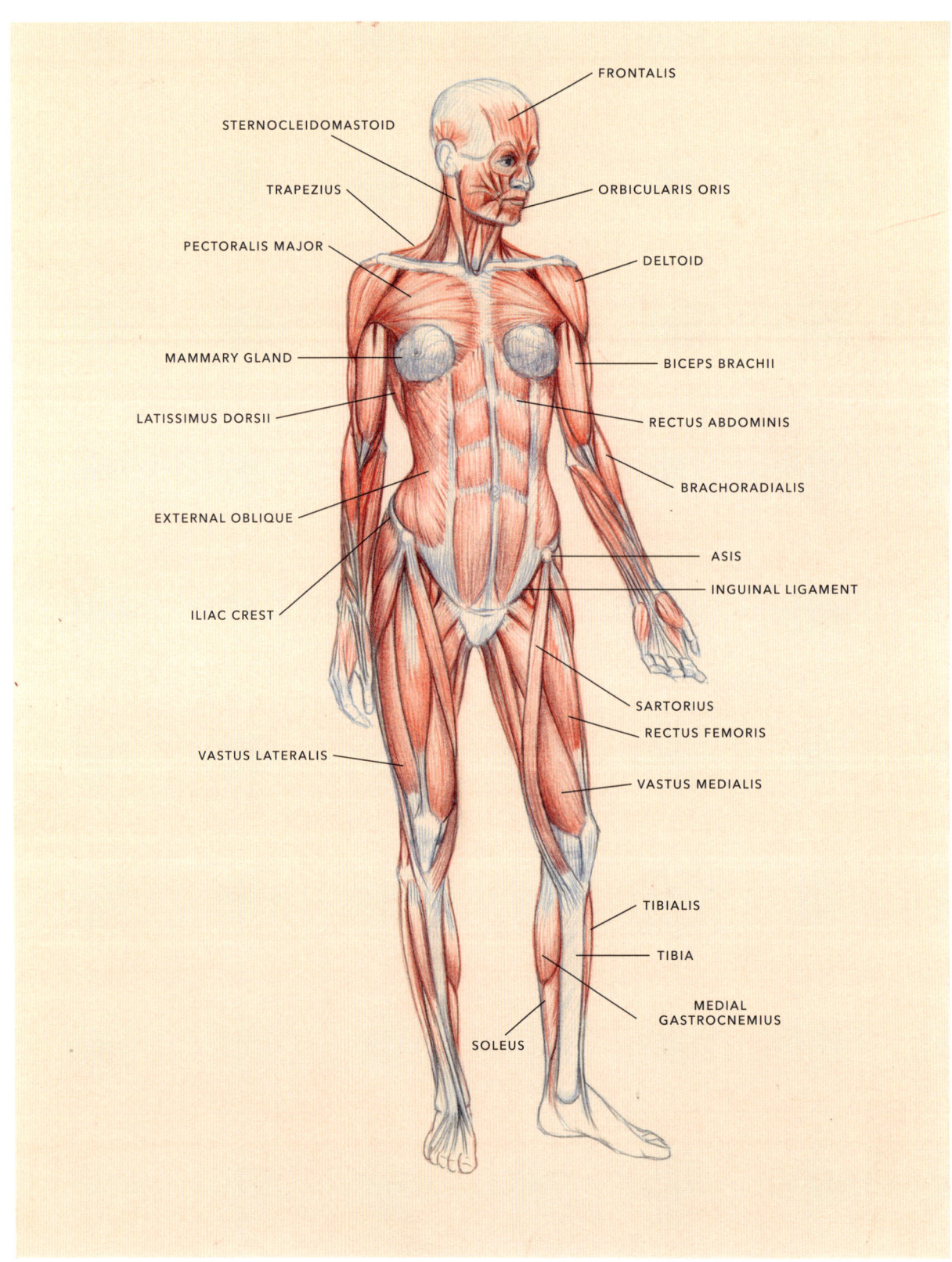

FRONTALIS

STERNOCLEIDOMASTOID

TRAPEZIUS

ORBICULARIS ORIS

PECTORALIS MAJOR

DELTOID

MAMMARY GLAND

BICEPS BRACHII

LATISSIMUS DORSII

RECTUS ABDOMINIS

BRACHORADIALIS

EXTERNAL OBLIQUE

ASIS

INGUINAL LIGAMENT

ILIAC CREST

SARTORIUS

RECTUS FEMORIS

VASTUS LATERALIS

VASTUS MEDIALIS

TIBIALIS

TIBIA

MEDIAL
GASTROCNEMIUS

SOLEUS

FEMALE FIGURE, BACK VIEW

Vilidian's softer forms provide a very good complement to the muscular definition of Andrea's physique. This posterior view shows very clearly the typical difference in width between the ribcage and pelvis in women, where the ribcage is usually narrower than the pelvis. Note how visible the dimples of the PSIS and the triangle of the sacrum below the spine are in this image.

STEP 1

COPY THE PHOTO

Copy the reference photo, identifying and labeling the landmarks and main muscular groups seen in the image.

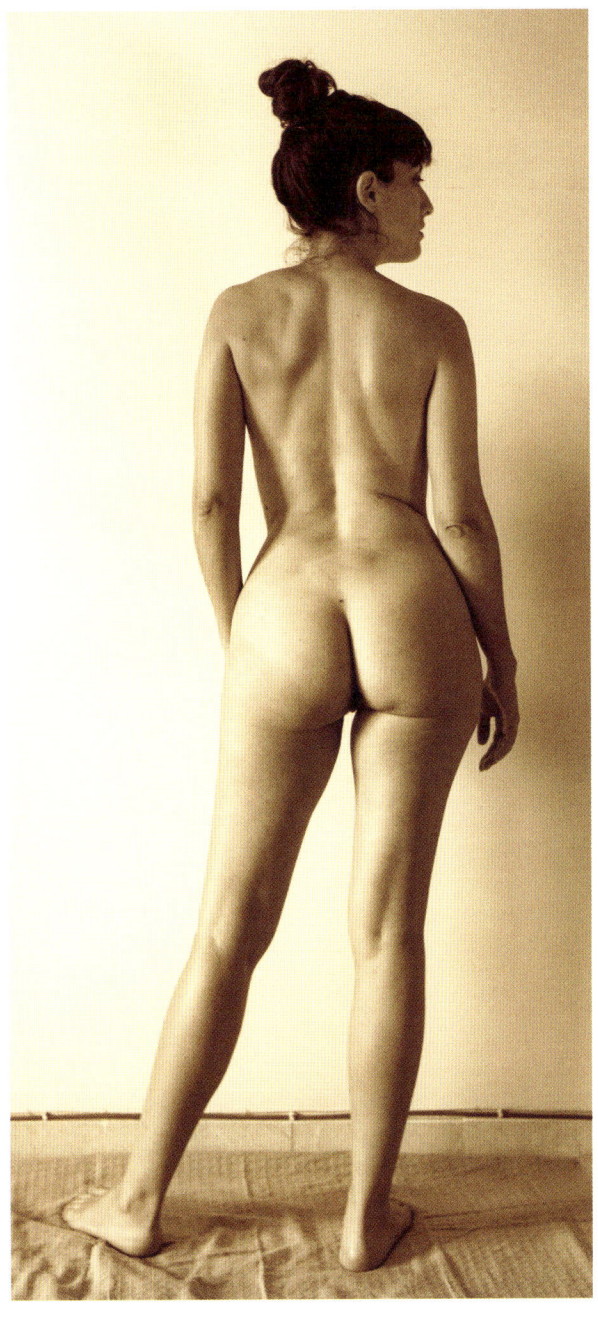

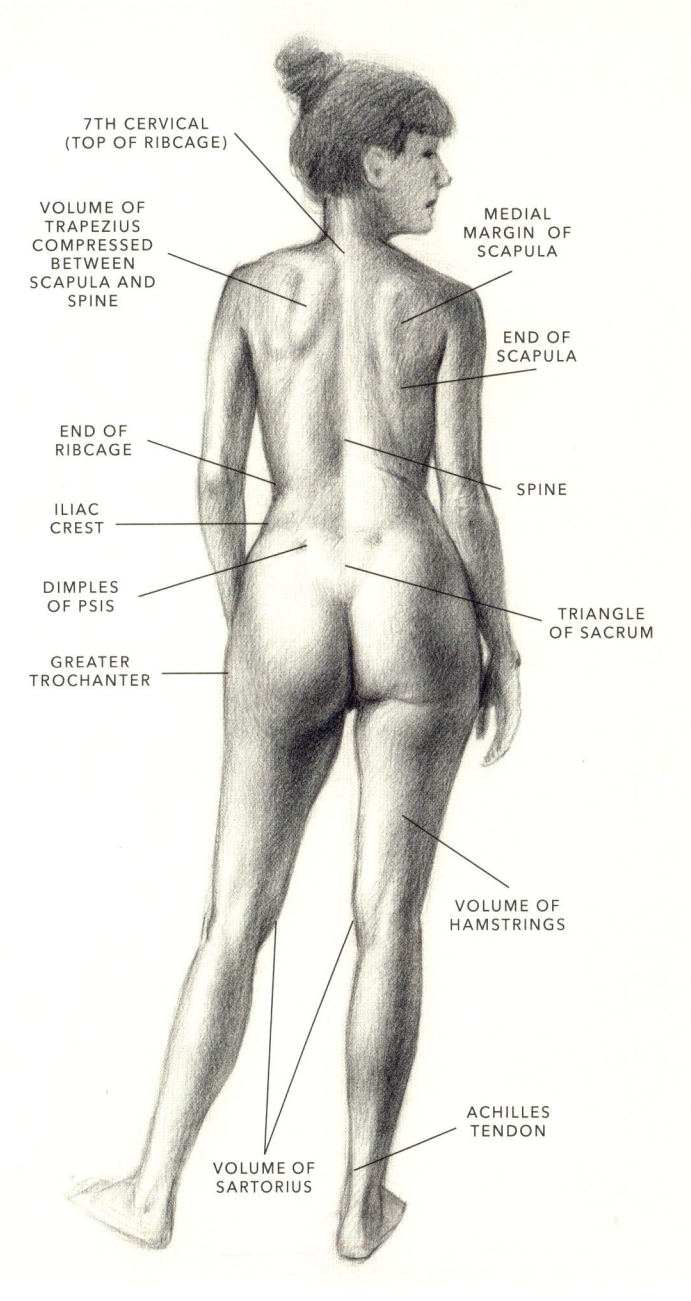

STEP 2

DRAW THE SKELETON

Reconstruct the skeletal structure
and add the arrows showing the
muscles' position and direction.

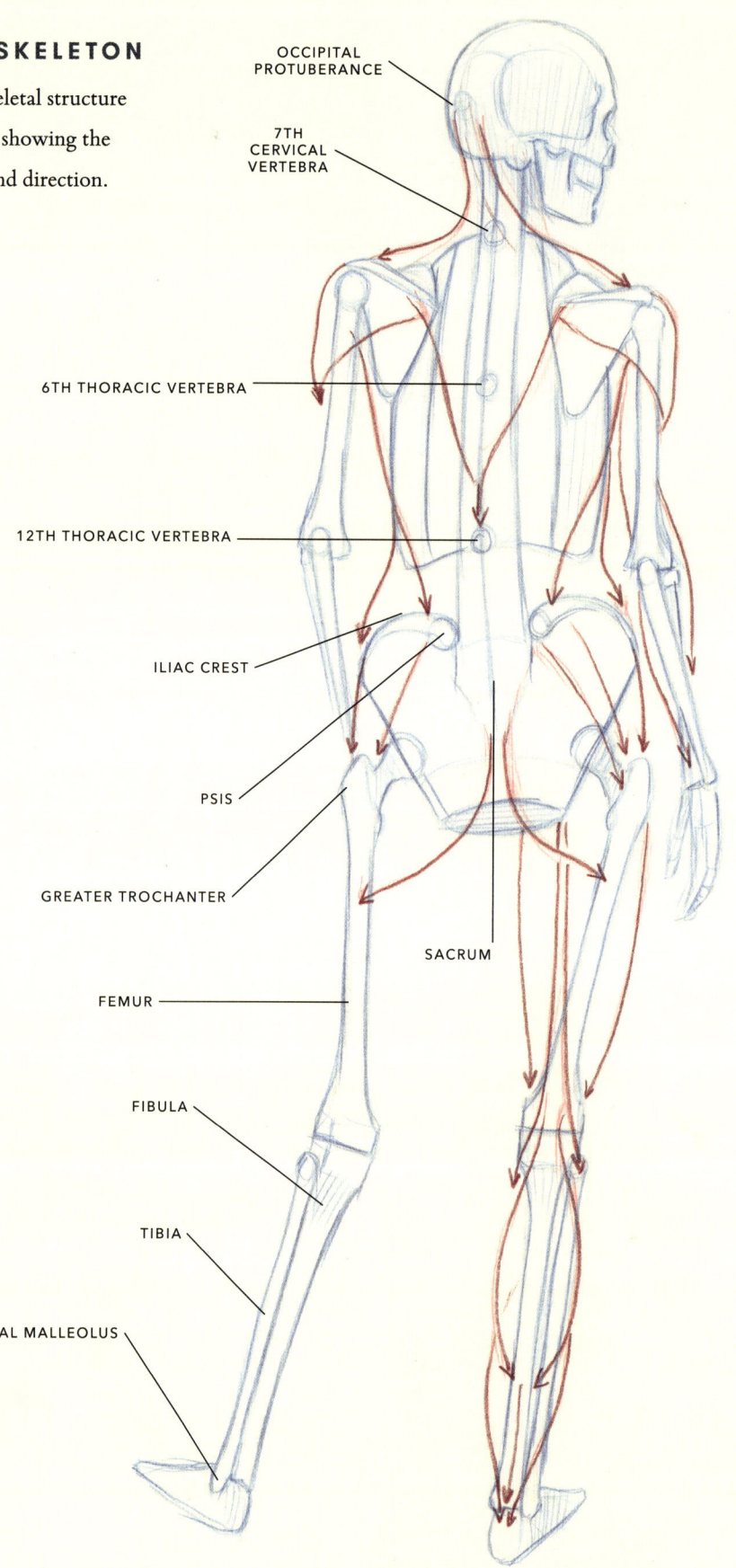

OCCIPITAL
PROTUBERANCE

7TH
CERVICAL
VERTEBRA

6TH THORACIC VERTEBRA

12TH THORACIC VERTEBRA

ILIAC CREST

PSIS

GREATER TROCHANTER

SACRUM

FEMUR

FIBULA

TIBIA

LATERAL MALLEOLUS

STEP 3

ADD THE MUSCULAR VOLUMES

Informed by the previous step, where the directions of the muscles are shown, add the muscular volumes to this figure.

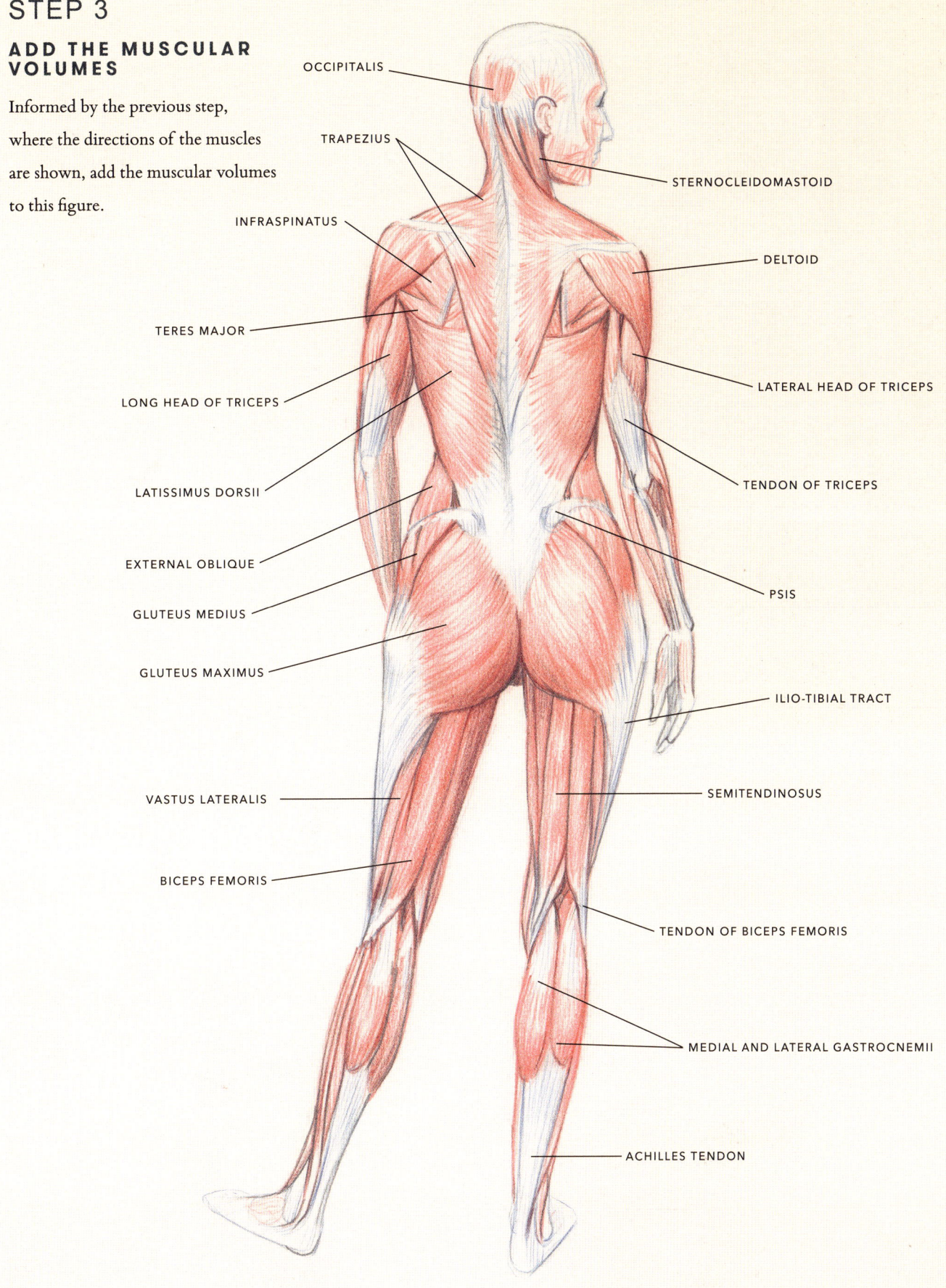

OCCIPITALIS

TRAPEZIUS

INFRASPINATUS

TERES MAJOR

LONG HEAD OF TRICEPS

LATISSIMUS DORSII

EXTERNAL OBLIQUE

GLUTEUS MEDIUS

GLUTEUS MAXIMUS

VASTUS LATERALIS

BICEPS FEMORIS

STERNOCLEIDOMASTOID

DELTOID

LATERAL HEAD OF TRICEPS

TENDON OF TRICEPS

PSIS

ILIO-TIBIAL TRACT

SEMITENDINOSUS

TENDON OF BICEPS FEMORIS

MEDIAL AND LATERAL GASTROCNEMII

ACHILLES TENDON

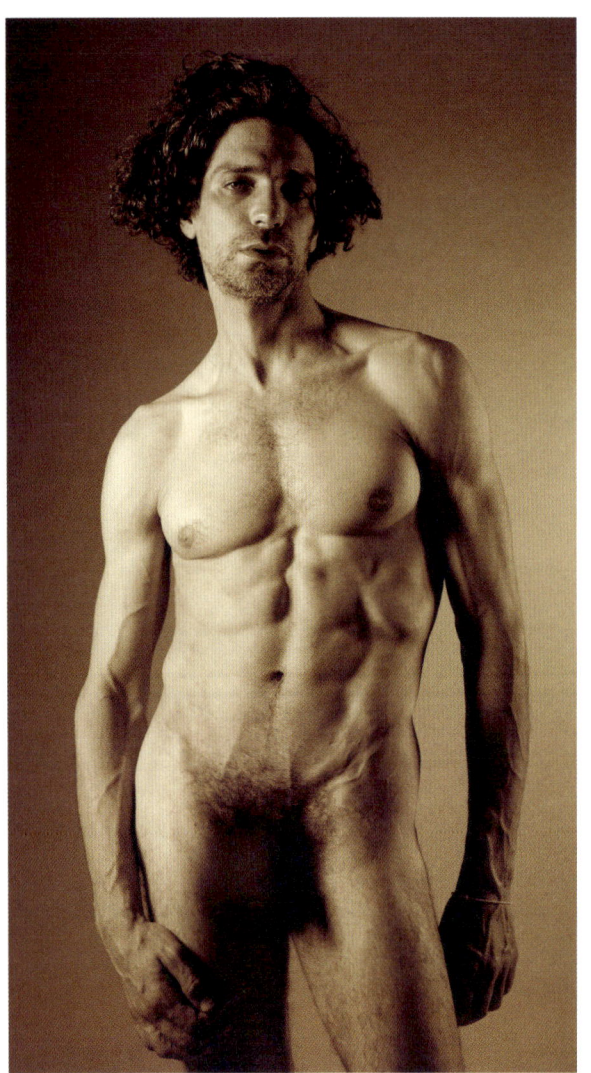

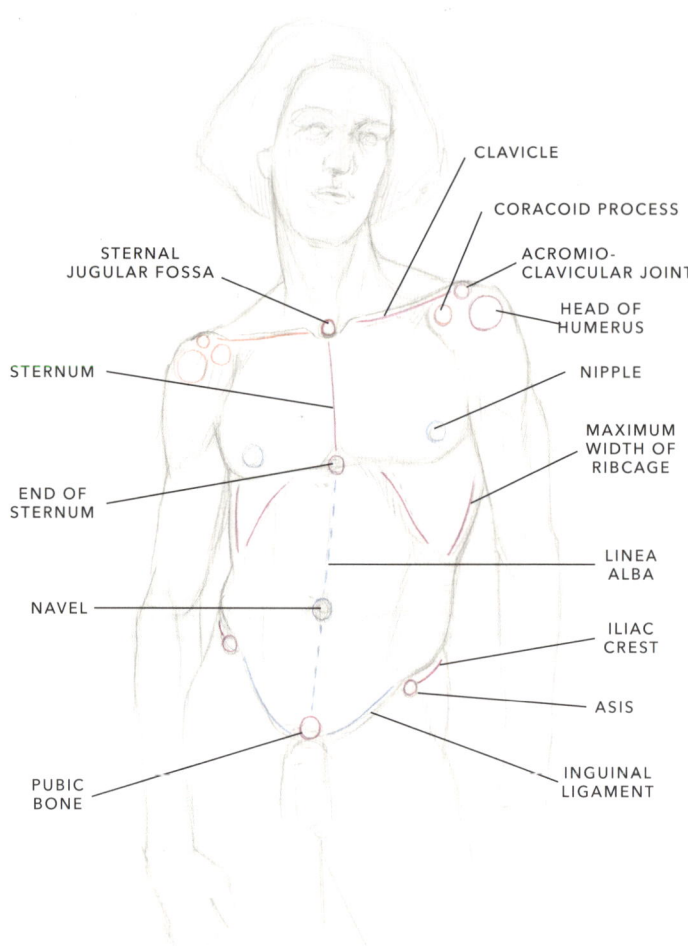

CLAVICLE

CORACOID PROCESS

STERNAL
JUGULAR FOSSA

ACROMIO-
CLAVICULAR JOINT

HEAD OF
HUMERUS

STERNUM

NIPPLE

MAXIMUM
WIDTH OF
RIBCAGE

END OF
STERNUM

LINEA
ALBA

NAVEL

ILIAC
CREST

ASIS

PUBIC
BONE

INGUINAL
LIGAMENT

EXERCISE 3.13

MALE TORSO, FRONT VIEW

This exercise focuses on the front view of the torso. The image offers a clearer view
of details such as the less-visible landmarks and the smaller muscles, leading to a more
accurate description of the muscular forms.

STEP 1

COPY THE PHOTO

Start by creating an accurate line drawing of the figure, and mark the skeletal and soft
landmarks, as shown.

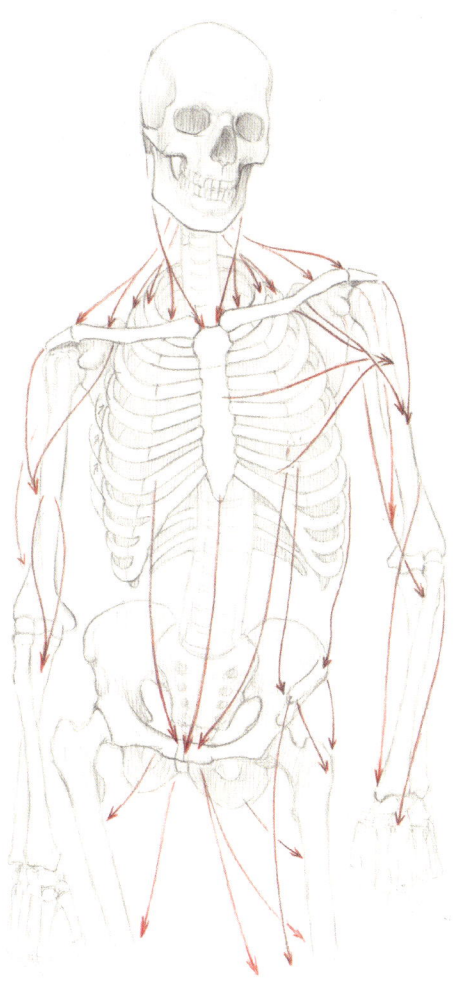
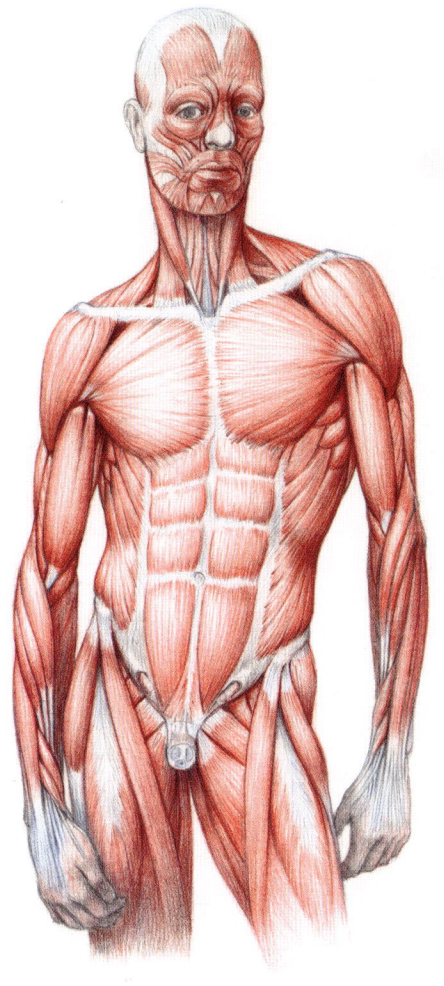

STEP 2

DRAW THE SKELETON

Next, layer a sheet of tracing paper over the line drawing, and, guided by the land-marks, recreate the skeleton. Add the arrows for the directions of the muscles, as shown in the image.

STEP 3

ADD THE MUSCLES

Now place a sheet of tracing paper over the skeleton and draw the muscles over it, using the image here as a reference. You have now created a flip chart with overlapping layers, one for the external forms and landmarks, one for the skeleton, one for the muscle.

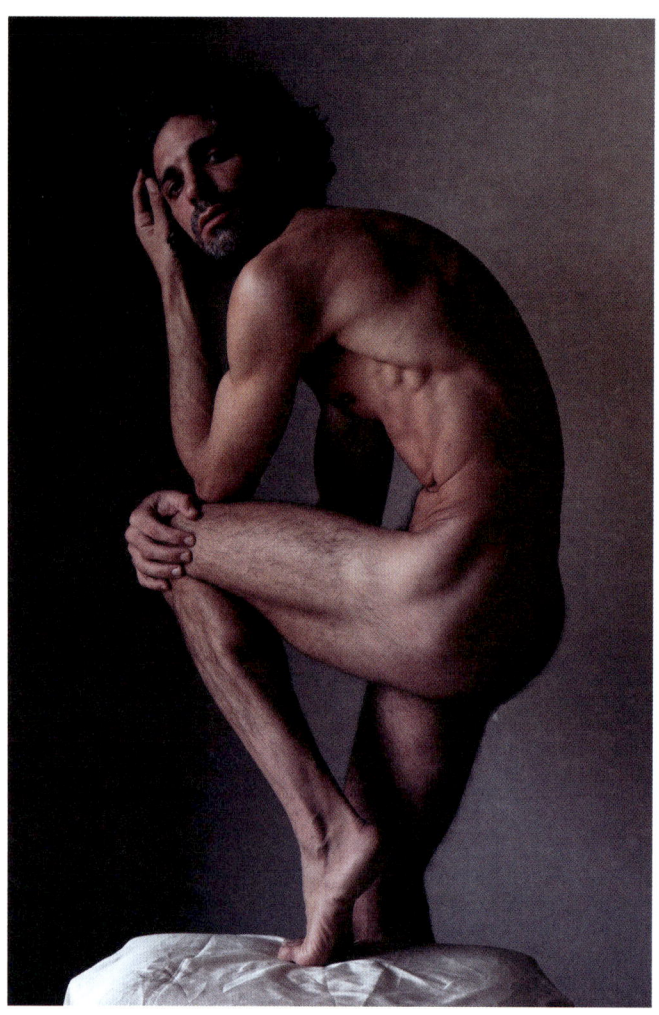
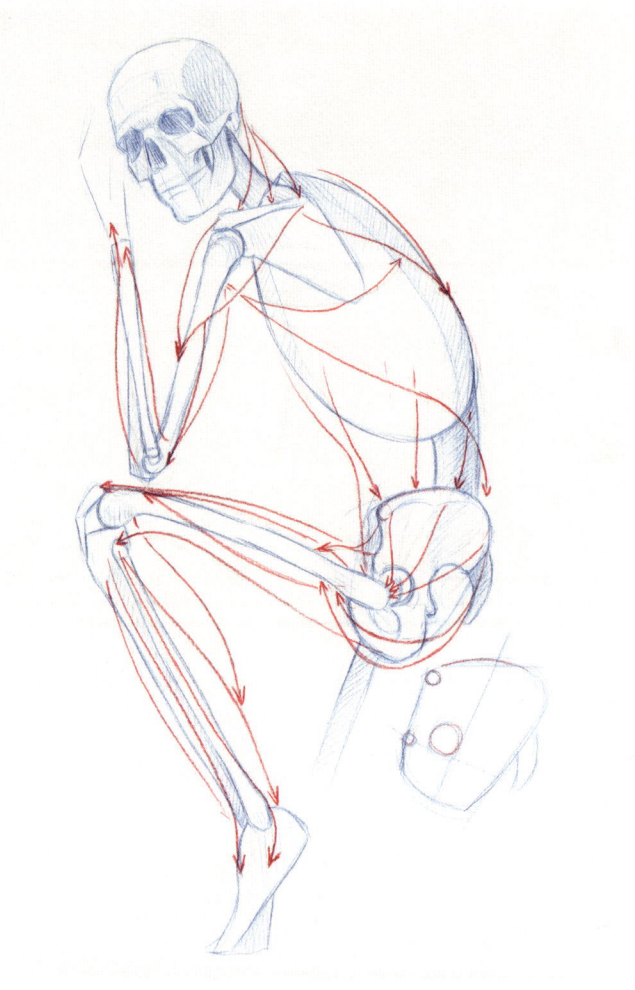

EXERCISE 3.14

MALE FIGURE, DYNAMIC SIDE VIEW

This exercise concludes level 3. Despite the challenging pose, Andrea's muscular definition will make it relatively easy for you to find landmarks. You'll recreate the skeleton and position the muscles over it, using the same approach as for the previous two exercises. And you may again draw on sheets of tracing paper to produce a "flip chart" of the layers.

STEP 1

LOCATE THE LANDMARKS

Identify the landmarks on this reference image to extrapolate the skeleton (step 2).

STEP 2

DRAW THE SKELETON

Now draw the skeletal structure as well as the lines of direction of the muscular volumes.

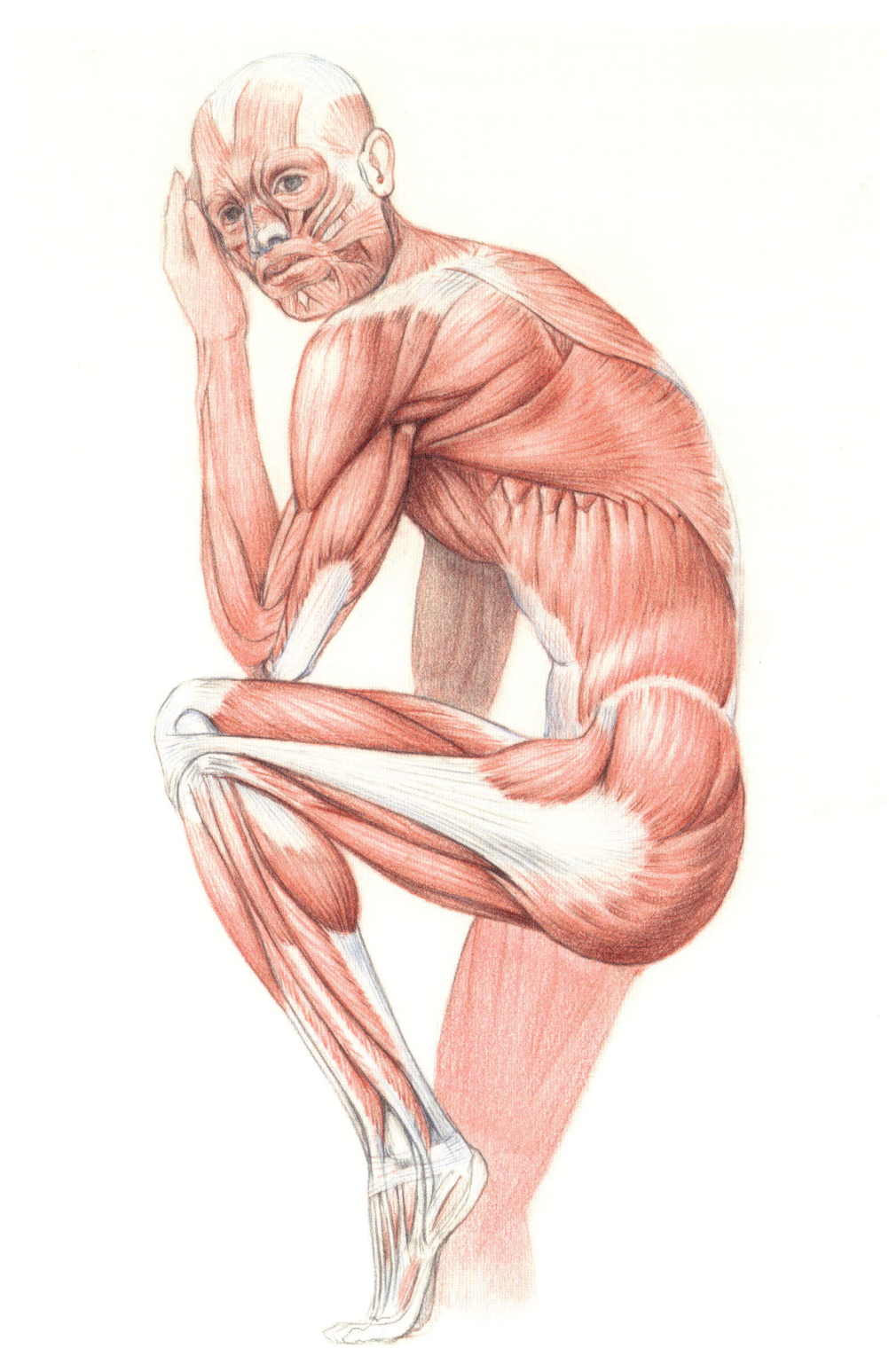

STEP 3

ADD THE MUSCLES

Finally, layer the muscles over the skeleton.

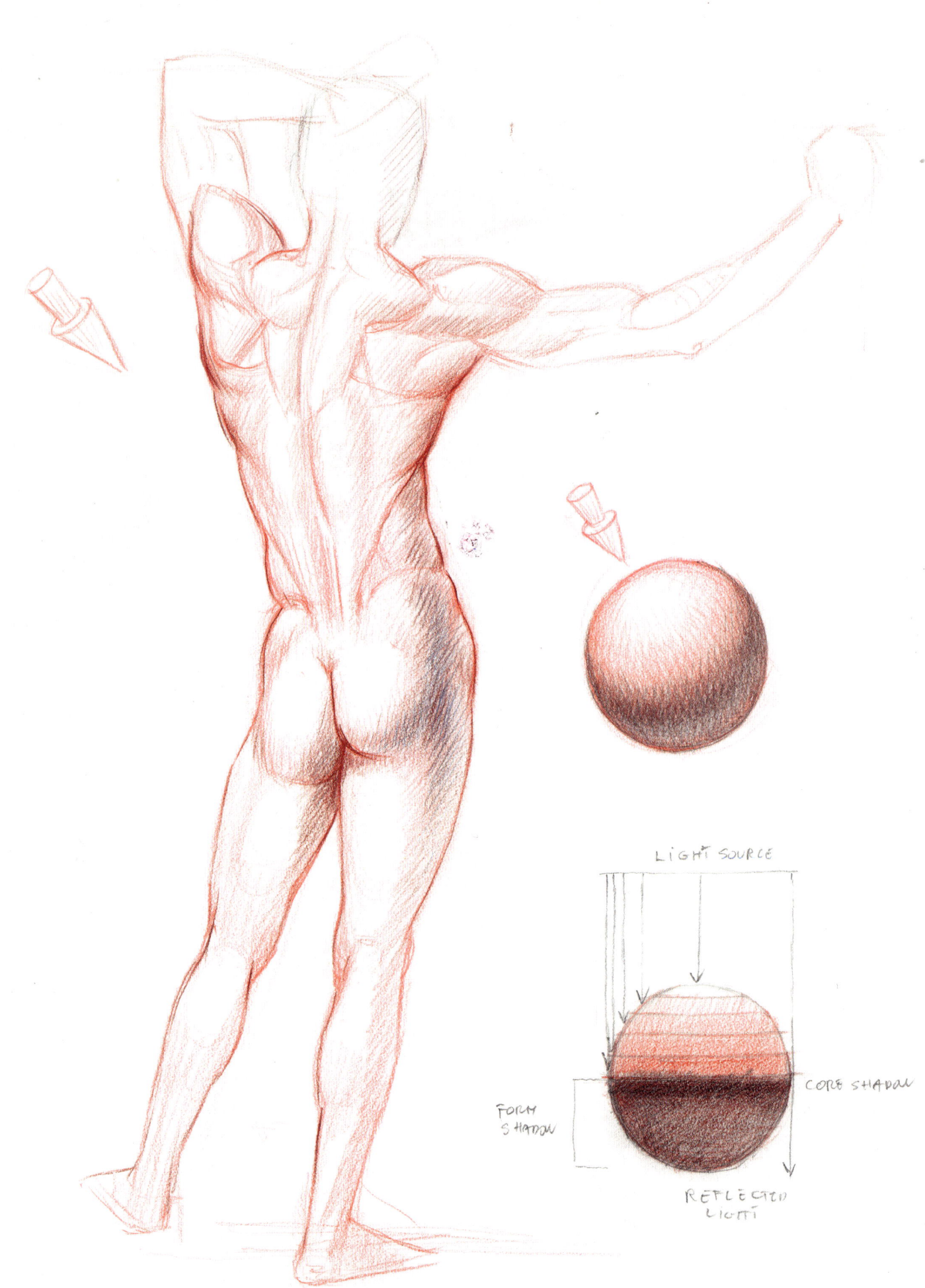

LIGHT SOURCE

FORM
SHADOW

CORE SHADOW

REFLECTED
LIGHT

CHAPTER 4

MEASURING AND DRAWING TECHNIQUES

Each drawing technique approaches a subject differently, focusing, for example, on contour, tonal range, structure, color balance, or another attribute. Practicing and mastering a number of techniques will improve your understanding of the subject and contribute to your aesthetic development and the technical refinement of your work.

The exercises that follow focus on methods that I consider indispensable for figure drawing and, in fact, drawing in general: graphite on white paper, charcoal and chalk on toned paper, the reduction technique, and the *trois crayons* technique.

Using graphite on white paper provides excellent practice for gradually learning to develop a tonal range from white to black, one value at the time. With this technique, each value has to be carefully built and properly related to the other values in the drawing.

Practice and master different techniques

When drawing on toned paper, you need to find the values in the subject that are darker than the paper, lighter than the paper, and the same as the paper. You'll use charcoal for values that are darker than the paper and white chalk for values lighter than the paper; values that are the same as the paper's value are left unmarked.

With the reduction technique, you start with a sheet of paper, white or toned, that has been smeared with charcoal; you then proceed to lift the charcoal from the paper with a chamois, a kneaded eraser, or another erasing tool, creating a range of values darkest to lightest. This approach is the opposite of working with graphite on white paper.

The *trois crayons* technique is based on the use of three colors: red earth, black, and white on toned paper. With this technique, you can intervene on the chroma, value, tint, and tone of the colors.

LEVEL 1

MEASURING EXERCISES

The exercises here and in the following levels will improve your knowledge of anatomy and your skill in figure drawing by presenting a range of reference images, including foreshortened and dynamic poses. Some of the images add to the complexity through strong light-shadow contrast.

EXERCISE 4.1
MEASURING STANDING FIGURES

Follow the steps of this sequence to practice measuring a standing figure, using the proportional relationships between head and body.

STEP 1
DRAW THE STEREOMETRIC VOLUMES

Draw the figure on the left as a set of stereometric volumes, using the typical ratio 1:7½ to measure the segments. The figure on the right shows the specific proportions an actual live model may have, in this case about 1:7¾. Copying the right-hand figure will help you understand how to adapt the typical proportional relationships to the specific proportions an actual model may have.

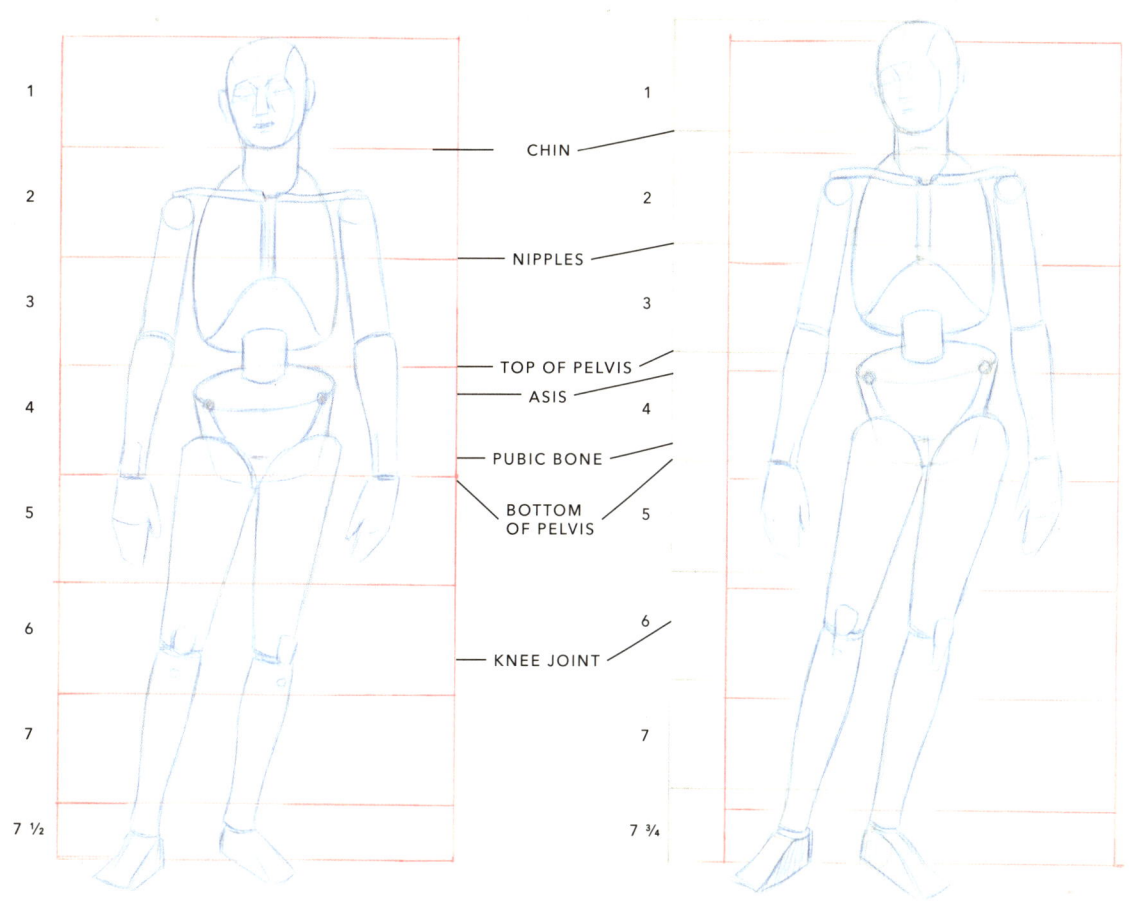

CHIN

NIPPLES

TOP OF PELVIS

ASIS

PUBIC BONE

BOTTOM OF PELVIS

KNEE JOINT

STEP 2

FROM STEREOMETRY TO REALISTIC FORM

Develop the stereometric volumes into more realistic forms. Break down the outlines of the main muscular volumes into shorter, measurable segments to impart a more realistic appearance to the figure.

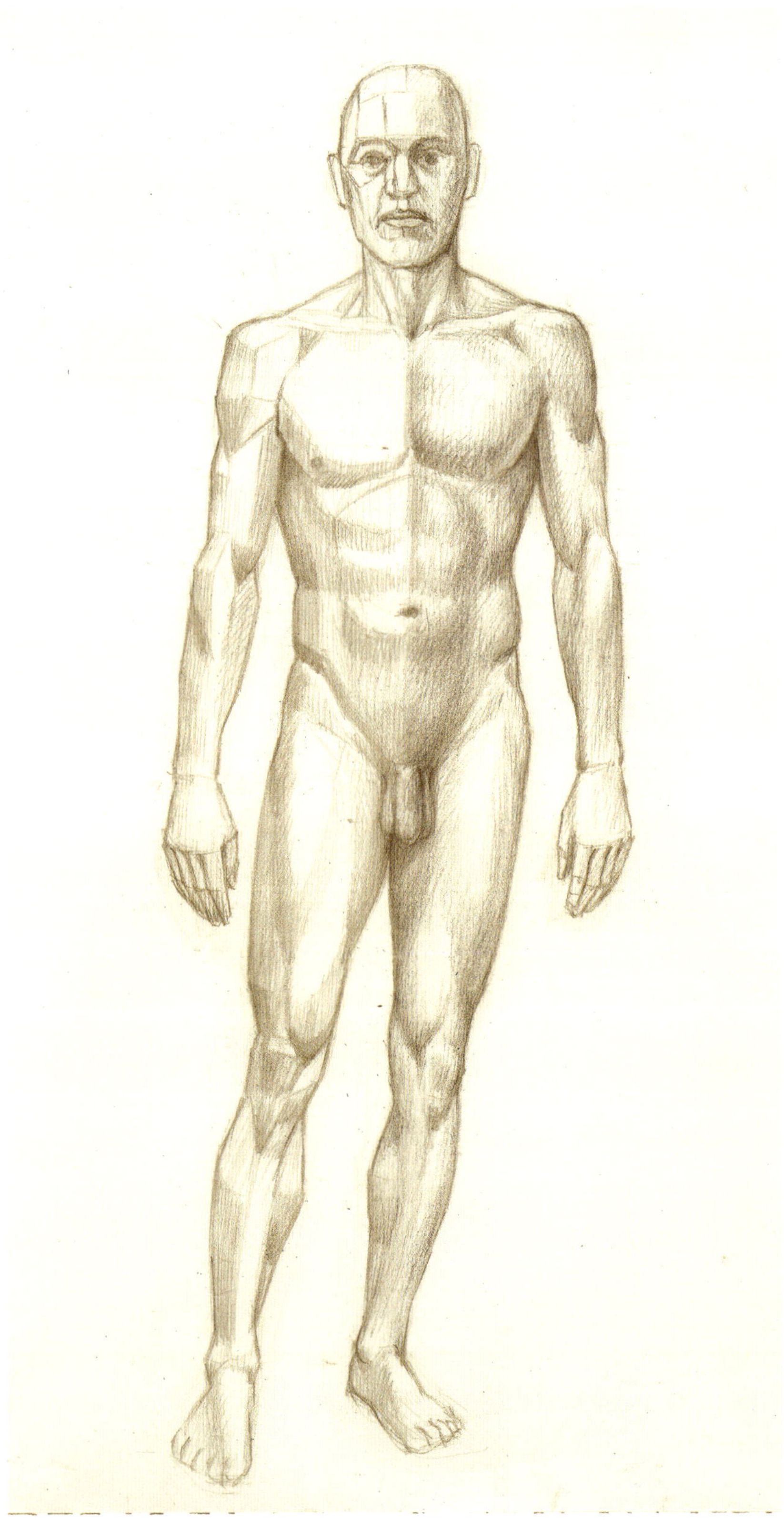

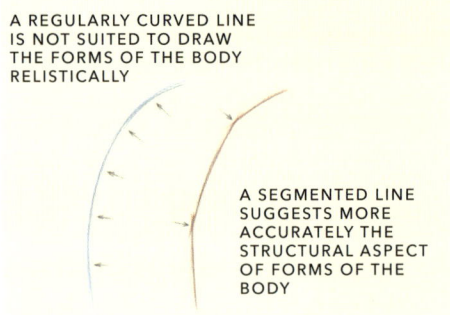

A REGULARLY CURVED LINE IS NOT SUITED TO DRAW THE FORMS OF THE BODY RELISTICALLY

A SEGMENTED LINE SUGGESTS MORE ACCURATELY THE STRUCTURAL ASPECT OF FORMS OF THE BODY

MULTIFACETED CURVES

When rendering the volumes of the body, avoid smoothly curving lines because they tend to create the impression of even pressure from the inside of the form (as might be the case, for example, with swelling caused by inflammation). Think of the muscles as multifaceted geometric solids, and draw the various planes of these solids as gently curved surfaces connecting with other gently curved surfaces. The subtle difference can be seen in the illustration above.

The points where the planes connect can be smoothed out to achieve a more realistic effect. In the figure drawing at left, I exaggerated this concept for clarity: the drawing shows the progression from body forms rendered as multifaceted geometric solids (left side of the drawing) to smoother and rounder forms, which still retain their geometric structural characteristics (right side of the drawing).

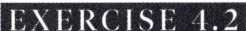

EXERCISE 4.2
MEASURING NONSTANDING FIGURES

The method used to measure this sitting figure can be applied to any other nonstanding pose. As you copy this drawing, notice how the measure of the head can be used to establish a comparison with the various parts of the figure even though this is not a standing pose. When the head is not visible, you can use any other part of the body as the basic unit of measure.

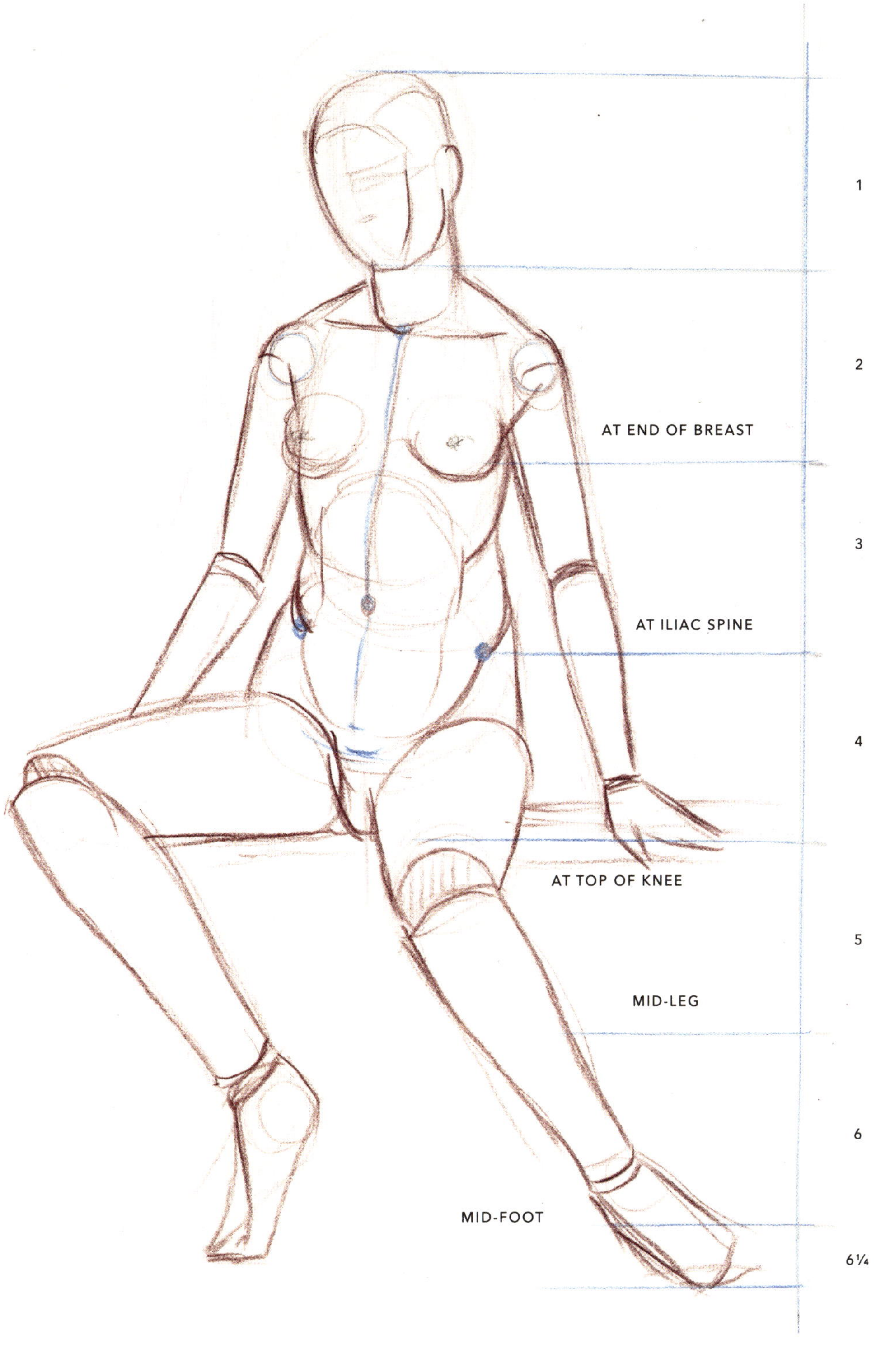

1

2

AT END OF BREAST

3

AT ILIAC SPINE

4

AT TOP OF KNEE

5

MID-LEG

6

MID-FOOT

6¼

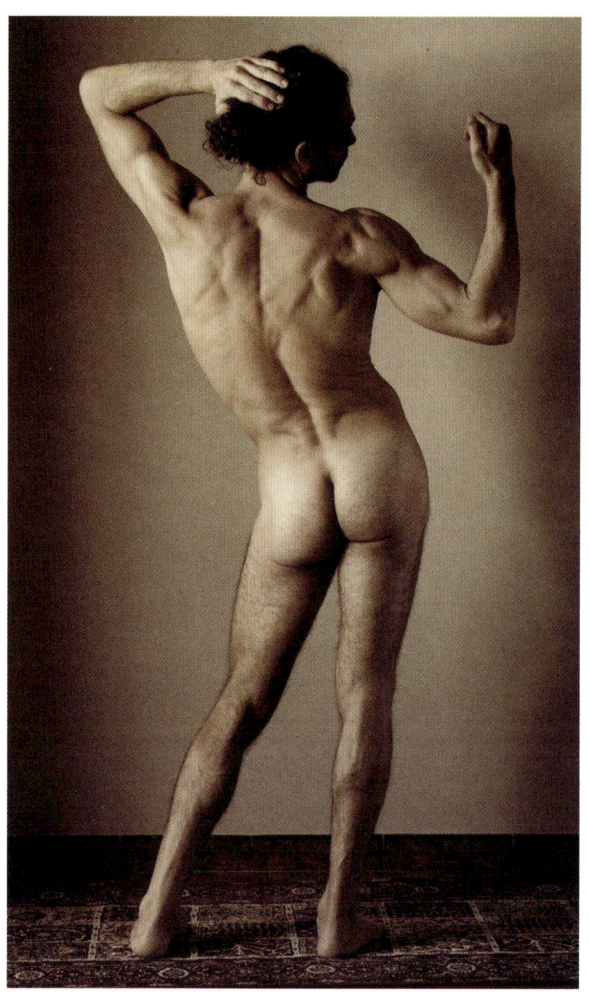

EXERCISE 4.3
FLORENTINE STRUCTURAL SYSTEM, MALE FIGURE, BACK VIEW

This exercise continues your practice with the Florentine Structural System begun in chapter 3, but it increases the dynamism of the figure and the level of structural and anatomical detail. This method can also be thought of as a "reverse dissection."

STEP 1

COPY THE REFERENCE IMAGE

Copy the reference image using the proportional relationships method described in exercise 4.1. Remember to also use vertical and horizontal alignments, the angular profile of the form, and the line of the center of gravity. Find the landmarks, too.

STEP 2

RECONSTRUCT THE SKELETON

Reconstruct the skeleton using the landmarks identified in step 1 and paying particular attention to the landmarks of the scapula, shoulder, and arm.

STEP 3

"FLAY" THE FIGURE

Draw the flayed (skinless) figure, adding the muscles directly on the drawing of the skeleton you just made or drawing the muscles on tracing paper positioned over the skeleton.

STEP 4

REDRAW THE REFERENCE IMAGE

Now redraw the reference image to create a figure drawing informed by the previous steps, which have given you a deeper understanding of the body's anatomical forms.

MATERIALS

Materials for this exercise include the following:

- Lightly toned paper of your choice (I used an 11 x 14 sheet of light tan paper from a pad of Stonehenge Colors.)
- Colored pencils (I use Faber-Castell Polychromos colored pencils in black, white, dark blue, and a red earth color such as India red, Pompeian red, or Venetian red.)
- Graphite pencil, grade HB (for step 1)

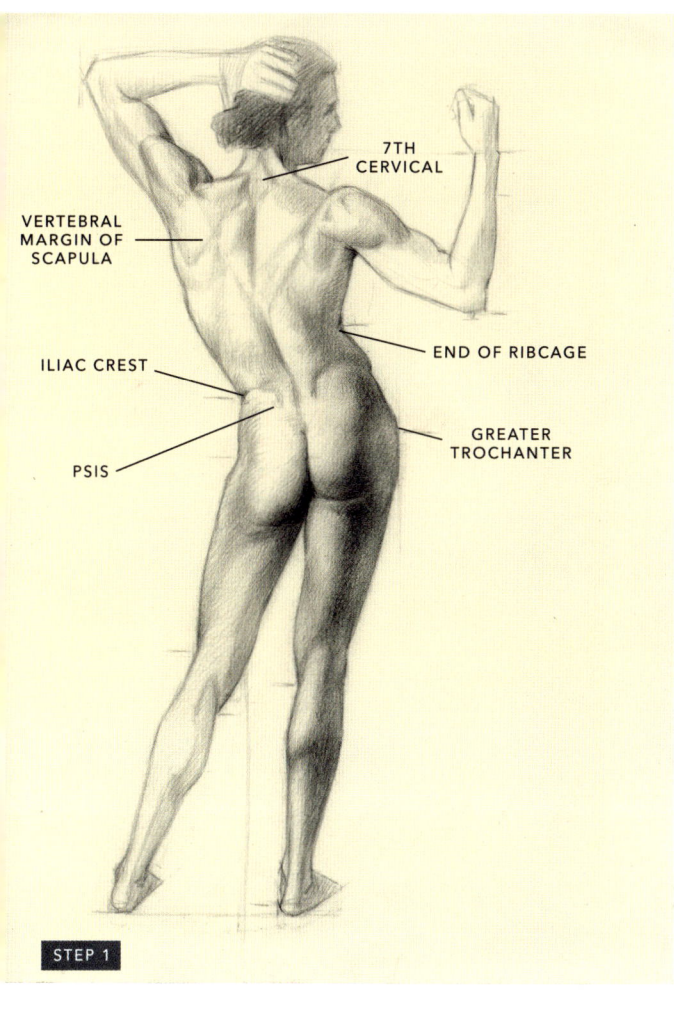

VERTEBRAL MARGIN OF SCAPULA

7TH CERVICAL

END OF RIBCAGE

ILIAC CREST

PSIS

GREATER TROCHANTER

STEP 1

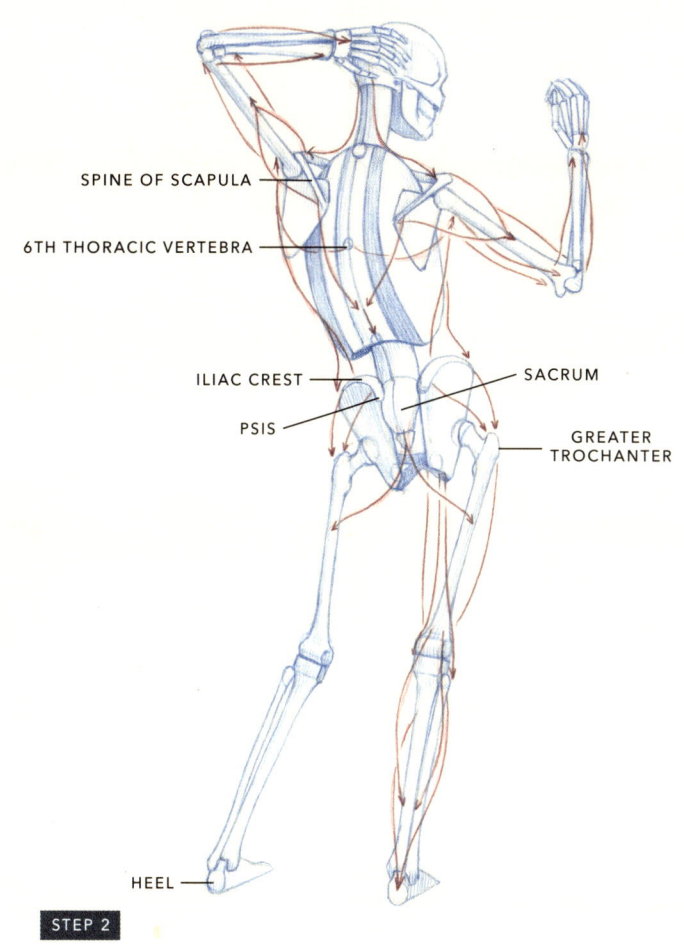

SPINE OF SCAPULA

6TH THORACIC VERTEBRA

ILIAC CREST

PSIS

SACRUM

GREATER TROCHANTER

HEEL

STEP 2

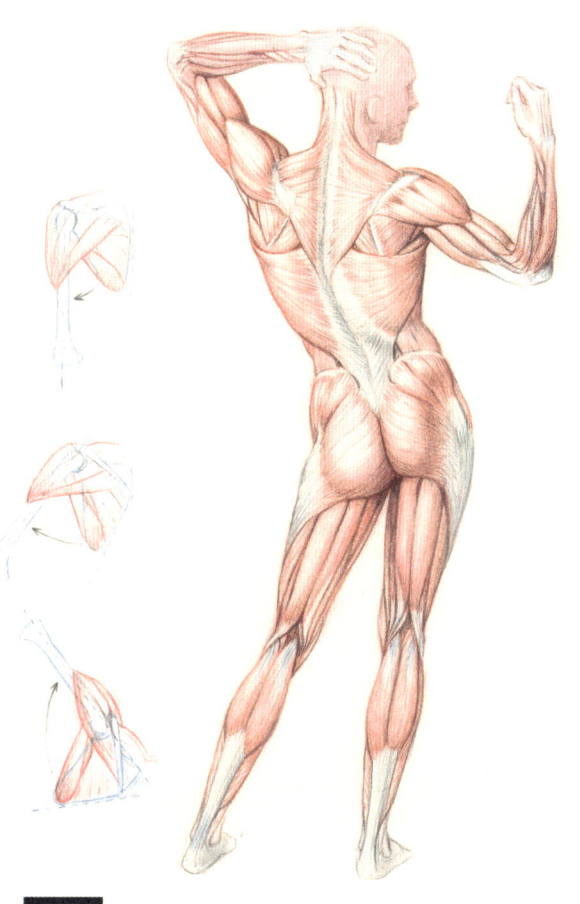

STEP 3

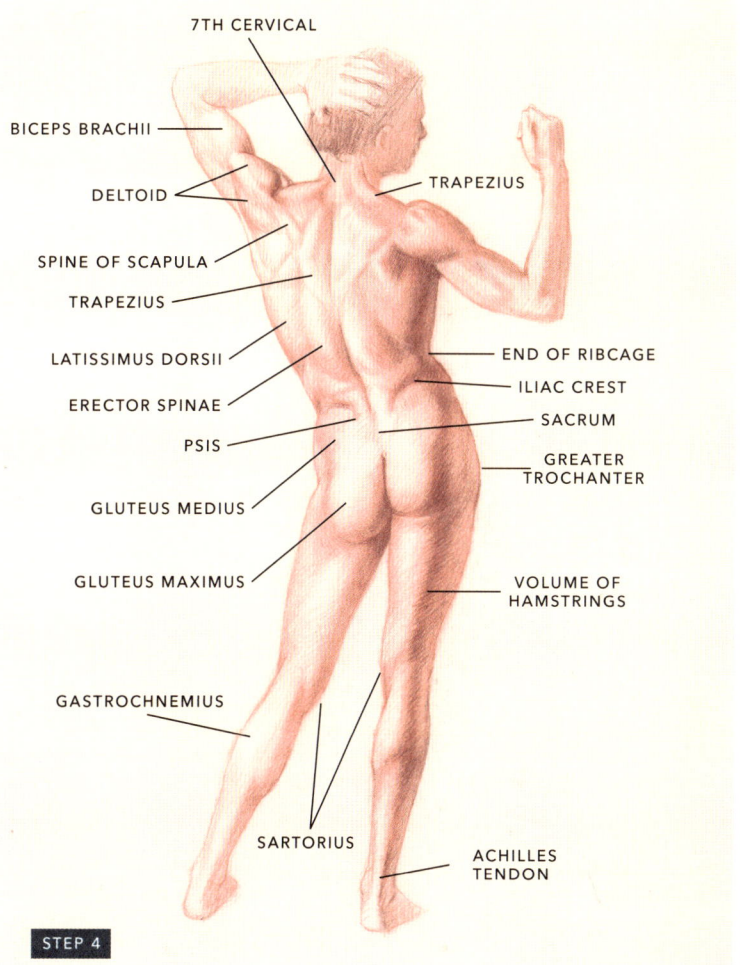

7TH CERVICAL

BICEPS BRACHII

DELTOID

SPINE OF SCAPULA

TRAPEZIUS

LATISSIMUS DORSII

ERECTOR SPINAE

PSIS

GLUTEUS MEDIUS

GLUTEUS MAXIMUS

GASTROCHNEMIUS

SARTORIUS

TRAPEZIUS

END OF RIBCAGE

ILIAC CREST

SACRUM

GREATER TROCHANTER

VOLUME OF HAMSTRINGS

ACHILLES TENDON

STEP 4

MEASURE AND DRAW THE FIGURE IN A DYNAMIC POSE

With this exercise, you'll practice measuring and drawing a figure in a more dynamic, non-erect pose. You'll still be using the method of proportional relationships to measure, but in a more fluid way. Instead of using just the head as the basic unit, you'll see how any segment of the figure can be related proportionally to any other part of the figure using vertical and horizontal alignments. As with the previous exercises, you'll identify landmarks and muscular volumes from the reference photo and, using them as guides, you'll reconstruct the skeleton and superficial muscles.

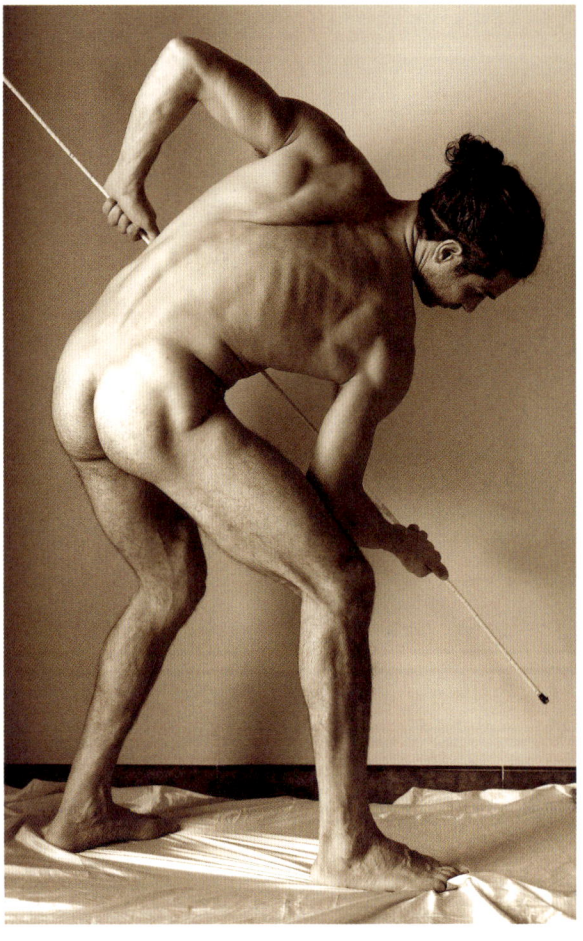

STEP 1

BLOCK IN THE MAIN VOLUMES

Block in the main volumes of the body with a few lines that capture its size, pose, and dynamism. Use vertical and horizontal alignments, as shown in the drawing, to adjust and perfect the pose. For this figure, I used only two lines for these alignments, one vertical and one horizontal, but you can use as many alignments as you need. I find horizontal and vertical alignments more reliable than angled alignments.

STEP 2

REFINE YOUR DRAWING

Gradually refine your drawing, using clean lines. This step is useful for improving your precision in drawing and gaining more skill in identifying and conveying proportions, landmarks, and muscular volumes.

STEP 3

DEVELOP THE DRAWING FURTHER

Now, develop the drawing further by refining the volumes and details of the figure, using framing lines (see page 188). Mark landmarks and label the muscles.

MATERIALS

Materials for steps 1 through 4 of this exercise include the following:

- A pad of white Strathmore Drawing paper, 11 x 14 inches, medium finish
- Faber-Castell Polychromos colored pencils in dark blue, black, and a red earth color such as India red, Pompeian red, or Venetian red
- For step 5, I used a lightly toned tan sheet of paper from a pad of Legion Stonehenge Colors and the same mix of colored pencils. Remember to keep your pencils sharp!

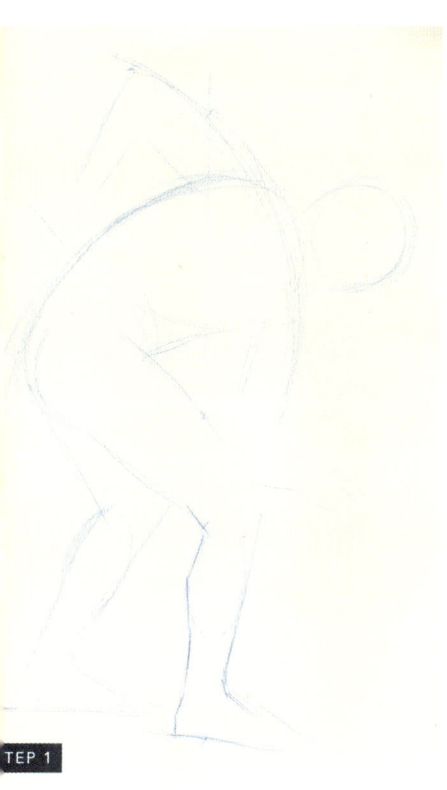

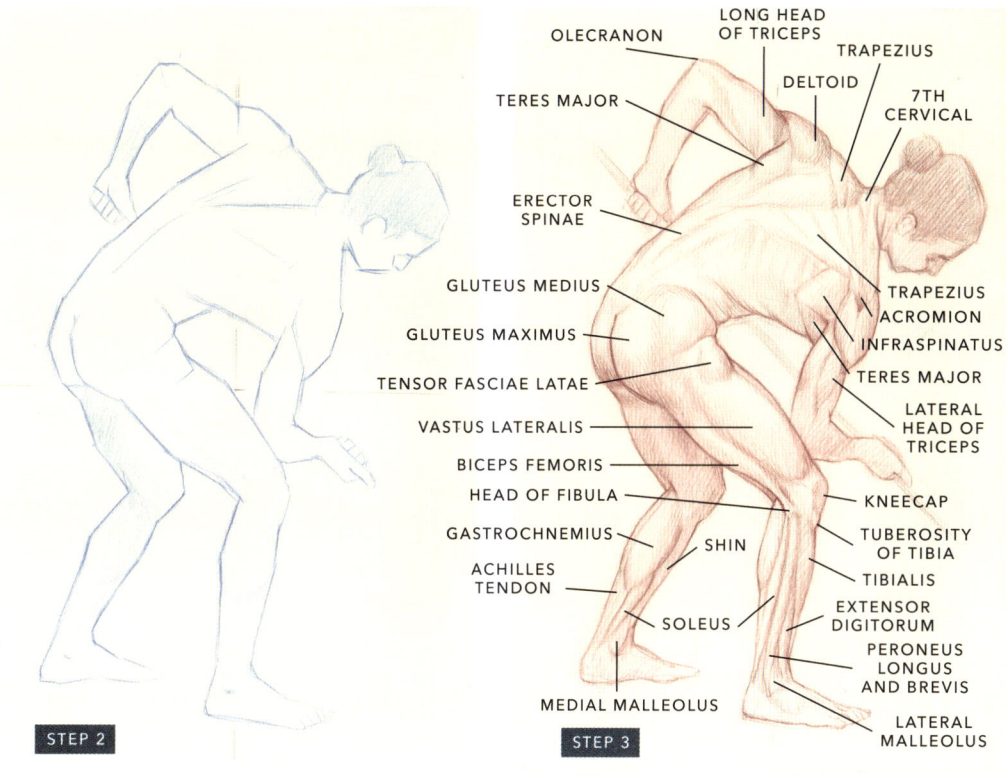

LONG HEAD
OF TRICEPS

OLECRANON

TRAPEZIUS

TERES MAJOR

DELTOID

7TH
CERVICAL

ERECTOR
SPINAE

TRAPEZIUS
ACROMION
INFRASPINATUS
TERES MAJOR

GLUTEUS MEDIUS

GLUTEUS MAXIMUS

TENSOR FASCIAE LATAE

LATERAL
HEAD OF
TRICEPS

VASTUS LATERALIS

BICEPS FEMORIS

KNEECAP

HEAD OF FIBULA

TUBEROSITY
OF TIBIA

GASTROCNEMIUS

SHIN

TIBIALIS

ACHILLES
TENDON

EXTENSOR
DIGITORUM

SOLEUS

PERONEUS
LONGUS
AND BREVIS

MEDIAL MALLEOLUS

LATERAL
MALLEOLUS

STEP 3

STEP 4

RECONSTRUCT THE SKELETON

Reconstruct the skeleton using the skeletal landmarks, as shown in the image here.

STEP 5

DRAW A FLAYED FIGURE

Create a flayed version of the pose using the images you created so far. You can draw the muscles over tracing paper positioned on the skeleton or redraw a very simplified rendering of the skeleton and layer the muscles directly over it.

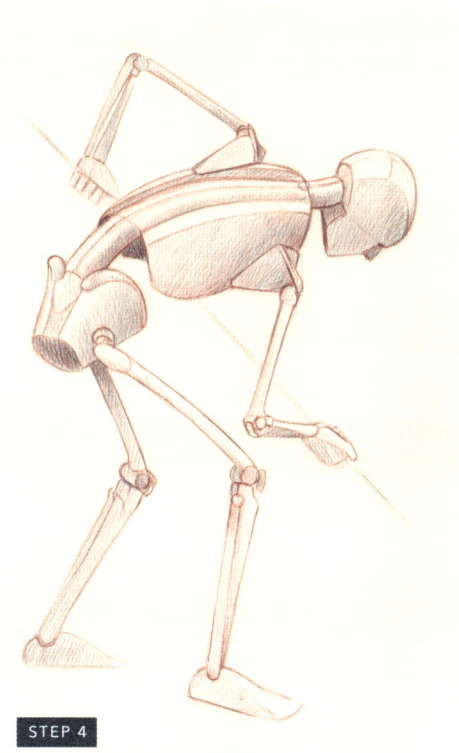

STEP 4

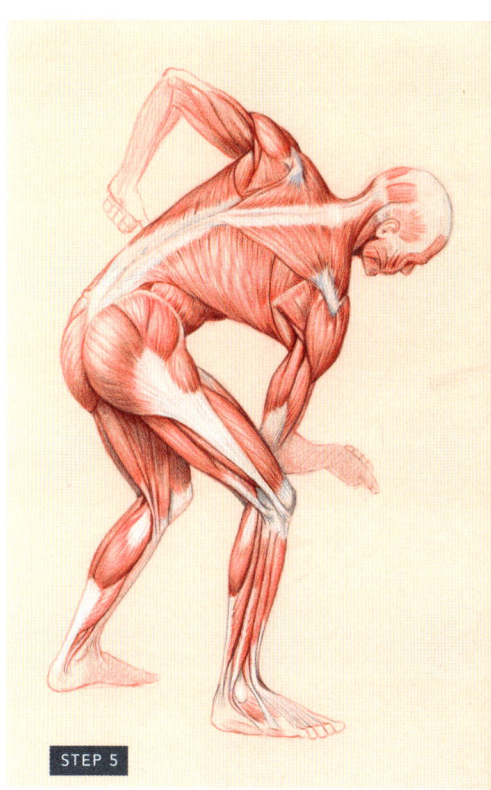

STEP 5

LEVEL 2

LINE OR VALUE?

Exercise 4.5 explores the use of the value, and exercise 4.6 the use of line for figure drawing. Value is particularly powerful when you want to focus on the effect of light on the form and obtain a mimetic, realistic result; lines are better suited to expressing the structural and topographic aspects of the form.

EXERCISE 4.5
THINKING TONALLY (USING VALUE)

The first question you encounter when developing a drawing tonally is, Where do I start? The multitude of values in a given figure can be confusing and may lead you to choose random values, starting with the darkest, most obvious ones instead of first anchoring the drawing in the dominant value—typically the weakest—and then gradually progressing toward the darker values.

This exercise, which returns us to Brian Booth Craig's sculpture *Flavia* (image at top right), approaches tonal rendering using a systematic layering of values, each obtained with regularly spaced, vertical parallel lines for a clearer visualization of the concept behind the technique. Eventually, you will seamlessly merge parallel lines to obtain a smooth, transparent layer, as demonstrated in Step 5 of this exercise (page 184). In the sequence that follows now, I use four or five values, obtained by gradually layering the vertical colored-pencil strokes. (You can also use charcoal or graphite.)

STEP 1

BLOCK IN THE ENVELOPE

Using a blue pencil, block in an "envelope"—an outline—that surrounds and fully contains the whole figure to its maximum height and width. (Here, I first measured the width, then found out how many times it fit in the height, in this case about 2.75 times.) Next, using a red pencil, refine the envelope a bit more, sketching in a slightly more precise outline of the figure.

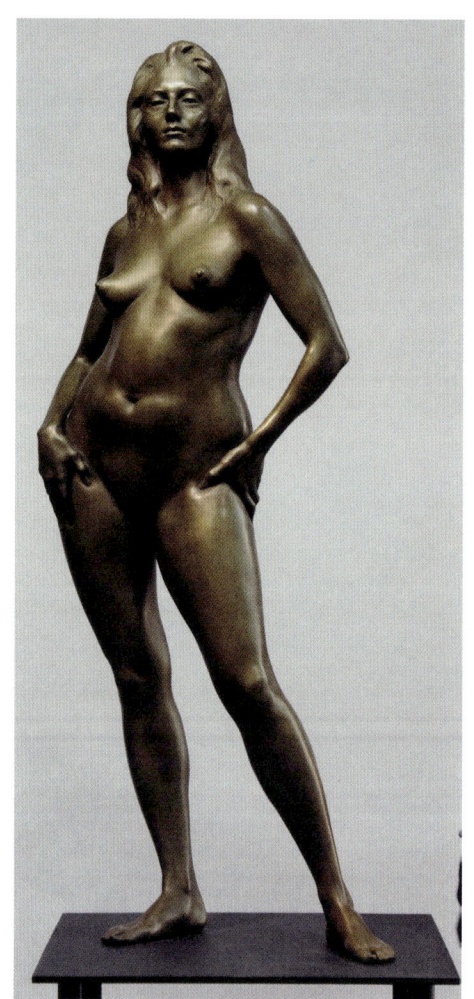

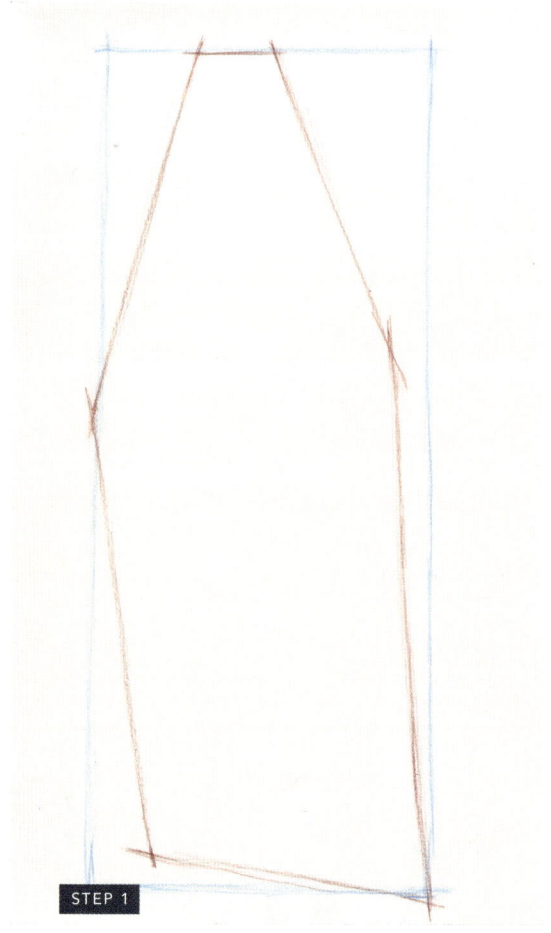

STEP 1

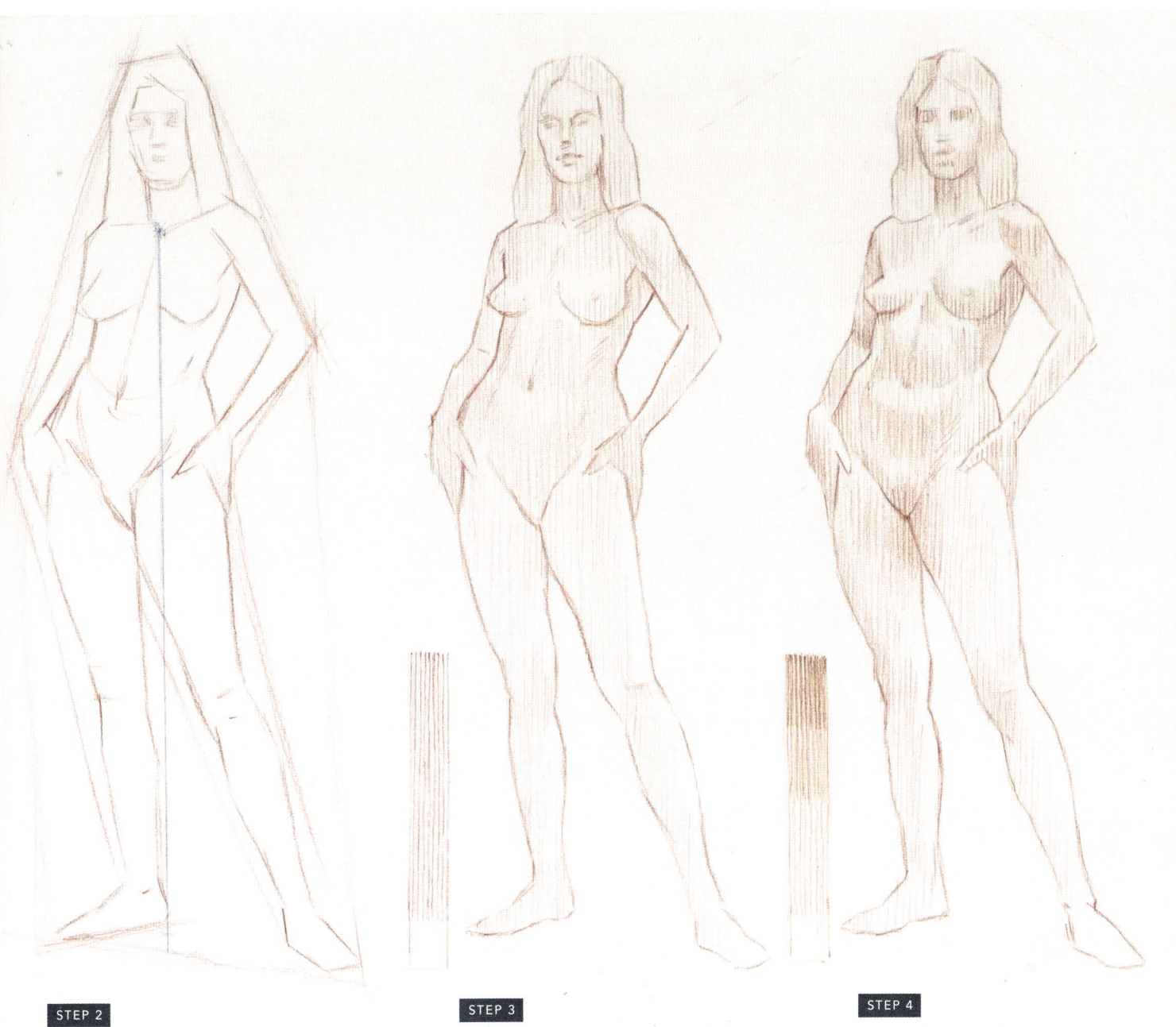

STEP 2

STEP 3

STEP 4

STEP 2

DEVELOP THE POSE WITH A SEGMENTED LINE

Develop the pose with a line drawing, using a segmented line. Focus on the proportional relationships within the figure, using the line of the center of gravity to properly align the figure's various parts. Here, the LCG is the vertical blue line that starts at the jugular fossa and ends at the model's right heel (at left in the drawing).

STEP 3

BLOCK IN THE WEAKEST VALUES

Using only vertical lines, block in the weakest value throughout the figure, first identifying the areas of highlights that you will leave blank and the positions of the darkest values to establish the tonal range.

STEP 4

GRADUALLY ADD DARKER VALUES

Gradually layer more values over the initial layer to obtain progressively darker areas.

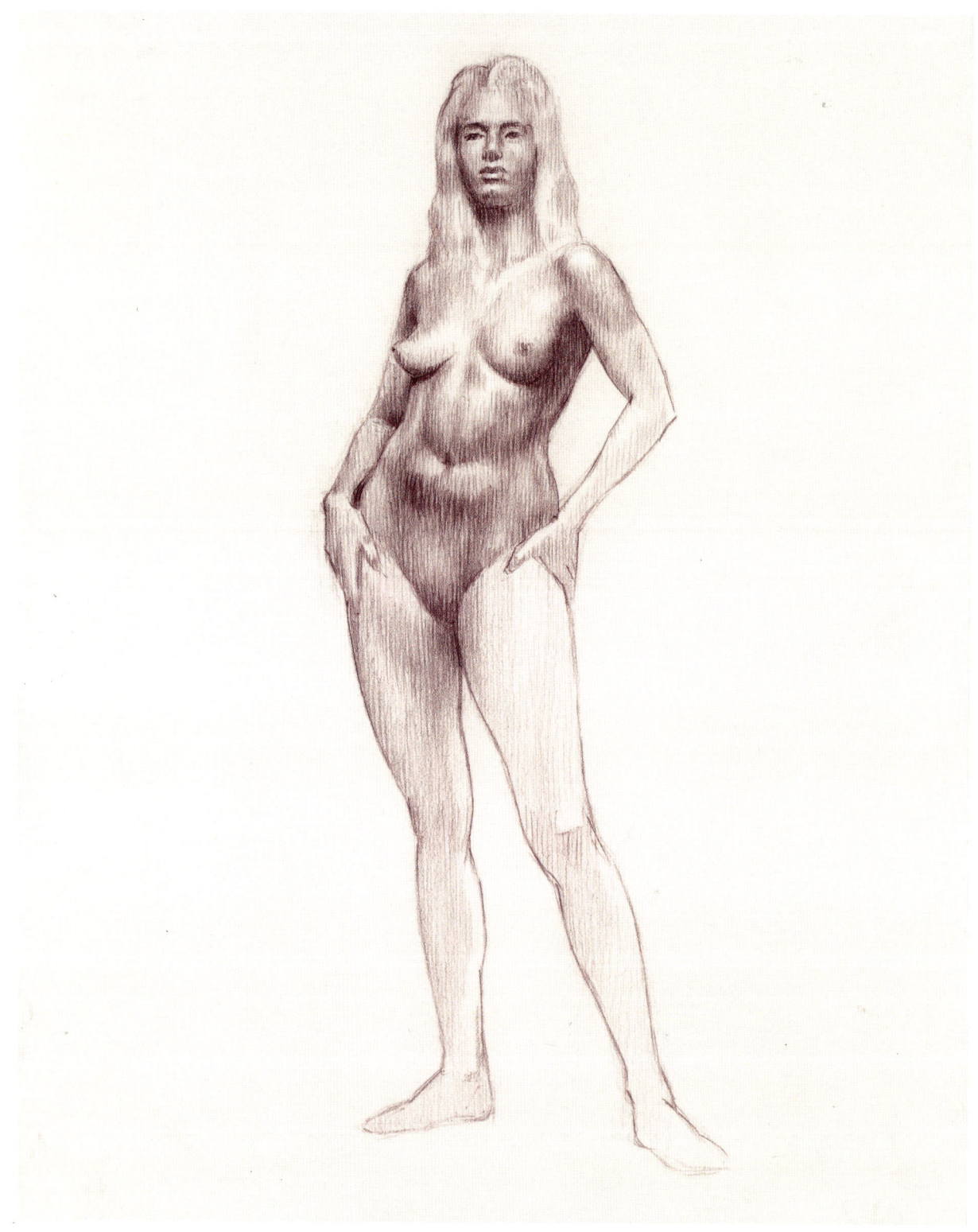

STEP 5

LAYER ON THE DARKEST VALUE

Layer on the darkest value. Use only four or five layers altogether to make it easier to obtain a progressive tonal development.

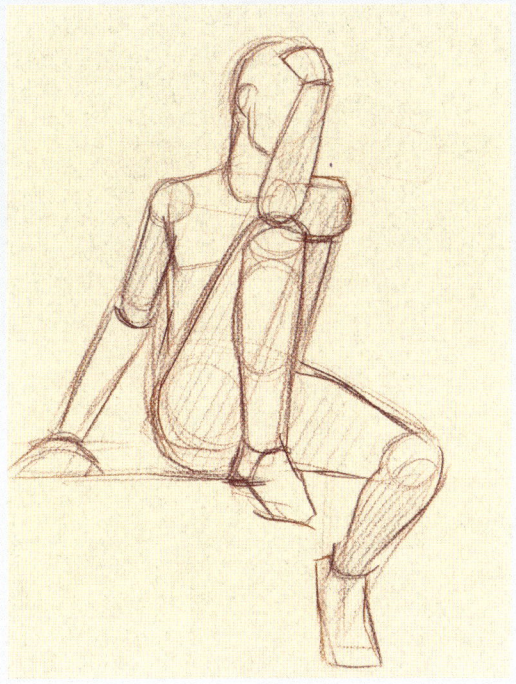

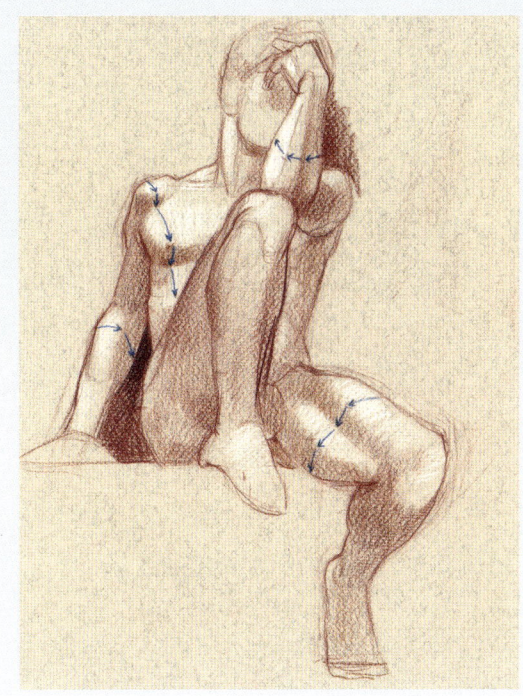

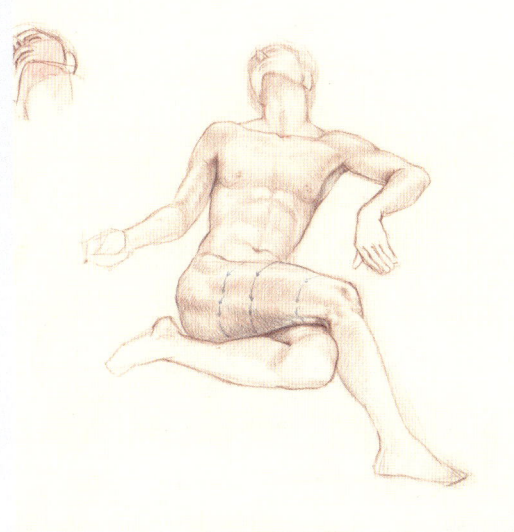

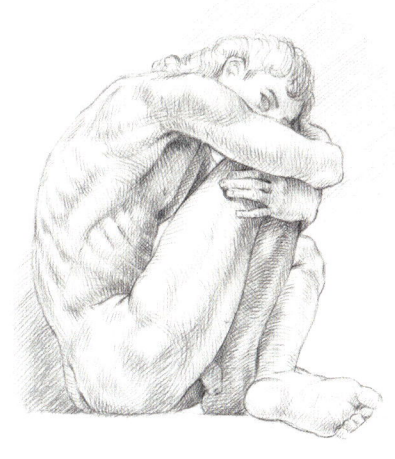

A MASTER OF LINE

American artist Paul Cadmus (1904–99) was a master of structural or framing lines, and all his drawings were created with structural lines to obtain a convincing sense of volume and tonal range.

The two drawings of mine at the top are both based on a drawing by Cadmus. In the image at top left, I reduced one of Cadmus's nudes to basic stereometric volumes, to show how line can clearly depict the main structural forms of the body. In the image at top right, I used blue arrows like cross-contour lines to visualize the three-dimensional aspects of the figure.

The image at bottom left shows a more detailed use of line to achieve a greater level of realism and more accurate depiction of the forms of the body. The blue arrows show the direction of the structural cross-hatched lines that

describe the turning of the forms and the various planes of the body.

Cadmus was also a master of cross-contour hatching, using it to create a very large number of figure drawings. The drawing immediately above is my copy of one of his drawings that very effectively demonstrate this method. You can find dozens of his drawings on line. To continue practicing cross-contour hatching look some up and try copying them.

ABOVE, BOTTOM LEFT: My copy of Cadmus's drawing *Male Nude, NM32,* 1967.

ABOVE, BOTTOM RIGHT: My copy of one of Cadmus's most famous drawings, *Male Nude, NM 165,* 1981, graphite.

THINKING STRUCTURALLY (USING LINE AND CROSS-CONTOUR HATCHING)

Line is efficient for visualizing and measuring the topography and structure of the form. The line became the perfect method for visualizing the world as filtered through the concept of "direct experience" at the core of the Italian Renaissance. Perspective, for example, relies on line to create clear pictures of the physical world. And the impeccable use of line is essential to the surgical clarity of Leonardo da Vinci's anatomical drawings.

Unlike tonal drawing, which focuses on light and produces a realistic effect, cross-contour hatching conceptualizes form with line. Lines travel across a form, or perpendicularly to the direction of the form, revealing its topography. To understand how this works, imagine yourself going for a hike on a hilly landscape, holding a spool of twine that unravels as you walk, recording your path up and down the hills. Then imagine yourself back in your studio, drawing your path: your pencil's line will describe the ups and downs of your route, producing a kind of relief map of your journey. When applied to figure drawing, cross-contour hatching conceives of the body as topography, and lines drawn across this "landscape" (sometimes called lines of section) reveal the planes and volumes of the form and can also describe the associated values.

For this exercise in cross-contour hatching, let's return to the Quirinal Boxer, whom you met in chapter 3, but with a twist. Instead of the ancient sculpture, you'll be referring to a modern, live-action version. As you can see in the photo at right, model Andrea Morani has adopted a relaxed sitting pose not very different from our pugilist friend's.

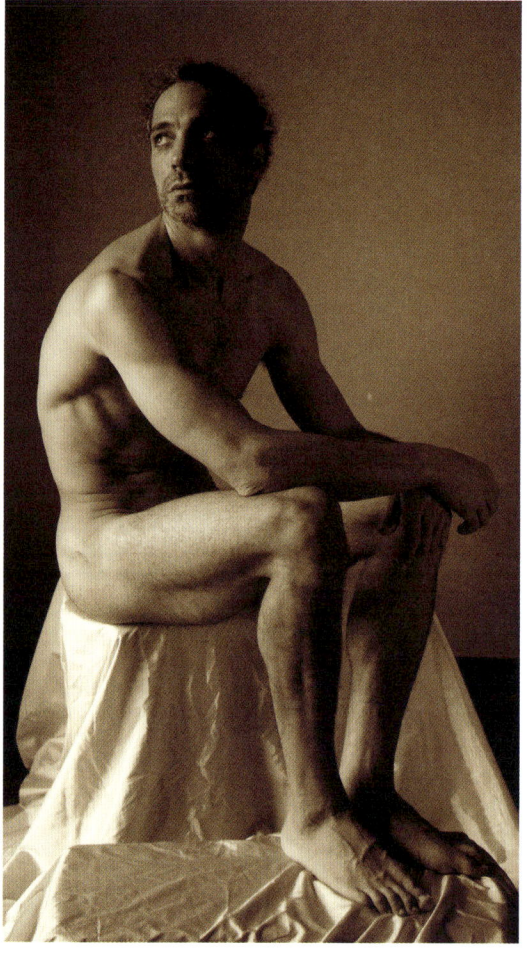

MATERIALS

Materials for this exercise include the following:

- A pad of white Strathmore Drawing paper, 11 x 14 inches, medium finish
- Faber-Castell Polychromos colored pencil in India red
- Graphite pencil, grade F
- Kneaded eraser
- Pencil sharpener

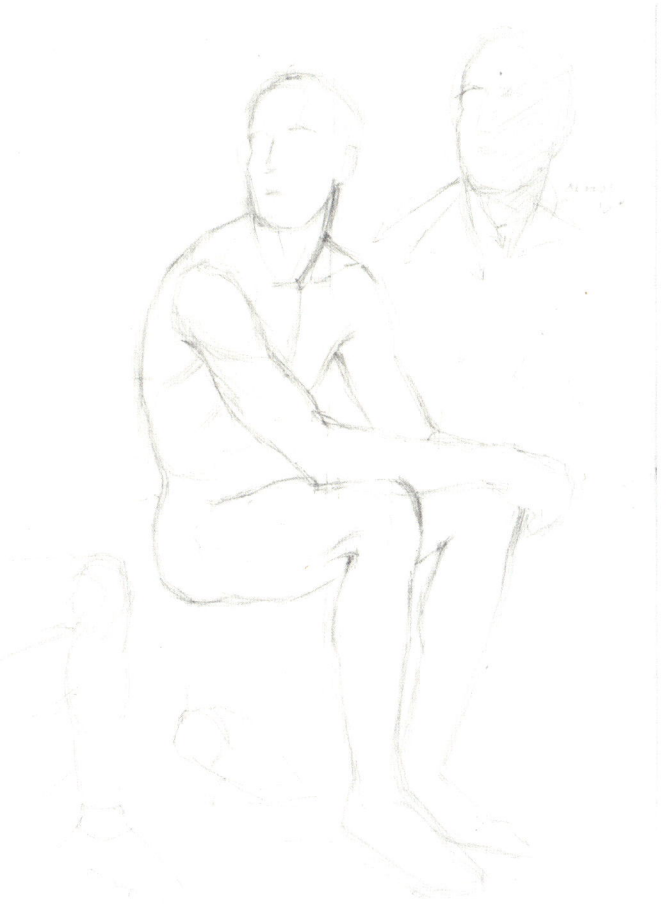

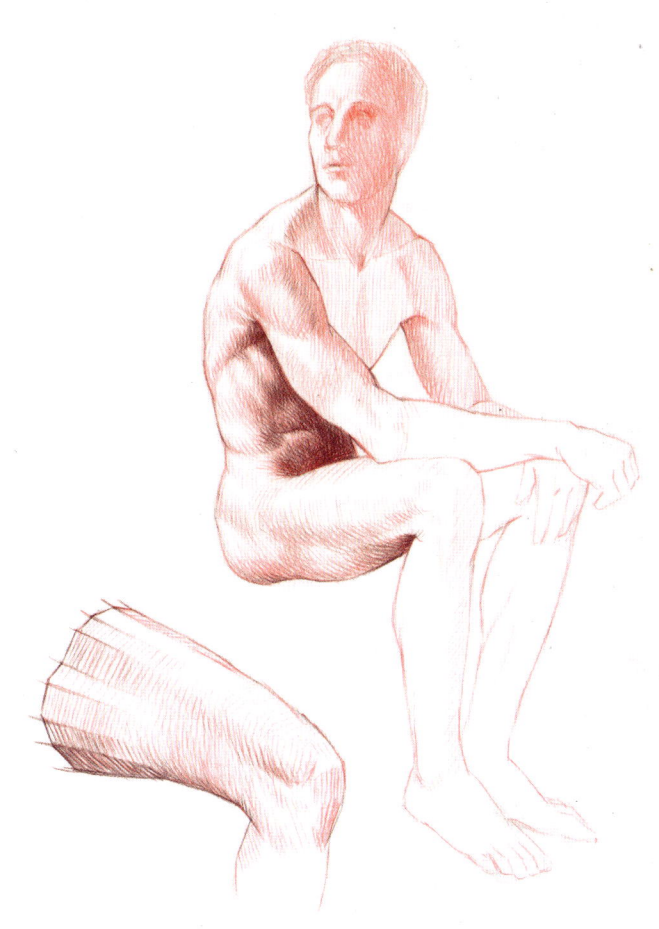

STEP 1

SKETCH THE FIGURE

To begin, sketch Andrea's "Quirinal" figure. I recommend using a graphite pencil simply because it is easy to erase, but if you prefer, you can use the red colored pencil. Keep lines very light to avoid creating too much visual noise. You may also prepare a few small studies of details of the figure as you see in the image here.

STEP 2

CLEAN UP THE SKETCH AND REDRAW

Now, clean up the initial sketch with a kneaded eraser to eliminate any smudges and unnecessary lines. Using the red pencil, redraw the figure, going over the faint lines of the initial sketch and making it more accurate. The image here shows the various stages of development of the drawing: the line drawing of the figure with differentiated lines; the straight parallel lines that create a uniform value that does not follow the form; and the layered cross-contour lines that develop the dimensionality of the form. The detail on the lower left provides a closeup showing how the cross-contour lines follow the form and reveal its planes and values. With practice, your cross-contour lines and cross-contour hatching will become smoother and more realistic.

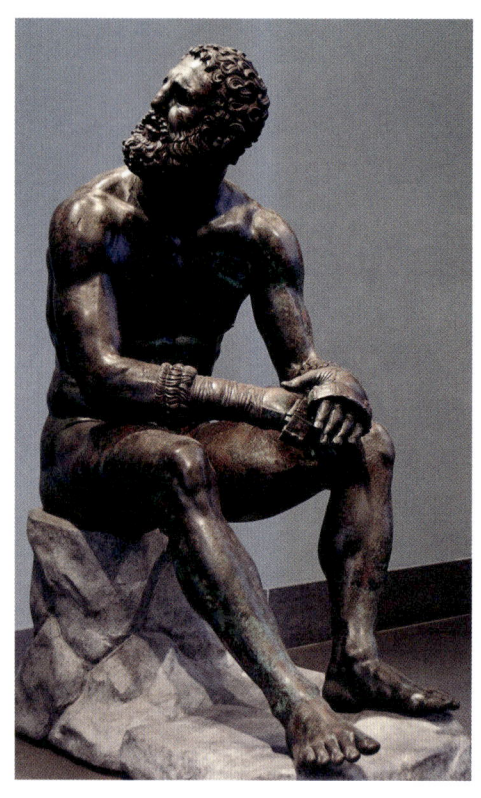

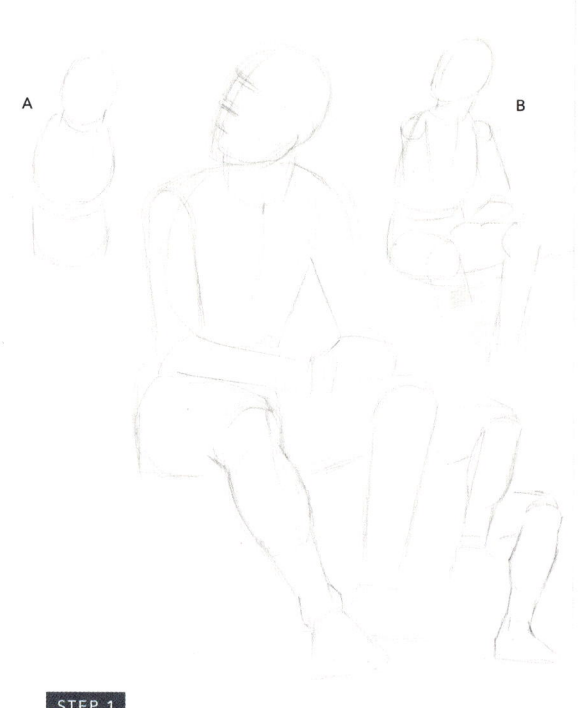

A

B

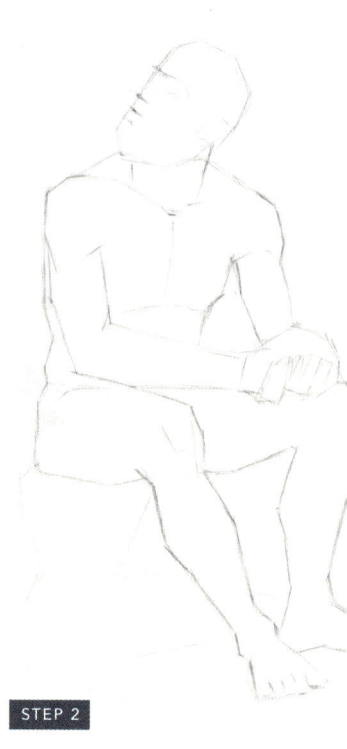

STEP 1

STEP 2

EXERCISE 4.7
TONAL RENDERING, QUIRINAL BOXER

With this sequence, you practice creating a tonal drawing using even, transparent layers of graphite or charcoal on white paper. Once again, you'll use the *Quirinal Boxer* as inspiration.

ABOVE: *Quirinal Boxer* (*Boxer at Rest*). Full information on page 156.

STEP 1
BLOCK IN THE FIGURE

Start by blocking in the figure with a rounded stereometric rendering. Use proportional relationships and vertical and horizontal alignments to draw this initial stage. Once the main volumes are sketched in (detail *A,* at lower left), you can gradually adjust and perfect them until you have a more precise stereometric scaffolding (detail *B* at upper right).

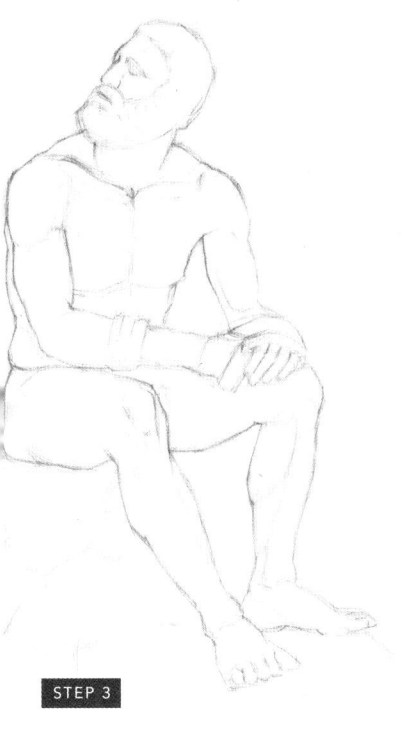

STEP 3

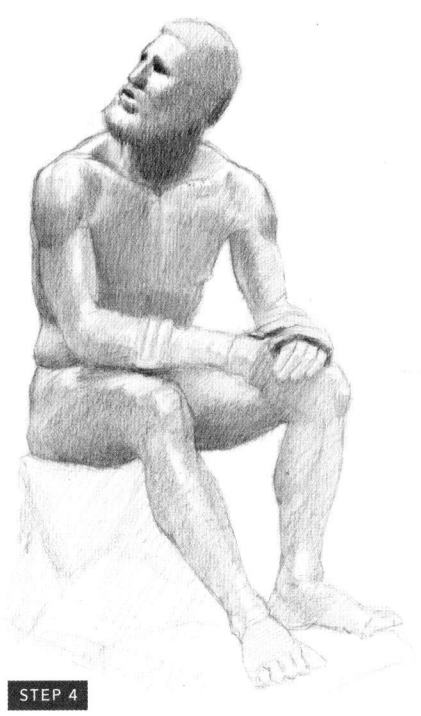

STEP 4

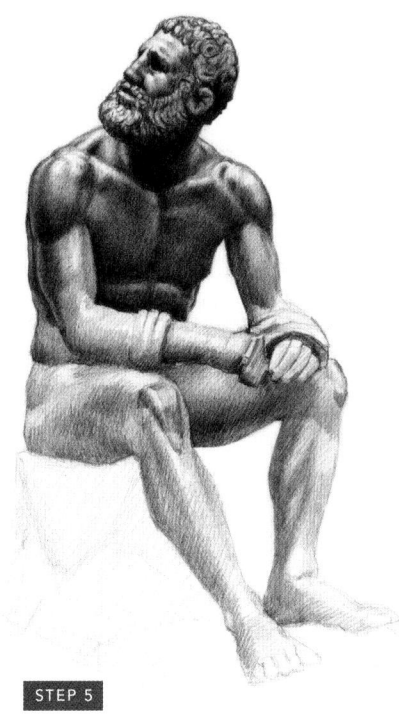

STEP 5

STEP 2

"SCULPT" THE MUSCULAR VOLUMES

Now refine the stereometric scaffolding by "sculpting" the main muscular volumes. Use segmented lines, as recommended on page 176.

STEP 3

FURTHER DEFINE THE ANATOMY

With the next pass, define the anatomy of the *Boxer* more accurately, ending with a clean, precise line drawing.

STEP 4

EXPAND THE TONAL RANGE

For this step—shown across the two images labeled *4A* and *4B*—proceed with the gradual layering of values as demonstrated in exercise 4.5 (see page 183). Leave the white of the paper blank for the highlights while gradually layering on graphite from a pencil to achieve a range of values. It's not necessary to use only vertical marks; let your marks go in any direction needed to obtain an even, saturated, transparent layer of graphite. (As you add graphite, the effect will progress from transparent to translucent to opaque.) Extend the tonal scale to eight to ten values.

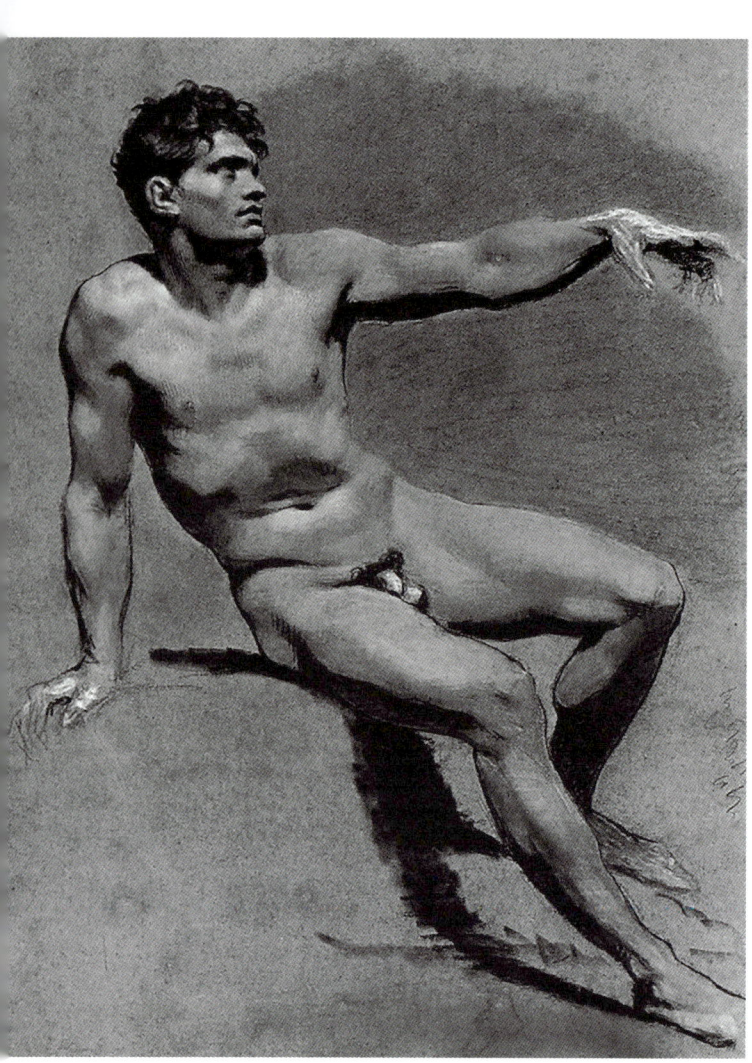

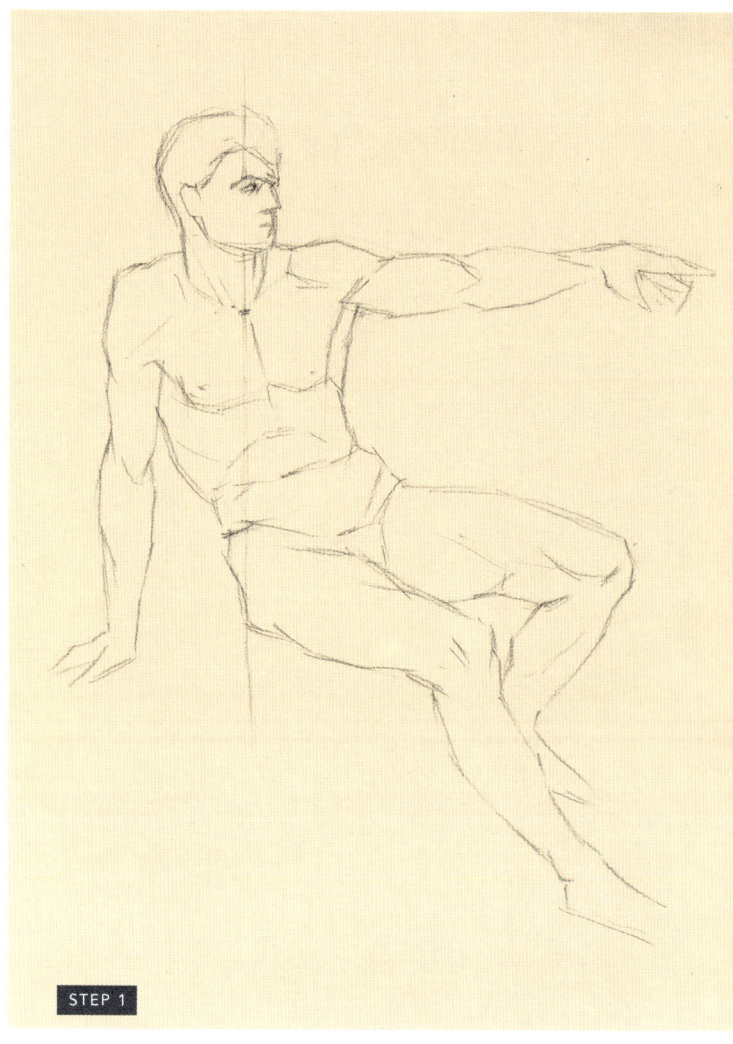

EXERCISE 4.8
COPYING FROM A MASTER DRAWING

Now let's turn our attention to drawing with charcoal and chalk on toned paper. This is one of the most effective techniques for figure and cast drawing. In this technique you'll use charcoal for the values on the model that appear darker than the paper and chalk for those that are lighter. You'll leave blank those areas that have the same value as the paper. For this exercise, let's return to the Prud'hon figure drawing first encountered in chapter 3 (page 134). Note, however, that we are not necessarily using his technical approach to measuring or tonal rendering.

STEP 1
BLOCK IN MAIN OUTLINES

Block in the main outlines of the figure using the method described in exercise 4.4. In the image here, note the main vertical line I used to find alignments between a few parts of the body: the corner of the eyebrow, the jugular fossa, the iliac spine, and the

MATERIALS

Materials for this exercise include the following:

- A sheet of mid-value tan toned paper (I used Fabriano Ingres.)
- Charcoal sticks in hard, medium, and soft grades (Nitram is a good brand. For this demonstration I used Wolff's carbon pencils in grades B, 2B, 4B, and 6B.)

ABOVE LEFT: Pierre-Paul Prud'hon, Seated Nude with Arm Extended, black and white chalk on blue-tinted (Gray: Le Musee Baron Martin)

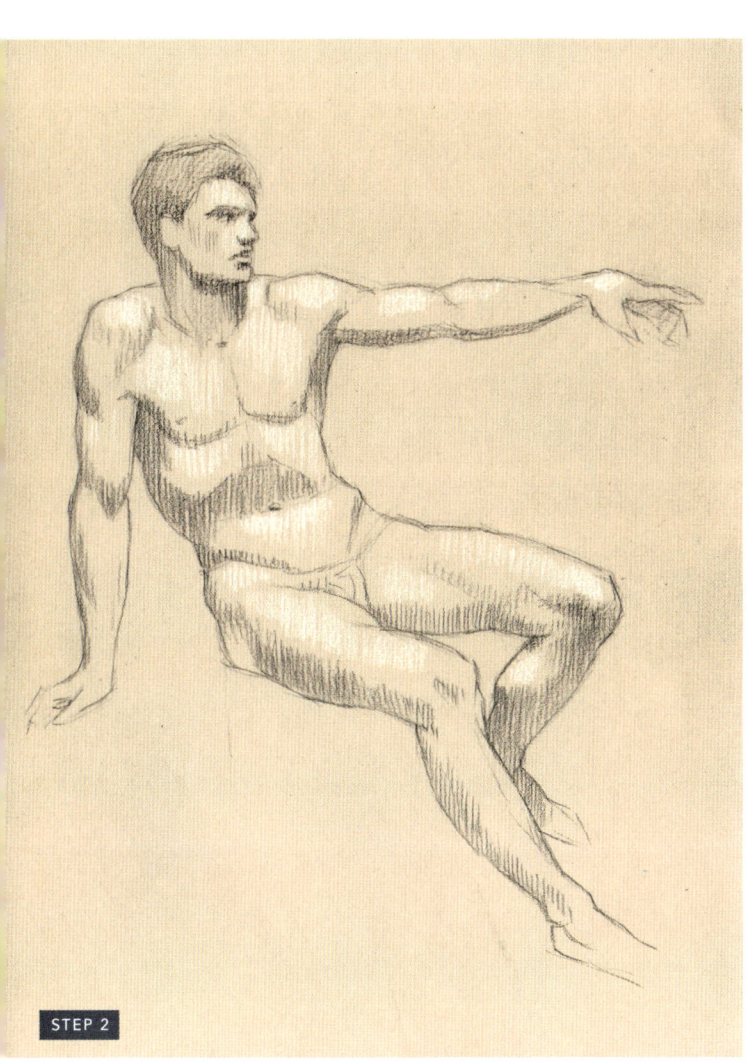

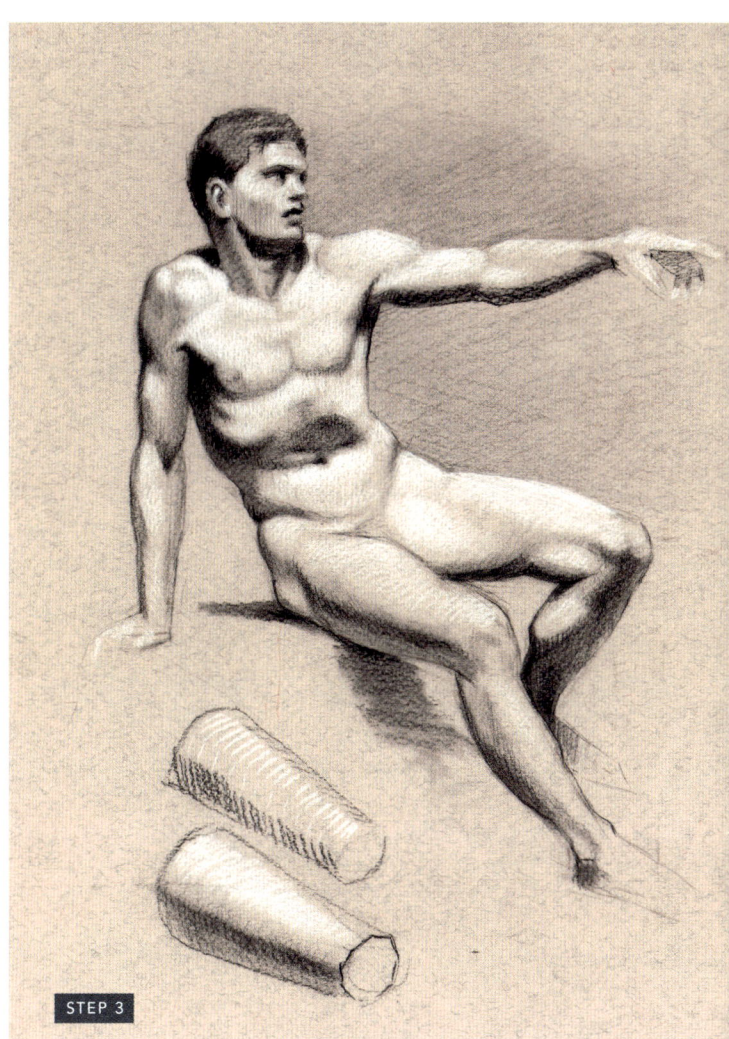

gluteus maximus. Use as many alignments as you need, but my advice is to stick with horizontal and vertical lines because they are by far more reliable than diagonal lines.

STEP 2
BLOCK IN SHADOW AND LIGHT MASSES

Block in the shadow mass with charcoal and the light mass with white chalk. Keep the values light, because at this stage you are just identifying the positions of the areas that are lighter and darker than the paper and not yet developing the tonal range.

STEP 3
DEVELOP THE TONAL SCALE

Develop the tonal scale, taking care to identify the darkest value and the highlight to establish the tonal range. Use the white chalk to develop the areas lighter than the value of the paper. You have to leave areas of transition blank, with the value of the paper providing the values between the values obtained with charcoal and chalk.

EXERCISE 4.9
USING CHARCOAL AND CHALK ON TONED PAPER

In this exercise you'll be drawing the plaster cast of *The Wrestlers* shown at right.

STEP 1
CREATE THE ENVELOPE

Create an "envelope" that contains the whole subject, using its maximum height and width to create the envelope. Then block in the main outlines of the sculptural group.

STEP 2
ADD THE FIGURES' VOLUMES

Refine the drawing with more details and accuracy in measurement.

STEP 3
BLOCK IN LIGHT AND SHADOW MASSES

Block in the light mass and shadow mass and identify the lightest and darkest values.

STEP 4
EXPAND THE TONAL RANGE

Expand the tonal range to about eight values, paying particular attention to the tonal transitions.

MATERIALS

Materials for this exercise include the following:

- Mid-value blue-gray toned Strathmore charcoal paper
- Wolff's carbon pencils in grades B, 2B, 4B, and 6B, or General's compressed charcoal pencils in hard, medium, soft, and extra soft grades

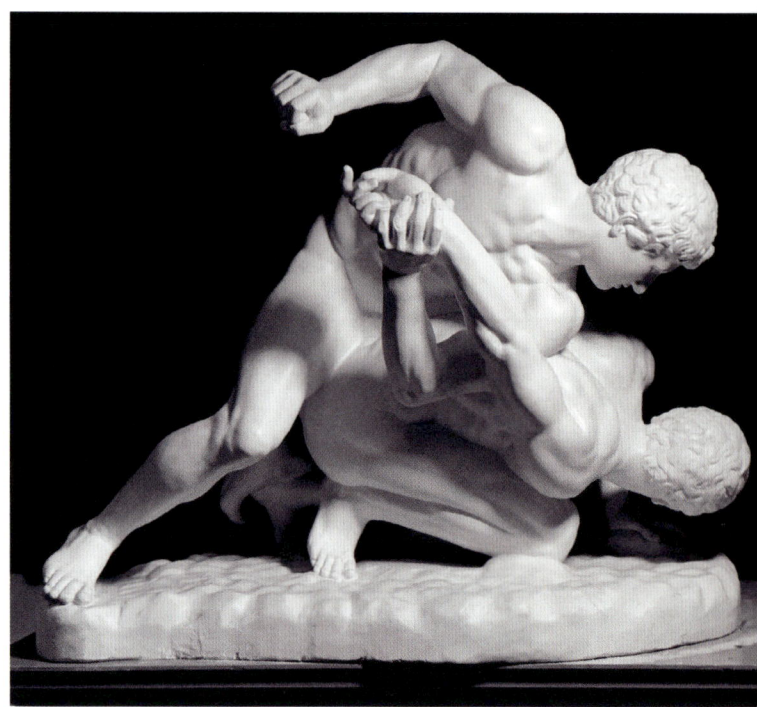

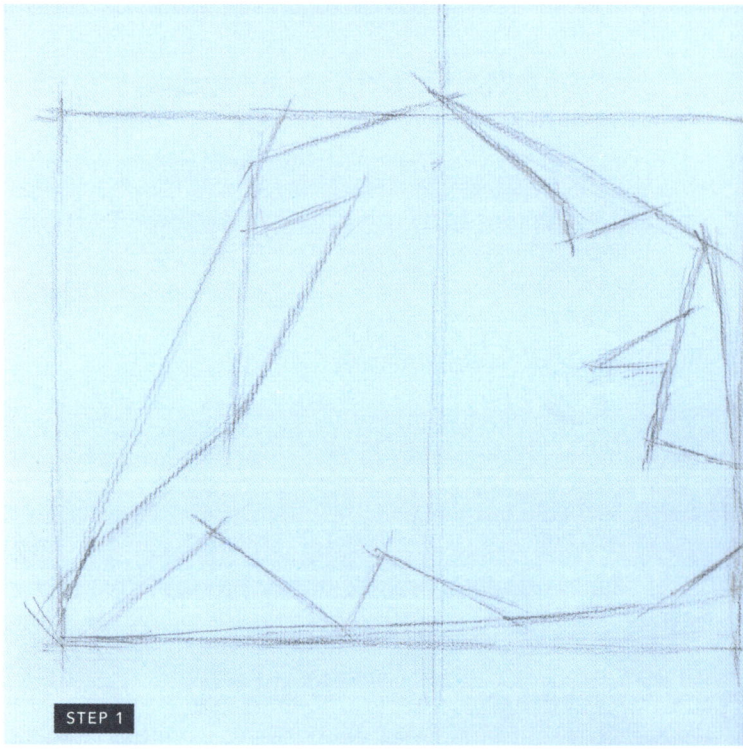

STEP 1

TOP: Plaster cast of *The Wrestlers,* a Roman marble sculpture after a lost Greek original made during the third century BCE. The cast is in the collection of the New York Academy of Art; the marble sculpture is in the Uffizi, Florence, Italy.

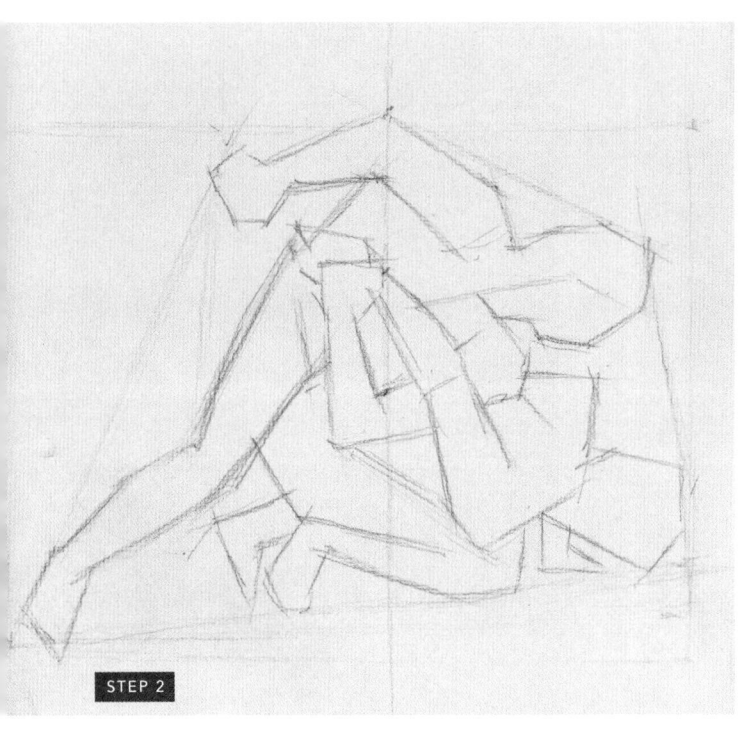

STEP 2

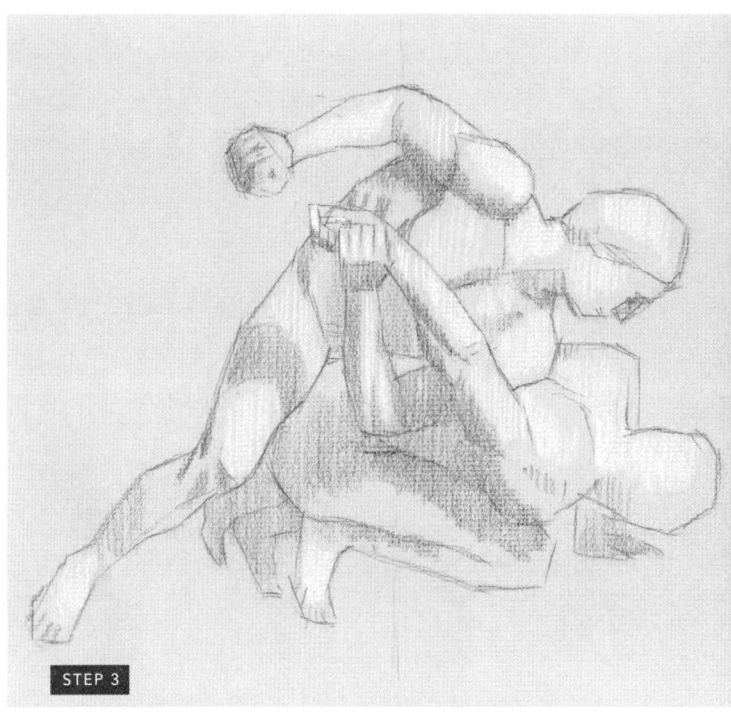

STEP 3

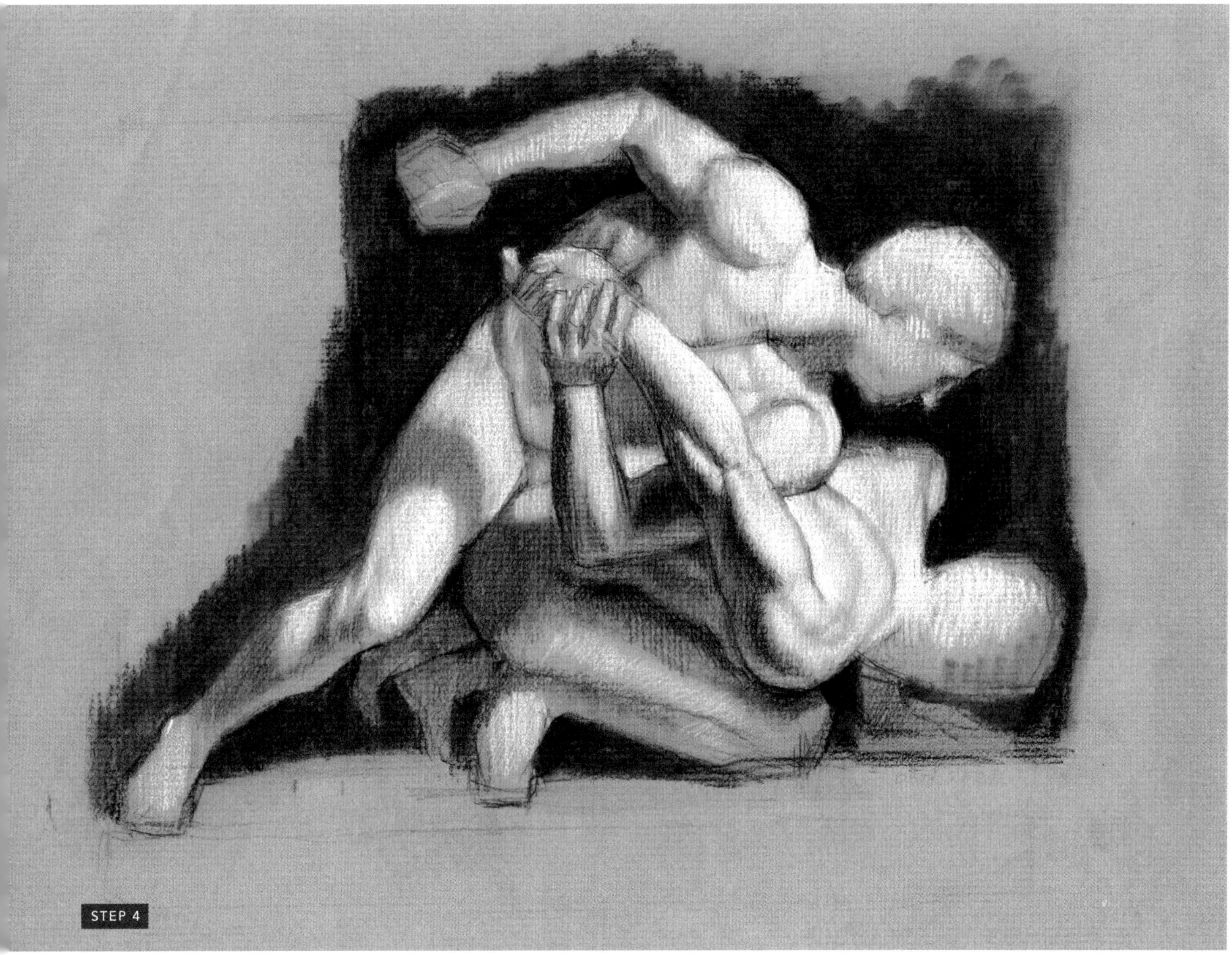

STEP 4

EXERCISE 4.10
REDUCTION TECHNIQUE, HYBRID VERSION

This sequence presents a hybrid version of the reduction technique. Usually, the result of the reduction technique is obtained only by removing charcoal that has been smeared on a sheet of paper, without adding charcoal and chalk afterward to create the darkest and lightest values. In the following sequence, however, you'll expand the tonal scale and sharpen the details with charcoal and chalk. The strong chiaroscuro of Andrea Morani's self-portrait makes this exercise more challenging, but the finished drawing is very rewarding.

STEP 1
APPLY CHARCOAL DUST AND BLOCK IN THE FIGURE

Prepare the paper by smearing charcoal dust or a soft charcoal stick on it, saturating the paper as much as possible. Push the charcoal into the paper using a soft paper towel or your fingers, followed by another application of charcoal. Before starting to lift the charcoal, eliminate any excess by blowing on the sheet and gently tapping it while holding it up vertically. (Do this out of doors to avoid dispersing charcoal inside your studio!) Then block in the main outlines of the figure with a charcoal stick or pencil.

STEP 2
BEGIN LIFTING CHARCOAL

Start lifting charcoal from the surface with the chamois cloth or kneaded eraser, establishing areas of light and shadow mass as shown here. You don't need to be too detailed at this stage.

STEP 3
CONTINUE LIFTING CHARCOAL

Continue lifting charcoal with the chamois or other erasing tool to extend the tonal scale in the light values range. Apply more charcoal to extend the range of the dark values.

STEP 4
DEVELOP THE TONAL RANGE

Continue developing the tonal range by gradually lifting more charcoal and adding values with white chalk for the light values and charcoal to make the dark values even d darker. Remember not to mix charcoal and chalk and to apply white chalk only in areas on the model that are lighter than the paper.

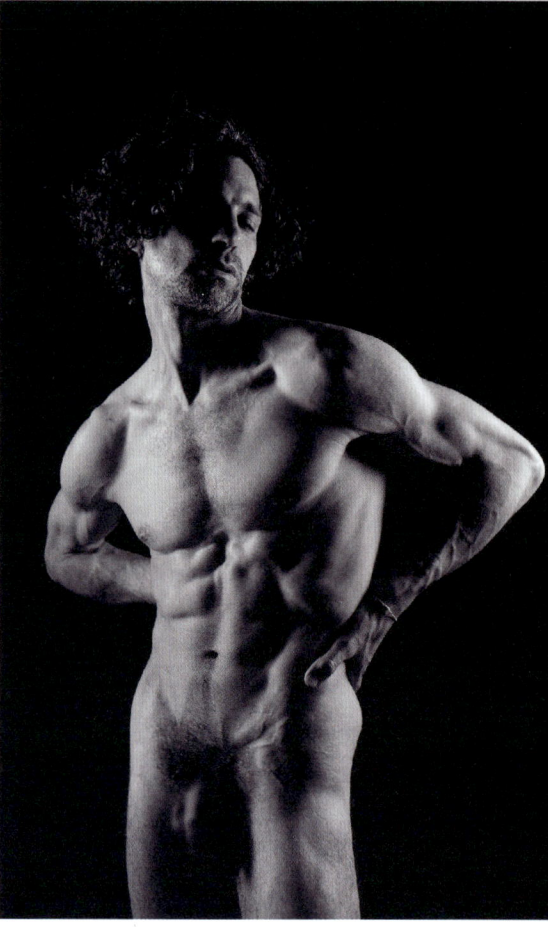

MATERIALS

Materials for this exercise include the following:

- A sheet of white Strathmore Charcoal or Fabriano Ingres paper
- A stick of soft charcoal or charcoal dust for the ground
- A piece of chamois, a kneaded eraser or a Factis eraser for removing charcoal from the surface
- Charcoal sticks in hard, medium, and soft grades for the drawing (Nitram is a good brand. You can also use Wolff's carbon pencils in grades B, 2B, 4B, and 6B or General's charcoal pencils in hard, medium, soft, and extra soft grades.)
- White chalk pencils or sharpened sticks (General's, Faber-Castell Pitt pastels, Conté, or Cretacolor)

ABOVE: Andrea Morani, *Self-Portrait*, 2023. Courtesy of the artist.

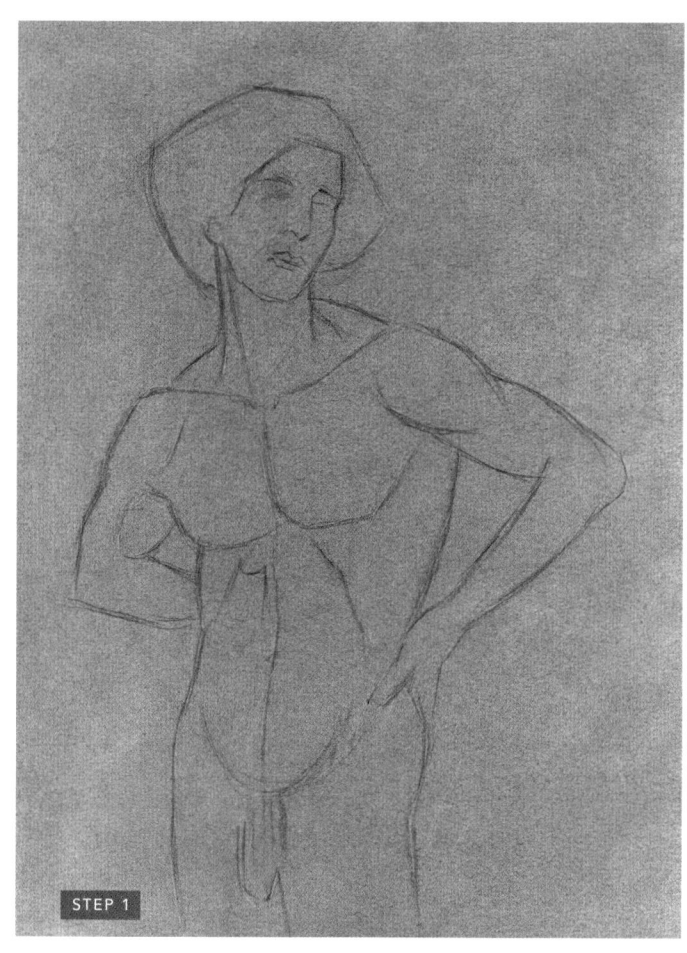

STEP 1

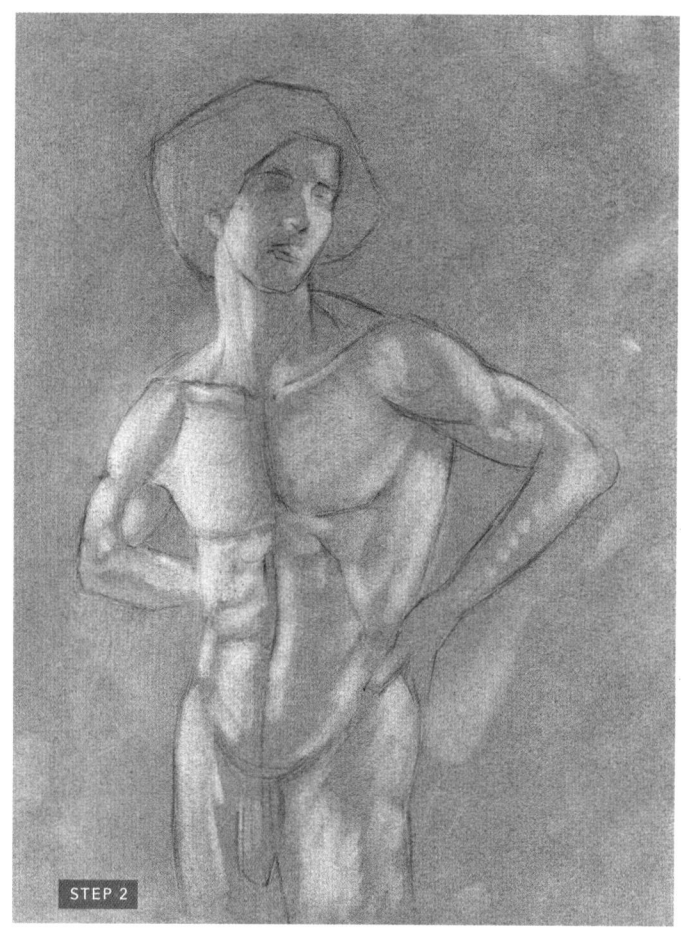

STEP 2

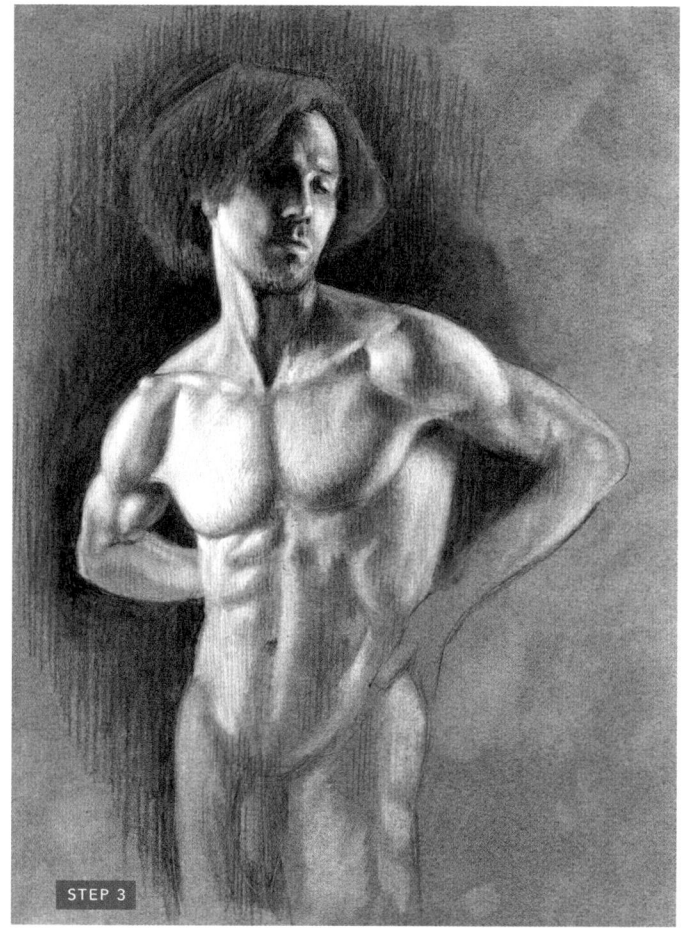

STEP 3

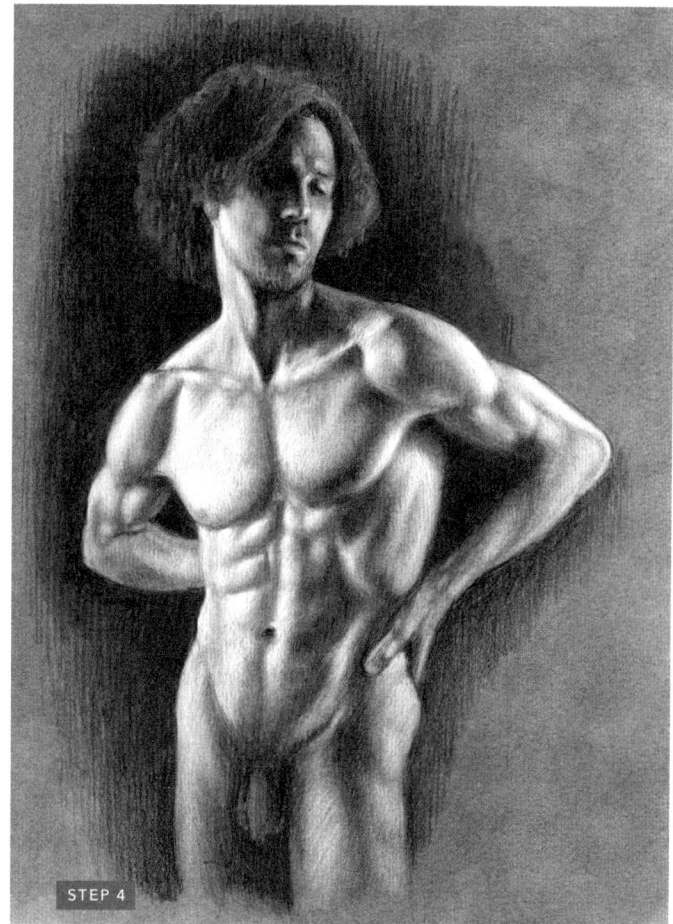

STEP 4

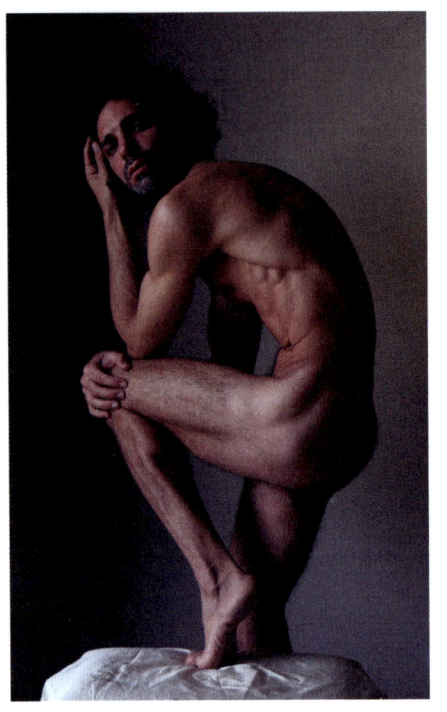
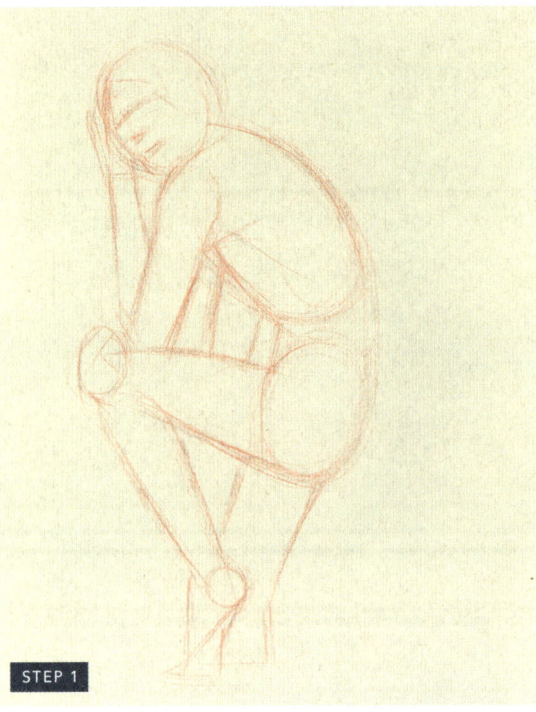

STEP 1

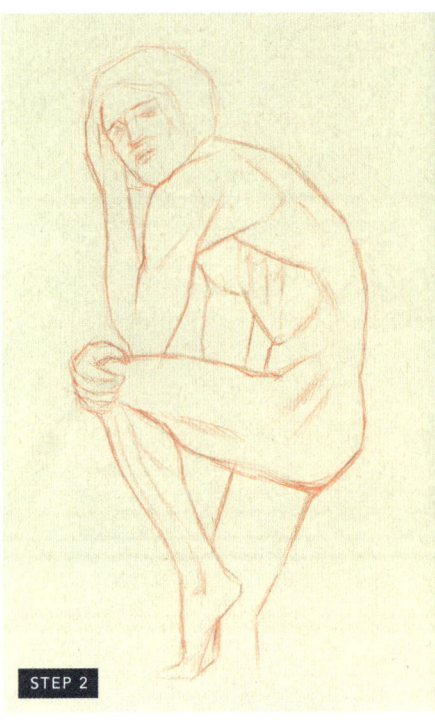

STEP 2

TROIS CRAYONS TECHNIQUE

The *trois crayons* technique uses three colored crayons: red, black, and white. Pastels or colored pencils can also be used, and charcoal can substitute for the black. The red member of the trio should be a low-chroma red, typically a red earth hue such as sanguine, Pompeii red, Venetian red, or India red. Many famous artists—Rubens, Carracci, Watteau, and Fragonard, to name a few—created lively, expressive works using this technique.

The *trois crayons* technique allows you to focus on three fundamental aspects of color: chroma, temperature, and value. You start drawing using only the red color, bringing it to a fairly high level of tonal development. The black is used for the shadow mass, layering over the red to lower its chroma, darken the value, and alter the temperature. The white is applied only in the areas that are lighter than the value of the toned paper you are using.

MATERIALS FOR TROIS CRAYONS

The media you can use for trois crayons are actually somewhat varied. Traditionally, artists have used crayon sticks in black, white, and a red earth color by manufacturers like Conté or Cretacolor. These also come in pencil form—or you can use colored pencils by other makers. Pastels in pencil form, such as Faber-Castell's Pitt pastels, are another possibility. And charcoal and white chalk can also be used along with crayons or pastels.

For paper I choose tan or gray toned paper, such as one of the tinted papers in the Strathmore Charcoal line, Fabriano Ingres, or Stonehenge Colors. But, really, you can use any other toned pastel or charcoal paper you like.

ABOVE LEFT: Andrea Morani, *Self-Portrait,* 2023, digital photograph. Courtesy of the artist.

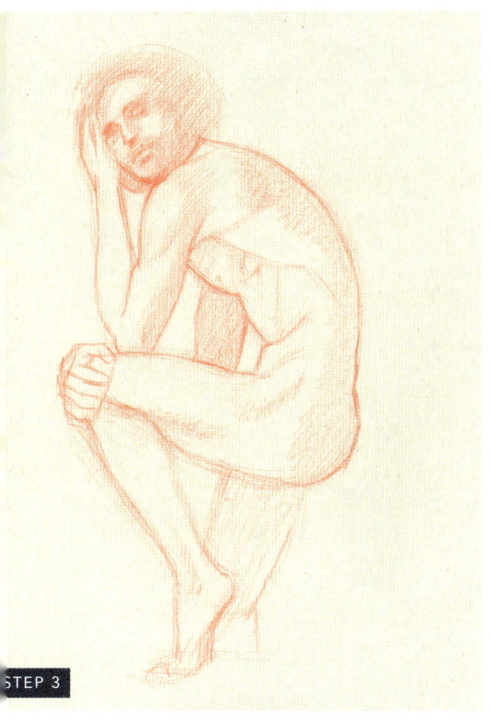

STEP 3

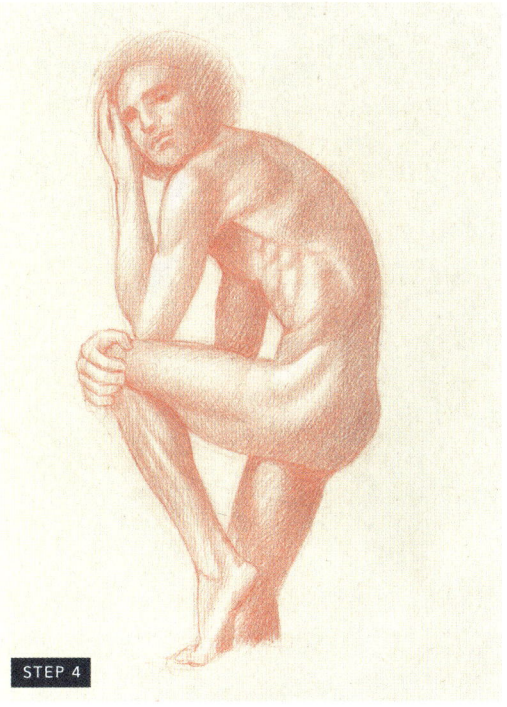

STEP 4

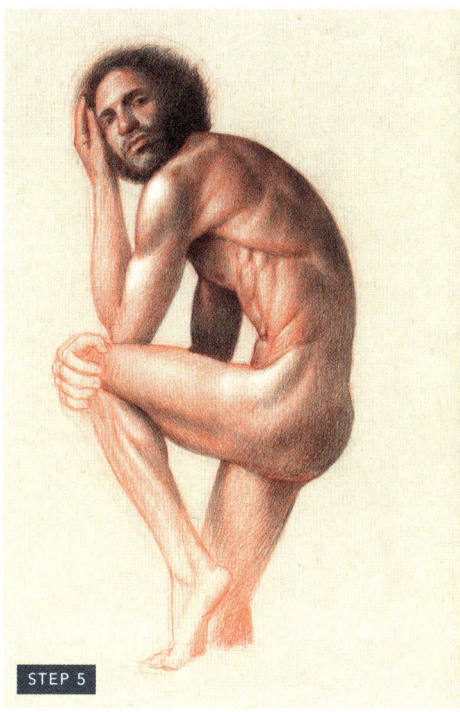

STEP 5

STEP 1

BLOCK IN FIGURE WITH RED CRAYON

Block in the main volumes of the figure using the red crayon. As usual, pay attention to the proportional relationships and alignments of the various parts of the figure

STEP 2

DEVELOP THE FIGURE WITH LINE

When the proportions and pose of the entire figure have been established, develop the figure in further detail with a clean, defining line drawing.

STEP 3

BLOCK IN SHADOW MASSES

Begin to block in the areas of shadow, which indirectly define the light masses.

STEP 4

DEVELOP THE FIGURE TONALLY

Start developing the figure tonally, still using the red crayon for the values that are darker than the paper and introducing the white crayon to establish the areas lighter that the paper.

STEP 5

INTRODUCE THE BLACK CRAYON

Now introduce the black crayon for the areas of shadow. This will lower the chroma, shift the temperature, and darken the value of the red. Keep developing the highlight areas with the white crayon. Remember that red and black can be mixed in the areas of shadow but not in the light mass, where you will use only red. The white does not mix with either the red or black and is used only in the areas that on the model are lighter than the paper.

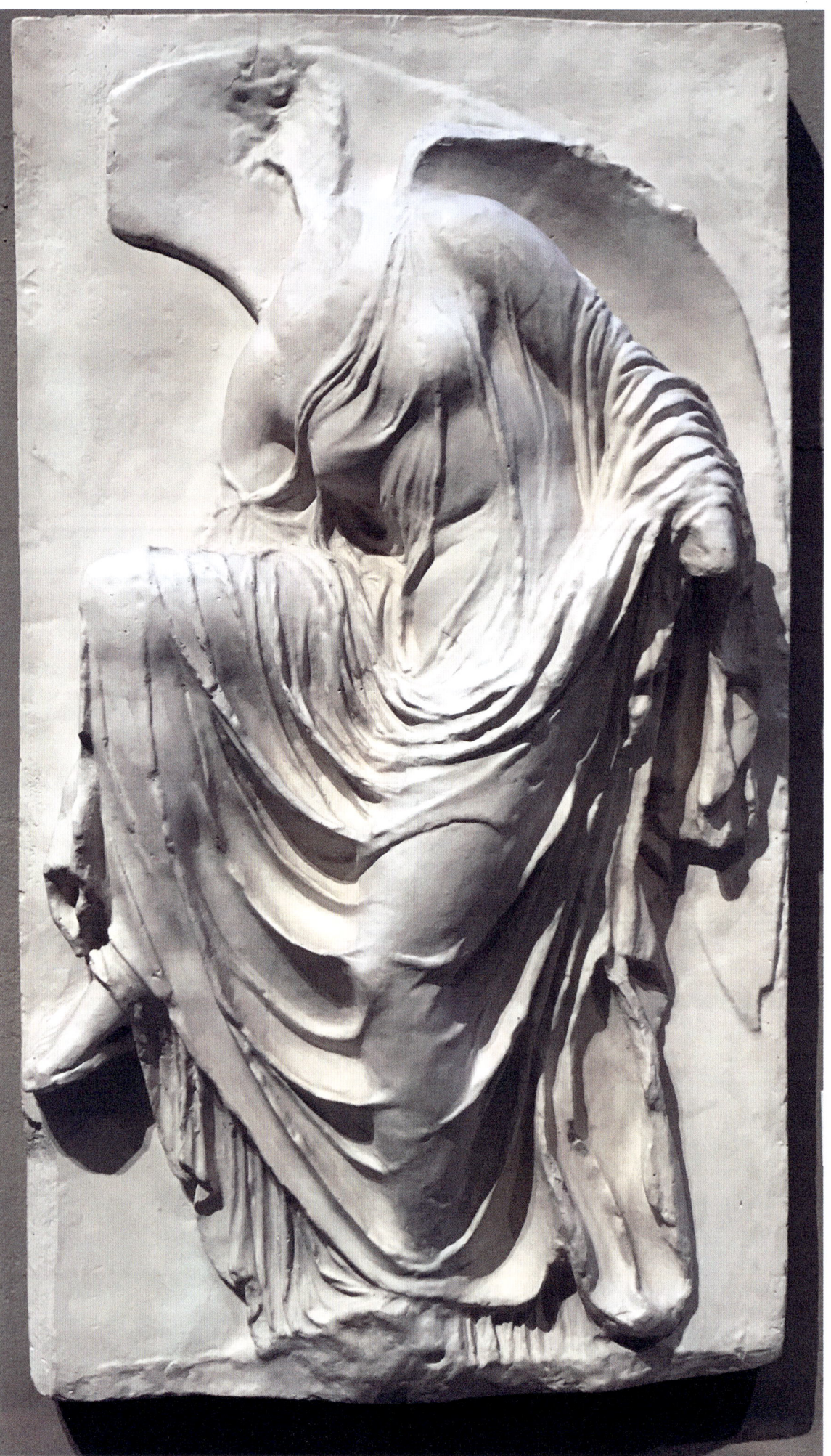

CHAPTER 5

AESTHETIC USE OF CLOTHES AND FABRIC

This last chapter explores how clothing can be used for aesthetic, compositional, and narrative purposes. **Clothing can guide the gaze of the viewer with a whirl of spiraling silk, or be used to suggest, reveal, disguise or conceal the human form.**

Now that you have acquired a good understanding of the human body—its proportions, landmarks, and forms—it will be easier for you to layer a garment or drapery over a figure while still suggesting its volumes or to create aesthetic interplays between the folds of clothing and the underlying body.

The artworks that explore these concepts in this chapter span two millennia, starting in the fifth century BCE and leading to the twentieth century CE.

OPPOSITE: *Nike Adjusting Her Sandal,* c. 410 BCE, marble, 42 inches tall. Acropolis Museum, Athens; originally from the south side of the parapet of the Temple of Athena Nike on the Acropolis. The fabric folds of this elegant artwork by an unknown artist delicately reveal the forms of the goddess Nike's body while contributing to the spiraling pattern created by the arrangement of the figure's torso and limbs.

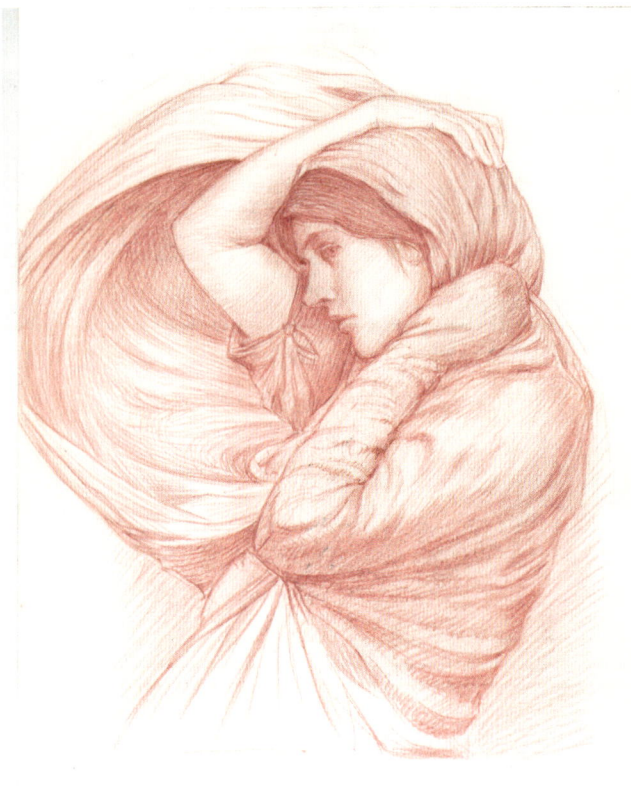

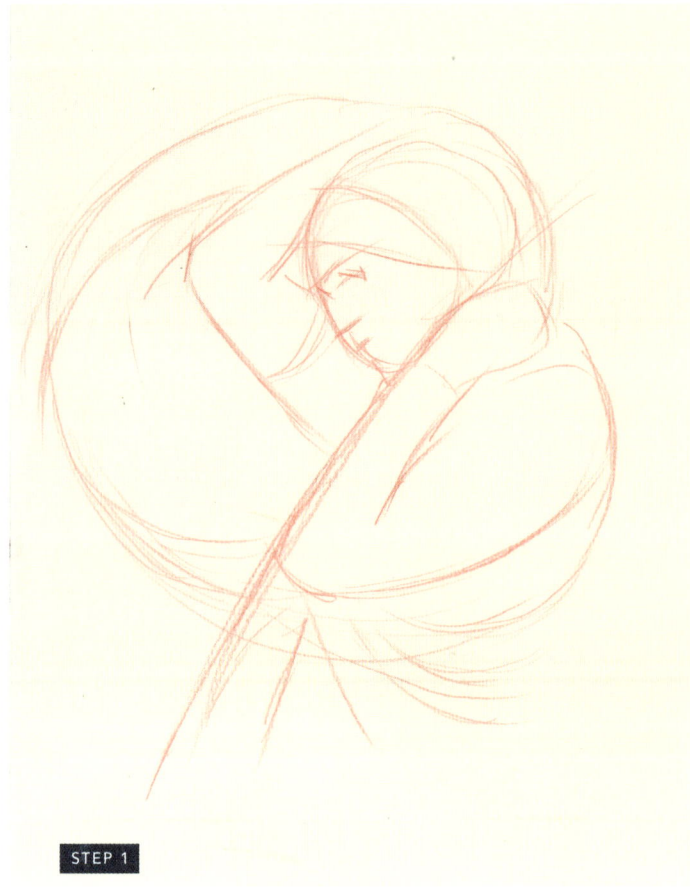

EXERCISE 5.1
FABRIC SUGGESTING THE BODY

The subject of this first exercise is a beautiful drawing by John William Waterhouse, prepared as compositional study for his 1904 painting *Boreas*. (In Greek mythology, Boreas is the god of the north wind and usually depicted as male.) We can appreciate how subtly the body is suggested and easily perceived under the spiraling folds: a good knowledge of the human body was fundamental to create this very convincing effect of clothing wrapped over and around the figure.

Copying this work will reveal aspects of the drawing that you might not otherwise notice, such as the composition, the play of the folds, the geometric construction, the structural and proportional aspects of the figure and, therefore, the time and effort Waterhouse invested in organizing this pose.

STEP 1
BLOCK IN MAIN OUTLINES

Block in the main outlines of the composition with thin, light, clean lines to capture the arrangements and proportions of the main volumes of the figure. I started this sketch by drawing a larger circle for the body, a smaller circle for the head and a diagonal line for the lower forearm and abdomen, then added a few more details.

MATERIALS

For this drawing I used white Strathmore Drawing paper 400 series, 11 x 14 inches, in medium finish and a Faber-Castell Polychromos colored pencil in Pompeian red. You can use any other red earth color, such as India red, sanguine, or Venetian red. Colored pencils produce finer detail and cleaner marks than red chalk, pastels, or crayons, and they are easier to sharpen. You might instead use red oil-based Pitt Pastel Monochrome pencils. Unlike regular pastels, oil-based pastels make finer, cleaner marks that are similar to colored pencils' marks.

ABOVE LEFT: My copy of John William Waterhouse's study for *Boreas,* original c. 1903, colored pencil on drawing paper.

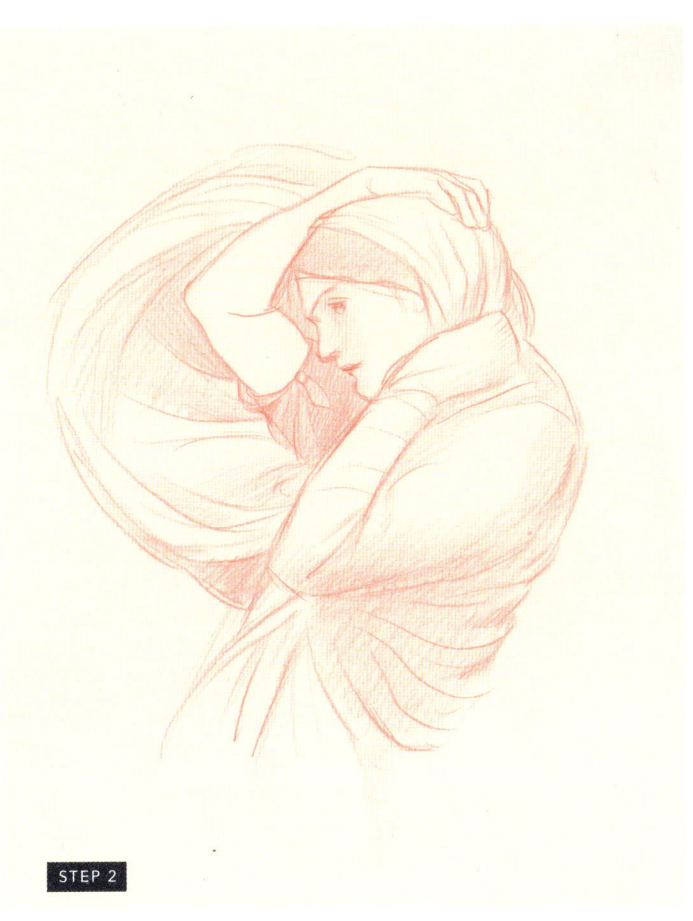

STEP 2

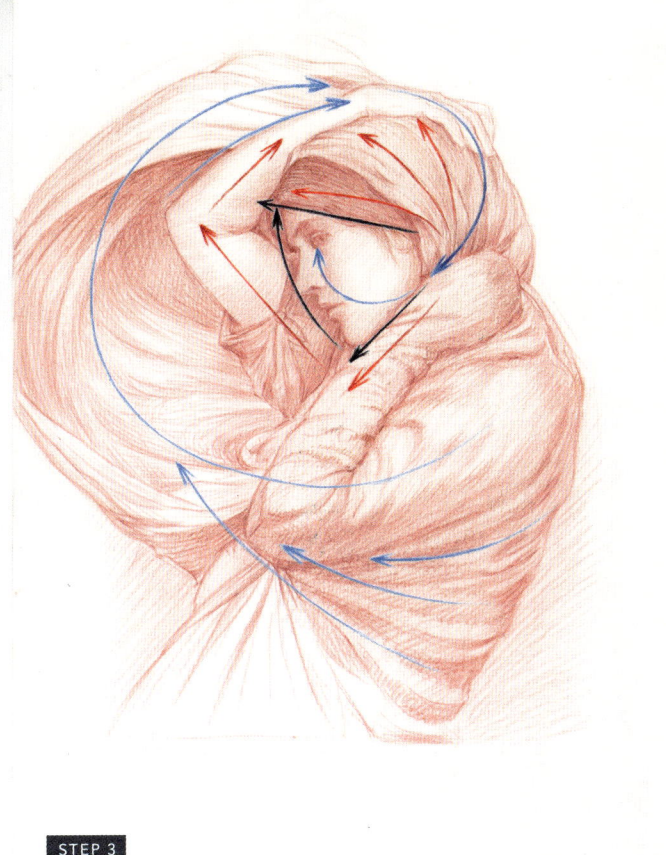

STEP 3

STEP 2

REFINE INITIAL SKETCH

Refine the initial sketch by measuring more accurately and adding details. Block in the shadow mass, which will indirectly define the light mass as well.

STEP 3

FINISH THE DRAWING

This final image shows the dynamism of the pose. Note the careful arrangement of the arms and clothing, elegantly organized in a spiraling pattern that leads to the eye of Boreas. Specifically, these movements identified by arrows in the image here:

- *Blue arrows:* The swirling cloth and curving right forearm direct the gaze of the viewer toward the top of the hand that frames the back of the head. From there, the visual path runs along the jaw and the profile of the face and stops at the eye of Boreas, the center of the composition.

- *Straight red arrows:* These arrows show the "fence" created by the forearms and right upper arm, framing the face.
- *Curved red arrows and black arrows:* The curved red arrows show how the hair that's visible and the folds of the fabric covering the head lead to the "wedge" that frames the face, shown here with the black arrows.
- *Blue arrows:* The figure's left upper arm and the folds of the cloth below it direct the gaze toward the "halo" created by the cloth that travels upward and leads to the top of the head and to the hand that frames the back of the head, as shown by the blue arrows.

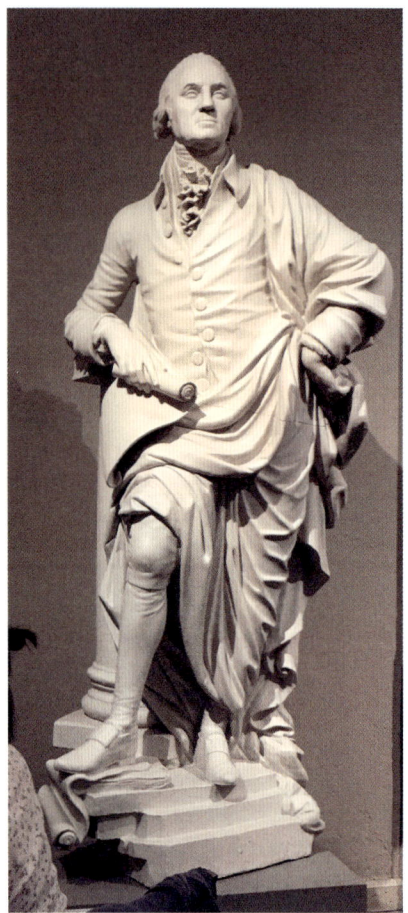

William Rush, 1756-1833, *George Washington*, 1815, painted pine, life size. Independence National Historical Park, Second Bank of the United States building, Philadelphia, Pennsylvania.

MATERIALS FOR EXERCISE 5.2

- Drawing paper (I recommend a pad of white Strathmore Drawing paper, 11 x 14 inches, medium finish.)
- Graphite pencils of grades HB or B
- Blue and red colored pencils

EXERCISE 5.2
FABRIC PARTLY DISGUISING THE BODY

This sculpture depicting George Washington, by the American sculptor William Rush, is the perfect work to study and draw because of the great variety of folds it showcases. The figure stands in the classical contrapposto pose, which is likewise true of the sculpture you will meet in the next exercise.

The term *contrapposto* (Italian for "counterpoise") describes a pose in which the various segments of the body are counterposed: the head, ribcage, and pelvis are tilted in opposite directions and aligned along a slightly *S*-curved line. Michelangelo's *David* (shown opposite) provides what may be the most famous example of a contrapposto pose.

Looking at my sketch of the George Washington statue, opposite, you can see how the forms of Washington's body are aligned along a slightly curving line of flow, traced by the blue arrow, that goes from the right side of his head (at left in the drawing) to his left foot (at right).

Starting from the right side of his jaw (at left), the flow gradually descends toward the foot following the inside margin of the lapel, which begins at about the level of the sternocleidomastoid, then travels down the line of buttons that correspond to the sternum and the linea alba, and then dives under the transversal fold that recalls the tilted pelvis. This line of flow then emerges from under these mid-body folds and continues along the engaged leg, ending at the foot. Even if disguised under a few layers of garments and partially hidden by folded cloth, the anatomical structure is carefully considered. In fact, this work demonstrates that knowledge of the anatomical and structural aspects of the figure is essential to obtain such a successful and convincing fully clothed figure.

As you draw George Washington from the photo and study the diagram, you will come to appreciate the variety of folds the sculpture displays: spiraling, catenary, wrapping, and radiating. If you wish, draw the figure using one of the techniques described in chapter 4.

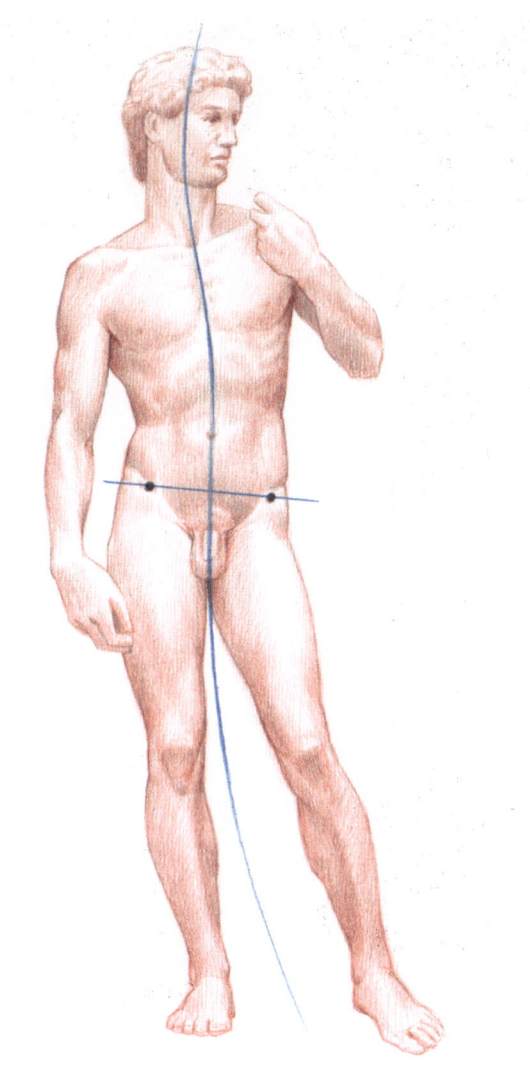

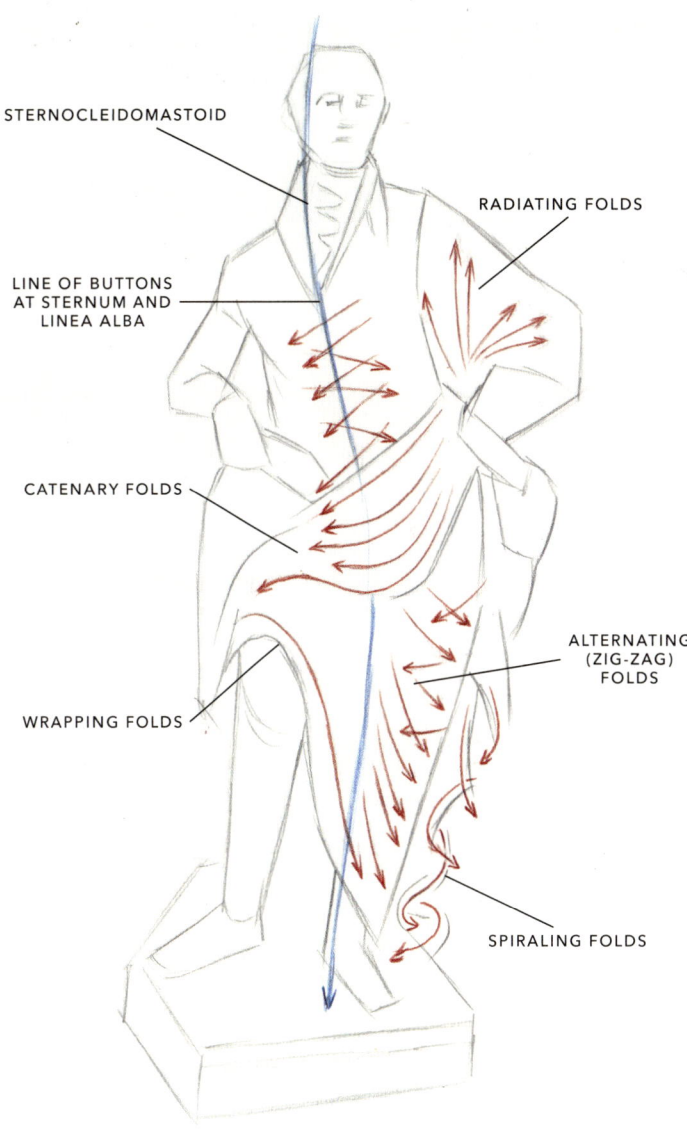

STERNOCLEIDOMASTOID

RADIATING FOLDS

LINE OF BUTTONS
AT STERNUM AND
LINEA ALBA

CATENARY FOLDS

ALTERNATING
(ZIG-ZAG)
FOLDS

WRAPPING FOLDS

SPIRALING FOLDS

The blue vertical line shows the gently curving vertical alignment of the segments of the body typical of the contrapposto pose, as it flows from head to toes.

As with the David, the blue vertical arrow here is created by the alternating tilted segments of the body. The red arrows show the various types of folds and their interaction with the forms of the body.

EXERCISE 5.3
FABRIC REVEALING THE BODY

About two thousand years separate this delicate sculpture, called the *Frejus Aphrodite,* from William Rush's statue of George Washington. Even if, at a first glance, the two sculptures cannot seem more unrelated, they do share the same contrapposto pose of Classical convention. Unlike the Washington statue, however, the Aphrodite is garbed only with a diaphanous veil that reveals the forms of the body instead of disguising them; the contrapposto pose of the *Frejus Aphrodite* is therefore much easier to identify than Washington's.

The blue arrow in the image opposite, which shows the alignment of the segments of Aphrodite's body, follows a path similar to that in the George Washington statue. The red arrows show how the cloth has been cleverly used to frame the legs and to create a triangular pattern that starts at the raised hand (to counterbalance the head, which leans the opposite way) and also to create a connection between the top of the figure and the bottom.

Draw the statue as it appears in the reference photo to discover the aesthetic and dynamic interplay between the folds of the cloth and the body. (You can also use the diagram as reference.) You can either create a line drawing in pencil or make a more detailed drawing with charcoal and chalk on toned paper, following the steps described in exercises 4.9 and 4.10 in the previous chapter (see pages 192–95).

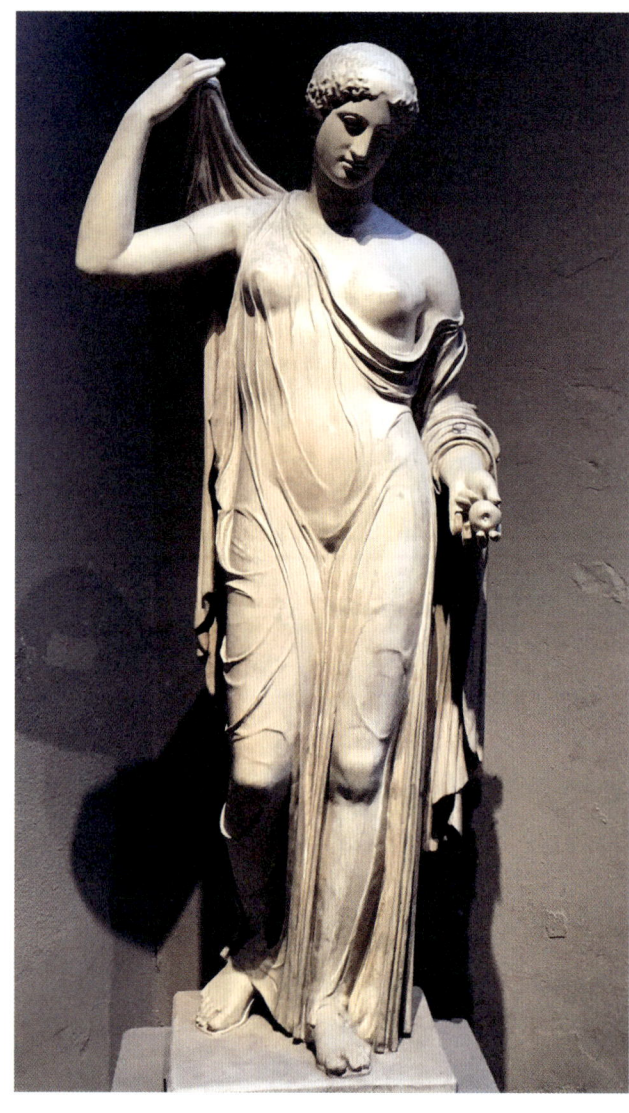

Frejus Aphrodite, late 1st century BCE–early 1st century CE, marble, Roman copy of a lost Greek original, 64 ½ inches (164 cm) tall. Louvre, Paris.

MATERIALS FOR EXERCISE 5.3

- Drawing paper (I recommend a pad of white Strathmore Drawing paper, 11 x 14 inches, medium finish.)
- Graphite pencils of grades HB or B
- Blue and red colored pencils

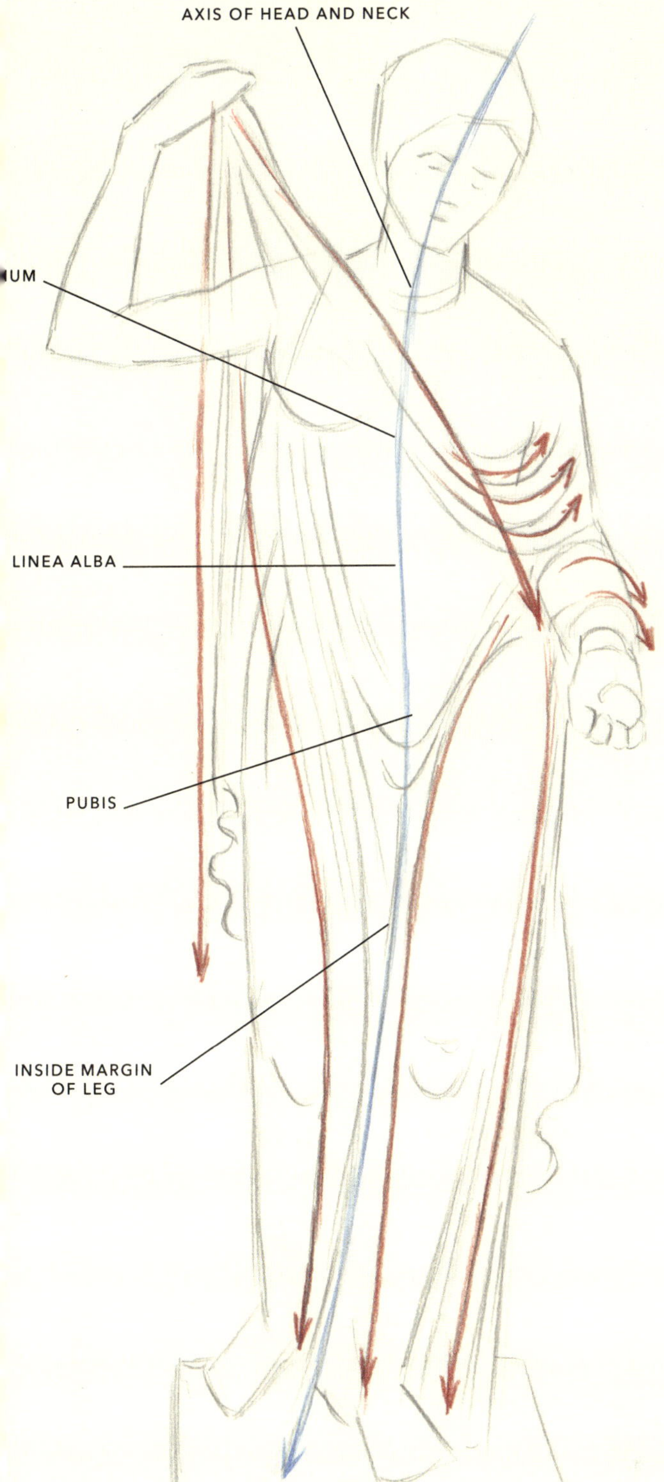

AXIS OF HEAD AND NECK

UM

LINEA ALBA

PUBIS

INSIDE MARGIN
OF LEG

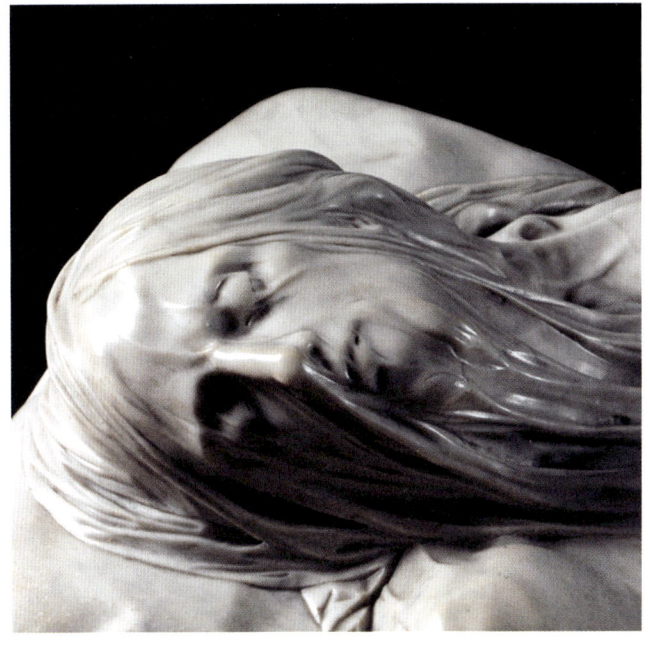

A TRANSPARENT VEIL IN STONE

Giuseppe Sanmartino was a Neapolitan sculptor of the
eighteenth century whose technical mastery enabled
him to carve the amazing statue whose head you see
here. The sculpture is unequivocally about death, but
the splendidly realistic veil that covers the dead Christ
softens the crudeness of the tragic event. It makes view-
ers think of the loss of the Spiritual Center in a more
conceptual, metaphysical way.

I encourage you to try to draw this challenging work.
If you do, the best technique to use is probably charcoal
and chalk on toned paper, though simple graphite on
white paper would also be fine. You can work either
in an additive mode or a reduction technique (pages
194–95).

ABOVE: Giuseppe Sanmartino, *Cristo Velato* (Veiled Christ; detail), 1753,
marble, 20 x 31 x 71 inches (250 x 80 x 180 cm). Cappella Sansevero,
Naples, Italy.

EXERCISE 5.4
FABRIC CONCEALING AND DISRUPTING THE BODY

In his masterpiece *The Ecstasy of Saint Teresa,* sculptor Gian Lorenzo Bernini encases the saint's body in a cocoon of crumpled and animated folds of fabric, both concealing and disrupting her physicality. It's an ingenious device that discourages an interpretation of physical pleasure while exalting the ecstatic experience.

Despite the disruption, this fabric exoskeleton still respects the segments, proportions, and alignments of the human figure, making us perceive the saint's physical being. Bernini evokes the convulsions of a body agitated by mystical experience while simultaneously showing the passions of the soul.

In my drawing of the sculpture opposite, note how the flow of any group of folds is interrupted by other folds that run perpendicularly. The unpredictability created by this organization of folds further disrupts the body of Saint Teresa.

Copy the sculpture from the reference photo. As you do, pay attention to the almost Cubist effect of the folds' broken planes and the figure's chaotic writhing. Refer to my drawing as a guide to the fabric's patterns.

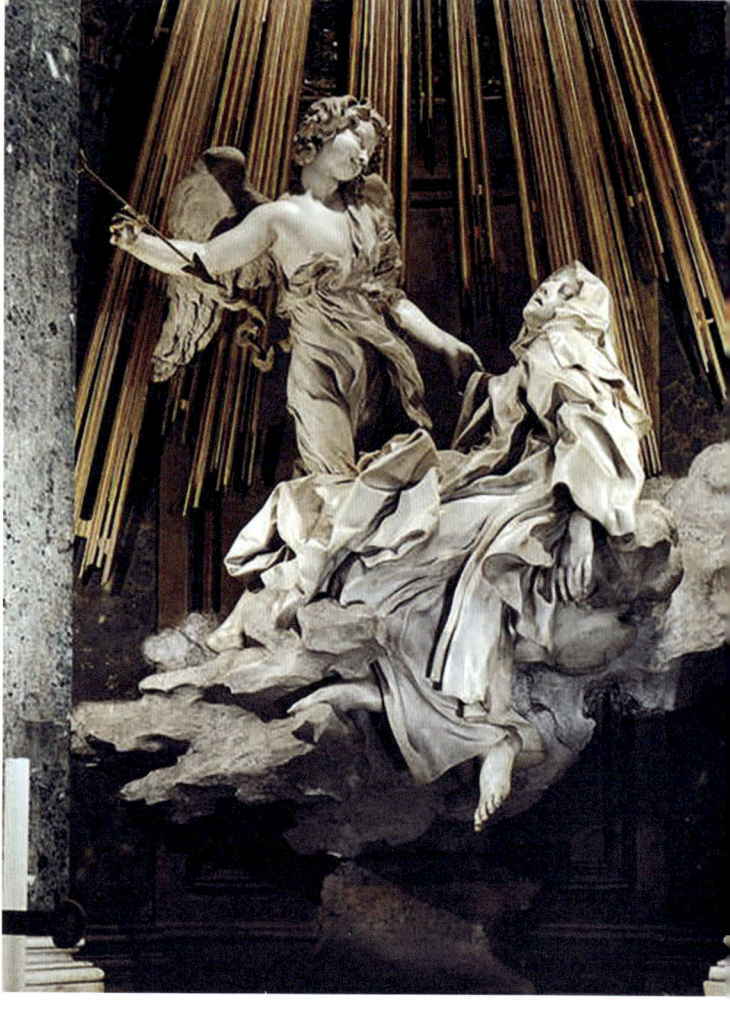

Gian Lorenzo Bernini, *The Ecstasy of Saint Teresa,* 1647–52, marble, life size. Church of Santa Maria della Vittoria, Rome.

MATERIALS FOR EXERCISE 5.4

For this exercise, use white drawing paper such as the Strathmore Drawing paper, 400 series, medium finish. A dark brown colored pencil works well; I used a sepia pencil from the Faber-Castell Polychromos line. Graphite pencils in grades F, HB, or B are also okay. Remember to keep your pencils constantly sharp: a dull point makes a dull drawing. You can touch up the point of your pencil frequently with a piece of medium or fine sandpaper.

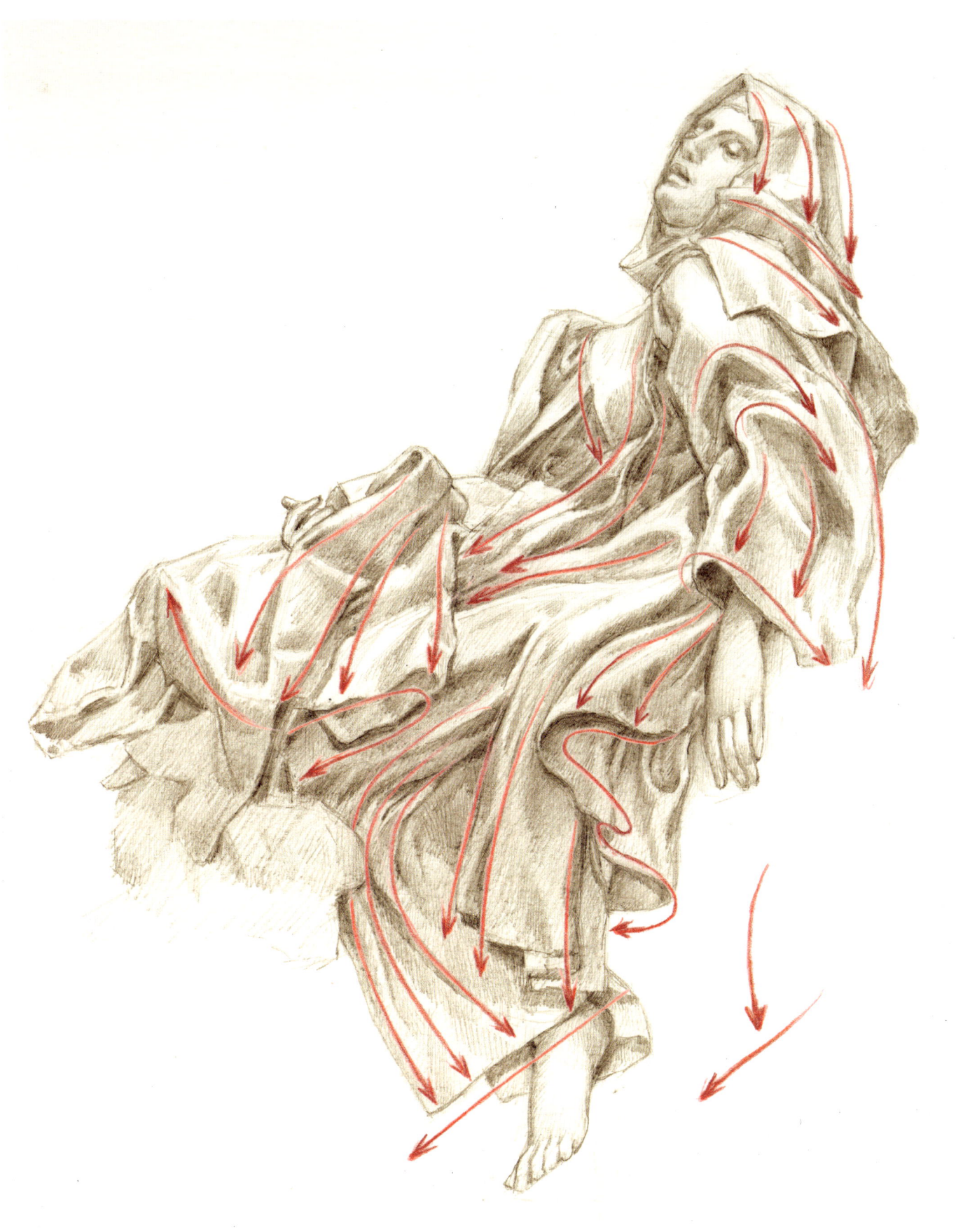

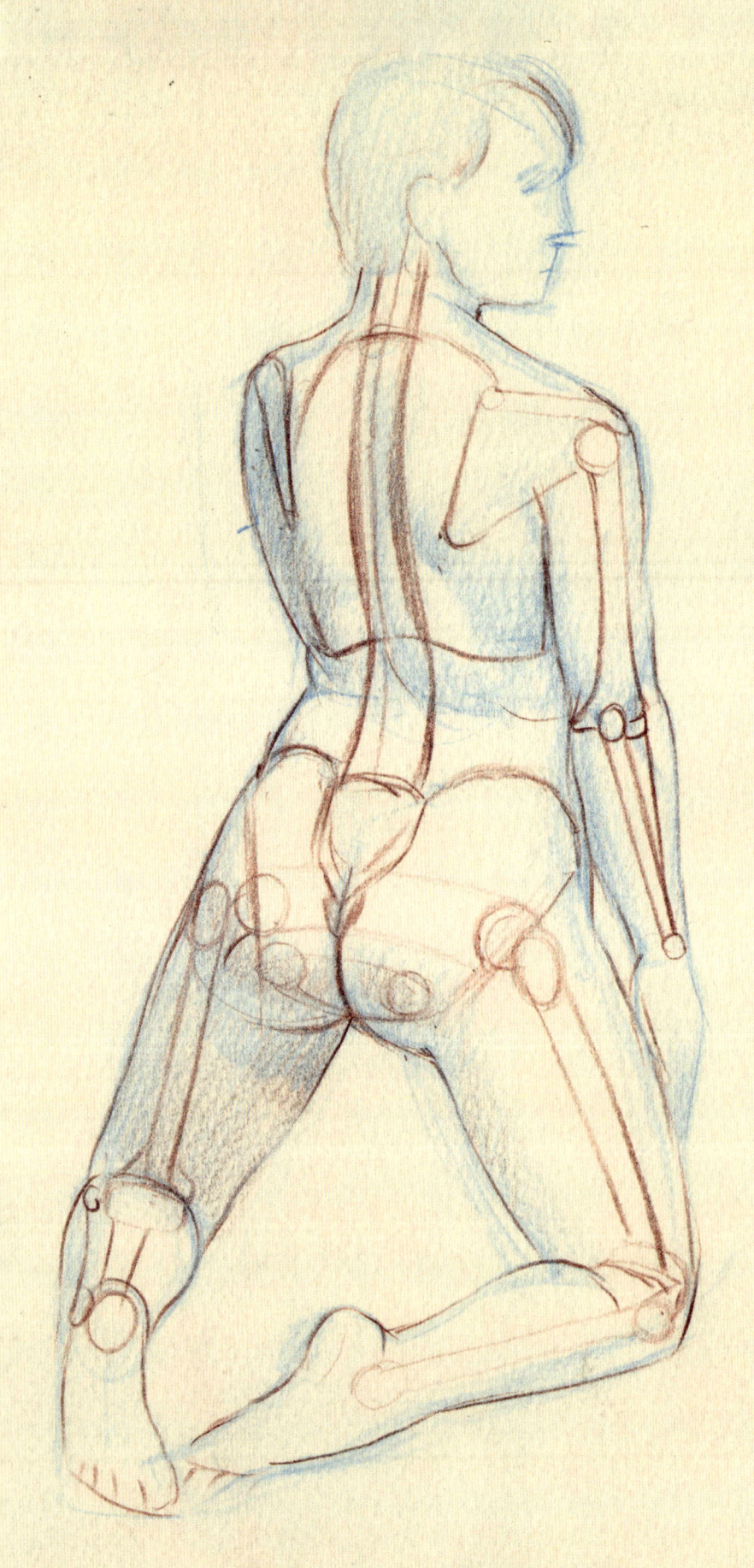